Psychodynamic Interventions in Pregnancy and Infancy

Psychodynamic Interventions in Pregnancy and Infancy builds on Björn Salomonsson's experiences as a psychoanalytic consultant working with parents and their babies. Emotional problems during the perinatal stages can arise and be observed and addressed by a skilled midwife, nurse or health visitor.

Salomonsson has developed a method combining nurse supervision and therapeutic consultations which has lowered the thresholds for parents to come and talk with him. The brief consultations concern pregnant women, mother and baby, husband and wife, toddler and parent. The theoretical framework is psychoanalytic, but the mode of work is eclectic and adapted to the family's situation and its members' motivation. This book details such work, which can be applied globally; perinatal psychotherapy integrated with ordinary medical health care. It also explains how psychotherapy can be made more accessible to a larger population.

Via detailed case presentations, the author takes the reader through pregnancy, childbirth and the first few years of life. He also brings in research studies emphasizing the importance of early interventions, with the aim of providing therapists with arguments for such work in everyday family health care. To further substantiate such arguments, the book ends with theoretical chapters and, finally, the author's vision of the future of a perinatal health care that integrates medical and psychological perspectives.

Psychodynamic Interventions in Pregnancy and Infancy will appeal to all psychoanalysts and psychotherapists working in this area, as well as clinical psychologists, clinical social workers and medical personnel working with parents and infants.

Björn Salomonsson, MD, is a psychiatrist and training and child psychoanalyst in Stockholm. His research at the Karolinska Institute concerns parent–infant psychoanalytic treatment and psychodynamic consultations at Child Health Centres, as well as the development of clinical practice and theory of such treatments. He is an internationally renowned lecturer on these and other topics in the field of psychoanalytic therapy.

"Some books do make a difference, and this is one of them. With knowledge and compassion, Salomonsson addresses how to help troubled parents and infants. The theoretical framework is psychoanalytic, integrated with research findings from various fields that may explain emotional states. He creates a comprehensive theory about the unique characteristics of the perinatal period, and provides rich clinical examples from work with mothers, fathers and babies, from pregnancy and through early infancy to toddlerhood. He also discusses how the external world and the therapist's internal world impact therapeutic work. These are complex issues, but Salomonsson writes in a way that draws the reader in to join him, his mentors and his patients in their explorations."

– **Tessa Baradon**, Consultant, Anna Freud Centre, London; Visiting Adjunct Professor, School of Human and Community Development, University of the Witwatersrand, South Africa

"A masterful, much needed and highly readable exposition of this flourishing field. The author's compelling clinical vignettes, that include his own emotional and counter-transference exchanges, bring to life his helpful formulations that bring forward new clinical knowledge and research. The book not only builds on his own consulting experiences in a Swedish health care context, but reviews work in other contexts, including clinical trials there and elsewhere. Wonderfully, the book also offers links to couples and family work as psychoanalysis is increasingly recognized as a two-person and relational psychology."

– **Robert N. Emde, MD**, Emeritus Professor of Psychiatry, University of Colorado; Honorary President, World Association of Infant Mental Health (WAIMH)

"Björn Salomonsson's excellent book is at the crossroads of four disciplines: neurosciences, obstetrics, neonatology and psychoanalysis. Through significant clinical examples, it deepens the understanding of the emotional turmoil raised by an infant's birth, and simultaneously proposes precise and elaborate theoretical developments for investigation in this new field. It also describes in detail how a psychotherapist should find his/her place in every unit of neonatology, both to teach the health care team and to help the families with their newborn."

– **Florence Guignard**, Training Analyst of the Paris Society and Past President of the COCAP/IPA (Committee on Child and Adolescent Psychoanalysis)

"The undeniable benefit of early psychotherapeutic interventions for infants and parents has come as a surprise to us all. Björn Salomonsson takes us on a riveting journey into the depths of his unique therapeutic work with babies and parents, beginning in the prenatal period and moving to the early postnatal development. He presents an astutely designed panoply of rich case reports and deep insights into psychoanalytic thinking against a sound backdrop of empirical research. With conceptual clarity and coherence, he bridges the clinical and scientific arenas, offering an excellent foundation both for therapeutic work and future research efforts."

– **Kai von Klitzing**, Professor of Child and Adolescent Psychiatry, University of Leipzig, President of the World Association for Infant Mental Health (WAIMH)

Psychodynamic Interventions in Pregnancy and Infancy

Clinical and Theoretical Perspectives

Björn Salomonsson

LONDON AND NEW YORK

First published 2018
by Routledge
2 Park Square, Milton Park, Abingdon, Oxon OX14 4RN

and by Routledge
711 Third Avenue, New York, NY 10017

Routledge is an imprint of the Taylor & Francis Group, an informa business

© 2018 Björn Salomonsson

The right of Björn Salomonsson to be identified as author of this work
has been asserted by him in accordance with sections 77 and 78 of the
Copyright, Designs and Patents Act 1988.

All rights reserved. No part of this book may be reprinted or reproduced
or utilised in any form or by any electronic, mechanical, or other means,
now known or hereafter invented, including photocopying and recording,
or in any information storage or retrieval system, without permission in
writing from the publishers.

Trademark notice: Product or corporate names may be trademarks or
registered trademarks, and are used only for identification and
explanation without intent to infringe.

British Library Cataloguing in Publication Data
A catalogue record for this book is available from the British Library

Library of Congress Cataloging in Publication Data
A catalog record for this book has been requested

ISBN: 978-0-8153-5904-3 (hbk)
ISBN: 978-0-8153-5905-0 (pbk)
ISBN: 978-1-351-11714-2 (ebk)

Typeset in Times
by Keystroke, Neville Lodge, Tettenhall, Wolverhampton

To the next generation: Noah and Leo, Hugo, Oliver and Ruben

Contents

List of clinical cases	ix
Author's preface	x

PART I
Clinic: Consultations and therapies at a Child Health Centre

1

1	In the beginning	3
2	The psychology of pregnancy	13
3	Circumventing primary maternal preoccupation	28
4	Delivery trauma and the maternal introject	36
5	Therapeutic technique in perinatal consultations	47
6	The external frame at the Child Health Centre	56
7	Supervising nurses at the Child Health Centre	64
8	The internal frame at the Child Health Centre	71
9	From panic to pleasure. Therapy with Debbie and Mae	80
10	Parent–infant psychotherapy: a review of clinical methods	87
11	Parent–infant psychotherapy: RCTs and follow-up studies	98
12	Brief interventions with parental couples – I	109
13	Brief interventions with parental couples – II	121
14	Extending the field to therapy with toddlers and parents	131

viii Contents

PART II
Theory: the mind of the baby – continued
investigations 149

15 A baby's mind: empirical observation versus speculative
theorizing 153

16 Naming the nameless: on anxiety in babies – I: Freud 165

17 Naming the nameless: on anxiety in babies – II: after Freud 175

18 Babies and their defences 187

19 Metaphors in parent–infant therapy 203

20 A vision for the future 217

References 223
Index 249

List of clinical cases

(When applicable, entries are indexed via the mother's first name)

'Beatrice' and 'Fran' 167, 176, 180–181
'Bridget', 'Ron', 'Walter', and 'Bruno' 132–146
'Debbie', 'Don', and 'Mae' 80–86, 89, 92, 110, 167, 176–178, 183–184, 186
'Donna' and 'Annie' 17, 28–30, 33, 40, 58, 81, 92, 220
'Doriane' and 'Pascal' 45–46, 81
'Douglas' (by L. Emanuel) 145
'Edna' and 'Leonard' 206–216
'Frances' and 'Paul' 30–31, 106
'Gail' 33–35
'Jane', 'David', and 'Ottilie' 74–75
'Joey' (by D. Stern) 183
'Karen' and 'Cristopher' 9–12, 14–15, 18, 35, 40, 55, 61, 67, 73
'Lena', 'George', and 'Yasmine' 37, 51–53, 80
'Leyla' and 'Jenny' 37–41, 47–50, 54, 58, 61, 81
'Lisa' (by J. Norman) 93
'Louise' and 'Eric' 122–126, 129
'Maria' (by Lieberman & Van Horn) 144
'Mary' and 'Phil' 7–9, 12, 14, 36
'Myra', 'Don', and 'Kirsten' 188–197, 199–201, 203
'Nancy' and 'Brent' 166, 168, 170–171, 173–174, 176, 180, 182, 186
'Nora' and 'Bess' 49–50, 51, 53, 72, 92, 106
'Pamela' (supervision example) 68–71
'Rita' (by M. Klein) 155
'Tilde', 'Salih' and 'Kevin' 110–120, 125–126
'Trudy' and 'Nancy' 32–33
'Uma' and 'Greg' 73–74

Author's preface

Some years ago, I published a book (Salomonsson, 2014a) on mother–infant psychoanalytic therapy. It was primarily written for psychotherapists but also for anyone interested in perinatal psychological well-being. The same goes for the present book, which relies on brief consultations at a Child Health Centre (CHC) in Stockholm, where I work as a psychoanalytic consultant. A CHC is a local health care unit for infants and young children and offers regular check-ups up to six years. The CHC health visitor or nurse is central in helping parents with "baby worries". Other countries have other names, such as Well Baby Clinics, and other systems; but in most of them, these conditions are taken care of by a team of professionals: a midwife, a nurse, a doctor. Though I proceed from a Scandinavian experience, my model of work is not restricted to these countries. The idea of placing a competent psychotherapist at similar units can be applied to any country and any health care system.

I see families in a consulting room next to one of the CHC nurses' offices. Also, I provide regular supervisions with the team of nurses. The aim is to inspire them to observe symptoms of emotional disorder in parents and children, and to become aware of their personal emotional reactions when they meet the families. To psychotherapists, it is no novelty that a clinician is inundated with strong and sometimes incomprehensible feelings vis-à-vis the patient. As we will see in this book, this phenomenon of "countertransference" can be used to great advantage in work with babies and parents. Supervisions also aim to encourage nurses to bring up with the parents any concern they might have regarding them or the baby. If this leads to a plea for help from the parent(s), the nurse can suggest a consultation with me. The fact that I work at the CHC makes it easier for mothers to climb the threshold to my office and talk about their baby worries.

The book's first section on the clinic suggests how to address the mother's anxieties, how to include the father in therapy, and how to observe and address distress in infants and toddlers. The second section on theory continues my efforts at integrating clinical experiences with psychoanalytic theory. Psychodynamic therapy with infants and parents (PTIP) is a rather new empirical field and we need to build a coherent theory that takes into account findings from therapeutic encounters and infant researchers' lab studies. Otherwise, theory will hang in the air and the therapeutic mechanisms will seem mysterious or fuzzy. The book ends with a vision for the future of perinatal psychological care. I have noted the positive impact of therapeutic interventions offered in a relaxed and easily accessible setting at the CHC. This has made me a convinced advocate of such treatment at perinatal health care units. There is a paradoxical discrepancy between today's widespread awareness of the negative repercussions of postnatal depression on maternal and infant mental health and, on the other hand, the scarcity of accessible and high-quality PTIP options. If the book can contribute to diminishing that discrepancy, and inspire such work to be implemented more widely, I will be more than pleased.

A second aim is to inspire therapists to work with the "infant within the adult" patient. Psychoanalytic discourse relies much on reporting *verbal* interchanges between patient and analyst. Sometimes, this downplays our understanding of the non-verbal communication with patients. Here, experiences from parent–infant therapy come to our help. They help us perceive communication *beyond words* and understand more deeply what it means to *contain* a patient's anxieties. More about this later! The book also comprises stories of parents and babies whom I interviewed in a randomized clinical trial (RCT). In the published reports (Salomonsson & Sandell, 2011a, b, 2012; Salomonsson & Sleed, 2010) the dyads were amassed in figures, tables, and graphs. The study comprised more than 200 interviews using a semi-structured format with a psychoanalytic lens. The mothers told me stories, the babies displayed communicative behaviours, and the analysts whom I also interviewed reported their experiences. All went together to increase my knowledge about the background to "baby worries" and how parents and babies may experience them. This book includes several such cases. Throughout, quotation marks (") are used for citations of authors or patients, whereas apostrophes (') illustrate imaginative formulations of the baby's or the parent's representations.

Every scientific publication ends with two sections: "limitations" and "acknowledgements". First, what does this book *not* contain? A book with a psychoanalytic perspective gains credibility if it is based on the analyst's personal experiences. This book's cases are thus my own. The reader may miss others, such as adopted babies or those born in LGBTQ relationships. The reason for their absence is that I have little experience with such cases. Most of the families here are middle-class, which has to do with the catchment area of my CHC and with the recruitment procedure in the RCT. These families were motivated to remain in a study or a therapy, which enabled a deeper understanding of their problems. I am grateful for their willingness to reveal embarrassing matters and face painful insights, and I believe this may help families in less advantageous circumstances to benefit from our amassed knowledge. A comparison comes to mind from Freud's days; his patients had the means and interest to participate in psychoanalyses, which helped him build theoretical concepts and clinical recommendations that we today can apply in our daily work with less privileged patients.

xii Author's preface

As for acknowledgements, I wish to thank warmly all the patients who gave permission to publish de-identified material from our joint work. My deep thanks also go to my wife, colleague, and research collaborator Majlis Winberg Salomonsson. Our discussions and collaborative research efforts have been stimulating and great fun. Warm thanks to the staff at Mama Mia CHC and my colleagues at the Infant Reception Service of the Swedish Psychoanalytical Association. Especially, Daniela Montelatici Prawitz has done a giant work administering a grant from the Swedish Inheritance Fund, which enabled ten analysts to be placed at CHCs in Stockholm for three years. This project is now evaluated systematically by Katarina Kornaros at Karolinska Institutet.

A host of colleagues have stimulated my thinking. In Pavia, Nino Ferro. In Los Angeles, Joe Aguayo, Ethan Grumbach, Julie McCaig, and the late Jim Grotstein. In Boston, Lawrence Brown. In Tel Aviv, Miri Keren. In Sao Paulo, Rogerio Lerner, and Elizabeth and Elias da Rocha Barros. In New York, Christine Anzieu-Premmereur and Talia Hatzor. In Berlin, Christiane Ludwig Körner. In Paris, Françoise Moggio, Bernard Golse, Sylvain Missonnier, Elsa Carlberg Phamgia, and Florence Guignard. In Geneva, Irène Nigolian and Jacques Press. In Munich, Susanne Hauser. In London, Tessa Baradon, Angela Joyce and the PIP team of the Anna Freud Centre. In Toronto, Elizabeth Tuters and Sally Doulis. In Leipzig, Kai von Klitzing. In Stuttgart, Michael Günter. My colleagues in Stockholm, Arne Jemstedt and Björn Sahlberg, gave valuable points of view on Winnicott and Aulagnier, respectively. Thanks also to my research colleagues at the Unit of Reproductive Health at Karolinska Institutet in Stockholm, headed by Helena Lindgren and formerly by Eva Nissen. Finally, I extend my gratitude to the Bertil Wennborg Foundation; a generous grant helped me to write this book.

Five chapters (10, 11, 14, 15, and 18) are amended versions of previously published papers. Acknowledgements are duly provided at the end of each chapter.

Part I

Clinic
Consultations and therapies at
a Child Health Centre

Chapter 1

In the beginning

In the beginning God created the heavens and the earth. Now the earth was formless and empty, darkness was over the surface of the deep, and the Spirit of God was hovering over the waters. And God said, "Let there be light", and there was light. God saw that the light was good, and he separated the light from the darkness. God called the light "day" and the darkness he called "night." And there was evening, and there was morning – the first day.

Genesis: I, 1–5

In the beginning egg and sperm met to form an embryo; maybe in a passionate embrace of two lovers longing to become parents. Or it just happened, or a man coerced his exhausted wife into having yet another offspring, or a woman persuaded her partner to have a child he was not very keen on. Or it happened in an IVF lab or at a clinic with a single mother fertilized by an anonymous donor. In any case, egg and sperm united and multiplied; 2, 4, 8, 16, 32 cells . . . The foetus settled and started growing in the womb. Everything was hazy and without visible forms. Buzzing sounds were everywhere, and the foetus' budding nervous system could register the resistance from the uterus wall as it kicked and moved about in its habitat.

The Bible begins in a similar mystic, dark, and watery cosmos. Only after the sky had been erected did life on earth become possible. Light separated from darkness, day from night, matter above heaven from matter beneath, land from water, sun from moon. In this cosmic birth scene, numerous acts of separation took place before our planet became hospitable and friendly. The future mother may also feel that her womb is a cosmos where unknown and uncontrollable things occur. Whether she enjoys or fears it, pregnancy has its long and due course. She will start creating *internal images* or *mental representations* of the foetus. In her mind, it becomes more and more of an individual – though some women cannot, due to internal and external tensions, let their minds fly away in "silly fantasies".

Finally comes birth, the great act of separation. It may be quick, prolonged, nice, terrifying, wonderful, or painful – or cause less feelings than expected. Whatever happens, the memory of it will be engraved in the mother's mind. Then comes a time when she and the child form a unique relationship; confluent and coalescent, with passions running up and down the emotional thermometer. Yet, parenthood also implies separation. Unless the parents realize that their baby will leave them one day in a distant yet imaginable future, emotional problems will ensue sooner or later.

This balance of emotions around *confluence and separation* illuminates why pregnancy, delivery, and infancy make up such challenging eras of our lives. Another factor is that many things are concealed to the future parents yet arouse intense feelings. To illustrate, I am calling the foetus "it", though thanks to ultrasound images the parents might already know if it is a boy or a girl. Yet, such knowledge is different from grasping *emotionally* what kind of human being will one day become their Tim or Lucy. Metaphorically, the parents also live in a formless universe shrouded in darkness. They google on the internet and prepare for delivery in maternity classes. The future mother avoids alcohol, drugs, and unsuitable food, and goes to the gym to make her fit for delivery. The father talks to his pals about what it means to become a dad and looks for the smartest pram on the web. Yet, these respectable efforts cannot fully illuminate this misty and unchartered landscape. Information from parents, midwives, friends, brochures, and web-sources dispel some worries but also tend to engender new qualms and questions. The full impact of the baby's arrival cannot be felt until delivery. And not even then . . .

One day the foetus says, "Let there be light", and floods of sound, light, odour, and temperature thrust towards him – or her – from outside the mother's womb. Still, it is not clear to the newborn and the parents what it means to have entered infancy and parenthood. Whether delivery takes place at home, in a taxi, or in a hospital delivery ward, the newborn meets an unknown world. In our biblical paraphrase, life in the womb was "night" whereas the new existence is "day". And now there is breastfeeding and sleep and awakening and crying and breastfeeding again – the first day. And the parents look at the baby and at each other in awe, amazement, anxiety, doubt, joy, hesitation, strength, weakness, exhaustion, resolve, and fear. Or, even more painful, they "feel nothing".

This stage in life is crammed with emotional changes that may bring about the parents' best assets, but also their limitations. It has a forward direction; parents prepare to take care of a future life embedded and embodied in the expectant mother. They mature and feel responsible, and they shift from egocentric preoccupations to caring for their young. But this era also has a backward direction. Seldom in life is the pull of *regression* – a movement towards more immature functioning – so insistent and distressing. This is because the parents' implicit memories of babyhood are stirred up. In other terms, *attachments* to their own parents reawaken and affect their relationship with the child. Such recollections and patterns also contain painful and upsetting memories, which up until now were repressed more solidly; their childhood's impotence, fears, isolation, and sadness. Now they may emerge – rarely as clear memories but as dark clouds that obscure their vision and prevent them from relishing their baby and enjoying parenthood.

In the words of the psychoanalyst Therese Benedek (1959), the mother was once herself a child who *introjected* – she instilled in her personality – from *her* mother what it felt like to be fed, nursed, and cared for. In her present mothering experience, she will relive with her baby "the pleasure and pains of infancy" (p. 395). Such phenomena constitute what Fraiberg (1987) called *the ghosts in the nursery*: "the visitors of the unremembered past of the parents; the uninvited guests at the christening" (p. 100). Unconscious fantasies can coax her into believing that she will not be a good mother, have a healthy baby, or enjoy parenthood.

Other periods in life may also be marked by regressive and progressive fluctuations. When we get ill, we may shrink to childlike behaviours and emotions and become helpless and whining. In adolescence, the skills and securities painstakingly acquired during childhood may crumble and we might feel indecisive, stupid, embarrassed, and flawed. To be true, imminent danger or positive possibilities can also make us progress and become courageous and enterprising. What then constitutes the perinatal period's peculiar psychological characteristics? One answer is that *progression and regression occur simultaneously*. The parents feel weak and strong, certain and uncertain, silly and wise – all at once. As we shall see when discussing the concept "primary maternal preoccupation" in Chapter 2, parents need to go through such vacillations to become competent, loving, and reasonably secure in their identities. A second answer is that the perinatal period compels them to shift from love of oneself to love of the child; in other terms, from *narcissism* to *object love*. To accomplish this without feeling annoyed, disappointed, or angry is not easy. A third reply is that the mother's body, including its sexual aspects, is involved from conception and onwards. If this was a thorny subject to her, it may interfere with her becoming a mother. The father's sexual maturity is also challenged. While he perhaps feels proud of having conceived the child and become a dad, he may simultaneously feel uncertain as a man, competitive with his partner, and jealous of the child.

We will return to the issue of regression and progression throughout this book and a brief example will suffice here: A common cold can make anyone feel pitiable and weak. For a woman going through all the corporal changes during gestation, such a pull can be all the more powerful. Any man can feel resentful when his wife speaks appreciatively of her male colleague. It is all the easier for him to feel left out when pondering what goes on inside her body! But, pregnancy can also be a time of pride, joy, and progress for both parents. As Benedek (1959) puts it, "parenthood utilizes the same primary processes which operate from infancy on in mental growth and development" (p. 389). I would add that in parenthood the *primary processes*, that is, the more primitive levels of psychic functioning, are enforced and may take the upper hand. Our task is to understand the clinical consequences of such an imbalance and how we can treat them in psychotherapy, whether at length or – as is the focus of this book – in brief consultations.

Union and separation

Let us return to the Bible story. After completing the creation of cosmos and earth, it centres on the making of man. Unexpectedly, separation is now expressed as a force that promotes development. When Adam has been severed from a rib and Eve is created, the text concludes: "That is why a man leaves his father and mother and is united to his wife, and they become one flesh" (Gen. 2; 24). If we condone the text's masculine bias, it conveys an important message: The creation of man and woman opens up the possibility of a future love relationship, but it will not come about unless they separate from their parents. In a love relationship, confluence and separation are intertwined and cannot exist without each other.

Other religious texts give more tragic renditions of separation. The pregnancies of the mothers of Moses, Jesus, and Muhammed were darkened by death and the threat of murder. In the book of Exodus, the Egyptian Pharaoh ordered all newborn Hebrew boys to be slain. Moses' mother hid him for three months and then set him off in a basket on the Nile. He was saved by Pharaoh's daughter who allowed a wet-nurse – Moses' mother in disguise – to feed him. After weaning, their second and final separation occurred. Her pregnancy and his first months of life were thus marred by the fear of infanticide and abandonment.

In Matthew II, Herod orders all newborn boys to be slaughtered, but Joseph's family flees. Like Moses, Jesus begins life in the shadow of infanticide. In Muhammed's case, his father died during his mother's pregnancy. When he was 5 years old, she fell ill and died. His grandfather became care-taker but soon died as well. Why have the three religions chosen such dreadful "in the beginning"-stories for their founders? The texts do not connect their childhood trauma with later achievements and personalities. In view of psychoanalytic theory, attachment research, and clinical experience their prognosis was grim. Their parents' internal worlds must have been filled with fantasies of death, loss, and humiliation, and one may wonder how a secure attachment could come about in a child born in such dire straits. The authors must have intuited that intra-uterine life and the first years can be of decisive importance for the future. The enigma is how they imagined that the hero's beginnings linked with his later deeds and personality.

I will use the spiritual leaders to illustrate a recurrent question: How are we to understand the *cause* of a psychological reaction? It is easy to imagine the perinatal stress of Moses' mother. But can we claim that the calamities in his infancy *caused* later character flaws and emotional problems, such as his hot temper, lack of impulse control, and speech difficulties (as mentioned in Exodus)? In broader terms, what are the causal mechanisms behind a phenomenon, reaction, feeling, idea, relational pattern, etc.? We can approach such questions from the neuro-scientist's lab, the sociologist's data sheet, the social psychologist's questionnaire, and the psychotherapist's caseload. Each method yields data with different kinds of validity, reliability, and generalizability. No method is inherently superior, none more true or "scientific". The point is to (1) know on which method the investigator construes his/her findings, (2) report which instruments were used to amass the findings, and (3) comprehend that each method may use the same term but define it in divergent ways.

To illustrate, depression is said to be "one of the most common complications of pregnancy" (Marcus et al., 2011, p. 26). This statement relies on epidemiological data derived from questionnaires. The statistics showed that pregnancy is paralleled by depression more often than we have realized – and that we must consider this when we plan health care for future parents. Such studies search for *general* truths, while a therapist searches for *individual* truth. I may say that two patients are depressed but their stories, personalities, symptoms, behaviours, etc., diverge – and they will do so the more I get to know them in therapy. Therapists need to clarify to patients and health service policy makers that *individuals are individual.* Accordingly, when a psychoanalyst sets up hypotheses based on clinical phenomena, s/he should know that their validity is restricted to the present case. Then it is up to the readers to let it inspire – or not – their work. Consequently, this book contains many cases and you will have you to judge whether they cohere into a meaningful knowledge.

I will also present systematic research studies on the emotional sufferings of parents and infants. And, I will present psychoanalytic theory, because what I just wrote is not entirely true, namely that psychoanalytic validity is confined to the individual case presented. Therapists are often criticized by scientists for relying on "anecdotal evidence". If we submit a vignette of a successful case and then claim that this is evidence of the general efficacy of our intervention, this is anathema to the scientist. "One swallow doesn't make a summer". In defence, we might claim that we applied it to several patients with good results. Yet, this would not satisfy the scientific mind, since our memory might be biased. There is, however, another argument that supports the validity of case vignettes. If they harmonize with the psychological theories underlying therapeutic work, this supports the efficacy of the treatments. If not, we need to refine or reject the theory – or the therapy mode. Thus, when I wrote that you must judge if the vignettes are meaningful to *you*, I did not imply that any psychological theory is OK. It needs to be complex, diversified, and clear so we can discern where it needs to be refuted or developed.

Mary's "delossery"

Let us now focus on clinical work. To understand how some individuals feel when they are "in the beginning", let me introduce *Mary*. She is in her 40s and is in psychoanalysis due to recurrent anxious and depressive moods. One concern is her relationship with *Phil*, her firstborn 12-year-old son. He is obsessed with computer games, engages little in family life, and his personal hygiene is not a success. School is boring and the teachers have voiced concern about his academic results.

Mary is discontented with her son, but she also resents *her own* behaviour with him. The two run into squabbling dialogues, in which he pushes her to yield

8 Part I: Clinic

to demands such as postponing homework for another day. Mary gets angry and raises her voice until he starts crying, unable to understand her indignation. Phil is bestowed privileges to which the family has slowly adapted. Not until an outsider, in this case me, her analyst, shows surprise at her story does reflection get started. She starts pondering why she and her husband accept habits in Phil that they do not condone in themselves or in his younger sister.

> Mary: *"With his little sister there's no problem! My husband is also concerned about Phil but he doesn't get upset. There's a distance between Phil and me, there always was, no, that's not true . . . Not when I was pregnant. I wanted a child so MUCH! My husband wasn't that committed and I felt lonely during pregnancy. But God was I beautiful! I felt complete, full of life, filled with life. Then, at the delossery something happened. Everything went well from a medical point of view, but . . ."*
>
> Analyst: *"You said 'delossery'. What comes to your mind?"*
>
> Mary: *"'Delossery'. . . It sounds like a combo of 'delivery' and 'loss'."*
>
> Analyst: *"A child was born. You had been longing so much. Yet, maybe you felt it was a loss, too. Delivery and loss at the same time."*
>
> Mary: *"I recall feeling sad when Phil was a baby. I also felt ashamed. It had nothing to do with him! He was a sweet boy and my husband soon became a devoted father. I still can't grasp that shame."*

I know from our previous work of Mary's shame of herself. She has often felt awkward and unfit. Like Phil she hated school, felt clumsy and stupid and did not grasp the teachers' instructions. She is intelligent but sometimes she dissembles as a silly person. Like our biblical heroes mentioned earlier, Mary was born under the sign of death; when her mother was pregnant with her, an elderly family member, who was loved by both parents and was a maternal figure to Mary's mother, suddenly died. Her parents' marriage capsized when Mary was only 2 years old. She recalls switching between the homes of her parents, who soon became bitter enemies.

Mary's story provides a background to her feeling of loss during delivery and her shame with Phil. During pregnancy, she felt wonderful and beautiful. But after delivery, her lifelong tattered self-image of a rag doll and a silly schoolgirl re-emerged. She felt ashamed of herself and of Phil, though her embarrassment blended with love and care. I do not know why Phil has issues with restlessness and attention. But I do know that today, Mary's corroded self-image weakens her ability to help him. When she sees him handling an object in a clumsy way, it awakens her own "ghost in the nursery" (Fraiberg, 1987, p. 100), whispering that *she* is silly and maladroit. When this hated self-image re-merges, she is overcome with hatred of Phil as well, which reinforces her shame. Her slip was telling; she was delivered with a child but lost an illusion of perfection which she, as long as pregnancy lasted, had used to counter her ragged self-esteem. The story shows that a mother's emotions during pregnancy can be deeply influenced by her life history. We will now introduce a woman for whom a medical emergency during pregnancy caused an emotional upheaval.

Who's going to die: Karen or the foetus?

I met *Karen* and her son *Cristopher* a few months after a delivery that had been preceded by disastrous events. Her story made me ponder; when do we become parents? When the child is born? Fair enough, but *when* is s/he born? When egg and sperm meet? When the fertilized egg settles in the uterine wall? Or, when the child leaves the womb and gives his first birth cry? From a psychological vertex, the answer is somewhere in between. Once the parents learn about the pregnancy, mighty expectations, fears, wishes, and anxieties are set in motion. How is "it" going to be? Like me? Like my partner? Will it become handy, sporty, intelligent, mischievous, malformed, beautiful . . .? Will everything be fine during pregnancy or will something bad happen?

Karen, a 35-year-old woman, had been together with Johnny for several years. Both were successful professionally, liked travelling, and had many friends. Now it was time to have a child, although Karen "never was the child type". The child was conceived quickly and everything went well, but during the 20th week of pregnancy she got severe abdominal pains. At the ER at the hospital an ileus was diagnosed, that is, the intestinal passage was blocked. A CT-scan revealed a retroperitoneal tumour, which might be malignant and lethal. A less grave scenario was a benign tumour but if so, what about the child? It was too late for an induced abortion and besides, Karen and Johnny really longed for a child. What should Karen do?

> For three weeks, while waiting for the cytological diagnosis, I asked myself: 'Who's going to die, me or the child?' If I wouldn't survive, neither would the child. I decided to be the first survivor. It was appalling to prioritize my life rather than the child's!

Three weeks later the pathologists were convinced; the tumour was benign. The surgeons planned a Caesarean two months ahead of her due date. Karen, who had just escaped from an impending death sentence, did not want to complain that she had expected a vaginal delivery. "The important thing was that the baby and I made it!" Yet, breastfeeding did not start. "I was too stressed. But I was so grateful that we survived that I didn't want to grumble."

When I see Karen and Cristopher at the Child Health Centre (CHC), he is 2½ months old. The health visitor has told me that Karen is worried and sad.

Karen:	*"So, everything should be fine now, I guess."*
Analyst:	*"If everything were OK you wouldn't be here. I've understood from your health visitor that things aren't easy for you."*
Karen points at Cristopher:	*"I panic when I am alone with . . . him . . . After delivery, when my husband was still at home with me, everything was fine. But now he's resumed work, and the moment he leaves home I get anxious. I get into a tizzy, just waiting for Johnny to come home."*
Analyst:	*"Do you have any hunch about what your panic is all about?"*
Karen:	*"No . . . I can already leave Chris to a baby-sitter. I don't feel anything special, but my mum friends get withdrawal symptoms after one hour! They're normal, not me! They chat about the joys of motherhood, but I've never experienced those things."*
Analyst:	*"Maybe your 'feeling string' was broken. Chris had a navel string until recently. All kinds of good stuff were flowing through it. Similarly, feelings and fantasies were flowing from you to him."*
Karen:	*"Are you intimating that this 'string' was broken? How do you know!?"*
Analyst:	*"I don't know, and I didn't say that. We can only speculate about how things were for Chris. But we do know that your expectations of a wonderful pregnancy were cut off."*

Now and then during our first conversation, Karen is looking at her boy. It is a special gaze; searching, thoughtful, and a bit awkward, as if she does not know what to do with their contact. He is a sweet boy who looks at length into his mother's eyes. He does not seem negatively affected by his mother's struggle to fall in love with him. He seems to lie waiting for her to decide: 'Well, Mum, when are you finally gonna discover what a cute guy I am?'

I turn to Chris:

Mum went through some horrible times. She thought you were going to die in her tummy. She didn't know if she was ever going to hold you in her arms. She didn't even know if she was going to survive herself. It was just terrible.

With a searching look, Chris observes me. He neither smiles nor seems depressed. It is as if he is sitting in the waiting room of a railway station, wondering when the "love train" will pick him up. Meanwhile, Karen tells me that the doctors have recommended her not to have any more children. The tumour was removed, but a new pregnancy might restart the process. Karen now becomes sad in a more clear and unrestrained way and Chris whines a while. I wonder if this is due to the changed state of Karen's mind. I share this thought with Karen and we continue talking. When asked about what she wants me to help her with, she replies: "I want to *enjoy* being with Chris!"

Karen comes from a "normal" family; no big problems, good support from her parents, "though talking about feelings is perhaps not their favourite game". Sports were always important. Today, her parents are happy to help the new little family. Karen is very fond of her husband, loves her work, and goes to the gym several times a week. "It's a bit like a drug. I guess I'm a bit restless. At the gym, they speak about endorphins . . ."

Analyst:	*"You speak of some restlessness that you keep in check with your gym classes. Is that feeling connected with the panic at home with Chris?"*
Karen:	*"The other mums at the CHC spend cosy moments with their babies. They just can't take their eyes away from them! But I get nervous and check my diary. In the morning, if I realize that there are no entries I go nuts. When I look at him I don't know what I'm feeling!"*
Analyst:	*"Like now? It's as if you're looking at someone you don't really know."*
Karen:	*"I don't know him! The other mums, we meet regularly in a group, their babies are of the same age but . . ."*
Analyst:	*"I think they're some months older than Chris."*
Karen:	*"No no, they're the same age."*
Analyst:	*"Right, but their feeling strings were not cut off like between you and Chris. So they're ahead of you. You learnt about the tumour. Maybe the foetus, maybe you, were going to die. When you learnt it was benign you had to start all over again and glue the string together."*
Karen is crying softly:	*"He's such a cute boy, I know that. What if I could feel it one day!"*

Our contact lasted eight sessions over a period of a few months. The bulk of our work took place in the first two sessions. Returning for the second hour, her way of looking at Chris had changed. There was a glow in her eyes. Sometimes it faded when she spoke about worrying things. But then the curtain withdrew and her love of the boy emerged.

> *Karen:*   *"I thought a lot about our conversation. I've been so rational. Everybody kept reassuring me that I should be happy now that we made it. Your way of listening helped me grasp that the things Chris and I had been through were horrible. Earlier I thought, 'We made it so just get on with it'. As if life is a gym class and you grit your teeth to make those final minutes on the cross-trainer!"*

The pregnancies of Mary and Karen were quite different. What, however, united them was that they soon repressed how the events and the emotions impacted on their relationship with the foetus and, subsequently, the child. Mary was so pre-occupied with her wondrous condition that she, perhaps, allowed less space for thinking and dreaming about her future child. Karen was terrified and absorbed with carrying a catastrophe in her womb. Psychotherapy helped the women become aware of the emotional impact of these matters. This enabled the two, one with a preadolescent son and the other with a baby boy, to chisel out their *projections* onto the child.

We could summarize our work by stating that they both came *closer to*, and *further away* from, the child. Let me explain the paradox. When I use the term projection, I refer to the mechanism by which one person ascribes his own traits or intentions to another person. Of course, our negative projections are more problematic since they, so to speak, invent our own enemies. When we get hold of our projections, by therapy or other interchanges, they become manageable and we can look at the other person and at ourselves with less hackneyed and prejudiced eyes. Mary and Karen became less enmeshed with their sons. When Mary and I put words to her old "romance with her pregnant self", she started looking at Phil with fresh eyes and as an individual. Karen was released from a freeze that prevented her from discerning Chris as a vital and lovely baby boy, not a relic of a foetus that menaced their lives. In this, the two mothers got closer to the boys. In parallel, they got more distant in that they allowed their sons to become individuals in their own right and less tainted by projections. We will return to them in the next chapter when discussing some concepts that are necessary for understanding the psychology of pregnancy.

Chapter 2

The psychology of pregnancy

"The cultural stereotype of a pregnant woman suggests that her primary emotional state is uninterrupted bliss and serenity" (Slade, Cohen, Sadler, & Miller, 2009, p. 25). I agree: Think of all the paintings with Virgin Mary smiling in wonder at her child, which make us forget that "the vulnerability of this period cannot be overstated, both from the mother's as well as the unborn infant's mental health" (p. 22). To grasp this blend of bliss and vulnerability and the unconscious implications of pregnancy, we will start by consulting the etymology of the word *pregnant* and synonyms in other languages. One source, www.etymonline.com, introduces an ambiguity; pregnant means "with child" as well as "cogent, compelling". The first signification stems from "before birth" (from *pre* + *gnasci* = be born). The second is rooted in the Latin *premere*, implying "press" and "squeeze", which has yielded denotations of "significant", "salient", and "protruding". In Swedish, the ancient word was *havande* or "having". Today, we use *gravid* from the Latin *gravis* or "heavy". Similarly, in French *grossesse* stems from *gros* or big and fat. A synonym, *enceinte*, is rooted in *ceindre*, "to rim" or "to wrap" (www. cntrl.fr). The German *Schwangerschaft* relates to words implying "bent" and "curved" (www.woerterbuchnetz.de) and to *schwingen*, or *swing* in English.

Our findings point in various directions. Many words indicate the woman's changed physical state and movement pattern when she is *havande* with a child in her body. Does *have* imply that she is an active *subject* involved in a process – or an *object* harbouring another object inside herself? The answer will waver according to what she feels about her pregnancy for the moment. This chapter will stay with this *double entendre*. We now turn to another English synonym; *expectant*. This word also has passive and active connotations. Compare "I expect a thunderstorm tomorrow" with "I expect to study these documents tomorrow". The complexity of pregnancy lies in the unique mixture of psychological activity and passivity, preparing and waiting, doing and being, cognizing and dreaming. The woman needs to "integrate reality with unconscious fantasy, hopes and daydreams" (Pines, 2010, p. 63). Also, she prepares to "meet the demands of a helpless creature who represents strongly cathected areas of self and non-self, and many past relationships" (idem). It is felicitous that parents have three quarters of a year to integrate these facets before receiving the newcomer!

14 Part I: Clinic

In Chapter 1, Mary had blissful expectations about her future child. Much of this went to pieces at Phil's "delossery", and her ensuing shame and sadness complicated their relationship. Karen, in contrast, started pregnancy with positive expectations that crashed as she learnt about the tumour and must face excruciating existential decisions. The relationship with her son Chris became intricate but in a different way than for Mary, in that her "feeling string" was cut off. In psychoanalytic terms, her *internal relation* to the object "My Future Child", initially filled with warm and positive expectations, suddenly became fraught with death, murder, despair, and loss. In other terms, there was a severe threat to her *foetal attachment* (Cannella, 2005; Sandbrook & Adamson-Macedo, 2004), a concept we will soon discuss.

Research on maternal distress during pregnancy

Did the tumultuous events during Karen's pregnancy affect the foetus? No one knows and, as said, Chris seemed alright over the months that I followed him. To reiterate from Chapter 1, we must differentiate between quantitative evidence garnered from statistical samples and qualitative evidence amassed through individual encounters in psychotherapy. Researchers have established many links between emotional stress during pregnancy and negative effects on the foetus and the newborn. They also understand much of the physiological basis, although "the precise mechanisms of communication of stress between the mother and fetus are unknown" (Sandman & Davis, 2010, p. 678). The most well-studied biochemical mechanism is the LHPA (limbic-hypothalamic-pituitary-adrenal axis). For depressed patients, this stress-regulating system seems to be in an "overdrive" state regarding adrenal and cerebral activity. Newborns whose mothers were depressed during pregnancy had higher levels of adrenocorticotropic hormone (ACTH) at birth (Marcus et al., 2011). It is released from the brain's pituitary and stimulates the adrenals to increase production of the stress hormone cortisol. These mothers' babies did *not* have a higher cortisol level, but perhaps their constantly increased ACTH level disabled the feedback loop by which cortisol normally diminishes ACTH production. For a recent review of this field, see Seth, Lewis and Galbally (2016).

Babies of mothers who were depressed during pregnancy are also more hypotonic and habituate more quickly to auditory and visual stimuli. This tallies with findings (Field, Diego, & Hernandez-Reif, 2009) that these mothers' neonates are less responsive to faces, voices, and, later, to still-face exposure. Studies show connections between pregnancy distress and diminished foetal growth and increased motility (Conde et al., 2010), sleep disorders and crying in the newborn (Field et al., 2007), problems with affect regulation, premature birth, and conductive disorders (Martini, Knappe, Beesdo-Baum, Lieb, & Wittchen, 2010), delayed motor and mental development (Huizink, Robles de Medina, Mulder, Visser, & Buitelaar, 2003), and impaired cognition (Sandman & Davis, 2010). A recent review (Suri, Lin, Cohen, & Altshuler, 2014) summarizes such findings. I omit listing how pregnancy stress also links with adversities during delivery and future medical problems in the child. We cannot dismiss these findings by claiming that prenatal depression is rare: "In most studies, the prevalence has hovered somewhere between 30% and 40%" (Field, 2011, p. 2). Prenatal emotional suffering is thus even more common than its postnatal counterpart.

I use "distress" for stress and depression because for a clinician, the conditions are hard to differentiate. Cf. our biblical cases in Chapter 1: Who could tell if the expectant mothers of Moses, Jesus, and Muhammed were depressed or stressed? Probably, there was depression due to impending loss *and* stress due to the impact on their daily lives. It has been suggested (O'Connor, Monk, & Fitelson, 2013) that the arrival of SSRI drugs (Selective Serotonin Reuptake Inhibitors – drugs typically used to curb depressive and anxious emotions) has led to a focus on depression more than on stress. I argue that any woman who is worried, moody, stressed, sad, angry – in short, who expresses a need for help – should be offered a consultation with a therapist. The aim is to tease out how *she* perceives *her* distress and how it is "influenced by many factors including genetics, social support and personality" (Sandman & Davis, 2010, p. 676). Such subjective factors, plus the timing of the onset of stress, make it impossible to forecast an individual child's development. O'Connor et al. (2013) suggest practitioners should pay attention to these findings and view neurobehavioural development as beginning already *before* birth. I completely agree, especially since longitudinal data are accumulating, indicating that maternal prenatal anxiety and depression predict behavioural and emotional symptoms in childhood and adolescence (O'Donnell, Glover, Barker, & O'Connor, 2014).

Should we interpret the studies to indicate that a child's future mental health is determined and set at birth? I think not. A study (Bergman, Sarkar, Glover, & O'Connor, 2008) showed a link between maternal prenatal stress and infant fearfulness at 17 months. It also demonstrated that an insecure-ambivalent attachment at this age accentuated the link. Thus, "postnatal parenting may moderate the adverse effects of antenatal stress" (p. 1089). I venture that if prenatal or mother–infant therapy had been instituted promptly, fearfulness and insecurity *might* have decreased. As for Karen, she contacted me when Chris was 2½ months old. When I observed him and listened to her, he seemed alright. But, if her anxious and ambivalent relationship with him had lasted and her worried and depressed mood had continued, this *could* have affected him negatively.

Primary maternal preoccupation

If we can neither establish neurophysiological causalities nor speak with the foetus, one channel remains for psychoanalytic investigations: to talk with the pregnant woman about how she is feeling. To this end, we need a theory about emotional changes during this period of life. One concept, *primary maternal preoccupation*, was coined by D.W. Winnicott (1956a). He departed from the psychological difference between "on the one hand, the mother's identification with the infant and, on the other, the infant's dependence on the mother" (p. 301). His concept refers to a mother's identification with her infant – "conscious but also deeply unconscious" (idem). This "very special state" develops gradually into "a state of heightened sensitivity, especially towards the end of pregnancy" (p. 302). Later, she will repress the memory. Were she not pregnant, we might mistake it for an illness like "a withdrawn state, or a dissociated state, or a fugue" (p. 302).

Pregnant women tend to complain of being "soft", dreamy, scatter-brained, and forgetful. One reason is that they are preoccupied with the child's future: "Did I eat unhealthy food? Whom will the child look like? How will my parents react?" In contrast, one study indicates that new mothers perform *better* on cognitive tests (Pereira & Ferreira, 2015). A Canadian study (Gonzalez, Jenkins, Steiner & Fleming, 2012) showed their performance to be positively associated with their sensitivity to the baby's emotional signals. Maybe, the mothers need cognitive functions "to recognize and attend to their infant cues and to integrate environmental demands with the needs of their infant" (p. 679). Despite these indications of cognitive acuity, new mothers do appear "woozy" sometimes. Perhaps, they have simply begun to identify with the baby. Before pregnancy, it was important to know the day of the week. Now, they consider such knowledge petty. In this, they resemble the baby. S/he needs Mum to grasp the emotional import beneath his "little sorrows" and "soft desires" (Blake, 1994) rather than if it is Tuesday or Wednesday. Her muddle thus represents an empathic identification with the baby and thus, maternal preoccupation contains much *creative alertness*.

Another background to mothers' "fog" or "breastfeeding brain" is "the re-emergence of previously repressed fantasies into pre-consciousness and consciousness" (Pines, 2010, p. 49), for example, of carrying a devouring foetus or disgusting worms inside. No wonder, such unconscious fantasies will disturb her focus on worldly matters. Yet Pines states, like Winnicott, that they do not signal severe pathology. It is as if "the reality of the kicking baby" (idem) affords the ego a security, whence it can let go of such "follies". Pines detected these fantasies in women in psychoanalysis, where she offered them the security of containing their anxieties. This enabled her to link anxieties, like a mother's ambitious preoccupation with correct food intake, with unconscious fantasies of, for example, ambivalence towards the intruder. Pregnant women who do not get such help often feel lonely and exposed to demons they cannot comprehend. We will learn more about them in Chapter 3.

The French analyst Monique Bydlowski (2001) compares pregnant women's internal situation to adolescents, with their inward look and egocentricity. They easily shift between orienting towards reality and fantasy life – similarly to what she calls the "psychological transparency" between the pregnant woman's conscious and unconscious mentation, and between herself and the surrounding world. To Winnicott (1956a, p. 303), these changes provide:

> a setting for the infant's constitution to begin to make itself evident, for the
> developmental tendencies to start to unfold, and for the infant to experience

spontaneous movement and become the owner of the sensations that are appropriate to this early phase of life.

We now realize that the beneficiary of these psychological changes in the mother is *the baby*. Gentile (2007), a US analyst, points to a paradox; by giving up parts of her adult identity, the mother helps the infant to create *his/her* own identity. She negates her own mind and offers the baby her "unimpinging subjectivity" (p. 556). If we stop at Gentile's words, it is no wonder that mothers can have very mixed feelings towards the child. In the words of another analyst (Harris, 1997), "mothers hate babies for their impact on the mother's life and liberty, hate them for the extraordinary control and self-management that being a parent requires" (p. 320).

Primary maternal preoccupation is thus a double-edged concept. It signifies that "the mother is so identified with her baby's needs that her own recede, if they do not disappear altogether" (Slochower, 1996, p. 198). On the other hand, it comprises her sound anger with the foetal "occupant". Gentile (2007) points out, like Arietta Slade in this chapter's beginning, that the literature tends to emphasize the self-forgetting and symbiotic aspects of maternity and to downplay the reverse of the medal; the future mother is also angry with the infiltrator who disrupts her narcissistic equilibrium, autonomy, and bodily integrity. Mothers who are anxious, depressed, or insecure find it especially unacceptable that they would be angry. It falls upon the therapist to help differentiate between sound and necessary anger, and destructive, disruptive, and vehement rage. Chapter 3 will portray Donna, for whom these issues began during pregnancy.

One difficulty for a pregnant woman to enter a "state of regression in the service of the baby" (Bergman, 1985) is that although "the foetus is present in the mother's body and mental preoccupations, it is absent in her visible reality. Though it is actual, it is only representable by elements of the past" (Bydlowski, 2001, p. 42). Thus, how can a mother mentalize this "it" inside of her? To answer, I transfer Bion's (1962a) model of mother–infant interaction onto the mother and her fantasized interactions with the foetus (see also Gaddini, 1981; Ogden, 2004). In Bion's model, which we will learn more about later, the baby swarms the mother with undigested mental waste products that he calls β-*elements*. In other terms, the baby's "wild thoughts" (Bion, 1997) are searching for a thinker and find one in the mother. In a state of *reverie* she receives, reflects, digests, and returns them to the baby as more comprehensible messages or α-*elements*. Such *containment* is possible because she is in a "state of mind which is open to the reception of any 'objects' from the loved object" (Bion, 1962a, p. 36). In parallel, the pregnant woman tries to get to know the foetus via a fantasized communication. True, it does not answer her stroking the tummy, talking, or dreaming, so the traffic is one-way. But, she can fantasize a dialogue between herself and the foetus. This can include a traffic of her own "waste products" or β-elements being superseded by messages that are more acceptable and lenient. She might go from thinking "Ouch, my back hurts, I'm sick of this hefty monster" to "Imagine, in one month's time I'll be a mother and will talk to him". She can also extend such interchanges into a "trilogue" (Fivaz-Depeursinge & Favez, 2006) with the future father and the two can dream together. My application of Bion's containment model helps explain how *foetal attachment*, a concept discussed in the next section, comes about.

What happens to primary preoccupation when a mother suffers trauma? Sally Moskowitz (2011), a New York analyst, movingly describes mothers who lost their husbands in the 9/11 disaster in 2001. They were facing the excruciating task of mourning their spouses while focusing on their pregnancy or newborn. Every expectant mother fears losing control of her body, but such apprehensions received further input in these women who were powerless in preventing their husbands' deaths. Some scheduled their delivery earlier, with induced labour and full anaesthesia, because they longed to see the baby who "represented all that was left of their husbands" (p. 232). Yet, when thinking of their babies it was under the spell of sadness, grief, anxiety, and lost hope. The therapists had difficulties in addressing the mothers' traumatized states and grief while simultaneously helping them interact with their babies.

Moskowitz (2011) reminds us that trauma always implies "a radical break from normal experience [and] the usual structures of meaning and categories of thought are not available and do not apply" (p. 235). This applies to Karen in Chapter 1, who went to hospital with a banal tummy ache and left with the doctors' ominous words ringing in her ears. This was an egregious, overwhelming, and un-metabolizable experience. Freud (1920) suggests that when we are unprepared for anxiety the "stimulus barrier" crashes and "the inflowing amounts of excitation and the consequences of the breach in the protective shield follow all the more easily" (p. 31). Karen did not crash but entered a hyper-factual state of mind: "First I do the examinations and the doctors will advise us, then we will decide." These deliberations, indeed respectable efforts at self-containment, were criss-crossed by swarms of anxiety, despair, and ethical considerations. The tumour thus expelled her from primary maternal preoccupation. The result was her fumbling relationship with Chris and her panic attacks.

The mystery of the father

So far, I have described the mental state of the future *mother*. When I asked students what might be Mother Nature's intention with promoting such a brittle mental state in someone who is about to take care of a helpless creature, some men observed: "When the future father notices that his partner is helpless and unstable, he becomes protective and supportive." They had a point; his caretaking impulses are triggered by the mother's preoccupation. Should we even stretch their argument into suggesting a *paternal preoccupation* similar to Winnicott's conception of the mother?

When we theorize about fathers, a major problem is if we speak of a physical person or a psychological function. When conceiving of mothers, it was easier to criss-cross between both alternatives, because what happens in her psyche is interwoven with her bodily changes. She cannot hide her pregnancy to herself and others and thus, she is *certissima* or very certain as the old Latin adage goes. But to become a father, whether he acknowledges fatherhood or not, is initially a more abstract experience. Thus, the Latin term describing paternity, *semper incertus* or always uncertain, refers not only to a biological fact but also to a psychological condition. Is this why psychoanalysis has had less to say about the father's experiences? Freud did write extensively about the father, but it was "the historical oedipal father, the object of desire, or a figure arousing destructive rivalry" (Eizirik, 2015, p. 343). In the words of Diamond (2017), "psychoanalysis has largely neglected the *actual* flesh-and-blood father while privileging the *symbolic* oedipal father" (p. 298). In *Totem and Taboo* (Freud, 1913b), for example, the main character is the dead/absent father, not the expectant man accompanying his partner to the antenatal clinic. Yet, Diamond brings out a contrasting opinion in Freud (1930) who could not "think of any need in childhood as strong as the need for a father's protection" (p. 72). Freud's focus on the father's adversarial role in the boy's Oedipus complex obscured, perhaps more so in his theorizing than in his observations of daily life, a more friendly and supportive aspect of him.

Especially French analysts have extrapolated the Freudian father into "a psychic formation characterized by his third-party role as a separator of mother and child, and should be understood as a *father principle* . . . [which] develops through exchanges with the primary object" (Eizirik, 2015, p. 343). One major function is to inhibit the drives roaming in the mother–infant dyad. Diamond and others criticize analytic theory for restricting the father to such an *incertus*, dead or third-party position, rather than to one where he is involved in conceiving, fantasizing, and taking care of his progeny. Yet, we must avoid confusing the concrete man with the abstract function. The physical father's impact on the child's emotional well-being has been demonstrated (Vreeswijk, Maas, Rijk, & van Bakel, 2014), but such studies tell us nothing about what goes on *inside* him. Genesoni and Tallandini (2009) portray modern men's dilemma in their transition to fatherhood. They view themselves as part of a "labouring couple" and join their partner in midwifery exams, etc. They do want to bond emotionally with the future child but also suffer from "feelings of unreality, arising out of the lack of tangible evidence of the existence of their unborn child" (p. 313). Their outsider position might explain why Vreeswijk et al. (2014) found fewer balanced representations (Zeanah, Benoit, & Barton, 1986) of the future child among expectant fathers (44%) than among mothers (62%). Fathers were thus "less able to describe their relationship with the unborn child in detail or could not give descriptions of the infant's personality" (p. 76).

To explain Vreeswijk et al.'s findings, I would invoke the facts of biology; the woman carries the child. In my view, any efforts at equalizing fathers' and mothers' preoccupations will collapse in front of this fact. If it can be difficult for expectant mothers to create fantasies of an unknown and unseen creature inside their bodies, how much harder is it for fathers? A man of today can be 100% certain about fatherhood – but psychologically he will remain more *incertus* than the woman. Today's fathers perceive a "disequilibrium in the relationship with their partner" and experience difficulties in making "a core identity shift from the role of partner to that of parent" (Genesoni & Tallandini, 2009, p. 313). They seem caught in a dilemma; they struggle with being outsiders while also feeling that they must be strong and supportive of the partner and that their worries are minor compared with hers (Stavrén-Eriksson, 2016).

Even though I clarified earlier that evidence garnered from dialogues with therapy patients is not on par with what is collected in lab studies, some recent neurobiological research (Feldman, Gordon, & Zagoory-Sharon, 2011; Swain, Dayton, Kim, Tolman, & Volling, 2014) inspires my thinking of what might differ between fathers' and mothers' psychological setups. These researchers found that *both* parents undergo neurophysiological changes during pregnancy and afterwards. Feldman's group showed that mothers of babies aged 4–6 months showed higher amygdala activations that correlated with oxytocin levels. Fathers showed greater activations in social-cognitive circuits, which correlated with vasopressin. In their conclusion, the mothers' "enhanced limbic-motivational activity . . . may point to the deeply rooted, phylogenetically ancient role of mothering, whereas fathers' enhanced social-cognitive activations may reflect the more culturally *facultative* role of fathering" (Atzil, Hendler, Zagoory-Sharon, Winetraub, & Feldman, 2012, p. 805, italics added). They also found that the two parents' brain-to-brain synchrony when responding to the baby's signals paved the way for the child's attachment development. The parents' emotional cooperation thus mattered a great deal.

The italicized word in the preceding paragraph, "facultative", points to a problem that is also revealed by "*pater semper incertus est*". Far from all men are willing to, or capable of, supporting their spouses in this process and becoming the child's "primary playmate" (Roggman, Boyce, Cook, Christiansen, & Jones, 2004). The price paid by the child becomes evident if we consult the *activation relationship theory* (Paquette, Coyl-Shepherd, & Newland, 2013). The father helps the child open up to the outside world, which furthers "the development of autonomy and the management of risk-taking . . . the development of physical and social skills, self-assertiveness, anger management, and academic and professional success" (p. 740). To Swain et al. (2014), he provides *stimulation* encouraging the child's interaction with the outside world, and *discipline* which sets limits to maintain his/her safety (p. 396). But, if the father feels *incertus*, remote, frustrated, or angry, the paternal function may crumble.

Returning to Winnicott's preoccupation concept, he reserved it for women. In fact, fathers appear rarely in his descriptions of infant development. I agree with the critique (Rutherford & Mayes, 2014) that he viewed the father as a mere "holding environment for the attunement of the mother-infant dyad". Today, a father's role differs from the Zeitgeist in Winnicott's days. Being a father is perhaps more fun and more difficult nowadays. Fun, because men have progressed from being breadwinners to co-workers in the commitments of parenthood. Difficult, because gender roles are still vacillating – and nature forces men to reach emotional contact with parenthood later and more indirectly. It is a paradox, but no coincidence, that Genesoni and Tallandini (2009) report pregnancy to be a most stressful time for men. Draper (2003) outlines their dilemma; lack of knowledge about the process, feelings of isolation, inability to engage in the reality of the pregnancy, sense of redundancy, and "frustrations at not being able to directly feel what their partners were feeling" (p. 70).

We clinicians must consider the future father's experiences of detachment, surprise, and confusion (Chin, Hall, & Daiches, 2011), or apprehension and helplessness (Poh, Koh, & He, 2014). We may call them examples of *paternal preoccupation* – as long as we remember the differences between the origins and qualities of such experiences in men and women. Now, if expectant and new fathers also may suffer, why are there so many mothers in this book? First, it focuses on the psychology of pregnancy and the first year of life. For this brief period, as I argued, the two parents impact differently on the child and their personal experiences also diverge. Another explanation is that I have less therapeutic experience with expectant fathers. Certainly, this may reflect a bias in psychoanalytic theory and training programmes with an "exaltation of paternal power and marginalization of fathers from the fabric of family life" (Freeman, 2008, p. 113) which, if so, would stymie my grasp of their contributions. Freeman criticizes an alleged tendency in psychoanalysis to define the father in terms of absence and see him "as an unwelcome threat to the maternal dyad [which] occludes the possibility of early paternal intimacy and love" (p. 120).

Freeman's critique has a point – and is unfair. Some analytic authors did highlight warmer and friendlier aspects of the father's role from the 1950s and onwards (Abelin, 1975; Blos, 1985; Loewald, 1951). Yet, they centred more on the young *child's* unconscious image of the father than on what we are discussing: the *adult* man's vision of being a father. Her critique against the notion of the father as a threat to the maternal dyad I would counter by arguing that this is indeed so – and that it should be so. Lacan, one of the analysts Freeman criticizes, refers to a function and not a person, when he speaks of the Name of the Father (*Nom-du-Père*). In his condensed language, "the father, to the extent that he promulgates the law is the dead father, that is, the symbol of the father" (Lacan, 1998, p. 146). It has two purposes. One is to prohibit; this is the *Non-du-Père*, as in the Oedipal law *though shalt not*. In instituting discipline, to use Swain's term (2014), he is an unwelcome threat to mother and baby who try to maintain a perfect and illusive bliss. When he commands the individual to assign *names* (*Nom-du-Père*) to his desire, that is, to accept the symbolic order he, to once again quote Swain, stimulates the child to use language to discover the outside world.

The message of the paternal function is thus twofold: "No, Mum is my woman, I have a special right to her, we had a relationship long before you were born." And, "No, life has no magic wands, you and Mum are wonderful but you are subject to the same reality as we all are. We have to speak to mediate our wishes." Evidently, I now switched to the real father. Indeed, many tasks fall upon a man just turned father. One is to support, encourage, and concretely relieve mother and baby from various pressures. Another is to send messages to the dyad; to claim his rights and dissipate mutual illusions of perfection. But, importantly, these tasks do not fall only on him. The mother, too, needs to represent the Name of the Father. Books and the internet have taught many ambitious parents about attachment and infant development, and they believe that unless they are stalking and appeasing the baby's wishes, development will be stunted. The baby is stuck in the role of an insatiable insomniac whose parents are food and diaper providers with no other interests in life. Sooner or later, this will collapse – unless they come to terms with this illusion often shared by both parties. Such couples have problems with instituting the Name of the Father in the family.

Green (2004) paraphrases Winnicott's (1975) famous words, "there is no such thing as an infant" (p. xxxvii) into "there is no such thing as a mother-infant relationship". He thus reminds us of the father's role. In the beginning,

> the baby relates exclusively to the maternal object, [but] this is no reason to conclude that the father has no existence whatsoever during that period . . . the good enough quality of the relationship with the mother hinges on the mother's love for the father and vice versa.
>
> (p. 101)

Her love for him is blended with, and almost overturned by, the feelings that the newborn arises in her. She is overwhelmed, enamoured, exhausted, frustrated, and frightened by the newcomer's arrival. No wonder, the regressive pull is strong. Therefore, it should be easier for the man to keep a cool eye and represent reality and the *Non-du-Père*. Here is one reason why I meet many bewildered fathers in couple therapy. They define fatherhood negatively: "I don't want to be like my Dad, never at home, just working." The reason they find it harder to define it positively is, once again, their *incertus* position. In brief, *maternity is concretion, paternity abstraction*. Men, initially that is, find it hard to establish a solid paternal role. In an interview study, a first-time father of a 1-month-old baby said:

> You are very worried that you will hurt it . . . they have tiny, tiny, tiny hands and tiny feet . . . my hand gets right in his face . . . and you know that he understands right away – that this person has no idea what he is doing, so it screams all in.
>
> (Stavrén-Eriksson, 2016, p. 3)

To sum up my views, attachment and unconscious internal relationships with the future child build up earlier in the expectant woman than in the father because she carries the foetus inside her body. The rumble from the Unconscious of the future father is discernible but more hazy and hesitant in the beginning. When the baby is delivered, shrouds of uncertainty begin to lift off and, little by little, he will feel that "the" baby becomes "my baby" and "our baby".

Research on phenomena related to primary maternal preoccupation

When Winnicott coined his concept, he gleaned observations from extensive clinical encounters. He wanted to portray pregnant women's behaviour and mood and what went on in their Unconscious. Some sample studies on pregnant women can be said to support his concept. One study (Frank, Tuber, Slade, & Garrod, 1994) submitted 25 expectant mothers (gestational age was not indicated) to *Rorschach tests* and measured their "Primary Process Integration" (PPI), that is, how much responses to the ink blots were coloured by primary process thinking and how adaptive and accurate they were. In other words, how optimal were their defences? Responses were boiled down to a PPI score (Holt, 1968). A high score meant that a woman could access affectively charged material without compromising reality testing.

When the children were 14 months old, their attachment was assessed in the Strange Situation Procedure (Ainsworth, Blehar, Waters, & Wall, 1978). As in most samples, about two thirds were securely attached. During the pregnancies, these children's mothers had higher PPI scores than mothers whose children became insecurely attached. The women in the high group responded to the Rorschach by giving "voice to frank and uninhibited expressions of sexual, aggressive, and illogically conceived material and integrat[ing] such affectively laden content into a perceptually convincing gestalt" (p. 484). Responses often centred round maternal themes and were not "weird" but counterbalanced by adequate and flexible defences. Their primary occupation was balanced, which paved the way for becoming sensitive to the infant's needs. The authors suggest that "*the psychological birth of the securely attached infant takes shape many months before the infant will be ready to survive on its own* – originating, perhaps in part, in the symbol laden world of his mother's unconscious fantasy life" (p. 485, italics added). Parallel findings were made in a study (Porcerelli, Huth-Bocks, Huprich, & Richardson, 2015) where the maturational level of the woman's defensive functioning assessed in an interview during the last trimester predicted the child's attachment security at 2 years old.

Another psychological phenomenon shows that the unconscious activity of (first-time) pregnant women is focused on maternity and the mother–child relationship. *Dreams* with such content increase as pregnancy progresses (Lara-Carrasco, Simard, Saint-Onge, Lamoureux-Tremblay, & Nielsen, 2013), which the authors interpret as the women's remodelling of the representations of the unborn baby and herself. Approaching delivery, the dreams contain more morbid elements and focus on the delivery process. "Dreams might thus be part of a 'working through process' that enables pregnant women to be more psychologically prepared to face childbirth" (p. 11). This "may be reflected indirectly in a more dysphoric emotional tone in dream content" (p. 10). In my assumption, as delivery is approaching, the mother becomes unconsciously more ambivalent to the child. Until now she has, figuratively speaking, been in full mental control of the foetus;

her fantasies have met with no reality correction. Soon, she must interact with a real and responding human being for whom she is responsible. This shift frightens many women, as we shall learn more about soon.

Fantasies, like dreams, have unconscious and conscious tributaries. As pregnancy progressed for first-time mothers, their fantasies about the child's psychological and behavioural traits increased (Sorenson & Schuelke, 1999). In contrast, fantasies decreased about the child's gender, malformations, and its status as "godlike" or not. The authors advise us against judging the fantasies as normal or not, but that we should focus on the woman's *rigidity* in her expectations of the maternal role and the baby's characteristics. This is in line with the referred Rorschach study.

Maternal–foetal attachment is another way of studying the mother's emotional relation with her foetus. The term refers to the pregnant woman's emotional relationship with her foetus; specifically, if she engages in behaviours that represent "an affiliation and interaction with [her] unborn child" (Cranley, 1981, p. 281), such as differentiation of self from foetus, interaction with it, attributing to it characteristics and intentions, giving of self, role-taking, and nesting. Cranley developed the Maternal-Foetal Attachment (MFA) scale. Though it also taps the woman's emotions, such aspects were more emphasized by Muller (1993) who defined MFA as a "unique, affectionate relationship" (p. 201) between woman and foetus. She constructed items in her Prenatal Attachment Inventory (PAI) like "I feel love for the baby"; "I get very excited when I think about the baby"; and "I imagine what part of the baby I'm touching". With a similar emphasis on affects, Condon and Corkindale (1997) brought out two underlying dimensions in their Maternal Antenatal Attachment Scale (MAAS); the *quality* of the woman's attachment, including her conception of the foetus as a "little person", and the *strength* or *intensity* of her preoccupation with the foetus. Only the first dimension was related to psychological distress, whereas the second was related to how busy the woman was.

Alhusen (2008) concludes that many studies associate MFA with the mother's psychological well-being/distress (p. 323). But, a meta-analysis (Yarcheski, Mahon, Yarcheski, Hanks, & Cannella, 2009) did *not* find such links. The latter authors cite Lindgren (2001): "Clinicians should be cautious in interfering with maternal-fetal attachment, a process about which little is understood" (p. 214). Despite this warning, the Yarcheski study ends by recommending clinicians to be concerned about low MFA, especially during "the third trimester of pregnancy when the magnitude of the [mother-foetus] relationship is expected to be the strongest" (p. 714).

It has also been shown that MFA predicts a mother's interaction with *the baby*. Siddiqui and Hägglöf (2000) found that pregnant women who felt affection for and fantasized about the foetus were more involved when interacting with their 3-month-old babies. On the other hand, Muller (1996) found only modest correlations between the future mother's foetal attachment and the attachment to her 2-month-old baby. Unfortunately, these studies did not investigate the *infant's*

The psychology of pregnancy 25

contribution to the interactions. After all, babies can vary substantially in their propensity to communicate – in other words, they have different temperaments and social aptitudes.

How does MFA relate to the future baby's health? One group (Alhusen, Gross, Hayat, Woods, & Sharps, 2012) collected a sample of low-income, mainly African-American pregnant women. Low MFA scores were associated with low birth weight and pre-term birth. When the children reached 1½–2 years, MFA linked with mothers' reports of the children's emotional and social functioning and with their own attachment style; mothers who had had low MFA scores were now more often avoidant or anxious (Alhusen, Hayat, & Gross, 2013). An Iranian study (Maddahi, Dolatian, Khoramabadi, & Talebi, 2016) also found associations between the MFA scale and neonatal outcomes such as birth weight.

Researchers on *attachment*, finally, studied "the transmission gap" (van IJzendoorn, 1995), that is, how attachment patterns are transmitted across generations. If a mother's sensitivity to her infant predicted attachment entirely, every receptive and understanding mother would have securely attached children, and vice versa. But in fact, sensitivity only accounts for a quarter of the variance of the baby's attachment pattern. Which factors account for the rest? Focusing on the context of this chapter, I underscore the links between how *expectant* mothers talk about their childhood attachment experiences in the Adult Attachment Interview (AAI; George, Kaplan, & Main, 1985) and their infants' security in the Strange Situation Inventory (SSI). One UK study (Fonagy, Steele, & Steele, 1991) found that pregnant women's attachment classifications predicted the infant's SSI pattern in 75% of the cases. Similar associations were found in samples from Canada (Raval et al., 2001) and Texas (Shah, Fonagy, & Strathearn, 2010). Thus, the baby's attachment not only depends on the mother's sensitive *behaviour* with him/her, but also on her own *feelings* about her parents.

Slade's group (Slade, Grienenberger, Bernbach, Levy, & Locker, 2005) found only a modest link between maternal and infant attachment. Instead, they stressed the mothers' *reflective functioning* measured by the Parent Development Interview (PDI; Aber, Slade, Berger, Bresgi, & Kaplan, 1985) as more important for a child's attachment. Since AAI and PDI ratings were associated, they concluded that mothers who could "coherently describe their own childhood attachment experiences were more likely to be able to make sense of their children's behavior in light of mental states" (p. 293). They argued that:

> a parent's capacity to describe and contain complex mental states within the context of a relationship that is full of current feeling (not all of which is positive) is particularly crucial for a range of later developments in the child.
>
> (p. 293)

This echoes the studies on Rorschach (Aber et al., 1985) and on defences (Porcerelli et al., 2015); it is advantageous for a child if the mother can access a spectrum of feelings and defend adequately against the ones that cause overwhelming anxiety.

Another method of measuring the mother's attachment to the child is the Working Model of the Child Interview (WMCI; Vreeswijk, Maas, & van Bakel, 2012; Zeanah, Benoit, & Hirshberg, 1996). When applied to pregnant women, associations were found between WMCI classifications and children's attachment security at 1 year of age (Benoit, Parker, & Zeanah, 1997; Crawford & Benoit, 2009; Dayton, Levendosky, Davidson, & Bogat, 2010; Huth-Bocks, Theran, Levendosky, & Bogat, 2011).

Returning to the concept of primary maternal preoccupation, this section looked for studies that might validate it via outcomes on women's variables during pregnancy. It also sought connections between these variables and the infants' behaviours. We found studies of women's Rorschach responses, foetal attachment, defences, dreams, fantasies, and attachments to their parents and future babies. Many measures predicted their involvement with, or reflective functioning about, the infants – and/or the infants' attachment security at 1 year of age. Other studies did not find such associations. So, how are we to make sense of these divergences? This research area springs from the attachment tradition and from the concept of a short sensitive period of bonding after delivery (Klaus & Kennell, 1982). Such studies have led to expectations that if we could influence mothers' attachment to their foetus it would yield beneficial effects on the child's development.

It is doubtful whether these divergent findings motivate grand scale efforts at promoting every future mother's attachment to her child. Muller (1992), an influential researcher, calls for caution. She brings out problems with the validity of the concept of maternal–foetal attachment and adds that we must also consider "characteristics of the maternal personality" (p. 18). For a therapist, this sounds reasonable. First, the studies were made on samples in which the individual person is concealed. Second, they did not tap the mother's unconscious experiences of pregnancy and her future child, except the ones by Frank et al. (1994) and Porcerelli et al. (2015). Let us interpret these studies sensibly; they point to possible connections of a woman's relationship to her parents, her fantasies about the child, and his/her future well-being. Clinically, I would not recommend casting a vast net over all pregnant women but, rather, to be alert to those who signal distress. For them, these studies could give us the backbone to suggesting psychotherapy; for their own good and for the future of their babies. Alternately, and here I must confess I have not made up my mind, would it be reasonable to suggest a questionnaire on foetal attachment to all pregnant women, like depression questionnaires are used today? Not as a diagnostic tool, but to start a dialogue between the midwife and the expectant mother. If she is unaware of how much she worries about her child's future – or how little she feels about "it" – then such a device might be of considerable help to start a therapeutic process.

Concerning our question whether the studies could validate the primary maternal preoccupation concept, I would accentuate the studies on Rorschach (Frank et al., 1994) and defences (Porcerelli et al., 2015). If a mother can access primary process functioning without losing contact with reality, and defend against it in an adequate and flexible way, this might positively influence her baby's attachment. We could learn more from studies using projective tests on pregnant women – and men, too, for that matter. Unfortunately, only a few such studies exist (Bellion, 2001; Belot & de Tychey, 2015; Hart & Hilton, 1988; Klatskin & Eron, 1970; Vartiainen, Suonio, Halonen, & Rimón, 1994).

Chapter 3

Circumventing primary maternal preoccupation

In Chapter 2, we learnt about systematic research on the psychology of pregnancy. Now we will return to its clinical phenomena. I suggested earlier that the expectant woman's narcissistic equilibrium, autonomy, and bodily integrity are at stake during pregnancy. Sooner or later, she realizes that someone is forcing himself/herself onto her and will soon demand her full attention. This threatens the balance between *love for herself and for the child*. Such challenges also apply to the future father but he can, at least unconsciously, deny it when the baby is "just inside her". After delivery, such self-deception becomes impossible when the baby screams through the night, breastfeeding doesn't work, and curious rashes appear on the baby's face. Furthermore, only the woman is affected, and sometimes overtaken, by bodily alterations. Amenorrhea, nausea, fatigue, weight gain, hormonal changes, symphysiolysis, in short, the burden of *la grossesse* or "bigness" all confront her with challenges: "Who's most important in my life, me or 'it'? Who's running my life, me or that unknown being growing inside me? What happened to my body?"

Donna and her daughter Annie

Donna is a 30-year-old woman whom I interview with her 5-month-old, *Annie*, as part of a randomized clinical trial (RCT) to be reported in Chapter 11 (for a follow-up see also Salomonsson & Winberg Salomonsson, 2017). She starts right away:

> I'm no good at this parent–child thing! I don't like being off work, just rolling the pram. Guess I feel guilty. I know this isn't politically correct. I like to work hard. It's new being unable to compensate by working harder. I didn't feel well during the latter part of pregnancy. The doctor wanted to put me on the sick-list. I told him I don't have time. 'That's just your problem', he said. Delivery wouldn't start so they made an emergency Caesarean. I woke up after five hours. That 'immediate mother-baby-contact' never appeared. She never liked breastfeeding, just threw herself backwards. I got fantasies of throwing her out of the window. Everybody praises breastfeeding, but there's no scientific evidence that it's better than a bottle! When my husband resumed working I panicked. Alone with the baby . . .

Circumventing maternal preoccupation 29

I video-record Donna and Annie's interaction, which is hectic, tense, ironic, and sad. After the recording, Donna deplores she cannot have that "loving feeling" for Annie. She looks sad, but then claims her real problem is that she cannot fulfil society's expectations about maternal happiness. She switches between brief moments of realizations of her painful relationship with Annie and lengthier periods when she accuses society of extorting faulty attitudes from mothers. Yet she does not regret having become a mother: "At one phase in life one has to go through this thing with someone being totally dependent on you." Donna's relationship with Annie is "functional. I'm the one who understands her needs". I ask how she thinks the girl would respond if I asked her the same question. "Mum has too little patience, she's split and absent-minded." Then she caricatures the girl, "I want attention ALL the time, Mummy!" Donna maintains a brisk and jaunty attitude, but when I ask about her husband she is moved and tearful. She misses such positive emotions with Annie but also shrinks back from the sensual aspects of parenthood. Taking care of Annie is more like a work-task that she must perform in obedience to societal norms. I guess her references to such standards reflect her efforts at ridding herself of guilt.

Donna has been ambivalent about motherhood throughout pregnancy. Many authors acknowledge mothers' mixed feelings towards the foetus and the baby (Harris, 1997; Hoffman, 2003; Pines, 2010; Trad, 1991; Winnicott, 1950). Hoffman thinks it is time to "normalize the omnipresence of ambivalence in the psychology of women" (p. 1219). Trad argues that the caregiver's resentment may become aroused "during periods in the developmental process that herald infant separation from the caregiver and threaten severance of the bond of intimacy" (p. 46), as in weaning. In contrast, Donna's sarcasm seems to reflect both her disappointment at their faint intimacy as well as her efforts at avoiding closeness with Annie.

Donna is a concerned, responsible, and caring mother who is conscientious about her child's future. Why was pregnancy so difficult? Some themes during the interview throw light on the question. She talks about her mother:

> We've a close and frequent contact . . . I've an academic education but my parents haven't exactly read Strindberg . . . My Mum is rather hasty, she doesn't think things through. I once asked her if she thought in any special way when she had me. She replied: 'Was I supposed to think anything special? I just did what I did. Everything's gonna be all right, don't brood on your troubles'.

A vital dimension is lacking; Donna cannot speak with Mum about the qualms that started during pregnancy.

Donna describes her mother as a dismissive person. Filled with guilt, vexation, anguish, and shame, Donna would need a mother who received her emotions, accepted, reflected, and talked about them. To interpret their interaction in object-relational terms, we could bring in Bion's (1962a) model of *containment* from the previous chapter. I conceive separately of its maternal and the paternal components

30 Part I: Clinic

(Salomonsson, 2014a). In the maternal, we "hold" (Winnicott, 1965) the other's anxiety by our patience, empathy, imagination, and dreaming in order to receive and process her anxieties. In the paternal aspect (Quinodoz, 1992), we represent the human order. We convey to the patient that interactions are regulated by language, conventions, and laws, and we must use words and unequivocal non-verbal signs to convey our messages. This is linked to Lacan's concept of the Name of the Father mentioned in Chapter 2. But Donna's mother's down-to-earth philosophy caricatures this principle and is not counterbalanced by a comforting and warm maternal containment. This imbalance has coloured their relationship long since. During pregnancy, Donna's foetal attachment was probably down to earth and far away from a sound preoccupation. This seemed akin to her mother's preoccupation with Donna. Thus, intergenerational transmission was unbridled.

Becoming a mother without having a mother: Frances and her son Paul

Though the contact between Donna and her mother was factual and barren, the mother was alive and well and there was no major trauma among the generations. What if a catastrophe occurs in the relationship of a young mother and her own mother, for example, if mother's mum dies? The answer depends on their former relationship but in any case, the decease implies that containment by the older generation will be absent when a woman's contact with her mum is essential.

Frances, the mother of 9-month-old *Paul*, speaks vaguely of problems with breastfeeding, his bowels and his coyness with new people. She also mentions her loneliness and worry. "I can't put my finger on it . . . I lost my Mum in an accident, less than a year before Paul was born. I've lost some close friends as well." Frances vacillates between being sad and restrained, laughing and earnest. Paul listens attentively and avoids looking at me. "I'm worried and I fear it might affect Paul. In my teens, I loved horses and dogs. They could sense when I was nervous or scared. Maybe it's the same with babies, maybe he feels I'm sad."

The interview is part of the RCT and the dyad is assigned to mother–infant psychoanalytic treatment. In the interview after therapy, Frances is more explicit about her feelings after Paul's birth. "My husband was away at work. It felt difficult asking others for help. I didn't let them in. I got lonely, I guess." Therapy challenged her to do what she feared yet longed for; to accept help from another person. I also interviewed the therapist, who described a parallel from her consulting room. At first, the boy was distressed and screamed but did not lean towards his mother. Similarly, the mother did not "lean towards" the analyst and confide in her. Slowly, this "frozen shock" melted and Frances talked about mourning her mum, her sick dad living in another city, and her husband who travelled much in his work. She also realized that the boy's bowel problems, harmless according to the doctors, had aroused fears that she would lose him just like she had lost her mum.

Any mother's capacity to think clearly may be threatened after her child is born. This is part of her maternal preoccupation. In such a situation, her own mother may be of great help, now that the two have become "colleagues". But Frances had no mother to talk to. She could not unburden her fears and get comfort or sympathy. I think this froze her maternal capacity and made her an easy victim to various worries about the boy. Once she could "lean towards" the analyst, her thoughts and feelings started thawing. I also met Frances and Paul at the follow-up project when he was 4½ years old, some 3½ years after therapy:

Frances:	*"My mum is gone now, and she was gone already when Paul was born. I was so insecure then! My husband, too. We were insecure together! Yet . . . my mum is with me all the time. Every passing day or year, I understand her in a different way. She and I still have kind of a relationship."*
Interviewer:	*"She's like a little piece-of-LEGO-lady inside you?"*
Frances:	*"Exactly!"*
Interviewer: (noticing a tear in her eyes)	*"Did you get sad now?"*
Frances:	*"No, not really . . ."*
Interviewer:	*"What do you think of the analysis today, in hindsight?"*
Frances:	*"Some support, I guess. Seeing things with someone else's eyes. Guidance, sort of."*
Interviewer:	*"Do you think of your analyst today?"*
Frances:	*"To be honest, no."*

The "LEGO-lady" was my metaphor for how Frances had internalized a supportive and empathic maternal figure. The two had "kind of a relationship", which made her feel less lonely. The analysis comprised 22 sessions across five months. A fair guess is that it meant more to Frances than she acknowledged. First, the analyst could account exhaustively for the therapeutic process. Thus, Frances' term "some support" from her therapist seemed an understatement. Second, therapy also involved and helped Paul, according to both interviewees. Third, Frances tended to avoid strong affects with me in the interview. If she had admitted that she was fond of and had learnt much from her analyst, feelings of regret and mourning might surge anew. Vital parts of maternal preoccupation, shattered because of her mother's death and further dilapidated due to her son's bowel problems, were thus restored in treatment. To this was added her discovery that she had not let people in to help her. She began to lean on her husband and ask him to be at home more.

Therapeutic technique during pregnancy

The nine months of pregnancy contain many changes and upheavals. Regressive and progressive movements alternate, which we need to consider when we receive a pregnant woman for a consultation. Joan Raphael-Leff (2005), a British child

32   Part I: Clinic

psychoanalyst and expert in the field, emphasizes that pregnancy is "not a condition – it is a process" (p. 60). She divides the future mother's fantasies into three phases which centre on *fusion, differentiation and separation*. At first, she experiences the foetus as part of herself. She takes responsibility by avoiding alcohol and smoking while "it" is yet quite an anonymous character. The *differentiation* phase begins when she starts feeling foetal movements. They clarify to her that a human being is actually in there. For the father this comes a bit later and, as stated earlier, in a more displaced way when he can feel the kicks with his hands. This yields fantasies about "its" character – in both parents. Will it become a football player, a scientist, a dreamer, a fighter . . .? One often hears future parents drawing parallels between the foetus' movement patterns and its personality.

During the *separation* phase, preparations for delivery commence; from practical considerations, such as packing the bag for the delivery ward and arranging who is to take care of the older siblings at home, to fearful ruminations about a painful delivery and thoughts about Life and Death. Raphael-Leff's "separation phase" refers to the imminent divorce between mother and foetus. A vast array of feelings culminates and may overwhelm the woman; confidence, anxiety, joy, and pain – to name but a few. They surge during delivery, a unique crossroads of farewell and welcoming, fear and ecstasy.

I interviewed *Trudy*, the mother of 1-year-old *Nancy*, in the research project. She was still preoccupied with the delivery:

> I started thinking about death, which became much more important than before. I felt as if my skin was peeled off and I was a big heart walking about. I was so anxious: Had I made the child out of egoistical motives?

I read her comments as eloquent articulations about universal aspects of human existence. Neither pregnancy nor delivery are carefree and completely successful passages in life. Catastrophes still occur today. Trudy also articulates that birth is the harbinger of death, the beginning of the end of the road. Parents are happy and full of expectations, and if the midwife was to address them about the child's future demise they would be outraged. But Trudy reminds us that there is no life without death, no joy without sorrow. No one can tell if the mood swings and regressive preoccupations in her and other women bring about these existential insights – or if it is the other way around. Whichever notion we hold on to, her story reveals phenomena that any therapist must consider once s/he undertakes treatment with a parent in the perinatal period.

Winnicott, like Bion, compares the therapist's task to that of a mother. Yet, there are differences. The therapist learns, through years of studies and supervised casework, to help the patient towards a regression that is benign (Balint, 1979) or in the service of the ego (Kris, 1956). Via this "organized return to early dependence or double dependence", s/he supports the patient in achieving "a new sense of self", "a new progression", "an unfreezing of an environmental failure situation", and "a new position of ego strength" (Winnicott, 1955, p. 22) Mothers have no

Circumventing maternal preoccupation 33

such training. They may have attended maternity classes and spoken with friends, parents, and nurses. But these preparatory steps cannot delete the elements of surprise and alarm that form part and parcel of every pregnancy.

A further complication is that from a psychoanalytic vertex, the mother is not only the little inhabitant's "caregiver", a term used in the attachment literature. In moments of regression, she also wants to be the "care-receiver". To feel like a helpless baby *and* an adult responsible for her newborn; such an equation was not easy to solve for Mary, Karen, Donna, Frances, and Trudy. This pendulum is one reason why psychotherapy during pregnancy demands special consideration. Another point to reflect on is that a mother may seek consultation "just to get tools for handling my anxiety". Little does she know – and neither can we forecast – that sessions may extend beyond her apparition as "an ordinary pregnant woman" who just wants to get "tools". Suddenly, we may reach topics like the meaning of life, death's inevitability, and old ghosts from the family album.

One might think that a woman in primary mental preoccupation would be an excellent case for psychotherapy; she is highly motivated to accept help and her regressive state can make her accept deep interpretations already during the first session. This is true but also knotty. Due to her pressing anxiety, a woman may promptly address her ambivalent feelings about the foetus, her partner or parents. The therapist may, almost as quickly, find his/her ideas about the psychodynamics confirmed by the woman's story. Her confidence may also trigger a need for narcissistic confirmation. This may lead him/her to overestimate the "working alliance" (Greenson & Wexler, 1969) and the woman's motivation for comprehending why she is so afraid or moody.

In the void between sessions, women may face difficulties accepting that they have come to depend so quickly on a therapist. Dependency may appear in reverse; as a disappointed and resentful feeling that "these sessions lead me nowhere". Not only may she find it hard to grasp that such feelings reflect her negative transference onto the therapist. Should she intuit this, she might still find it embarrassing to address the "weakness" (H. Freud, 2011, p. 113) that for her goes hand in hand with therapy. This is one reason why some pregnant women leave therapy after a few sessions. Another reason is that they want to be in charge. The work of delivery lies ahead and they want to feel empowered and in charge. This "urge to progress" also applies to mothers after delivery, but at no time is it as evident as during the anxieties of pregnancy.

Gail was in the middle of a pregnancy that she was deeply ambivalent about. She had never desired a romantic relationship, even less to form a family. But things changed. "I met him and he persuaded me to have a child". Like Donna, she accused society of foisting positive expectations about motherhood on her. She knew she was expecting a girl but named her "it" or "this ET". She thwarted the necessary and salutary regression of pregnancy by diving into work, resenting that the child would "force" her to stop working for a while. She found comfort in unburdening herself to me about her deep ambivalence. I listened without judging, to understand her blunt refusal to emotionally accept the foetus. We came closer

34 Part I: Clinic

to grasping this when she began talking about her lifelong feeling of alienation in her family of origin. She and her mother had a distant, even frosty, relationship but they also shared similar interests "in worldly matters". As for love and devotion, her older sibling had got "so much more from mother". I suggested *she* had felt like an ET in the family, which she confirmed with some emotion. Such feelings now reoccurred in relation to the foetus, which made her scared and ashamed. When, after a handful of sessions, we discovered this connection she said: "I don't have the stamina for therapy now and I want to focus on the delivery."

What went wrong in this brief therapy? Or – *did* something go wrong? Perhaps Gail got as much help as she could accept at this point. After all, she had not contacted me to work through her relationship with her mother but to get help with an ambivalence to pregnancy, which grossly impinged on her ability to endure or enjoy it. She felt relieved when I listened with interest and without treating her as an ET. In consequence, she began to talk more openly about her feelings towards motherhood. Yet, I failed to grasp the depth of her fears of being an ET – in the family and in society. When we touched on the parallel between her lifelong ET-feelings and her view of the foetus as an ET whom she felt forced to love and care for, it became too hard. Possibly, one aspect of the negative transference was not resolved; she may have suspected that behind my intention to help her I was chiding her as an unsuitable ET-mother.

In fact, I was not convinced that Gail would become a disengaged mother. First, she could talk with me and her husband about her ambivalence, which of course was better than being unaware or silent about it. Second, there was a chance that the newborn would one day seduce her into becoming a devoted mother. But these are mere guesses. We have learnt that mothers' representations of the foetus may relate to their interaction after birth and to the baby's attachment. Gail's foetal representations were clearly disengaged, coloured by an emotional distance and indifference. But, every person is unique and we must also consider the flexibility of Gail's personality, the support from her partner, parents and peers, socio-economic factors, etc.

It is possible that our work provided Gail with an experience that she could talk about her "ET" thoughts and feelings with a psychotherapist – perhaps also in the future if problems should arise with her or the child. In Karen's case, the outcome was more successful. Though she already had delivered Chris when we met, the bulk of our work centred on her pregnancy and its near-death character. At the end, I asked what had helped in our contact. She replied:

> Earlier, I had talked to my husband and parents and friends. Everyone was understanding. But I guess they thought I was tedious. Some tried to cheer me up, 'now that everything had gone so well', as they said. You listened and you didn't cheer me up. And you don't seem stressed when I get worried.

The time has come to summarize my recommendations on therapeutic technique with pregnant women. By and large, they are the same as for any psychodynamic

Circumventing maternal preoccupation 35

therapy. I address the patient about what I intuit are her unconscious intentions and fantasies. The aim is to help her become acquainted with them and connect them with other aspects of her person, life history, and present relationships. Equally important is to convey my commitment, attention, and non-judgemental attitude. This double helix of promoting insight and conveying acceptance constitutes psychodynamic therapy. When Bion (1962a) described containment in mother–infant and therapist–patient relationships, he used a metaphor of food metabolized in the intestinal canal. In perinatal therapy, I receive the mother's "food", "taste" it, and process it. After a while I return it similarly to when a bird processes food before expelling it into the chicks' beaks. The term "food" signifies the mother's emotional communication with me in all its verbal and non-verbal aspects. In Gail's case, I "tasted" what it felt like to be pregnant with a creature that one regards as an ET to be dispelled to a distant galaxy. I also tasted how she might feel like an alien who, just like in the movie, is moaning and longing for "home". As for "putting back the food", I told Gail that these feelings must be tormenting and shameful to her.

Containment cannot merely imply to emotionally receive, "taste", and hold the patient's anxiety. Neither can it be to simply echo the patient's words. We also need to *translate* (Salomonsson, 2007a) and provide *new meaning* to the patient's communications. These terms must be understood in their broadest sense. I might tell an anxious mother who says in trepidation, "I think I'm a bit . . . frustrated with my little Jeremy" something like "I think you're *angry* with him and it scares you". Here, I clarify (Greenson, 1967) the impulse (her anger) and the malfunctioning defence (her scare). I thus translate her word "frustration" into "angry", which describes her frightening feelings more accurately. At other times, I use spontaneous metaphors and enactments (Lebovici, Barriguete, & Salinas, 2002), empathy (Emde, 1990), and "co-thinking" (Widlöcher, 2001) or co-construction (Beebe & Lachmann, 2002) with the patient. Talking with Karen about her "feeling string" was such a metaphor. I will devote Chapter 19 to this aspect of analytic work, not the least since therapeutic work during the perinatal period often engenders such metaphors.

In brief consultations, it is also essential to sort out what *not* to broach, and when to terminate treatment. During our eight-session contact, Karen picked up what she wanted and at her own pace. I kept a focus on her relationship with Chris, since that was why she had contacted me. Some topics we never delved into, such as her tendency to be over-active and restless. After all, she had neither considered this to be a problem nor expressed that she wanted help with it. To state it more generally, *the focus is on the parent–child relationship and what interferes with it*, whereas characterological problems are left to another occasion – if the mother should wish to do so. It often happens that a handful of sessions focusing on a mother's premonitions about the relationship with the child will ignite her interest in a lengthier therapy or analysis of her own. In general, she will wait to embark on this until some years later, when she has become more settled in her role as a parent.

Chapter 4

Delivery trauma and the maternal introject

There is something odd about the many synonyms of the word *delivery*. It has a concrete and prosaic meaning, as when a freight company delivers a package to your door. *Deliverance*, on the other hand, implies being saved from danger. It has a biblical overtone in that God is the rescuer, as mentioned many times in the Book of Psalms. The Swedish word *förlossning*, which Mary in Chapter 1 replaced by the slip "förlussning" or "delossery", carries a similar ambiguity. The root "loss" is the same as "loose" in English; "to unload" or "to loosen". But when a Christian calls Jesus his "förlossare", he means "redeemer" or "saviour". *Loss* and *salvation*; why these contrasting implications for one and the same thing? Mary's slip indicated that she suffered the loss of an emotional state and a foetus that she had idealized during pregnancy. Thus, delivery was a loss. But this loss is also a prerequisite for rapture; a tiny human being has appeared on earth and his family rejoices in bright expectations. Perhaps this explains the links between delivery and redemption. Not only has the foetus been saved from its mysterious, uncontrollable, and perilous existence in the womb; it also carries promises of bringing something better to the world.

A delivery is also the beginning of the end. Trudy in Chapter 3 captured this with her thoughts about death and "the reverse of the medal". One might suggest her words merely indicate a realistic insight that delivery can end in a catastrophe. But I do not think this explains all. Delivery brings parents nearer to an incontestable and relentless duality of our existence; life and death are intertwined and one does not exist without the other, as poignantly described in the Book of Ecclesiastes:

> To every thing there is a season, and a time to every purpose under the heaven:
> A time to be born, and a time to die; a time to plant, and a time to pluck up that which is planted;
> A time to kill, and a time to heal; a time to break down, and a time to build up;
> A time to weep, and a time to laugh; a time to mourn, and a time to dance . . .

There is a third root to the word delivery; the French word *accoucher* and the German *Niederkunft* are both anchored in the body: "Coucher" means to lie down and the German term literally means "coming down". Avowedly, delivery has a concrete and meaty aspect to it with blood, sweat, and tears – and urine, faeces, and colostrum. It comprises both a physical dimension with crying and laughing, groaning and bearing down, as well as an existential and spiritual dimension that may suddenly turn the labouring woman and her partner to contemplating philosophers.

The act of delivery itself allows no time or space for consultation work, so my experiences are restricted to stories from consultations and therapies. I have met many women who were afraid or terrified of the upcoming delivery. Even more mothers told me retrospectively about deliveries that they experienced as terrifying, heavenly, sad, or blissful. Emotions seem to run up and down like a roller coaster when it comes to childbirth. Many women will remember forever what they felt and can detail every event. This is true for mothers whose deliveries were smooth and normal, and even truer when they were complicated. There are two main situations in which one may suggest therapeutic consultations. Some women had a delivery during which a misfortune occurred; an emergency C-section, the vagina needed to be sutured, etc. From a medical point, everything went well but an emotional scar remained, gnawing at the mother's self-esteem and interfering with her joy and pride. Often, one or two consultations can help her overcome the shock, humiliation, resentment, and self-accusations to move on in life. Later on, "Lena" will exemplify such a case. In the second group, a medical trauma punctured someone who carries, in her historical and characterological luggage, items that make her ill prepared for dealing with the obstetrical misfortune. The next case illustrates this category.

A stillborn baby who came to life: Leyla and her daughter Jenny

Leyla is a 30-year-old social worker who has addressed the CHC nurse about her panic. She begins her consultation with me by relating a terrible experience. At home, when delivery was approaching, her body temperature peaked unexpectedly. Upon arrival at the maternity ward, the staff monitored the foetus with cardiotocography (CTG). Suddenly, its pulse decreased sharply and an emergency Caesarean was performed in a few minutes. A girl was born with no registrable pulse and an Apgar score of 0, 0, 0. The child was thus stillborn. Leyla, still under general anaesthesia, was taken to the post-op unit while her husband remained with the child:

> I lay dizzy after the Caesarean, convinced that my child was dead. In my thoughts, I buried her over and over again. I *knew* she was dead. After one hour, my mother came and told me the girl was all right. I just cried and cried.

We talk about this at length. Then I ask what her problem is right now.

38   Part I: Clinic

> *Leyla:*   *"It's not so much these memories of the delivery. I just can't stop worrying about* Jenny! *At night, I get up every hour to check her pulse. The doctors keep telling me she's OK and unless I stop checking her I won't be able to enjoy her. But I can't stop it!"*

Leyla's background is a peculiar mix. She was born in Sweden of Middle East immigrants and grew up "in a ghetto where nobody studied at the university – except me! My father encouraged me to get a solid education. My mother didn't care much . . . We've a more restrained relationship." Leyla seems rough, cheeky, and defiant, almost like a teenager – but she is also a reflective and earnest adult.

> *Analyst:*   *"Do your parents know about your panic and that you keep checking Jenny?"*
> *Leyla:*   *"I could tell Dad. But it would put him in an embarrassing position, because he'd feel he must tell Mum and I don't want him to. Fred, my husband, knows. Our families are from the same area."*

I am, needless to say, shocked by Leyla's delivery story. Thoughts of all kinds tumble around inside. How do such events impact on the parent–child relationship? Like Chris's parents in Chapter 1, Leyla and Fred were confronted with the death of their child, but in their case it was "for real", at least for an hour. How could it happen? Is the girl damaged for life? How will I feel when I meet her? To Leyla, I convey that this has been an appalling experience and that she needs time to digest it. I also wonder to myself if any other issues might lie beneath her panic. I am curious to meet with Jenny and I ask Leyla to bring her to the next session.

Some days later I meet Leyla and Jenny, now 10 weeks old. She is sweet and smiles happily at me from Mum's lap. Most of the time she is asleep. It is neither my task nor competence to perform a neurological examination, but nothing in her appearance worries me or makes me suspect that her development is deviant. I reflect on the countertransference: My fear that Jenny is brain-damaged paralyzes my thinking! Meanwhile, Leyla talks about herself. She labels herself a "control-freak". Then she moves on to talking about her relationships.

> *Leyla:*   *"*Fred *is my first serious love relationship. Before, I didn't dare falling in love, couldn't let go."*
> *Analyst:*   *"To fall in love is scary, like standing on a diving-board, not knowing if there's any water beneath. Should you jump or not? Fall in love or not?"*
> *Leyla:*   *"I* know *I love Jenny – but I can't feel it. I only feel that way about my younger siblings. But I do care about people. At my unit, I work hard to help battered children."*

Delivery trauma and the maternal introject 39

What started as a crisis intervention due to a near-catastrophic delivery has already turned into a dialogue about Leyla's fear of falling in love with the baby; not so much because of the near-stillbirth but because of Leyla's dread of becoming intimate. Jenny, now awake, is looking at her. But Leyla is preoccupied with her story and does not notice it. Later, she looks at her daughter who by now has closed her eyes. When one is seeking contact, the other does not notice or avoids it. This sombre observation is complemented by my still extant worry that something terrible and irrevocable has occurred to the brain of this sweet little girl. Indeed, both Leyla and I are on a roller coaster, whereas Jenny does not seem affected at all!

Some weeks later, Leyla triumphantly reports that she stopped breastfeeding. "I decided it against the know-it-all people who claim breastfeeding is mandatory . . . To tell you the truth, I stopped for egoistic reasons!" Here, another aspect of the countertransference emerges. Leyla challenges me by portraying herself as a selfish mother who oppugns against professionals' advice. Like a rebellious teenager she invites me to become an admonishing parent who tells her: "Stop being self-centred and start breastfeeding again!" I remain silent and she shows another aspect of her personality.

Leyla:	*"Only lately did I begin to enjoy being with her – a little bit . . . I think she melted the ice inside."*
Analyst:	*"Melted your ice. That's a powerful image."*
Leyla:	*"That's how it feels."*
	The girl wakes up, whines a little, the mother puts the pacifier in her mouth before I've had time to suggest she wait a little. I turn to the girl.
Analyst:	*"Jenny, you've melted Mum's ice, have you."*
Leyla:	*"Yeah. But you know, I can't stand being idle. I hate weekends! Even now, on my parental leave, I take on missions at work. I'm ashamed of being a bad mother, putting myself in the first place. I don't like being a mum . . . No, that's not true. Last week, I enjoyed stroking her cheek. The other morning, we stayed in bed and cuddled a bit. That never happened before. At work the other day, I longed for her and when I came home I wanted to hug her. Then I read blogs about Mums who just adooore their cute babies. Bah, I don't feel that way! I decided to stop googling and just follow my nurse's advice. That's good enough. I hate when people paste their opinions onto me!"*
Analyst:	*"So there's a triangle; you, Jenny, and 'all the others'. But isn't it an excuse when you claim that people paste their ideas onto you? Isn't it rather that you're feeling insecure as a mother? At work, you care for vulnerable and exposed children but you don't know how to love your own child."*

Leyla:	*"It took me two months to realize I was pregnant. At first I was crying, I didn't want to get fat!"*
Analyst:	*"You mentioned 'hug' earlier. That's a word about love. I wonder how you have been feeling loved in life yourself."*
Leyla:	*"Whoops, a tough question. I get completely blocked in my head . . . How did you feel loved?"*
Analyst:	*"I could answer. But you reacted strongly to my question. Couldn't you think a bit about it?"*
Leyla:	*"I can't, it's STOP, I must bring it home and think further."*

Of course, there was a link between the gruesome delivery, the conviction that Jenny was dead, and Leyla's anxious need to check her child's pulse. But I did not content myself with these explanations. At first, I took no position on the genesis of her panic. I just conveyed that delivery must have been a ghastly experience. But I got curious when Leyla spoke of the restrained relationship with her mother and her fear of falling in love. In Chapter 1, I talked to young Chris about his waiting for Mum's "love train". Leyla addressed previous difficulties with such a train in her relationships, and she embraced my metaphor of falling in love and hopping from a diving-board.

Falling in love has many similarities to the overwhelming, searing, and yearning emotions whirling about between parent and child. In thousands of pop tunes the singer cries out, "Oh baby, I love you so," or asks "My baby", where did "our love" go?. Manifestly, they refer to adult love but we can also apply them to the emotions between parent and child. Perhaps the dual meaning (lover/infant) points to the unconscious links between adult and mother–baby love. In Leyla's case, she could not sing "Oh baby, I love you so" to her daughter. She had a long-lasting fear of letting go, losing control, and falling into the abyss of love. The previous chapters told of other mothers with similar issues; longstanding as in the case of Donna, or recent as in the case of Karen who might lose her foetus. Leyla's delivery experience might lure us into attributing all her panic to that trauma. But if that explanation were sufficient, why was she still so distressed? After all, the girl had been alright from the second hour of her life and onwards. Soon, we discovered other factors beneath her panic; her narcissistic preoccupation, fear of surrendering to warm emotions, and efforts at circumventing these issues by being a workaholic. These solutions had functioned earlier in life but Jenny's arrival, in fact already her conception, smashed them to pieces. Not so much because she was a stillborn baby coming to life, but because her presence ignited the mother's longing for, and fear of, a love relationship.

As Leyla's relationship with Jenny warmed up, similar changes occurred in the relationship with her mother. Leyla began confiding in her, revealing she was seeing a therapist. To Leyla's surprise her mother responded, "I think that's very good for you and Jenny". I was not so amazed at this warming up. In Chapter 2,

I mentioned that the previous relationship between a woman and her mother will impact on her primary occupation. During pregnancy and afterwards, matters are often brought to a head between the two. In Leyla's case, projective mechanisms seemed to colour her view of mother. Indeed, there were similarities in Leyla's character and her description of her mother; efficient, rational and anything but mawkish. This might be accurate but also be coloured by Leyla's projections onto her mother of traits she found unbearable in herself. As therapy progressed, Leyla became warmer and, in parallel, she began to see similar assets in her mother. We can express this in terms of a change of balance in her identifications; Leyla progressed, from identifying with harsh and blunt aspects of her mother to those that indicated empathy and wisdom. In the first section of Chapter 5, we will follow this treatment to its end.

The maternal introject

I introduced Leyla and Jenny as a case where the delivery trauma punctured someone whose history and personality contained so many thorns that she was ill prepared for dealing with it. Leyla could hardly sleep, take a walk, or leave Jenny in bed; death lured everywhere, threatening to take her child away. Anxiety among new mothers is common and any line between normal and pathological anxiety is artificial. I take a pragmatic stance; if an anxious woman asks for a consultation, she deserves attention. This does not prevent me from wondering why anxiety is so common among parents and what is it all about? Answers commonly refer to evolution. Females, whether elephants, bears, or humans, protect and anxiously look after their offspring. Yet, this explanation does not illuminate the clinical phenomena we are discussing. Remember that Leyla was not just sheltering her daughter from realistic dangers. *Everything* was menacing and she was constantly terrified.

We thus need to go deeper to interpret the constant and debilitating anxiety in some mothers. I will start with what I believe it is *not* about – at least not as often as I used to think. Earlier, I tended to attribute such anxieties to *reaction formation*, a mundane defence mechanism. For example, two girls approach their classmate: "Sue, we don't wanna be nasty but *really*, your new hair-cut is sooo old-fashioned." The girls *do* want to hurt Susie, an intention they cover beneath their sweet assurance. Their display is thus *reactive* against aggressive unconscious impulses. The point with such hypocrisy, like with other defence mechanisms, is to make a compromise between your official persona and the one you are underneath. Enough steam gets out to make you feel relieved and affect the other, but little enough for you to seem polite and remain unconscious of the full import of your emotions.

When I began meeting mothers who feared harming their baby or that he would die, I used to conceptualize such apprehensions in terms of reaction formations. Sometimes I did have a point – but I needed to wait a long time until they were ready to accept such an interpretation. They were indeed angry, but to feel that way

42   Part I: Clinic

with a little helpless creature is frightening and shameful. It is true that aggression, envy, and ambition percolate in parents' psychic life. These feelings signal that their narcissistic equilibrium is threatened. It is as if they feel that the baby will obstruct their freedom, impoverish their resources, and lay a hand on all the good that their own infantile self yearns for. Simultaneously, they are eager to take care of the baby. The two currents, narcissistic and object-libidinal, crash in every parent and must be dealt with. A mother's anger with, or envy of, her baby may crash, not only with her sincere wish to take care of him, but also with a harsh super-ego or an extorting ego-ideal. The formula runs, "One must not be angry with a baby" or "Nice girls are never angry". Reaction formation emerges as a "solution" but takes up much psychic energy and is never completely successful. Some anger or vexation emerges anyway and engenders anxiety. Thence the terrifying fantasies that the baby will fall from her bed or be hit by a bus on the road.

Yet, often I was wrong in linking maternal anxiety to reaction formation. It took time to discover and conceptualize another root. The formula can be described:

> I fear that I am a wretched mother. In fact, I always feared I don't have enough love, skill, calm, and self-confidence to take care of a little creature. Therefore, I don't deserve to relish my baby and enjoy motherhood. All that's left is panic.

To understand such fantasies, we must look for their roots in the mother–daughter relationship. The generation after Sigmund Freud, especially his female colleagues (Horney, 1926; Klein, 1928; Lampl-De Groot, 1928), started this search. Freud, who thought female psychology was enigmatic and once exclaimed that he had never been able to answer "What does a woman want?" (E. Jones, 1955, p. 468), read their publications with critical interest. One, Ruth Mack Brunswick (1940), noted that the little girl has a long pre-oedipal attachment to her mother. Later, it will merge into an "active Oedipus complex" (p. 296), in which the mother is the love object and the father the rival.

The girl needs to traverse "a long and complicated route" (Mack Brunswick, 1940, p. 296) before the father becomes the "King" of her heart and mother the rivalling "Queen". The journey starts with the baby girl being fed by the mother, that is, she is in a passive position. Over the months, she will learn from and identify with the mother's activities, for example, by learning to eat by herself. This makes mother less indispensable to the child but also more prone to set limits: "Don't throw the food on the floor, Julie!" This can make Julie outraged with mother whom she experiences as almighty and stern. Her self-esteem is smashed, a vicious circle is set in motion and thus "the relinquishment of the first love object of the girl is accompanied by tremendous embitterment" (p. 312).

Hendrika Freud (2011) singles out Electra, the antique Greek mythological character, to exemplify such resentment. Her mother's lover Aegisthus murdered

Delivery trauma and the maternal introject   43

her father Agamemnon. While claiming to righteously avenge him, the real target is her mother Clytemnestra. Electra feels rejected by her mother's infatuation with Aegisthus and sacrifices her sexuality, maternity, and future to get rid of mother. The fixation on her contains bottomless hatred *and* attraction. To H. Freud, Electra is a metaphor for many women's painful oscillations between an illusion of eternal symbiosis with the mother and the abysmal and infinite separation from her. The symbiosis has a clearly parasitic quality; "a duo chained and addicted to each other, out of a feeling of guilt more than of love, and the signs of affection are never sufficient" (p. 11). Mother's love demands that the child surrenders to her wishes, to keep her "vulnerable sense of self-worth intact as much as possible" (idem). H. Freud discerns this mechanism behind a mother's fears of anger towards the child. It is as if she were thinking that *her* mother will begrudge her the baby. The formula is: "I may not become a mother for then my mother will be jealous" (p. 120). Unconsciously, the baby is blamed for having disrupted mother's and grandmother's illusion of a wondrous relationship. If only the baby were gone, all would be normal again . . . Such hateful thoughts are frightening. True, all new parents are challenged with liberating themselves, as best as they can, from their parents and "move up a generation" (p. 123). The thornier this previous relationship was, and the more the new care-taker unconsciously wants to be a "care-receiver" (see Chapter 3), the harder this move will be.

H. Freud suggests that to understand why motherhood is difficult for some women, we need to look at their internal relationships with their mothers. We can conceptualize this in terms of "*the internal maternal object*" or, more simply, "*the maternal introject*". The term "internal object" refers to "an unconscious experience or phantasy of a concrete object physically located internal to the ego (body) which has its own motives and intentions towards the ego and to other objects" (Hinshelwood, 1989, p. 68). I think Fraiberg (1987), when coining the term "ghost of the nursery", had this concreteness in mind though she did not use the term internal object. A ghost is nowhere and everywhere, it is here now and a revenant who will always return. Mothers who are in the grips of this ghost feel that their present inferno is everlasting, the past cannot come to help with memories of good mothering, and there is no hope for a future better relationship with the baby.

The introject can sometimes be visualized in dreams and mothers' experiences of their midwives. One interviewed woman said, "During delivery I had a wonderful and caring midwife. Then the night shift arrived and I got a second one. A total bitch, yelling and ordering me about, like molesting me." Her description seemed influenced by two opposing internal characters; one saint-like, the other diabolic. Internal objects are also influenced by experiences of the external object, in this case, the "actual" behaviours of the two midwives. The tricky issue is that internal objects "also contribute significantly, through projection, to the way the external objects are themselves perceived and experienced" (Hinshelwood, 1989, p. 68). As Klein (1946) put it, our relations with others are formed by interactions "between introjection and projection, between internal and external objects and situations"

44   Part I: Clinic

(p. 1). We can thus grasp how the interactions between this woman and her midwives spiralled, first in a positive and then in a negative direction.

The maternal introject comprises a woman's unconscious fantasies about maternity, femininity – and her own infancy: "I want/I do not want to mother the way I was mothered myself". The introject thus covers imaginations about her mother *and* about herself as baby *and* mother. In fact, we should perhaps speak of "the mother–infant introject" since it is composed of various interactions between the two. Writers and artists have portrayed women who represent this introject in its malignant version. *The Queen of the Night* in Mozart's *The Magic Flute*, the pianist mother *Charlotte* in Ingmar Bergman's movie *The Autumn Sonata*, and *Emma Bovary* in Flaubert's *Madame Bovary*. All three are portrayed in conjunction with a child who is terrified, humiliated, and neglected; Mozart's Pamina, the pianist's daughter *Eva*, and Emma's daughter Berthe. Common to these mothers is their self-centredness and volatile interest in their daughters, in short, their narcissistic predilections. In this book, think of how Leyla (earlier in this chapter) and Donna (in Chapter 2) described their mothers; not as nasty or ill-willing, but as self-preoccupied and unable to comfort and listen to their daughters' woes.

To comprehend the internal situation of Donna, Leyla, and others, we must go beneath their mothers' manifest behaviour. If the structure underneath – that is, their unconscious introject – is harsh, contradictory, or cold, this colours how they experience grandmother's comments. Leyla's and Donna's introject are too unyielding to provide a flexible and empathic support. But they cannot locate the cause of their anxiety to this shaky psychic structure. Only rarely do these women automatically blame their mothers for their anxiety and "silly thoughts". No, they think *it is all their fault*. They are "bad mothers" who cannot take care of their baby. They are ashamed of their agonies while being convinced that every other mum is jubilant, devoted and self-assured. Therefore, they cannot open up to anybody and feel painfully lonely. No matter if they speak with their partners, in the end they feel they must be their own emotional support. But, since the maternal introject is harsh and demanding, they are never content with how they take care of the baby. "Just another look to check if he's asleep or dead, a glance at the poo to see if he has some dreadful disease, one can never rest assured . . ."

If we describe Leyla's and Donna's maternal introjects in these terms, we realize the mistake in conceiving their worries only in terms of a reaction formation. They are at war internally, struggling with the maternal introject. To suggest that they might be angry with the child will be felt as another accusation by this introject: "It is all your fault". In a deep sense, they are victims of an internal war. I agree with H. Freud that much of this war relates to unconscious anger with baby and grandmother. I only add that their brittle self-esteem – they really feel "I'm a lousy mother" – makes them extremely sensitive to a premature interpretation about such emotions, especially towards the baby. It can easily lead to the flaring up of a negative transference, especially in brief consultations. The mother may then feel rejected and humiliated and, in a worst-case scenario, break our contact.

Doriane and her son Pascal

One mother, *Doriane*, portrayed this kind of maternal introject. After delivery, her son *Pascal* had a brief cramp and then everything seemed normal. Regrettably, the doctors gave contradictory information. Pascal had suffered no harm, but . . . there might have been a slight cerebral oedema and any possible sequelae could not be ascertained until he was 6 months old. This would be too much to bear for any parent and thus, Doriane's anxiety was easy to explain. But why was she convinced that Pascal had a brain tumour or a developmental retardation? She repeatedly brought him to the paediatric ER and, every time, the specialists assured her he was alright. In contrast her husband, whom I also met, was convinced that nothing was wrong with their son.

Doriane, Pascal, and I met nine times, once a week, starting when he was 6 months old. At first, I asked her why she was worried since, after all, he had been alright all his life and all tests were fine. I built on a rational argumentation, but since this kind of anxiety is never entirely built on rational grounds, it did not work. Then I said, "Perhaps you are 6 months, too? You feel so little, inexperienced and helpless. It must be terrible to feel that way and be in charge of a tiny person who in fact *is* week and feeble." Now, she started listening. My idea was to convey empathy by suggesting that her fearful and overwhelming fantasies might be similar to those of a panicking baby. At this point, she seemed to feel she had met someone who perceived "the baby within her".

Doriane seemed gentle and warm, so the idea of unconscious anger towards Pascal seemed far-fetched. I was led to another track when she spoke of an incident in her teens. She was studying abroad, staying with another family. "Suddenly the father there had to leave for an important mission and I was left with his . . . cutting wife." I asked about the unusual word "cutting". It seemed to cover "acute", "pointed", "sarcastic", and "unfriendly". She now moved on to talk about her mother.

Doriane:	*"I long to cuddle up in her lap and hear that everything's fine with Pascal. She says nice and warm things, and she really means it, but she sounds so stressed. Something about her voice doesn't match with her words. She has so many interests in life."*
Analyst:	*"Did you ever talk about this?"*
Doriane:	*"I thought of it, but then I'd start weeping and feel embarrassed."*
Analyst:	*"Weeping in front of your mum would make you feel like her baby again?"*
Doriane:	*"It would be shameful! I'm not a child, I should take care of a baby, not to be one myself."*
Analyst:	*"And then we have this thing about you being keen on taking care of others, too. You always greet me by asking about my state of health – rather than talking about your own."*

> During this dialogue, I happened to have a plastic mug of coffee on my desk. Now I pointed at it.
>
> Analyst: "If someone pierces that mug with a cutting object, it'll leak. Maybe you want your mother to just hold you and carry all that scares you about Pascal and comfort you by saying that you're a good mother. But you feel she's cutting and then all your panic leaks out."
>
> Doriane: "Lately, Mum's voice has indeed changed, she sounds warmer,
> (crying) nicer, just the kind of voice I've been missing."
>
> Analyst: "So, maybe you could talk with her now about your resentment?"
>
> Doriane: "Now that our contact is becoming warmer, I don't want to criticize her."
>
> Analyst: "On the other hand, now you might have a chance of a deeper dialogue."

Doriane described her mother as "cutting" and stressed and showing a slightly contrived interest in Pascal. Instead of judging this lady, we should recall that the description was provided by a mother who in several ways felt as little as her baby son. Doriane was in a regressed state, in which her needs of being taken care of had accelerated. Just like a baby, she wanted someone to speak warmly with her and promise that nothing would go wrong. Pascal's father also needed to, and in fact did, comfort her – but that was not enough for Doriane. Before pregnancy, the balance between her and the mother had worked well, because during those years such needs were in the background. She was then a cheerful, competent, and likeable woman in her relationships and jobs. Becoming a mother pushed her towards responsibilities for a helpless newborn while she felt like a newborn herself. In such a situation, the maternal introject is crucial. It needs to "hold" Doriane who then holds her son. This three-generational link was beautifully portrayed by Leonardo da Vinci in *The Virgin and Child with Saint Anne*. The serene faces of Jesus' grandmother Anna and mother Mary radiate tenderness, concern, and love as they look at the child. Leyla, Donna, and Doriane demonstrate that not all descendants of Mary feel this kind of "backward support" when they touch down in the agonies and trepidations of parenthood.

Chapter 5

Therapeutic technique in perinatal consultations

In the previous chapter I dwelt on some cases to illustrate how traumatic events and their sequelae may be entangled with the mother's life history. Another aim was to pursue the track of therapeutic technique. Consultations during "in the beginning"-period deal with life and death, hope and fear, power and impotence, strength and weakness. Other features are, as I suggested, that the primary preoccupation renders parents more open and susceptible to therapeutic work, and that they seldom seek help for longstanding emotional difficulties. Their main preoccupation lies elsewhere; to become a parent and take care of the child. Their motivation for deep-reaching therapy is thus limited – at least initially, because the paradox is that such work is sometimes necessary, possible, and fruitful. For sure, when we met the first time, Leyla had not expected me to focus on her fear of love or the relationship with her mother. Yet, I wanted to inspire her to probe deeper into why she was so worried. From this flowed the connections between her anxiety and her relationship with the mother – and the necessity of talking about it.

What can a therapist do when a patient (1) does not seek deep-reaching therapy, (2) has debilitating symptoms, (3) wants to quickly get out of the regressive state, (4) implicitly signals that deeper work is needed, and (5) the therapist has few practical possibilities of a lengthy therapy? My idea with consultation work is to consider all these contradictory factors and turn them into substantial work, in line with techniques submitted by Lebovici et al. (2002) and Winnicott (1971a). With Leyla, I spoke of falling in love and jumping from a diving-board. Such metaphors will be discussed in Chapter 19. Sometimes, my technique is a bit venturesome as when I, via Leyla's word "hug", asked her how she had felt loved herself. This question was neither premeditated nor well thought through, and it threw her off balance. The key to intuiting if such a question will be felt as blunt, stupid, perky – or challenging and worth thinking about – lies in how I assess our contact. With Leyla, I felt that whether she would reflect on my question or not, she was not going to feel snubbed.

A less innocuous example was when I, after Leyla had said she hated people pasting their opinions onto her, suggested that this was an excuse and that she in fact felt insecure as a mother. The comment did not beat about the bush. I would

48 Part I: Clinic

not have used it in an ordinary psychiatric interview, and in a psychoanalytic treatment I would have waited longer. But parent–infant consultations are different. I do not condone rudeness or intrusiveness, but the mother's emotional state and the situation's urgency often invites the therapist to be outspoken. This suggestion must of course be handled with judgement, otherwise the patient may feel put off and break off the contact. I soon noticed that Leyla wanted to be honest with herself and expected the same from me.

Still, Leyla was more brittle than she or I realized. After a handful of sessions my schedule was crammed. I suggested we finish after some further weeks' work. "Sure, I understand completely", she said. The next session she cancelled. The following one, the skin of her face had deteriorated and she had pimples. I brought up this at once.

> *Analyst:* "*What happened? You look different and your skin doesn't seem OK.*"
> *Leyla:* "*I thought a lot. I just accepted you said we'd stop. I know you've other patients but . . .*"
> *Analyst:* "*. . . but you just swallowed my decision, right?*"
> *Leyla:* "*I discovered another thing: I'm doing such things with my boss as well. I just do what people tell me to do, without thinking about what I'm feeling.*"
> *Analyst:* "*I was rough with you without seeing it, and you didn't want to see it. I guess I was rash suggesting we stop working together. I'll try to make room for you, even if it can't be once a week.*"

Leyla was grateful and wanted to continue in therapy. The negative transference flaring up due to my suggestion to end therapy and our working it through led her to scrutinize her present job situation. Her relationship with the boss resembled her negative transference with me. She said "Amen" to all his demands. She worked way beyond any normal working schedule while feeling humiliated, enraged, and exhausted – but she also relished in being the Obedient Good Girl. Now she rebelled and quit his department. It had been more difficult to rebel against her own ego ideal and accept that she had become a mother, a full-time job in itself. Parenthood revives old conflicts but also offers a chance to grapple with them. Leyla gained courage from motherhood and from therapy and finally told her boss to go to blazes.

All in all, we met for 20 sessions during a half-year period. The case began as a story about "a stillborn baby who came to life". Our focus veered to analyzing how Leyla's rash and love-fearing personality reacted to Jenny's invitations to a passionate relationship. The caption about the stillborn baby could be used metaphorically; one part of Leyla's personality was, if not stillborn, then suffering from asphyxia. Ever since childhood she had allowed little room for playfulness,

Perinatal consultations   49

leisure, and daydreaming. This continued into her tendencies to block maternal preoccupation, work like a slave, and be emotionally unprepared for delivery. When things went so terribly wrong with Jenny, it crushed her visions of a smooth and efficient start in life. The rest was just pure anxiety and panic.

Sundry emotions: Nora and her daughter Bess

When a mother reacts strongly to delivery, her sundry experiences seem intense, contrasting, and rapidly changing. Not only may she discover affects that seem brand new to her, but she may also perceive old feelings that surge anew with a frightening intensity. *Nora*, a participant in the RCT, could not come to terms with her envy towards her husband, which was a feeling that hit her promptly after delivery. Her daughter *Bess* was now 2 months old.

> Nora: *"When I was about to deliver the child, her pulse went down so they decided on a C-section. It wasn't fun anymore. I wanted to be delivered like a real woman! I had no say in it. I lay four hours at the post-op while she and her dad were alone. They got this wonderful contact that I missed out on and other mothers get instantly. I'm just a food machine! At home after surgery, I could hardly move due to the pain. They didn't give me enough painkillers. I'll never go to that hospital again I tell you."*

Both parents take part in the interview. They are convinced that the first hours with Bess were decisive for his contact with her and the present problems with Bess; she easily whines and breastfeeding is knotty. "But, he can give her the bottle which makes life easier for me . . . Still, I've a hard time really grasping it's my child." This is an underprivileged couple concerning economy and education. "I've failed in most things in life", says Nora. She had hoped delivery would come out as one of the few things she was good at, but the Caesarean smashed those expectations. She seems to have given up on motherhood. "Earlier, I panicked when she whined. Now I let her cry a while, it doesn't harm her." This insensitivity and resentment is also seen on the interaction video. She has just breastfed Bess but when the girl whines, mother pokes her lip and says in a teasing tone of voice: "You're hungry, right?" Nora does not seem devoted to finding out if the girl really is hungry, which she is probably not, or if there is another reason for her whining.

Nora was assigned to psychoanalytic treatment with Bess. Post-treatment, the analyst described to me Nora's negative relationships with the girl and herself. When Nora offered the breast, Bess often rejected it and whined, to which Nora would snort, "that's just her baloney". An overweight woman, Nora remarked that she had used the pacifier herself up to age 7. In my assessment prior to therapy, she seemed to feel abandoned by anyone she was leaning on. She expected to have

50   Part I: Clinic

such feelings taken away by the therapist rather than working together to understand their psychological roots. Nora experienced the analyst's contribution similarly to other instances in life; *never enough*. She suspected the analyst was "in it for the money". She saw no real gain from treatment, except "it was good to get that C-section thing off my chest". At first, the analyst did not notice that Nora's expectations of treatment deviated from what she intended to offer. Then she tried to repair it but without great success: "It was not quite clear to me who was the baby, Nora or Bess."

Leyla and Nora both had emergency C-sections. Objectively, Leyla's trauma was far greater; her child was near death whereas Nora suffered a separation from Bess for four hours. But trauma strikes individuals differently. Leyla could have felt massive envy towards all mothers who did not face their child's imminent death – but she did not. Instead, problems with her love of Jenny and others emerged as a major problem and she was willing to put it on the table with me though it caused pain, shame, and disappointment. To Nora, the C-section and the separation from Bess confirmed a longstanding experience that she was not entitled to good things in life. She must support herself and could not trust people who were willing to help her, like her analyst.

It seems that Nora's and Bess' analyst did not succeed in establishing a good working alliance (Greenson, 1967). Nora's suspicions about the analyst's greed and her experiences that, metaphorically, she did not get a pacifier she needed pointed in this direction. Sessions were free of charge but she thought the driving expenses were costly. How much of this reflects her economic reality and/or her discontent with treatment is impossible to tell. But one knowledge can be extracted. Analysts sometimes think "the more the better"; high-frequency therapy is a *sine qua non* for enabling deep and substantial work. I believe this is true concerning psychoanalysis, but Nora wanted something else; to get rid of resentment at the delivery, her anger with the doctors and nurses, and her envy of the child. At an unconscious level, I think she wanted to be fed by the analyst, and any suggestions to see her more often than Nora wanted was felt as forced feeding. Judging from Nora's obesity and the pacifier story, this must have been a hot issue for her.

When a patient seeks insight and wants to develop as a person, a high frequency is facilitating. I stick to that principle in my analytic office, but at the CHC I work with people in a very different situation. There, I offer my services to the parents, tell them briefly about how I work and then suggest we begin with some two sessions. I also ask how often we should meet. After those encounters, we will evaluate what we have achieved and whether it is enough or more work needs to be done.

Normal not to be normal: Lena and her daughter called what?

I will relate a brief consultation to illustrate that perinatal issues do not always need a lengthy and deep-reaching therapy. Sometimes we swiftly find the "hot spot" on which to direct attention and do meaningful and substantial work. Here is a two-session consultation with a mother who wanted to talk about a mishap during delivery that had marred her relationship with the baby.

Thirty-year-old *Lena* is married to *George*. She gives a capable and friendly impression. Pregnancy was normal and she intended to deliver vaginally. But like Nora,

> nothing happened at the delivery ward. The cervix wouldn't open up. Finally, they made a C-section. They promised me local anaesthesia, so I knew I was going to see my baby immediately. But the pulse of the foetus went down, and suddenly I was under general anaesthesia and they took her out in a minute.

Like Nora, Lena was overcome with envy towards her partner who was alone with the baby for four hours:

> George got an advantage by having the first contact with her! I feel stupid and childish, but that's how I feel. She and I don't tick. I've read a lot about attachment and it doesn't work! I take care of her but I don't feel any joy. This isn't normal!

The field lay open for an extended psychoanalytic investigation of Lena's envy. We might also focus on signs of distress in the girl, now 2 weeks old. Yet, I was not worried about the girl, and Lena seemed to be in good contact with her emotions. So, I tried a shot.

Analyst:	*"You envy and resent George because of his contact with the girl, and you envy her of the closeness with Dad. At other times of life, one might say, 'This isn't normal!' but in this situation, after the C-section, I'd say, 'It's normal not to be normal'."*
Lena:	*"Believe me, I am happy that she got such fine contact with her dad from the start. But there is a thorn inside me because I wasn't there!"*

Lena seems content with telling me her story without receiving any condemnation from me that she is childish and selfish. When I ask her, she wants to come back three weeks later.

Lena:	*"I'm in love! The whole thing is different from last time we met. I was hung up 'cause she hadn't been born the normal way. I kept ruminating, 'why wasn't I there from the start?'. I didn't see her as an individual! Now I'm so happy about Yasmine. At home, we call her 'The Sparrow'."*

Analyst:	"Yasmine . . . Last time, you didn't use her name."
Lena:	"Well, no, hm, Yasmine and Sparrow sounds more personal than 'she', I guess."
Analyst:	"You've changed . . ."
Lena:	"Time passed and I feel more secure today. It started after we met. I told George, 'I'm normal, you know'. He looked staggered and said, 'I know that!' I explained what we'd talked about here. I needed to tell you about the C-section and how I felt about George and her . . . I mean Yasmine. For the first time, somebody confirmed that I'd been into serious, even abnormal, things and that it was quite normal to think that way. I guess talking with you made me take my feelings seriously."

We now come to speak of envy in general. Lena relates that she envies George of another thing; he can go see his pals while she is breastfeeding Yasmine. I suggest she feels unable to look at it from another angle; she is the only one who can breastfeed their daughter.

Lena:	"Actually, I don't want to go out that much, I want to stay home and cuddle with her. But it's complicated, because George and I – or I and George, well, whatever – we always considered equality to be essential in our relationship."
Analyst:	"Maybe you confound equality with identity. Equality is about having the same rights and value. That's important. But identity? You and George aren't identical. Only you can breastfeed Yasmine. Is it a drawback or a privilege? It's true that only George can leave home easily at present since it won't affect Yasmine's hunger. You envy George his privileges but don't see your own."
Lena:	"Like what!?"
Analyst:	"Breastfeeding! You said you want to be home and cuddle with Yasmine."
Lena:	"You know, George and I met when we were quite young. We've been a bit like brother and sister who wanted to be fair to each other."
Analyst:	"And that balance needed to be reworked now that you've become parents."
Lena:	"It's only me who has that super-closeness with Yasmine. That puts him in the shade, right!"
Analyst:	"Yeah, but your envy of George prevented you from enjoying that thing which only you can do; breastfeed Yasmine."

I ask Lena about how she thinks of our future contact. She reflects and responds that she is fine. "I think we can stop now . . . To be on the safe side, can I come back if there are new problems?" "That's OK with me", I reply. In fact, I never heard from Lena again.

Let us compare with Nora. Had I suggested that she might look at something from various angles – like I did with Lena about breastfeeding – she might have regarded it as a cynicism delivered by someone living where the grass is greener. Further, she did not show the distance or reflective functioning towards her envious thoughts that Lena demonstrated. Nora felt she had been deprived of something essential during delivery – and in life in general. The only thing that could, at least partly, redeem such feelings was if she were given something by the therapist. Perhaps, if she had been provided with a more "generous", yielding, and supportive response, Nora might have felt more satisfied. Still, her deep-rooted feelings of being wronged by life would not have had much chance of being transformed during a brief treatment. Lena, too, seemed to have a characterological issue with envy but to a much lesser extent. She did not evince any general sense of being injured by Existence. Two other assets gave her important advantages to Nora; she quickly got confidence in me, and showed an ability to reflect on her contrasting emotions. These resources made her "swallow the food" with greater speed and appetite than Nora did with her therapist.

Conclusions concerning technique

If we survey our cases so far, we understand deeper the difficulties in knowing beforehand the course of a psychotherapy. A referral, no matter how accurate or well-founded, from a CHC health visitor can never presage its psychological complexity, which therapeutic approach is optimal, or how long it will last. Some cases seem initially alarming, but when I see the family everybody has emerged from the regression. It is like when a flock of black crows scatter in the sky and the sun breaks through. The reverse also exists; when seeing the nurse, the mother quenches her bewildering emotions and keeps a stiff upper lip. She starts her first session with me: "Well, nothing really, the health visitor thought I should see you but I'm alright." If allowed time and space, she will reveal that all is not sunshine. To exemplify, memories of an earlier miscarriage keep swarming her head and darken the relationship with her newborn. Such links between past events, significant but hitherto unrecognized – and present symptoms, diffuse but taxing and disabling – tend to emerge quickly in perinatal consultations. It is one consequence of the primary maternal preoccupation and one reason why such work can yield substantial results in a relatively short time.

In many cases the nurse has neither time, mandate, nor training to pick up these links between acute symptoms and past history. When the family visits her, many tasks need to be handled like weighing, inoculations, etc. In combination with a sometime embarrassment or unfamiliarity with listening and talking to anguished people, she may be tempted to overlook these signals. In general, we tend to brush

54   Part I: Clinic

aside distress signals from a baby more often than from a mother. The explanation is probably that "it is only the limitations in our ability to identify with the baby that leaves him, in our thoughts, denuded of mentality" (Meltzer & Harris-Williams, 1988, p. 16). The sight of a baby in distress stirs up buried infantile memories in all of us; implicit, unconscious, and fossilized by primal repression (Freud, 1915c), they do not exert their influence via an overt recall but by an attitude of dismissal; we react acutely and strongly to a baby's distress – and we hope it will pass away as quickly as possible.

The therapist needs to meet parent(s) and baby with a fresh and unprejudiced mind. The first interview provides a wealth of material. Impressions come from all sensory modalities: vision, hearing, smell, etc. We must use them all plus a rich plate of mental modalities: thinking, intuition, personal memories, and creative imagination. They form the basis for making a personal assessment and talking to the parents about it. Therapists have learnt a competence of staying with distressful situations, reflecting on them, using creativity in understanding them, and communicating with parent and baby. Such skills are demanded of any therapist, regardless of method, diagnostic category, or age group. To hone such skills is more crucial than learning a plethora of therapy methods that see the day each year and rapidly claim to be "evidence-based". It is regrettable when experienced therapists bow to outside demands of allowing only X number of sessions, or using only the Y method for the Z diagnosis. Administrators and politicians may demand such compliance in the name of rationalization. I call it "*irrationalization*". Every therapist builds up from life experiences, training, and clinical encounters a personal repertoire and method that becomes enriched and refined over the years. As experiences accumulate, the professional identity becomes more solid and the way of working more flexible. Donald Meltzer's words half a century ago are still valid:

> Every analyst must work out for himself a simple style of analytical work, in time arrangements, financial agreement, room, clothing, modes of expression, demeanour. He must work well within the limits of his physical capacity and his mental tolerance. But also, in the process of discovery with a patient, he must find through his sensitivity the means of modulation required by that individual within the framework of his technique. In a word, he must preside over the setting in a way which permits the evolution of the patient's transference.
>
> (Meltzer, 1967, p. xiii)

One might object that the facilitation of transference is not part of brief consultations. To be true, a full-fledged analysis of transference is neither possible nor desirable here, but the phenomenon is present nevertheless. If we follow Meltzer's advice, I think it paves the way for the patient to come up with immediately relevant material. Think of how quickly Leyla, in response to my innocuous questions about her background, addressed the constrained relationship with her mother and her problems of loving. Her question about how I had felt loved did have transference connotations, but we did not dig into this topic because it would be out of bounds in a brief therapy. In this context, presiding over the setting implies to allow material to emerge on parenthood, the relationships with the baby, one's partner and parents, etc. The therapist should be aware that these stories may be coloured by the patient's experience of him/her, and try to figure out how. But, bringing them up with the patient is another thing and is often redundant in brief encounters – except when a negative transference obstructs further work. I recall Karen's indignant question if I insinuated that the "feeling string" between Chris and her was broken. That topic had to be addressed swiftly. Similarly, if I sense that a patient feels hurt or provoked by me, I need to ask.

To sum up my thoughts about the technique so far: Any therapist working with perinatal consultations will meet with women like Nora, Lena, and the like. The art of such work consists of getting in contact with the patient, getting a grip on her personality, and treating her accordingly. Another aspect is to assess, get in contact with, and communicate with the baby. So far, that kind of work has not been portrayed but the last chapters will illustrate it. See also the first book (Salomonsson, 2014a).

Chapter 6

The external frame at the Child Health Centre

Perinatal consultations generally take place in a public health care setting. Organization and integration with other professions are therefore crucial issues, which will be discussed here and in the final chapter. If we cannot create a strong and sensitive network around distressed parents and babies, our skills may be of little value. We will never see the patients, either because the problems were not observed by the staff or because nobody dared to address the parents about them.

Stern (1995) observed that parents with baby worries seldom regard themselves as mentally ill but as being in a crisis or a state of shock. They have been walking steadily towards an eagerly awaited goal; to become a parent! Suddenly they have tumbled into a hole. The ground may have been brittle earlier due to character problems, neurotic symptoms, and relational frailties. But their defences have functioned reasonably well until now. We only need to recall the mothers from the previous chapters. When they fell into the abyss of primary maternal preoccupation they became helpless, bewildered, little, and shamefaced. I have met many such mothers who were recommended a psychiatric specialist service. Their reaction was: "But I'm not sick, I need to *talk* with somebody!" Certainly, psychiatric services should be available for chronically ill mothers. They need to have specialized health visitors or to cooperate with the CHC staff. But I dare say that most mothers with baby worries fare better if treated by a therapist with a special interest and competence, and who works at a parent–infant *general* health care unit. I have italicized the word general, because many of these mothers do not stick out from other women – at first sight. It is only when they get a chance to talk with a health visitor prepared to listen that the gates to their inner turmoil open up. This raises the challenge of nurse–therapist cooperation, an area covered in this chapter.

The therapist can gain the nurses' confidence more easily if s/he works at her unit. Once the nurse becomes interested in the therapist's approach, this attitude will extend to the parent(s), who then will find it easier to accept, and be more motivated towards, a therapeutic consultation. This argument also applies to health care of pregnant women. In many countries, they are taken care of by midwives and gynaecologists at antenatal clinics. Here, too, I suggest that medical and psychological health care should integrate treatment methods and localities. Parent–infant health care is differently organized around the world. Every country has some system overseeing that infants grow and hopefully remain unaffected by disease, injury, or handicap. It also surveys the parents' physical and mental health. In poor countries such care is left to the families, with the support of family, friends, and neighbours (Berg, 2003; Cooper et al., 2002). In countries with more optimal economic conditions, infant health care systems are legislated and institutionalized. A paediatrician or a family doctor may be in charge or, as in Scandinavian and other countries, a nurse who shoulders the main responsibility; a midwife, a paediatric nurse, or a health visitor. These systems are efficacious; global infant mortality has diminished enormously (United Nations, 2015), largely due to the professionals' patient, unobtrusive, and affectionate work. They teach parents about baby-care, survey the baby's growth and development, institute immunization programmes, and, if needed, refer the child to specialist care.

What about parental care? Maternal death rates due to puerperal fever have declined steadily since 1847, when Ignaz Semmelweiss advised midwives to wash hands before deliveries. While deleterious effects of infectious diseases and malnutrition have largely vanished in the Western world, perinatal *emotional* problems have emerged more clearly. Still, in my view many suffering parents remain undetected. There is also a relative ignorance or unfamiliarity with handling *infant* mental health issues. This is surprising, since most professionals know about perinatal depression and its possible links with infant mental health. I have already touched on some explanations; from organizational factors to feelings of embarrassment among professionals. Indeed, they observe issues with infant crying, attachment, breastfeeding, sleep, etc., but obstacles remain which prevent such problems from receiving full attention. I have deduced recommendations on how to institute an external setting that enables anxious mothers, bewildered fathers, and unhappy babies to receive help.

The problem with detecting "baby worries" or perinatal emotional problems

One might assume that well-organized health care systems would be well-fitted for taking care of perinatal psychological issues. Still, why are they not detected more often? Lack of resources? Such explanations do not take us very far. A dearth of public awareness? No, today most people know that postnatal depression is not a shameful disease but a condition which one can and should do something about. Many have also absorbed that an infant's development may be affected by it. The last two sentences contain words that indicate why many cases go undetected; *shame* and *infant development*. Now, there is "group shame" and "individual shame". It is one thing to educate the general population and nursing students to be tolerant. Much meritorious work to dissolve group shame is done in universities, maternity classes, and media. Another matter is to alter it in an individual up to a point where she will change her actual choices and behaviours. At the end of the day, what really counts is if a mother dares to mention to the nurse that "something is wrong with me".

58 Part I: Clinic

What is "wrong" is perhaps not merely that she feels sad which, after all, is not so reprehensible. Harder to disclose are thoughts like "I don't love my baby", "Other mothers are more devoted and loving towards their child", and "I never should have become pregnant with this guy". The thoughts cause shame – and they are *bound* to yield such feelings. Parents with such feelings are dimly aware of an internal thorn they want to ward off. Their conscious feelings for the baby – positive, tender, and caring – are true and concord with their ideals about parenthood. Such ideals clash with feelings of *not* loving the baby, regretting his existence, and deliberations of divorcing his father. Such clashes cause critical emotional problems, as for Donna in Chapter 2 and Leyla in Chapter 4.

We could apply two perspectives to the parent's negative and agonizing thoughts: They are symptoms of a mental disease for which s/he is as little responsible as for a physical condition; or they reflect an inner crash between feelings. The second perspective need not delete the first. Hormonal changes around delivery make the mother more unstable, and her genetic setup may also make her susceptible to depression. We also know that postnatal depression is linked with earlier episodes of depression in a woman's life (Norhayati, Hazlina, Asrenee, & Emilin, 2015). Applying a psychoanalytic perspective on a mother's ambivalence towards the baby or the impact of the maternal introject on her self-esteem does not neglect biological factors. Neither do I point fingers. Parents, like any other human beings, are subjects who desire, detest, love, vacillate, mourn, and rejoice – but who do not know very well *why* they have such mixed emotions. In short, they are *responsible subjects* but feel like *passive objects*.

The analyst's task is to sort out what caused the crash and help the parent get back into the saddle to take charge of what feels like a restive, unreliable, and dangerous horse inside. Before this is feasible, the parent needs to overcome the shame of his/her "forbidden" feelings. S/he also needs to handle the worries that one's personal turmoil can affect the child's development. To be true, such suspicions have been confirmed in sample studies (Chronis et al., 2007; Field, 2010; Murray et al., 2010; Murray & Cooper, 1997; Olson, Bates, Sandy, & Schilling, 2002). Depressed mothers exhibit more negative affects towards the baby (Field, Healy, Goldstein, & Guthertz, 1990; Tronick, 2007a), less optimal dyadic states of consciousness (Tronick & Weinberg, 1997), and regulate their babies' affects less well (Reck et al., 2004). They also have less optimal affiliative behaviour, attachment representations, and distress management (Feldman, Weller, Leckman, Kuint, & Eidelman, 1999; Leckman, Feldman, Swain, & Mayes, 2007). Their infants indicate less social engagement and play (Edhborg, Lundh, Seimyr, & Widström, 2003), less mature regulatory behaviours and more negative emotionality (Blandon, Calkins, Keane, & O'Brien, 2008; Feldman et al., 2009; Moehler et al., 2007; Weinberg, Olson, Beeghly, & Tronick, 2006), and less propensity to develop secure attachment patterns in early childhood (Toth, Rogosch, Manly, & Cicchetti, 2006; Toth, Rogosch, Sturge-Apple, & Cicchetti, 2009). Such studies, summarized by Stein, A. et al. (2014), point to associations between maternal depression and infant distress.

The external frame at the CHC   59

Nothing becomes better by turning a blind eye when one observes a baby avoiding Mum's eyes or her being overly anxious. The better we become in helping such families, the more relevant and beneficial it is to put such issues on the table and suggest help. Yet, some parents keep quiet about their worries because they are ashamed of "nonsensical fantasies". Also, they fear that once they voice their worries they will be assured or accused that the baby's development has already been irrevocably affected; a nightmarish fantasy.

Shame about "silly thoughts" and worries that "nothing can be done": These are the main motives why parents tend to conceal their emotional turmoil. Paradoxically, a nurse and a doctor may avoid seeing it for the same reasons. If we want to get in contact with such a parent, we must breach a wall. This demands an effort – emotional rather than intellectual – of overcoming our own resistance. Here is a comment I have heard from nurses at the CHC: "For some time, I've felt this mother isn't OK. But when I wanted to bring it up I started thinking of something else or felt uncertain whether my observation was reasonable or just a fancy." The remark reflects the nurse's perspicacity in detecting emotional problems – and her sudden pangs of guilt, self-depreciation, doubts, or discomfiture. Chapter 7 will approach this problem and suggest supervision as a remedy.

The external frame

Now we know more about emotional obstacles among parents to disclosing their emotional problems, and amid health care professionals to detecting and addressing them. These hindrances are intertwined with health care organizational problems. That is why I suggested integrating perinatal physical and psychological health care. The more we are facing an anguishing, complex, or chaotic situation, the more we need a solid framework to contain emotions, whether in ourselves or in the patient. Think of this simile: Go to a park and stand on one foot, as in yoga. Arduous! Look at a distant tree and it will be easier. Then go home, stand in your bath tub and fix your gaze on the intersection of some tiles. Now, you can stand upright for minutes! In the park, you felt adrift. In the bathroom, the fixation point is closer and you are surrounded by supporting tile walls. This simile brings out the distant tree as *hope* and the tile walls as the *structured aspects of containment.*

A second simile brings in the other person: Civil air traffic contains rituals and standard uniforms to dampen our anxiety when we enter an aluminium container and place our lives in the hands of a team of strangers. The air stewardess says soothingly: "In the unlikely event of a fall in pressure, oxygen masks will be released . . ." Such an approach in unison with a firm and professional framework make us feel safer on board. Parents with a baby may discover that they have boarded an "emotional aircraft" from which there is no refund or escape. Their "container" (Bion, 1962a, 1970; Malone & Dayton, 2015; Quinodoz, 1992; Salomonsson, 2011a) is unreliable. They feel like standing on one foot, but in a desert rather than a bathroom. They signal commotion and helplessness and try to "push" it into the nurse, that is, via projection. One prerequisite for her ability to handle this challenge is that she works in an organization that ensures a steadfast and reliable framework.

Perinatal mental health is organized in various ways. Specialized units, "Infant Mental Health Centres", do an immense job helping families with severe parental mental health problems or infant developmental disorders. These clinicians make ground-breaking efforts to change the trajectory of standard child and adult psychiatry. Such work is in stark contrast to earlier times, when psychiatrists took care of a depressed mother but paid little attention to other family members. Or, the baby was taken care of by expert paediatricians, who focused on developmental anomalies but were not equally attentive to the family's psycho-bio-sociological milieu. Great initiatives are now taken to treat perinatal psychological problems by involving the entire family. Yet, psychiatric care is sometimes "myopic". The following series of events is no rarity: A nurse meets a depressed mother and sends her to the GP who submits a self-report questionnaire. According to the results, she receives SSRI or is told that the depression will likely pass after a while. If things get worse, she may end up in a psychiatric ER overnight. She will leave with an SSRI prescription and a check-up appointment. The clinicians know they are treating a woman who just delivered a child – but this is too seldom transposed into a skilled care of the mother–baby dyad. What is needed is a holistic approach with adequate care routines to handle the tempestuous climate in these families.

The difference between work at specialized Infant Mental Health Centres and my practice is not the holistic outlook. It is rather the framework, since I work close to and in collaboration with the nurses at a CHC serving the local family population. In the RCT of "baby worries" (Salomonsson & Sandell, 2011a, 2011b), one question concerned the mothers' experiences of CHC care. Often, their emotional disorders remained undetected or were not handled in a sensitive and exhaustive way. To learn more about routine infant care, I started working as a psychoanalytic consultant at the Mama Mia CHC in Stockholm. The nurses are trained in paediatric medicine and have a keen interest in parental and infant psychology. I will begin by describing the patient material and then move on to talking about supervisions with nurses.

The most typical cases have been consultations with a mother or a couple with an infant below 1 year. Others were couple therapies with the baby present. Sometimes, families with older children run into difficulties; a 2-year-old must have it his way or cannot fall asleep, a 3-year-old is jealous of his newborn sibling, etc. I have developed such parent–toddler consultations out of parent–infant work and will present them in Chapter 14. I have also seen pregnant mothers and followed them up to delivery and afterwards in the postnatal period. In Sweden, pre- and postnatal health care is run at different centres which, nonetheless, are often located side by side, as in "my" CHC.

What about cases that I have *not* seen very much? As said in the preface, I have little experience with babies that were adopted or born in LGBTQ relationships. Babies with congenital metabolic errors and malformations, and those affected by malignant tumours, are taken care of at specialized units that also have expert psychologists. As Karen and Leyla illustrate in Chapters 1 and 4, I do meet with parents whose babies have been severely afflicted. In these cases, the child was well now and no medical follow-up was needed, but emotional problems did appear later.

As for socio-economic distribution, I wish I had experience with families from a wider spectrum of social milieus. Yet, as I will argue, this limitation is not an unsurmountable gap. Basically, we all struggle with similar challenges; we feel threatened by an affront to our self-esteem and our sense of safety, and we wish to be loved and to love, be strong and healthy, live and give life. We feel endangered when our anger, jealousy, envy, indifference, sorrow, and elation reach levels that are unacceptable or obnoxious to ourselves or to others. These threats loom in every family – whether poor or affluent. Low-income families also face economic worries, language problems, etc., but their attitudes to an insight-oriented approach do not routinely differ from those of other families. My middle-class patients sometimes emerge as naïve when asking for "tools" to deal with anxiety. Their reflective and associative thinking seems ousted by dreams of an expert quick fix. Furthermore, an analyst's expertise is to understand a patient's realm of imaginations and emotions. Since this internal world has more similarities than differences across the social strata, I believe lessons in this book can be transferred to other milieus though, of course, we must also consider external factors that might preclude therapeutic work. In my clinical work, I may treat a single mother and ask a social worker to help with economic support and contacts with other mothers in similar conditions. In other and more disadvantaged populations, special projects are launched to meet the need of education and information on infant care and parenting (Burström, Marttila, Kulane, Lindberg, & Burström, 2017).

Finally, cases of psychosis and substance abuse have not been common in my practice. I do work with postnatally depressed women who need hospitalization for some time. After returning home, we continue working together. Sometimes I prescribe SSRI, most often because she has been on it before and wants it again. As for introducing SSRI for the first time, I prefer to wait and see what therapy can accomplish by itself. I think it is more profitable to regard postnatal depression as a *life crisis* than as a relapse into a psychiatric disorder. If I can help the mother find new ways of handling it, she can gain substantially in self-confidence. Yet, she may still be anxious and desperate and request we add SSRI, which I then endorse. The important thing is not to be a zealot. Psychotherapy and medication are *not* incompatible. My hesitation weighs more on the argument that, if possible, I want to avoid sending the mother a message that she suffers from a disease. When we meet for the first time, she often has more internal resources than she is aware of, because until now she has felt lonely and in the clutch of regression. I want first to help her find and utilize the psychological capital hidden under the regressive helplessness and confusion.

Geography and collaboration

A Child Health Centre (CHC) is a special place. At the entrance prams, shoes, toys, and umbrellas lie higgledy-piggledy. In the waiting-room kids are everywhere; on the floor, on the sofa, and at Mum's breast. The ambience may be affable, reflecting the fact that a CHC is the abode of dawning life. Young people come here because they have experienced something unique; they have become parents and are filled with love, pride, and expectations about their little child. Yet, alternate and contrasting feelings exist as well . . .

Each CHC contains a handful of office rooms for the nurses and the paediatrician. I borrow one of the nurses' rooms and work next to a baby scale, a diaper changing table, and a stethoscope. An odd office for a psychotherapist! The physical proximity between the nurses' offices and my own is crucial. It makes a difference for a mother if the nurse says, "We have a therapist here. His name is B.S. and he's working next to my office", or if she writes a referral to another clinic. Why the difference? One factor is *shame*; if the parent knows I am part of the team, seeing me becomes more like the nurse check-ups and thus less embarrassing. Second, it is easier for a nurse to *trust* a professional whom she sees on a regular basis. She will transmit this to the mother, who will find it easier to confide in me. The third factor is *regression*. Just like a baby loves his teddy-bear or baby cot, the mother favours the CHC as her "home". We have learnt that although regression can run berserk and cause trouble for the mother, it is also essential for her contact with the baby's emotional world. I am thus not belittling her by calling her "homesick". She is closer to her "internal child" than during any other time in life. If we suggest for her to see a therapist at a faraway unit, we menace her needs of familiarity and intimacy.

When the nurse suggests to parents to see me, some are relieved while others hesitate. To make things easier for an anguished mother, I might suggest to the nurse to knock on my door with the parent to say hello and check me out. If needed, she can take part during our first encounter, though this is rare. A mother's expectations and attitudes towards me are always multi-layered. She might fear that I will condemn her lack of love for the baby or that I regard her as sick or repelling. A father may fear that I will collude with his wife's indictments of him. Or, he was expecting to get concrete "tools", but when I suggest we think together he may be disappointed. Such misgivings must be treated with respect but are rarely insurmountable. Freud (1913a) noted that clinicians think therapy will be easy if the patient shows "great confidence in psycho-analysis . . . whereas . . . another [patient] . . . will undoubtedly prove more difficult, because he has a sceptical outlook and will not believe anything until he has experienced its successful results on his own person" (p. 126). His point was that such misgivings have little importance for the upcoming therapy, where the real challenge is to dissolve "the internal resistances which hold the neurosis firmly in place" (idem). In consultations, parents' initial resistances often diminish with surprising speed. The mother's primary occupation and transparency and desire to get back on track with her baby quickly embolden her to approach her internal "hot spots", more so than in other phases of life. This also applies to couples in crisis.

The nurse's referral brings up the issue of professional collaboration, which is indispensable for functional teamwork. I have no expertise in medical infant health care, and the nurses are often astute observers of parent–infant interactions and the parents' relationship. Thus, they know many things that I am ignorant of. On my part, I get information and impressions during the consultations. Some of it I may need to convey to the nurse, so that she may grasp what goes on in the family. All in all, this would pave the way for a complete openness between me and the nurse. This clashes with issues about discretion and personal integrity. The mother should feel safe that there is no "hole in the wall" and be free to convey matters she wants me to remain silent about. This must be respected. Over the years such issues have been less problematic than I expected, due to the inter-professional climate built up during supervisions and quick chats. We get to know each other and a mutual trust develops. This gets transferred to the mother who feels taken care of by a competent *team*. Then it is not the end of the world if one confidence gets transferred between nurse and therapist. We can compare it to a *well-functioning family*, where the child feels safe to tell Mum or Dad about some embarrassing topic. S/he will know that this is treated with respect, even if one parent may transfer some of it to the other.

I may learn, for example, from a mother that her own mother is a heavy drinker. This affects her maternal identification and behaviour with her baby and constitutes important therapy material. I do not go into details about this with the nurse but only mention, "This mother has a thorny relationship with her mother and needs extra support". Should I deem it necessary to be more explicit with the nurse, I ask the mother beforehand. In contrast, I have not found it very useful to start up every contact with a programmatic statement, "Here at the CHC we work in a team and share information with each other". That would merely be clumsy and raise unfounded suspicions.

These recommendations are also supported by a submitted qualitative interview study from the Karolinska Institute, which was performed at several CHCs in Stockholm. The nurses were part of a clinical project, which placed psychoanalysts to work at these units. They emphasized their appreciation of cooperating with the therapist. But, if the therapist rigidly upheld her professional secrecy, this diminished the nurses' confidence and acknowledgement of her as a valued inspirational source.

Chapter 7

Supervising nurses at the Child Health Centre

Even if the CHC is the abode of dawning life, there is also a lot of anxiety. This puts the CHC staff under pressure. Parents with emotional problems tend to place their troubles in the nurse's lap. In fact, they *should* put them there – rather than in the baby's lap. After receiving this "placement", the nurse needs to sort out which parental comments reflect a passing annoyance and which ones signal a crisis. Which can be dealt with by a sympathetic rejoinder by the nurse and which merit serious considerations and actions? Another label for these "placing in the lap"-situations is *projective identification* (Britton 1992, 2013; Grotstein, 1999; Klein, 1946; Ogden, 1982; Sandler, 1993a; Seligman, 1999; Silverman & Lieberman, 1999). The parent is at the end of her tether and wants to relieve herself of the qualm, anxiety, and shame that weigh on her. She resorts to a mechanism we all use; we try to "push" our distress into another person so that s/he may feel, "under the skin", what it is like to be helpless, hopeless, and hapless. As Britton (2013) reminds us, Bion (1992) doubted that a patient will "ever accept an interpretation, however correct, unless he feels that the analyst has passed through this emotional crisis as part of the act of giving the interpretation" (p. 291). Bion spoke of psychotic and borderline patients, but it also applies to parents and babies in distress. Accordingly, a therapist or a nurse needs to succumb to and work through such a temporary crisis to grasp the parent's or the baby's vulnerability. As a result – and unsurprisingly – s/he may feel frightened, helpless, enraged, despondent, and filled with remorse and doubts.

The "receipt" that the parent's projective identifications have been efficient is the nurse's mounting incompetence, pessimism, anger, and misery. She has thus duly received the emotional mayhem that the parent has placed, unconsciously to be sure, in her lap. Such communicative modes have repercussions. She wants to help the families, answer questions, still their anguish, and heighten the parents' competence. But, she cannot do this with as many families and as thoroughly as she would like. The nurse is like a mother of a score of wolf cubs. She reaches for a whiner while another one starts screaming. Regression propagates down the road and she gets stressed and annoyed. She tries to hide it from the parents who may feel it anyway. Perhaps, they ask to see another "nicer and warmer" nurse. This adds to her regression and she may consider swapping to a calmer job. Yet, this is not an unstoppable landslide. Such emotional strain can be handled in supervisions with the team of nurses and within a strict framework. The following is a summary of my model:

1/ Supervisions take place regularly and in the same room. I prefer one-hour meetings every fortnight, but this can be adjusted to local conditions. The frame should be kept or changed only after mutual agreement.

2/ Anything talked about in sessions is handled with respect and professional secrecy.

3/ Supervisions focus on patients and the nurses' emotional reactions to these cases. Other issues, like working conditions, salaries, organization, or management are taken care of within a special "P-group" or personnel group. Its leader should not be the clinical supervisor.

4/ The session begins with my asking, in due order, who has a case to discuss. I estimate the time allotted to each, and one nurse then begins to relate her case.

5/ After a presentation, I invite the group to submit their reactions or points of view. To create a calm climate, I ask anyone who wants to speak to raise a finger. I then summarize reactions and viewpoints and add my own. I end by asking the presenter about her reactions to the discussion.

6/ There are risks when somebody presents difficulties with a case and the colleagues then submit their reactions. I have learnt from the "weaving thoughts" technique (Norman & Salomonsson, 2005; Salomonsson, 2012b), a format for therapists discussing cases in peer groups. Though it cannot be applied *in toto* to CHC supervisions, some lessons are useful: I try to preclude a question-and-answer dialectic between the presenter and her colleagues. Allowing the staff to associate to the material – rather than having a ping-pong debate with the presenter – yields two advantages. The group can toss up ideas in the air, without the presenter arguing for her case. Also, her position as listener diminishes the risk of feeling criticized.

The arguments for the frame in supervision are the same as when I talked about standing on one foot in the park or boarding an airplane. The nurse is subjected to anxiety and impotence. Feeling like a wolf mother with many cubs is enough to release such feelings. If, beyond this, a parent is depressed or ambivalent towards the baby and cannot bear such feelings but "pushes" them into the nurse, she will have a heavy burden. One common response among nurses is to overstep the framework. When 2 minutes remain of a routine check-up, the mother discloses her worries. The nurse wants to be kind and allows 15 minutes extra, which disrupts her working schedule and patience.

I discovered this tendency to overstepping the time frame in the supervisions. The nurses were often delayed to our sessions. I brought it up and various explanations were provided: "One mother 'just wanted some advice' when a few minutes were left. Her husband cheated on her and now she's considering divorce. I couldn't dismiss her. Sorry I'm late." True, if everybody does this with all mothers who prod the framework, the Centre becomes dysfunctional. Yet, such an argument can be rigid and rejecting. A more relevant claim is that the nurse, through her way of maintaining the framework, demonstrates to the mother her capacity of handling anxiety. By keeping a stable frame, the nurse conveys that a similar scaffolding is crucial for the baby's development. The baby is trying to "push" her distress into the parents. Their job is to take it in but also to counter it by maintaining the framework: "I know you don't like it's dark outside, but now it's bedtime, dear". Similarly, if this nurse told the mother, "I hear you're in trouble. I'm afraid we've no more time today, but let's set up an appointment as soon as possible", the message would be the same as to the babies: showing empathy and setting limits.

This maintenance of the framework could be labelled according to Jacques Lacan's concept the *Name of the Father* (Diatkine, 2007; Lacan, 1998; Marks, Murphy, & Glowinski, 2001). This function, introduced in Chapter 2, is the basis of the symbolic order and the representative of the Law. It is juxtaposed to what I call the *Principle of Boundless Maternity.* Here neither time, limits, nor constraints exist for the child's desire. Note that both concepts refer to principles, not to a parent of this or that gender. Also, none of them can exist in isolation. Rather, the task of the Name of the Father is "to unite (and not to oppose) a desire to the Law" (Lacan, 1966/2006, p. 698). Unmitigated and isolated, the maternal principle would signify psychosis and the paternal a fascist mental state. A "marriage" between the two principles is thus essential for the child's development, the parents' attitudes towards their baby, and the nurse's approach towards the parents.

The nurse is stretched in two directions; she is beleaguered by the Principle of Boundless Maternity as she receives e-mails from parents with requests for instant help, urges to overstep the times for appointments, and reproaches for not solving problems on the spot. Were she to yield to all these demands she would become annoyed and exhausted. She is pulled from the side of the Name of the Father which tempts her, in response, to become lecturing and harsh. We recognize the similarity with the everyday care of a baby; s/he needs to bask in the illusion of having all wishes fulfilled, like in a tale from *Arabian Nights*. Also, s/he needs to learn that life is no fairy tale but an evolving process with many people involved and with many limits. The CHC nurse can do a great job if she can impersonate a harmonious "marriage" between the two philosophies. This is why the frame is important yet difficult to uphold and continuous supervision is mandatory.

Many nurses want to pay attention to and help families with emotional problems (McCauley, Elsom, Muir-Cochrane, & Lyneham, 2011). Yet, they feel obstructed due to a "perceived lack of competency rather than a lack of interest" (C. J. Jones, Creedy, & Gamble, 2012, p. 216). They signal that they do have phronesis, or prudence. This Aristotelian term implies judgement based on practical wisdom and reflection (Aristotle, 1999). Yet, applying phronesis to their daily work at the CHC seems impossible and is thus relegated to the therapist. One reason is that nursing education and health politics have been overturned by instrumental and

Supervising nurses at the CHC   67

medical values (Kinsella & Pitman, 2012). Another reason, in my view, is that the nurses do not manage to uphold a sound balance between the paternal and maternal principles. They oscillate between being too harsh and too yielding and lose faith in themselves and in the families. This is where supervision comes in.

Bringing up and talking about problems

Supervisions aim at helping the nurses *detect* symptoms of emotional and functional disorders, *bring them up* with the parents, and *suggest* and institute adequate measures. Not all nurses are well trained in how postnatal depression can appear and link with infant disorders. Even if their academic knowledge is superior, they also need courage to bring up their intuitions about emotional problems in the family. The submitted interview study mentioned earlier sorted the nurses into three ideal types (Stuhr & Wachholz, 2001) regarding their attitudes towards taking care of perinatal problems at the CHC: "I don't want to", "I want to but I cannot", and "I want to and I can". Many of them chose their job due to its blend of medical and psychological questions. They wish to give advice on breastfeeding, baby food, or immunizations – and to support anguished families. Problems arise when a nurse observes a problem and needs to act. Embarrassment, uncertainty, a wish to be tactful, and an unease at meddling with others' affairs may interfere with her resolve to talk with the parents. Then, an attitude of "I want to but I cannot" may emerge. Here are some reactions vented in supervision.

Tanya:	*"I see what's going on between mother and baby, but it's hard to bring it up with her."*
I ask:	*"What makes it so hard for you to bring it up?"*
Tanya:	*"I'd like to tell her that I'm wondering how things are for them; she's looking sad and the baby seems unsettled. But if I'd tell her, how would she react? And what would I do if she breaks apart?"*
I ask again:	*"Would you feel guilty?"*
Tanya:	*"Actually, I should feel guilty if I remained silent! Maybe I'm afraid she'd become angry. Or, what if I'm wrong? Maybe their interaction is splendid! Then I would make a fool of myself."*
Karen:	*"My problem is not that I may be wrong sometimes. I know I am. I did bring up such things with one mother yesterday – but she started sobbing and I just didn't know what to do!"*
Andrea:	*"Maybe she had a postnatal depression!"*
Fran:	*"Sometimes I run into such situations but I hesitate and start talking about food or their kitchen ventilation aggravating the baby's asthma, even though I know it's beside the point!"*

68   Part I: Clinic

This interchange reveals what may prevent nurses from bringing up observations with the mother: guilt, fear of the mother's anger, concern of being wrong, the need to establish a diagnosis, and an unfamiliarity with handling emotional storms. Supervision aims at helping them get sight of these factors and become more explicit and courageous. Tanya fears she might be wrong about the dyad's interaction. Of course, she can be wrong! If she were to profess her observations in a dead certain manner, the mother would certainly feel humiliated. My alternative is to suggest to Tanya to tentatively convey her observations to the mother: "When I'm looking at you and Charlie, I wonder how things are for the two of you. What do you think, Katie?" This way, Tanya is merely hinting at a possible problem. Another road would be the "I think"-method: "I don't know what *you* think, but *I* think you look sad today." She would clarify that this observation emanates from her, not from anyone else. Nobody can take away her personal observations. The worst consequence would be a surprised, incredulous, or maybe even sour comment from the mother. Alternately, Tanya might have hit the nail on the head and mother Katie would start talking about distressing matters.

When painful matters have come up on the table, mother and nurse need to broach the problems. One factor to consider is the nurse's interest, personality, and education. Some nurses are keen on perceiving and talking about emotional things while others prefer to leave it to the "expert" therapist. Some have no psychological education apart from their nursing education. Others are trained in counselling (Holden, Sagovsky, & Cox, 1989), in which the nurse sees the mother for a handful of sessions. That method is more supportive and less insight-oriented than mine. In my view, a counselling nurse should suggest a main theme to the mother: "Let's meet a handful of times and talk about what makes breastfeeding so cumbersome." Sometimes, the two commence and terminate the project. Or, some issues emerge that necessitate further elaboration. If so, the mother can be referred to me or to a couple therapist with her partner.

A supervision session

This chapter ends with a detailed supervision, with the aim of illustrating what may come up at such occasions. Pamela is a nurse with some ten years of professional experience. She brings up a case.

Pamela:	*"I see a young mother who can't decide on breastfeeding or bottle. The baby is 4 months and doesn't gain enough weight. It's worrying me! Every call at the CHC I tell her: 'You must decide; either you breastfeed and then you'll have to work on it. Or, you can give it up and give the bottle."*

Supervising nurses at the CHC 69

Pamela impersonates the mother's whining voice, which sounds both submissive and rebellious: "Yeah, OK, I will breastfeed, but it's such big work." She continues with quotations indicating that she feels this mother is lackadaisical, nonchalant, and uninvolved: "She prefers to party in town rather than taking care of the situation". Clearly, Pamela is annoyed. I ask: "What do you feel here, and what do you think the mother feels when seeing you?"

Pamela answers by giving yet more examples of how the mother rejects her advice. She bypasses my question. I ask the group to reflect on our dialogue. Samantha and Beatrice simultaneously: "The two sound like a teenage daughter and her mother!"

Pamela in surprise: "I never told this mother I'm annoyed with her but I did think, 'Shape up, girl!'"

Pamela seems to think that her attitude was never noticed by the mother.

Marcia: "When the mother does like this with Pam, she doesn't really take responsibility of the situation. She transfers it to Pam, who gets to be the one who nags at her."

I intervene: "Well, what did you think about your mothers when you were teenagers?"

Everybody sighs and smiles in recognition.

I continue: "Responsibility, isn't it a major theme in adolescence? The girl claims that Mum's ideas about boys, the pill, drinking, etc., are old-fashioned. Yet, she expects Mum to take responsibility."

But Pamela claims she did not show the mother her vexation. She finds it hard to integrate this metaphor of a mother–teenager-daughter-like relationship.

I ask: "Perhaps, Pamela, you feel that I and the group criticize you now?"

Pamela: "No, I'm just trying to grasp what goes on between her and me, and how you people think."

I continue: "What if you asked the mother, 'I wonder why we get stuck in this kind of dialogue. You ask me about feeding, I give advice and that it's your choice and there's a certain risk for the girl at present'."

Pamela seems incredulous. Then suddenly she exclaims: "NO REALLY, you know what, let's take it from the beginning, we can't go on like this, you and I!"

I get startled, which Pamela notices.

Pamela:	*"You think I'm silly?"*
I reply:	*"On the contrary! I identified with your mother and felt, 'Wow, now you care for me!'"*
	Pamela becomes visibly moved and pensive.
Beatrice:	*"Yeah, you could convey to her that you've been thinking about what's so hard for her."*
Jenny:	*"Once, I quarrelled with my son about a party that I thought was risky. Finally, he admitted that I cared for him and that he . . . didn't dislike it. Then we could start talking without squabbling."*

This vignette can be viewed from many angles. One is Pamela's initial defensive efforts. Rather than looking at the problem from a relational perspective, she portrays the mother's contradictory communications. Yet, this is of no help for the mother or Pamela. Another angle is the adolescent metaphor, which emerges to illustrate the nurse–mother relationship. At first, Pamela is locked in the position of a mother confronted with a teenager's messages of rebellion, helplessness, passivity, and provocation. It was interesting to note the shift in Pamela's voice when she exclaimed, "Let's take it from the beginning". It was as if the Name of the Father entered our room and said "Enough! Something needs to be changed here." Another observation was the ease with which the nurses could identify both with the adolescent daughter and the resigned mother. Supervisions had made them more conversant with discussing countertransference and grasping that their life experiences, if acknowledged and talked about, can be valuable tools for understanding parents and babies. Some years later, Pamela told me that the mother had come to rely on her more openly, for example, by asking for advice and often also following it. She was still uncertain and a bit of a callow person, but she was not that prone to involve Pamela in hopeless controversies.

Chapter 8

The internal frame at the Child Health Centre

The two previous chapters focused on how to organize health care units and supervise nurses. As a transition to this chapter on therapeutic technique, I will argue that the therapist also needs to consider how the external frame at the CHC affects him or her. Communications, implicit and explicit, run zig-zag between parents, nurses, and the therapist. S/he is scrutinized in a way that may feel unfamiliar or uncomfortable. Doing therapy in any institution also carries the risk that the patient splits the transference. If we imagine that Pamela's mother patient in Chapter 7 had seen me for therapy, she might regard me as comforting while blaming Pamela for being a hag. Or, in reverse, a parent feels her nurse is "warm and understanding" while I am "critical and brusque". Whatever kernels of truths such splits may indicate, they need to be visualized. The good side of the coin is that one can learn a lot; once we can convince the mother to talk with the nurse about her misgivings, this can diminish her fears of broaching her ambivalence and critique. No doubt, such honesty will benefit the rest of the family.

The internal frame

The concept of the internal frame (Bleger, 1967, 2012; Faimberg, 2014) is related to that of the external. Yet, it is more abstract, implying an attitude and an ability to "think psychoanalytically", which gets transferred into clinical behaviour. The concept comprises "the role of the analyst, the set of space (atmosphere) and time factors, and part of the technique . . . [such as] fixing and keeping of times, fees, interruptions, etc." (Bleger, 1967, p. 511). It is a strategy, not a specific technique, which we need to "embrace the intensity and dependence that is necessary to contain the regression and impulse-pressure that is generated" (Künstlicher, 1996, p. 151) in our encounters with patients.

The therapist provides the patient with an external frame that is solid, reliable, and non-intrusive. This enables the patient to do that special thing called psychotherapeutic work or "play" (Künstlicher, 1996). Meanwhile, the therapist sets up an internal frame within which s/he is thinking, pondering, and daydreaming about what the patient says, does, and looks like – or does *not* say or do or exhibit. It is like reading a *palimpsest*, a manuscript where an earlier version is covered by

72 Part I: Clinic

one of later date. The "later", more polished and conformist, version is exemplified by a mother who assures that she just feels "sheer love" for her baby. An "earlier", more raw and anarchist, edition might be that *she* feels like a baby and envies him who gets everybody's attention. It would be erroneous to claim that this is the "true" version and that she "actually" is jealous. The truth resides in a mix of both. She loves her baby *and* is enraged with him, is happy about having conceived him *and* regrets it. It is easier to admit the positive version, which matches her ideals about motherhood.

One way of helping a mother to handle the tension between early and late editions, or between primitive affects and the defences against them, is to help her "thicken" the late edition; solidify repressions, encourage and convince her that she is a great mother. Such supportive practice is common among nurses, for example, in consultations using the Edinburgh Postnatal Depression Scale (EPDS; Cox, Holden, & Sagovsky, 1987) and in developmental guidance (Lojkasek, Cohen, & Muir, 1994) at child health units. It can also be endorsed from a psychoanalytic point of view. Every mother wants to hear that her baby is wonderful. She is in a brittle state and her self-image swings up and down. A friendly comment is thus "good medicine", especially for mothers who panic and do not wish to understand their unconscious motivations or earlier palimpsest editions. Perhaps Nora, in Chapter 5, would have benefited from such messages from her analyst. As she listened to Nora's grievances and her story about her childhood pacifier, she got an interior image of a screaming child in front of her. This was when she felt it was like having two babies in the consulting room. This made her adopt a more supportive and encouraging technique. Had she done this a bit earlier, it is not unthinkable that Nora would have nursed less grievance against her.

Most parents I see do not belong to this category. Rather, they get interested when I scrape on the surface edition to reach "texts" deeper down. Before exemplifying what goes on in an analyst's head, I argue that though I initiate this job, it can only be continued with a patient willing to participate. There are some similarities between an analyst and a detective; both want to uncover the truth – but the criminal opposes Sherlock Holmes' efforts while the patient, at least half-heartedly, wants to know more about herself. Unless she is willing to cooperate, it would be unwise and unfair to force interpretations onto her. Some mothers explicitly ask for CBT (Cognitive Behavioural Therapy) to deal with their panic. Some had it before and found it wholesome. If I meet with a decisive lack of interest or a negative attitude towards the "palimpsest project", I respect it and recommend her to a CBT therapist. There should be no prestige or dogmatic considerations in treatment recommendations.

Psychoanalytic pop-up comments: Uma and Greg; Jane, David, and Ottilie

Mothers who are interested in the "palimpsest enterprise" do not respond immediately with enthusiasm to a question like, "I wonder why you are so anxious about your child's health that you can't close your eyes at night". First, they need to feel some confidence in a stranger whom the nurse recommended. While this condition becomes partially fulfilled during our first minutes together, I get a chance to submit my first "pop-up comment", a hint that we could do some "scraping" together. To explain, when one heats up the popcorn machine, nothing happens. We all wait for the first pop. When it has occurred, the other seeds will follow along quickly. Does this metaphor imply that the mother, once "heated up", submits an avalanche of affects and insights? Wouldn't that risk releasing an emotional turmoil, more severe and enduring than the one she went to see me for? Certainly! I do need to explain what I mean by a "pop-up comment".

Any dialogue contains moments when cracks open up and unforeseen messages pop up from underneath. They offer the analyst a possibility of making a comment, posing a question, repeating a sentence, or just raising his eyebrows in surprise. He thus invites the patient to follow along deeper down, past the smooth surface. A banal example is Karen in Chapter 1, the pregnant woman with the tumour. During the first visit she related the calamities which, from a medical perspective, ended well. Then she said, "everything should be fine now, I guess". I responded, "If everything were OK you wouldn't be here". This incontestable and trivial comment merely reminded her of the obvious. It was an effort at encouraging *and* provoking her to focus on what chafed her.

Now to a more powerful "pop-up". *Uma* is a young mother of *Greg*, a boy of 11 months. She has been depressed on and off since she was 15 years old, and has had many treatments with medication and brief therapy, none of which were exhaustive or successful. At first, the boy is playing calmly on the floor. Meanwhile, the mother tells me she spent the other night at a psychiatric emergency ward. "Nobody understood me: They just sent me home with a prescription for my usual medication." Her partner has got tired of her ups and downs and has left her, though they remain in contact. As she is sobbing, the boy is stretching his arms towards her. She hands him a toy but makes no effort at contact. This happens again and I tell Greg, "I guess you want Mum to talk to you or lift you up". Uma gets the message and lifts him onto her lap. Instantly, he turns away his eyes. "He does this all the time", she says in a slightly accusatory tone. In Chapter 18, we will discuss gaze avoidance in babies.

A depressed mother feels abandoned by psychiatry and her fiancé. Also, she abandons her son by not reacting to his invitations – and feels abandoned when he turns away from her. In the countertransference, one might get saddened by such self-centredness and relative neglect of the boy. Yet, there is something appealing and earnest to her, which tempts me to probe deeper. I suddenly realize I feel provoked by her long eyelashes and I start elaborating on this theme within my internal frame. Why these artificial extensions? And why does he avoid her eyes? Any connections? Finally I venture, "You've got quite long eyelashes. What do you think about it?" Such a comment may be considered offensive, and I would not submit it until I had worked through my countertransference. When asking her, I felt friendly and curious. She startled: "I don't like when people look at me. It's

74 Part I: Clinic

as if they're seeing through me." I ask: "What do you think they'd see?" "Someone they don't like", she says. This little interchange became the start of a brief therapy, especially after I suggested, "I wonder if this thing about you being looked at could have something to do with the fact that Greg wavers between wanting to get close to you and avoiding your eyes".

My comment touched on some hot spots in Uma: Her conviction that she has a hereditary and eternal depression and is unfit for motherhood. Uma tries to conceal this negative self-image beneath her extended eyelashes, but it emerges in her choice of a job way below her intellectual qualifications. I knew nothing about this background when I made my "pop-up comment". It was an effort at creating a crack in the surface by inviting her to a dialogue that might scrape beneath her self-definition of "I'm depressed and nobody understands me".

This case shows a comment that "pops up" the mother's narcissistic defences. Such a resolute and warm attitude is often needed to bring people out of self-defensive entrenchments. In couple work, it is even more impending. One example is when the two have colluded on one sole perspective on their problem with the child or the relationship. They defend it behind a mutually consented defensive wall. Or, they fight like cat and dog and each one vindicates his/her position. To exemplify the first type, I bring up *Jane* and *David*, with their 7-month-old *Ottilie*. Both are ambitious and anxious professionals. Ottilie is their first child and no internet information about child care exists that mother Jane is unaware of. She is anxious about any trifling symptom in the girl.

In this family, the nights are "awful, like a circus". The girl wakes up, David puts her hand on her chest and she falls asleep for a while. Then she wakes up again, crying until she gets the breast. This goes on throughout the night. The girl is fine and the parents are exhausted. I suggest: "Ottilie is a fine and brisk girl who gives very good contact. What about weaning her?" This is anathema to the mother. "Every internet article says children should be breastfed at least up to one year, preferably longer. No way!" I respond: "You're here because you're exhausted. So . . .?" The father nods silently but she retorts: "Then give us the tools to make her sleep!" I shake my head:

> I have no such tools. The question is: Is it Ottilie or the two of you who shall rule the family? Will she remain Queen Ottilie and you two her subjects? Or, shall she be the Princess who knows there is a King David and a Queen Jane?

The mother starts laughing but also looks angry. I ask if she felt hurt but she responds that I've got a point. "Queen Ottilie . . . that's something! No, I don't want her to become queen. At work, I'm perhaps something of a queen. Damn it, it's much harder for me to be the queen in our own castle!" The couple had evidently colluded on one interpretation of Ottilie's insomnia. The imagery of the royal couple popped up in me. A month later they went on a week-long vacation trip, during which the father comforted the girl at night-time. David said afterwards, "Now she is breastfed during daytime only. It's nice to go to bed with your wife and wake up together". The royal bedchamber had been established and the princess slept in her own bed.

The rule of abstinence

In traditional psychoanalytic work the patient lies on the couch. While s/he is talking freely, the analyst sits behind and is pensive and rather silent, including answering questions about private life. This practice has a well thought through rationale since Freud (1915b) introduced *the principle of abstinence.* When we suggest the couch to a patient and decline answering questions on private life, we aim to facilitate regression in the hope of opening up her private, internal world. The idea is that:

> the patient's need and longing should be allowed to persist in her, in order that they may serve as forces impelling her to do work and to make changes, and that we must beware of appeasing those forces by means of surrogates.
>
> (p. 165)

She may be frustrated with the arrangement but will slowly understand that it is an act of respect; she is there to talk about and receive help with *her* private matters. This process often passes via fantasies about the analyst's life. Abstinence will enhance the transference and make her use it to mirror her own self and, in the end, become more able to handle her life in an autonomous and powerful way.

All this sounds good – and is good – if some conditions are fulfilled. The patient must be willing to engage in a high-frequency and lengthy therapy and have enough psychological maturity to tolerate the frustration. Freud pointed out that abstinence also exposes the patient to "a measure of real suffering through frustration" (1937, p. 231). Since a CHC parent's aim is not to be analysed we cannot expect her to accept such frustration. Having entered a new life phase, only to discover helplessness and panic, she wants to get back on track to parenthood NOW. Yet, quite a few parents wish to reflect on what worries them:

> It's strange that I can hardly take a walk with the pram. I *know* there is no real risk that a lorry will kill my baby, but I panic. Me, this tough girl who went hitch-hiking in India last year!

The "pop-up comments" and the "palimpsest project" aim at inspiring parents to explore beneath the surface. Such devices and aims are psychoanalytic – and so is my thinking and fantasizing with the patient – but the technical rule of abstinence cannot be adhered to as strictly.

As we take leave for the summer, a mother asks me where I'll spend my vacations. "In France", I answer and we talk about her fears of the upcoming summer. If she is panicking I may give her my cell-phone number to use if her alarm gets unbearable. In fact, I almost never get such calls. Another mother asks

76 Part I: Clinic

if I have children, to which I also may reply. Behind the question, another one may be hiding: "Are you capable of helping me? What do you know about children?" Were I merely to answer, "Yes, I have three children" and hope it would still her worries, I would be practicing an unduly naïve and supportive therapy. So, I follow up her questions to see what may lie behind. This reflects one aspect of the internal frame; the knowledge that no relationship is free of ambivalence. And, the more the distrustful, disappointed, annoyed, and jealous aspects of the relationship are brought up, the more honest will our dialogue be and the better I can help her.

Many analysts who criticized Freud's technique took as a starting point the mother–infant relationship. In a paper with the telling title "Confusion of tongues between adults and the child", Ferenczi (1949) argued that analytic technique could reflect "professional hypocrisy" (p. 226) when we silence our intolerance of a patient or a private concern. Better to discuss it openly with the patient, Ferenczi thought. One can trace a developmental line from him to Winnicott's (1971b) thoughts and the intersubjective school (Levenson, 2005/1983; Stolorow & Atwood, 1997). Many of the latter's adherents are infant researchers (Beebe & Lachmann, 2002; Lichtenberg, 1987; Stern, 2004) and we will return to their debate with more classically oriented analysts in Chapter 18.

The intersubjectivists question the rule of abstinence whereas the "classics" adhere to it. But which setting are we talking about? Behind the couch, I am musing on my countertransference towards a patient who sought analysis. This setting demands a classical technique, in my view. Sitting in front of a mother–infant dyad, I am more exposed. Subduing my personality would be felt as feigned, spurious, and unhelpful. The challenge is to transfer my psychoanalytic thinking to a CHC consultation. It may result in a classical interpretation or a spontaneous metaphor. All the time, my analytic thinking keeps ticking: "What happened? Why did I say that? Why is the girl not looking at Mum? How do I feel when I see that? Why did that man purse his lips all of a sudden?"

Flexibility and the setting

Let us go back to classical psychoanalysis. A female analysand talks time and again about her husband. "He's boring, makes mean comments, sits by his pc and accuses me of our insipid sex life!" Let us further visualize that I feel tempted to invite her husband for a joint session with his wife. Yet, our agreement is that she and I meet four times a week to talk about problems with herself and the people around her – including me. Thus I would rather think, "She really is discontented", "Why is she carping at her husband?", "What does that say about her self-image?", "What is she staging with me by this blame-game?" I would formulate some intervention around such themes. Perhaps she might recognize this pattern from earlier relationships and that she is repeating a sadomasochistic drama with me. She may then also understand that this relates to her negative and contemptuous image of herself, which she keeps aggravating through these

The internal frame at the CHC 77

scenarios. Or – she discovers that she has put up with a nasty fellow and now decides to leave him.

Let us transfer this scene to the CHC. The mother complains similarly about her husband. True, it might reflect her sadomasochistic tendencies. But, it may also signal that he needs to wake up and realize he has become a father. In such a situation, I often ask her to bring him for a session. The result has often surprised me. Among all husbands I have met, few matched their partner's one-sided descriptions. More commonly, they have voiced concern about her welfare, helplessness in supporting her, bewilderment in their new role as a father, tensions in relation to his or her parents, worries about combining job duties with family commitments, etc. I have often noticed a shift in the mother, from a plaintive appearance to one of appreciation and warmth. Sometimes, this leads me to suggest we switch to couple therapy, which we discuss in Chapters 12 and 13.

Another variation of the setting concerns the baby. A mother may come on her own. She wants to talk about her sadness, misgivings, fatigue, and anxiety. Then she reveals her ambivalent feelings for her baby: "I take part in a parental group at the CHC. The others speak about love at first sight in relation to their baby. I never felt that way. I'm not sure . . . if I . . . like him." It is easy to empathize with her; it is excruciating to conceive and give birth to a baby only to have these contradictory feelings towards a helpless creature. In response, I ask her to bring the baby next time. I would guess she wanted to come alone to her first hour to get space to talk about her resentment, without being interrupted by that little person whom she unconsciously might regard as a competitor for love.

I would have two reasons for inviting the baby. One would simply be to check on his state. If the mother has been depressed or overly anxious for some time, he may indeed be affected. There might be signs of gaze avoidance, a low-keyed mood, fretfulness, and other indications of malaise. The second reason is valid regardless of the baby's state; he is a partner in a relationship. If she complains about not loving him, he needs to be invited to our efforts at setting things right. I would even say – I am forestalling discussions in Chapters 18 and 19 – that *he* needs to know more about the mother's ambivalence. This is precisely what is holding their relationship padlocked and confined; the mother has this mix of feelings and thinks it will harm the baby irreparably were she to say it. The result is often the obverse; the baby notes that her ways of being with him are incomprehensible. She says nice things, but her hands are too firm when holding him. Or her mouth is smiling, but not her eyes.

Inviting father and/or baby; these are two examples of the need to be flexible about setting. This also applies further on in treatment. When a relationship issue with the baby gets dissolved through therapy, the mother may become aware of a personal difficulty, such as her limited access to warm emotions. The issue with the baby was thus a new edition of an old problem. When the baby has become free of symptoms and if the mother wants to work with her personal issues, it would be senseless to retain the baby in treatment. Such a shift to a personal therapy with the mother is often heralded by the baby losing interest in the mother–therapist dialogue.

78 Part I: Clinic

The internal frame: concluding remarks

To sum up my thoughts about the internal frame and its use in practice, the term refers to a mode of thinking that permeates my encounters with patients. It implies to "read between the lines", "read the text underneath", or to understand the unconscious currents beneath conscious messages. It has an ingredient of unmasking and translating, such as asking myself, "what does s/he want to say now?" This unmasking will meet with resistance. "Translation" may imply substituting more outspoken synonyms, from "I'm frustrated" to "You seem angry" or "To me, you look sad".

Unmasking and translating are two facets of the internal frame. This pertains to its paternal aspect, if we use that term similarly to when we explored containment in Chapters 2 and 3. There is also a maternal aspect to the frame; feeling compassion with anyone who has entered parenthood only to find hopes and expectations torn to threads by emotions surging from the depths like pristine sea monsters. To be true, panic and helplessness may hide beneath narcissistic and uncaring attitudes: "Wow, I can't go to the gym or have a glass of wine, I just *hate* breastfeeding!" Yet such attitudes, and the ensuing negative countertransference, soon dissipate when one starts exploring them from a position that is relatively free from prejudiced opinions. One may then learn that the mother's problem is not that she can't have a glass of wine but she can't have that loving feeling for her baby.

Earlier, when discussing abstinence, we spoke of the couch. One of its raisons d'être is to give the patient free reins to speak without anxiously scrutinizing the analyst's face reactions. Another argument is one that Freud (1913a) admitted was personal:

> I cannot put up with being stared at by other people for eight hours a day (or more). Since, while I am listening to the patient, I, too, give myself over to the current of my unconscious thoughts, I do not wish my expressions of face to give the patient material for interpretations or to influence him in what he tells me.
>
> (p. 134)

I would formulate his argument form a different angle. The work of translating and unmasking is an intellectual *and* an emotional endeavour. The analyst tries to reach a mindset that is unanchored to everyday and concrete matters and has more of a dreamy quality. Freud (1912b) recommended an "evenly-suspended attention" (p. 111) or, to better translate *gleichschwebende Aufmerksamkeit*, an equally hovering attention to the patient's communications. Bion (1962a) called it "reverie", which relates to dreaming:

> a state of mind which is open to the reception of any 'objects' from the loved object and is therefore capable of reception of the infant's projective identifications whether they are felt by the infant to be good or bad.
>
> (p. 36)

The internal frame at the CHC 79

This gives us another reason for suggesting the couch; to give *the analyst* free reins to exert this attention or reverie. Simply put, to be left in peace with one's thoughts and fancies and verbalize them at a time one finds suitable.

What happens in brief consultations in a nurse's office far away from a tranquil psychoanalytic office? Would that not overwhelm the patient(s) with a lot of perceptions of me and disrupt my reverie? Indeed, I may want to be left at peace with my deliberations to understand better what is going on. Yet, I would miss most of the valuable, even indispensable, information that parent–infant therapists need. Second, the presence of mother and baby provides stimuli that further my regression and inspires reverie. There is a lot of face-reading, smelling, and listening to the music of the mother's and the baby's voices. I said earlier that the classical frame provides the patient with the possibilities of a maternal holding. In parent–infant therapy, such possibilities are provided by the mere presence of mother and a baby. This inspires my maternal holding – and paternal delineation – and tints my analytic thinking with a serious yet playful, and a wide-opened yet dream-like, quality. No wonder, my spontaneity or my primary process is easily inspired. This may result in lapses, metaphors, and visual imagery that open up shafts into the unconscious communication between mother and baby. To sum up, the drawback of the absence of the couch is compensated by the presence of two people involved in a peculiar form of intercourse; the baby–mother interaction.

Chapter 9

From panic to pleasure. Therapy with Debbie and Mae

To illustrate brief mother–baby interventions, I have chosen the case of *Debbie* and her daughter *Mae*, because it illustrates many anxieties that run criss-cross in a dyad after delivery. I followed the two for seven months, an unusually long time at the CHC. There exists no "one-size-fits-all" treatment, and every case must be assessed individually. Lena in Chapter 5 needed to mourn the after-effects of her C-section. This was worked through in two sessions. In contrast, I quickly concluded that Debbie, a 32-year-old first-time mother, needed more help.

Debbie arrives alone the first time. Her rose-coloured outfit and her face give a sweet and slightly childish impression. Her daughter Mae is only 17 days old but already, things have gone terribly wrong, she says. "I was so happy being pregnant! Now she is getting at me!" She makes a gesture as if brushing aside some noxious insect from her sternum. "I always loved children and took care of my sister's girls." She is shocked by this emotional turnover but also recognizes it from other situations:

> I fell in love when I was 20. I was so happy – and yet, I just kept thinking of my acne! Similarly, our wedding was wonderful but the only thing that occupied me afterwards was if this or that guest held a fine speech or not!

She was in therapy and on SSRI medication during the period of her first love and the acne issue. When I suggest she bring Mae along to the next session, she hesitates. "I need to think. We talked about serious things today. I'm not sure if it's good for her to come with me." She seems eager to get quick help and I am far from sure that she will return.

Here are some thoughts simmering in my internal frame during the first hour: Her rose dress makes me think of a baby, an intuition strengthened by her hand's "get away"-gesture. I gather she is jealous of her baby who is now getting everybody's attention. I know this issue pesters many mothers and I have already mentioned a mother's many reasons for hating the baby. In his terse and gleeful language, Winnicott (1949a) listed up to 18 reasons for such hatred! This challenges the mother with the task of handling her ambivalence. Debbie, however, cannot accept such feelings. Everything about babyhood must be *la vie en rose*.

From panic to pleasure   81

I wonder how to help her with this and if the baby has been affected by mother's unsolved struggle.

The second session, Debbie comes with Mae. Today, she looks more adult and sad. Mae is breastfeeding calmly. Then she drops the breast, flails with her hands a bit and makes some noises. A banal reaction from her, I guess, but Debbie becomes unhappy and distressed:

> I told you last time I was happy while being pregnant. In fact, I wonder if I *was* pregnant! I didn't feel like it! I felt beautiful and appreciated by all, but did I really think of the baby to come? Then, at delivery they said I should touch her head with my hands, but I was only interested in whether the epidural anaesthesia worked or not . . . I can't take her to me, neither to my body nor to my heart. It's terrible, I feel so guilty.

Debbie moves on to talk about her handicapped sister. She had envisaged she would go on helping her parents with her, while the newborn would lie smilingly in the pram. It is easy to empathize with her hopeless double care-taking project. More difficult to talk about is the fact that Mae is fretting now. Any remark by me might be felt as blaming Debbie for the girl's distress. Instead, I utilize an internal image that comes to my mind: "When I'm looking at Mae at your breast, I'm thinking of driving a car and stepping on the gas and the brake pedals at the same time. Not very smooth driving . . . No good rhythm between you, right?" Towards the end of this second session the girl is lying like a frog on Mum's chest. I catch a smile on mother's face as she's saying, "Driving that car, I think we're gonna make it, right girl?"

Just like Donna, Leyla, and Doriane in Chapters 3 and 4, Debbie soon starts talking about her own mother. She has praised that Debbie is seeing a therapist, but after two sessions she claimed that no more sessions were needed since her daughter's anxiety was gone. This made Debbie feel misunderstood and annoyed. She did not vent it openly with her mother but smiled, went to the loo, and cried. "Anger isn't your favourite game, right?" I suggest and she confirms: "I'm always a nice girl, never much of a teenage rebel." I fill in, "Your sister got her handicap when you were 13. Not much room for rebellion." "I focused on taking care of her and my parents, making everyone happy." Debbie is carrying the baby while striding rapidly in the consulting room. Her shoulders tighten up, her voice is tense, and Mae is screaming. I speak with the girl about Mum's anger with Granny, that this may feel strange to her, and that Mum has many feelings. Mae pays attention to my voice and face and slowly becomes calmer. Mum complains: "It feels like a house arrest with Mae. Will I ever be able to leave home again?" She is walking around, bumping Mae up and down swiftly in a fruitless effort at calming her. She is sweaty and indeed, I feel a bit sweaty, too!

When the session is over and I leave the office I see *Donald*, Mae's father, holding her while Debbie is stowing the car. We say hello and speak a little about Mae. He is grateful for the contact with me. To compare with the setting in ordinary

82 Part I: Clinic

psychotherapy, I would nod politely to a patient's partner but not enter such a conversation. Here, we recognize the flexible setting addressed in Chapter 8.

A crisis in our relationship

The next session Debbie is upset. Mae never stopped crying after our previous hour. They went to the emergency room at the hospital, where they were assured that nothing was wrong with Mae:

> But I discovered that I need to find *my own* rhythm! It's good seeing you, but we need to come more seldom. To be honest, I googled on your name, and I understand you're a specialist. I really don't want you to feel that I don't appreciate our work but . . .

In fact, it was Debbie who had suggested we meet three times a week. As I happened to be available and she was anxious, I consented. Now she blames me for this frequency and it would be tempting to defend myself. But this would be pointless and prevent us from talking about her fear of anger.

Analyst:	*"Maybe you got angry with me because Mae got upset the last session and wouldn't stop crying. Then you wondered if I know what I'm doing. You were calmed by the info on Google and now you fear that I'm angry with your censure of me. Isn't that like when you get angry with your Mum – but you don't dare being honest with her."*
Debbie:	*"Damn it, must she constantly call me on the phone! I see her number coming up on my display and I go crazy. Then I answer anyway, because I feel responsible for her feelings!"*
Analyst:	*"Just as you feel responsible for mine. You claim you weren't critical of me, though in fact you were. Neither do you want me to feel offended by your wish to come more seldom. But it's my responsibility how I feel, not yours."*
Debbie:	*"I want to tell my mother that Don, Mae and I need to be left in our bubble for a while now and have our own life. But what if she gets sad!?"*
Analyst:	*"You're taking responsibility for your mother's feelings. By the way, you don't take into account that she might also be proud seeing you developing into a full-scale and capable mother."*

The greatest leaps in psychotherapy often take place during or after sessions that contained a breach of the frame or an emotional thunderstorm. In this case, the external frame remained intact, but there was a tone in Debbie's despair when Mae was crying that I did not capture well enough. Yet, I did grasp the connections between her rage towards mother and Mae, and the girl's ensuing reaction to Mum's insensitivity. One often needs to go through a rough and tumultuous hour, which arouses anxiety in the parent(s), the baby, and – last but not least – the therapist. In Bion's (1992) thinking, quoted in Chapter 7, a patient will only accept an interpretation if she feels the analyst has passed through an emotional crisis. Indeed, after the session I oscillated between thinking:

> I was insensitive . . . I should have stopped the girl's crying . . . Debbie needs to open up her anger with her mother . . . Now we see how Mae's distress is linked with Debbie's repressed affects . . . This is helpful . . . What if it's not helpful? . . . What if Debbie quits treatment and tells her nurse that I'm insensitive? . . . Debbie is insensitive to Mae because she's a dissatisfied baby herself.

This hour was followed by remorse, anguish, and doubts among the adults involved, and the girl's distress continued. Not until we all had gone through this purgatory could a true change be achieved in several inter- and intra-personal dynamics. The session led to the ER visit, the flaming up of Debbie's misgivings about me, anger with her mother, and her resolve to set limits vis-à-vis me and her mother. She decided how often she would see each one of us. I might have felt slighted by her rejection and/or interpret it as a sign of resistance and suggest we work it through while retaining the frequency. But in brief consultations especially, such a policy is doomed to fail and easily turns into belligerent discord. Besides, Debbie has an excellent point; "creating a family bubble" is her effort at emancipating from her family of origin. If she were to flush therapy down with her liberation war against her original family and her self-oppression, it would be unfortunate. But Debbie does want to continue and I ask how often she'd like to come. "Once a week", and I say "OK".

Before the next session, she texts a message asking to have it on phone. She has some visits planned to the paediatrician, her dentist, etc. Though I feel a slight vexation and wonder, "is this girl used to always having it her way?" I consent. On the phone, she is now speaking more honestly about her anger with the girl. "I thought everything was going to be like before; me and Don lying in bed and having a cosy time. Now, this one has arrived . . ." She also says he is annoyed with her, and I say that if she wishes he's welcome to a session. Once again, a change of frame. We also see confirmed my initial idea about her jealousy of Mae, the intruder into her relationship with Don.

Mother love or chocolate cream pralines?

The next session Debbie is standing calmly with the girl in a kiddy carrier, stroking her chin gently. "This carrier is a better invention than women's suffrage!" Next session, she is desperate again. "Don is googling a summer cottage while I'm looking up 'craving babies'!" I respond,

84 Part I: Clinic

Maybe there's a craving baby inside you. When Mae was born you became appalled. Little did you think that your 'baby inside' had to share time, love, sleep, and attention with that 'outside baby' Mae. And, men have much better conditions, you thought as you were joking about women's right to vote. The other side of the coin doesn't give you much; that you're housing, giving birth to, and feeding a baby.

This paves the way for a new theme; Debbie lives in "a world of chocolate cream. I got that image, thinking of boutiques selling luxury confectionery like chocolate pralines", as I put it. She fills in spontaneously: "Actually, I worked in such a store when I went to school! Funny that you mention it." I respond: "Chocolate is delicious but not as an image of everyday life with a baby." She hesitates: "There are more things where I strive for perfection: Don is wonderful. Yet, some things really needle me. His parents are bohemian with no academic education." "So, your craving baby inside is also a snob", I suggest. In embarrassment, she admits it while also seeing that with a jealous baby and a praline snob inside, things get quite rough with Mae. When she is whining, Debbie would like to say, "for God's sake, behave, little girl", which she realizes is a hopeless wish and an insensitive comment.

Debbie is now in the midst of therapeutic work. She asks me for a prescription of the SSRI medication she had some ten years ago: "Just for some time, to feel on the safe side". We talk about it and I see her mounting panic and helplessness vis-à-vis her baby as we now enter sore and painful topics. I follow the principles from Chapter 6 and prescribe SSRI for half a year. Debbie then reveals "awful truths" about herself. She is jealous of a friend who had a late miscarriage and was "liberated from the load of taking care of a baby . . . I'm totally appalling!" In parallel, we see a pattern in the interaction with Mae; when Debbie gets such thoughts her shoulders and voice rise and Mae gets fussy. I view this as a circle of bad projections: silly baby → silly Mum → silly baby . . .

At the same time, their contact is getting better and Debbie discovers something important: "Her fussiness is actually her . . . *temperament*! In fact, I recognize myself. I tend to go the whole hog. I'm not exactly moderated and suave when it comes to expressing my feelings . . . I think Mae got this from me." I nod in unobtrusive confirmation while noting that for the first time, Debbie looks proud when speaking of Mae. She identifies with an aspect of Mae's person, which up until now she could only see as a negative, annoying trait. This ability of seeing Mae from two sides is of good help to Debbie, now that she gets to work with her idealizations and de-idealizations. For example, her husband goes abroad to work for two days. She stays with her parents, "and we had the most *wonderful* days". Scraping away some chocolate covering, we discover that there was also some resentment between them. She also realizes the futility of her snobbish system; her husband once made a little error on his pc and she couldn't stop being annoyed and contemptuous. "It doesn't matter that there are so many domains where he is much more knowledgeable than me. He made this mistake and I despise him for it!" The wish for perfection is related to her concern about the acne in her 20s and to her family's bourgeois values about language and education. We cannot dismiss this as an innocuous character trait, because it harms her relationship with Mae. It is not easy to be 3 months old and behave perfectly . . . Debbie knows this too, and hates herself for this exigent trait of hers.

She develops a new appreciation of her husband; "Don's a sensitive and calm person who is not swept away by the childish things that harass me", she says. She also has serious talks with her mother about the family snobbery, and this leads to a new kind of maternal identity:

> I'm starting to feel like a mother. A mum is the utmost point of safety. Like in the Bataclan massacre in Paris 2015, I think I'd be a mother who noted that things were going wrong for her kid. At the end of the day, your mum is the person you turn to. I'm one of these mothers.

In this proud declaration, she chooses a metaphor of utter infantile madness. It would imply placing a too heavy burden on her were I to suggest the kinship between her enraged internal baby and the Paris murderers. Yet, I think there is some truth in it. The relevant point is that when talking about this destruction, she is also expressing something else; the emerging identity of a responsible, sensitive, and caring mother – a member of a group extant since the dawn of life; the maternal confederacy. This leads us to talking about her as a sexual woman:

> When Don pats me on the cheek I get bothered, though I don't want to. Sex . . . what if my breasts were to leak? Or, maybe it's just me who bothers and not him. That little Mae, she's an occupant – but I love her.

I respond that this challenge lies immediately ahead of them; combining motherhood with being the sexual partner and mate of Donald. He is facing the same challenge though, to be true, "Mae never was an occupant in *his* body", as Debbie calls it. Once again, she unwittingly uses an expression that is easily transferable to the world of terrorism.

To sum up the external frame of our work, we began working three times weekly and then changed to a once-weekly contact. After three months, we started seeing each other once a month and, when Mae was 7 months old, we terminated. Debbie had also chosen to end the SSRI medication without noting any increase of anxiety or anger. She had become curious to find out more about her "chocolate praline" ideal, the "enraged baby inside" as well as "the snob". She ended by musing on whether she would one day seek analysis or therapy,

> for the benefit of myself, not just because I need to be a good mother. I'm starting to feel I'm a good mother though I didn't feel that way when I first saw you. I really hated myself and felt so ashamed.

Postscript: Some weeks before starting her work again – Don was now going to stay home with Mae – Debbie asked for an appointment. She was anxious that her emotional turmoil during Mae's infancy might reappear at work. She was considering a personal therapy with me. Without being wholly committed to this idea, she then approached some issues between her and Don, which she thought stemmed from Mae's first months. "There's some resentment between us that we never dared talk about." In the end, she said:

> I'll go home and think it through. Perhaps a personal therapy is 'overkill' right now. After all, I feel confident that I'll do fine at work and Don will take good care of Mae. He and I might get back to you and talk through our issues with you, I don't know.

Some years have passed, and she has not come back.

Chapter 10

Parent–infant psychotherapy
A review of clinical methods

Two clinical applications at the CHC remain; working with couples and with parent–toddler therapies. Yet, the following two chapters will interrupt the flow, since I want to account specifically for various therapies with parents and infants. Efficacy studies will be summarized in Chapter 11, while this chapter surveys and compares various modes of PTIP, or psychodynamic therapy with infants and parents. There will be some emphasis on two traditions that are less well-known to the Anglo-Saxon readership; one is French (Cramer & Palacio Espasa, 1993; Dolto, 1982; Lebovici & Stoléru, 2003). The other was devised by a Swedish analyst, Johan Norman (2001), and was thoroughly explained elsewhere (Salomonsson, 2014a).

Two limitations will be pointed out at the start, which will lead us to two major questions. American authors often use "infant" for children up to 2–3 years of age. In contrast, Europeans generally restrict it to pre-verbal children. The Latin word *in-fans* means "speechless" or "not talking". In agreement with Winnicott (1960b) I will refer to infancy as "the phase prior to word presentation and the use of word symbols" (p. 588), that is, up to 12 or 18 months. This brings us to our first question: Can we call an "in-fans" a therapy patient? Does s/he take part in the therapeutic process to be affected by it? Our survey will yield different answers.

Second, I will focus on methods based on psychoanalytic theory. I will bypass some widely used methods in child health care: developmental guidance (Lojkasek et al., 1994), infant massage (Field, 2000), interaction guidance (McDonough, 2004) and Marte Meo (Aarts, 2000), since their aim is mainly to support the mother's ego and encourage her to change behaviour with the baby. I will focus on methods that help her grasp the *unconscious* ambivalence towards her child, her partner, or the maternal role. This sets off a second debate: psychodynamic therapy focuses on our conflicts between conscious and unconscious urges, but far from all therapists agree that this applies to an infant in therapy. The question is thus if unconscious factors are at work in a baby. The theories behind all PTIP methods agree that the *parent's* involvement constitutes a mix of *conscious* strivings to bond with the child and promote attachment plus *unconscious* and contrary urges. But, few authors speak of such factors in a *baby*. Positions on this point will influence technique.

88   Part I: Clinic

Psychodynamic therapy with infants and parents (PTIP)

Freud made astute observations of babies' everyday interactions with their mothers and used them to formulate cornerstones in metapsychology. He viewed the infant as emotionally affected by biological events *and* by the people around him; especially his mother seeks to silence his unpleasant experiences and offer him pleasant ones instead. Freud's baby is thus involved in passionate relationships from early on – though he rarely provided specific dates of development. He also intuited that there is an infant-like remnant in every adult's personality. In my mind, this partly explains why psychoanalysts have been reluctant to treat babies and why it took a long time for PTIP to develop. Countertransference in PTIP is often overwhelming. "It is not always easy to control one's reactions to [the baby's] positive or negative provocations" (Watillon, 1993, p. 1045).

Another explanation of the slow development of PTIP is the notion of psycho-analysis as a "talking cure" (Freud, 1910, p. 13). We think words are the main channel of communication, which leads us to overlook (Olinick, 1985) all other kinds of representations or signifiers in therapy. This may prevent us from viewing the baby as a patient with whom we can communicate. One would expect that Kleinian analysts who expanded Freud's baby speculations had promoted PTIP. But, they often refer to how infant-*like* parts of the verbal child's or the adult's personality emerge in the transference (Joseph, 1985; Meltzer, 1992; O'Shaughnessy, 1988). On "the other side", ego-psychologically oriented analysts warn against attributing mental capacities beyond the baby's developmental time-table (Fonagy, 1996). They rely on developmental models of how behaviour and facultative capacities change "over the early years in accord with emergent maturational biological changes in the context of a range of environmental prods" (Shapiro, 2013, p. 8). This makes them reluctant to view the baby as an active participant in psychotherapy.

Another reason for the late development of PTIP might be organizational. Analysts work in private practice and are contacted by people who acknowledge their emotional suffering. In contrast, many "baby worries" emerge at CHCs. A mother might complain about her child's somatic health or development without feeling that she needs psychotherapy herself. Or, she feels depressed or anxious and is suggested individual psychotherapy or pharmacological treatment. Neither case will result in PTIP. Nevertheless, though the delivery of PTIP was protracted many methods exist today.

Infant–parent psychotherapy

Selma Fraiberg, mother of the "ghost in the nursery" concept first mentioned in Chapter 1, was a psychoanalyst. She applied *brief crisis interventions* to problems arising from a "circumscribed set of external events and when the parents' psychological capacities suggest that they can make use of a brief focused intervention" (1989, p. 60). To illustrate, a well-functioning couple anxious about their newborn's well-being proved to be suffering from an unresolved mourning of another baby who had died earlier. After their mourning was worked through, they could attach to the newborn as a separate young person. My work with Lena in Chapter 5 belongs to this category. She needed to mourn the loss of contact with her daughter after delivery – rather than seeing herself as "not normal". After we had talked that through, she was back on track again.

Fraiberg's *interaction guidance* aimed at scaffolding parents with a limited psychological-mindedness. Though based on a psychoanalytic understanding of the family members, it did not aim at altering their fundamental psychodynamics. It was more of an "educational technique" (Sherick, 2009, p. 231). Similar techniques (Aarts, 2000; McDonough, 2004) adopt a "non-authoritative therapeutic stance, using treatment goals identified by the parents, emphasizing already-existing family strengths, increasing parents' satisfaction and enjoyment from interaction with their infants, and suggesting alternative interpretations of the infants' behavior" (Vik & Braten, 2009, p. 290).

Infant–parent psychotherapy, finally, was applied by Fraiberg when a baby reminded the parents of "an aspect of the parental self that is repudiated or negated" (1989, p. 60), for example, a childhood memory of a rejecting parent or a competing sibling. This unconscious "ghost" marred the parent's interactions with the baby who then got engulfed in, and distressed by, the parental neurosis. In Chapter 9, Debbie's issues with anger at her mother and me, and her "snob" ideal, marred her relationship with Mae. When these emotions overwhelmed her, Mae got distressed. In Fraiberg's words, "the pathology which had spread to embrace the baby" (p. 111) was withdrawn in therapy.

Fraiberg regarded the baby as a "catalyst" (1989, p. 53) in therapy, who intensified the emotional climate and could engage in "eloquent dialogue" with the family members and the therapist. Fraiberg did not aim to become a specific relational figure for the *baby* but sought to bypass the *mother's* customary perceptions of her child. Her followers explored parental "negative attributions" onto the child (Silverman & Lieberman, 1999): A mother complains that her baby is whining. Therapy reveals that her reproaches emanate from an unconscious suspicion that she is a cry-baby herself. When the baby internalizes such attributions and his self-image becomes that of a "whiner", the negative attribution has been "successful" from the mother's perspective. She feels less ashamed of her flaws, but the baby finds no way out of his whining and the mother's reproaches. A monograph describes infant–parent psychotherapy in depth (Lieberman & Van Horn, 2008). In RCTs (Cohen et al., 1999; Lieberman, Weston, & Pawl, 1991; Robert-Tissot et al., 1996) it proved to be about as efficacious as Interaction Guidance (Robert-Tissot et al., 1996) and Watch, Wait and Wonder (Cohen et al., 1999), though the effects were slower in coming. Compared with a non-intervention group, its results were superior (Lieberman et al., 1991).

A group of Geneva therapists have worked similarly, but with less disadvantaged families than Fraiberg. Its main figure is Bertrand Cramer. A book was published

90 Part I: Clinic

in French (Cramer & Palacio Espasa, 1993), and some works (Cramer, 1997, 1998; Espasa & Alcorn, 2004; Manzano, Palacio Espasa, & Zilkha, 1999) and an introduction (Zlot, 2007) in English. The difference with Fraiberg's therapy is subtle. The Swiss address the mother's psychopathology more consistently, such as her masochistic and narcissistic issues. Yet, their focus on "the conflicts of parenthood" (Zlot, 2007, p. 14) does not make them overlook the dynamics of the baby's symptoms, which might express "a repressed tendency in the parent" (Cramer & Palacio Espasa, 1993, p. 85). This "core conflictual relationship" between baby and a repressed part of the parent will be enacted and focused on in therapy. Though this approaches Fraiberg's notion of the "ghost", the Geneva therapists rather speak of the mother's "narcissistic scenarios" (Manzano et al., 1999), which prevent her from seeing the baby in his own right. The child then becomes involved in a relationship he cannot comprehend. The therapist confronts the mother about her misperceptions. By including the baby in his "joint focal attention" (Cramer, 1998, p. 156), he also aims to liberate her from the mother's "projective distortions" (Cramer & Palacio Espasa, 1993, p. 84). To sum up, Fraiberg and Cramer seem to view the mother's role similarly but phrase it slightly differently. And, Cramer seems to regard the baby as slightly less of an active therapy participant than did Fraiberg.

Therapeutic consultations with babies

In Paris, Serge Lebovici headed a child psychiatric out-patient clinic, Centre Alfred Binet, during the last decades of the previous millennium. His work resembled therapeutic consultations (Winnicott, 1971a) and brief crisis interventions (Fraiberg, 1989). We recognize Fraiberg when reading that the "mother's internal reality, her unconscious, constitutes the first world offered to the baby" (Lebovici & Stoléru, 2003, p. 289). Whereas Fraiberg focused on how a mother's *trauma* can build up to forming the "ghost", Lebovici focused more on fantasies stemming from her *infantile sexuality*. Their differences could depend on divergent theoretical foci, with Fraiberg oriented towards ego-psychology and Lebovici to drive psychology. He often interpreted to mothers how their unconscious sexuality coloured the relationship with the baby. One mother sought help for her 7-month-old son's insomnia. It emerged she had become frigid because she kept thinking about him during intercourse with her husband (p. 283). Lebovici noted that she held him in a way that restricted the distressed boy's ability to look around. He suggested she hold him with a hand between his thighs. The boy calmed down and their eyes met. Lebovici linked his insomnia and distress with their interactive *behaviour* that was compromised by the mother's sexual *fantasies*. For a similar example, I refer to Chapter 19, where I notice a mother's use of "vacuum" and "sucking".

Lebovici (2000) also unravelled what happens in the PTIP therapist's mind, notably in *enactment* (Fr: *l'énaction*) and *metaphors*. We will discuss this in Chapter 19. Returning to our question about the "in-fans" in treatment, Lebovici suggested the baby should be present in therapy to facilitate for the therapist to probe the unconscious meanings of a parent's behaviours or comments. The baby also stimulated the therapist's metaphoric function, but "Lebo" was not prone to intervene *to* the baby. As for an Unconscious in a baby, he would probably have claimed that it exists from early on, though without agreeing with his compatriot Dolto that a baby can understand verbal import.

Direct and brief mother–baby therapy

Françoise Dolto was a Parisian psychoanalyst active from the 1940s to the 1980s. Two books were translated into English (Dolto, 1971, 2013/1971). None of them covers her PTIP work but an English volume (Hall, Hivernel, & Morgan, 2009) covers some parts. Her walk-in facilities for mothers and babies were recently presented in English (Paglia, 2016). Long before infant researchers (Beebe & Lachmann, 2002; Condon & Sander, 1974; Stern, 1985; Trevarthen & Aitken, 2001), she spoke of the young infant's ability and efforts at communicating with his care-takers. In contrast to them and other PTIP therapists, she claimed that a baby understands some literal meaning of words. Before making conclusions about her clinical method, we need to know more about it and its theory.

Here is a case vignette (Dolto, 1985): A mother at the delivery ward with her fourth child learns from her husband that things are not going well with the children at home. Her worries are aggravated by the news that her own mother just died. The newborn stops breastfeeding and Dolto is called in for a consultation. She addresses the baby:

> Everything was OK when you were inside Mom's tummy. Then you were born . . . Mom had milk and you were calling for it . . . One day you heard, with Mom, Dad told you, that things weren't going well at home. Maybe you told yourself 'Poor little Mom, I'd better get back into her tummy, 'cause everything went well as long as I was there'.
>
> (p. 211)

Dolto thought the baby's refusal to suckle resonated with the mother's mourning and worries about the domestic situation. She even claimed the girl understood her intervention verbally. Dolto asked the girl to nod if she had understood. When the girl turned her head towards Dolto, she took this as a confirmation. Here, she was wrong; an overwhelming body of research (Karmiloff & Karmiloff-Smith, 2001) refutes that a young baby can understand spoken words literally. The baby *cannot* have turned her head because she understood Dolto's words.

Let us now go deeper into Dolto's arguments; if parents conceal embarrassing truths, it may stunt the baby's development. The mother tried to hide her mourning and worries. This created a paradoxical situation to the girl who, perhaps, sensed something unknown in her mother beneath her efforts at care-taking. Most PTIP therapists agree that a baby may intuit that "something is wrong" when parents are

92   Part I: Clinic

inauthentic, but they would address the *parents* and not the child. Dolto's reason for talking to a baby was that the mother's superego had been imposed on him/her, with the result that "instinctual urges whose affects have not succeeded in expressing themselves . . . disturb the child's somatic and cognitive functioning and engender anxiety . . . [The therapist's] role consists in re-establishing the flow between all this" (Dolto, 1982, p. 30). This, she claimed, should be done directly with the child.

We may agree that *toddlers* are sensitive to their parents' skewed communication but doubt that this also occurs with *babies and newborns*. This touches on a greater issue, namely, how one regards the infant's self-development. Winnicott (1960a) suggested that a good-enough mother enables the baby's *true self* to emerge. Dolto objected that s/he exists in a confusing tangle, with "little certainty about who or what is good, or good enough" (Bacon, 2002, p. 260). Talking to a baby not only indicates that there exists a mode which we use to bring some order to this confusion. Dolto went further and claimed that a *baby is formed in and informed by language*. Not only do words convey lexical meanings but they also inspire the baby to substitute *désir* with communicable demands. This turn is initiated by the parent's introduction of the symbolic order. Therefore, "a mother speaking to her infant is a nourishment more valuable than the milk she offers at the breast" (Dolto, 1994, p. 605). If we accept this position, we must nonetheless ask (Salomonsson, 2017a) why a *therapist* should talk to the baby. The answer is that his/her position is different from the parent's; s/he is freer to *parler vrai* or speak truthfully and genuinely with the baby. Thus, though Dolto was wrong about infant language comprehension, this need not force therapists to merely address mother about painful matters. We can also introduce the baby to a symbolic order that is *vrai*, which was difficult for a mother entangled in a contradictory relationship with her baby. I think the babies of Donna, Nora, and Debbie in Chapters 3, 5, and 9, respectively, were mixed up in such knotted bonds.

Mother–infant psychoanalytic treatment

Norman's technique (2001, 2004) was based on the following tenets:

> (1) that a relationship can be established between the infant and the analyst; (2) that the infant has a primordial subjectivity and self as a basis for intersubjectivity and for the search for containment; (3) that the infant has an unique flexibility in changing representations of itself and others that comes to an end as the ego develops, and (4) that the infant is able to process certain aspects of language.
>
> (2001, p. 85)

His Mother-Infant Psychoanalytic treatment (MIP), utilized the "disability" of every infant, that is, their ego immaturity. This made a baby prone to get involved

A review of clinical methods 93

in an emotional disturbance with mother *and* to look for containment from a therapist. This immaturity was thus a window of chance for undoing the effects of trauma. He explicitly addressed the baby about these processes, without agreeing that a baby understands words lexically. Another contrast to Dolto was that he worked in lengthy treatments whereas she worked in brief consultations.

Norman's 2001 paper submits a case of 6-month-old "Lisa" in therapy with her mother, who was depressed and hospitalized during Lisa's third and fourth months of life. She was devastated that the girl had not recognized her and shunned her eyes after her hospital stay. In simple words, Norman told Lisa what had happened and that she was now avoiding mother whom she felt was ruined and scary. Lisa cautiously began to contact mother by sucking her blouse. He concluded that her ensuing improvement resulted from Lisa having "managed to wake her mother up" (p. 89). This, he claimed, resulted from his containment of the girl's pain of separation and dread of rejection.

Norman saw a vicious interactive circle:

> Lisa's mother had a psychic pain that she could not bear. As Lisa's distress and sense of rejection increased her mother's own distress and pain, the mother was reluctant to open up the emotional links. As a defence against pain, mother was rejecting Lisa. The mother's capacity to symbolize was severely impaired and with that her capacity to metabolise Lisa's distress. Both Lisa and her mother appeared to feel threatened by the other's pain and rejection. They were locked in mutual avoidance.
>
> (p. 90)

I think Fraiberg and Cramer would have agreed, but Cramer might focus more on the mother's narcissistic affront by the child's rejection. Fraiberg would have recognized Lisa's avoidance but probably not addressed her as directly. She would rather help mother grasp the "ghosts" marring her contact with the baby. Norman's technique presupposed that mothers were motivated and willing to leave the baby "in his hands". To a mother with less motivation for insight-oriented work and who wants support and attention of her own, the therapist's baby focus might be felt as an abandonment. Such comments were heard from some mothers in an interview study on their MIP experiences (Winberg Salomonsson & Barimani, 2017).

Norman's infants were clearly distressed and containment aimed at directly modifying his/her emotional state. This raises questions not only about the baby's capacity of comprehending words, but also of the capacity of memorizing interventions and subjecting them to cognitive elaboration. If we, however, make explicit on which *levels of signification* the analyst–baby interchange takes place, some mystery of MIP vanishes. Human communication takes place on various levels, of which the verbal is only one – and every "talking cure" goes beyond talking (Salomonsson, 2007a, b, 2017a).

94   Part I: Clinic

The infant as subject

In Melbourne, a group of PTIP therapists work at the Royal Children's Hospital. Their young patients often suffer from physical illnesses. Akin to Norman, they emphasize the dialogue with the baby: A therapist explains to the parents that their 14-month-old boy is cross and addresses him too: "You're cross – and it'll be all right" (Thomson Salo, 2007, p. 964). She tries to "understand the infant's experience in order to enter treatment through the infant's world rather than primarily through the parents' representations" (p. 965). The aim of relating to babies in their own right, or recognizing them as a subject, is to bring about a "change in their thinking, feelings and behaviour, and the parents as well" (idem). Still, these clinicians' infant focus (Thomson Salo, 2007; Thomson Salo & Paul, 2001) is not identical to Norman's. They work with the infant to enable the *parents* to see that their fantasies of having damaged the infant "are not reality" (Thomson Salo et al., 1999, p. 59). This comes closer to Fraiberg's ghosts and Cramer's parental projections.

Another motivation for dialoguing with the baby is to create a "gap" (Thomson Salo & Paul, 2001, p. 14) between parent and baby. Such space did not exist previously, because the parent identified the baby with "some internal object in the parent's mind rather than [having built] an empathic relationship with the infant" (p. 18). When parents direct projections towards the therapist instead of the baby, s/he becomes a container "for the hate and the toxic projections for which the infant was previously the receptacle" (idem). Once again, we hear echoes of Fraiberg and Cramer. The Melbourne therapists do not contact the baby with the aim of encouraging his/her stormy feelings to flourish vis-à-vis mother *and* the therapist. Does calling the baby a subject imply that one regards the infant's negative and positive emotions as directed also towards *the therapist*? This was Norman's aim, while Paul and Thomson Salo (2007) seem more supportive: "Some infants relate positively to us from the first, as though they have left aside the difficulties with their parents" (p. 145).

Watch, Wait, and Wonder

This technique (WWW; Lojkasek et al., 1994) originated from the Hincks-Dellcrest Center in Toronto. It was compared with Fraiberg's mode in an RCT (Cohen et al., 1999; Cohen, Lojkasek, Muir, Muir, & Parker, 2002), where it seemed quicker in creating certain positive outcomes. The authors claim that most PTIP techniques focus on changing the *mother's* behaviour with and representations of her infant, whereas their method is *infant-led.* One foundation is attachment theory; unless a mother perceives and responds to her baby's signals, a secure attachment will not develop. This theory acknowledges how important the caregiver's physical presence is to the baby, so the authors emphasize the mother's participation in sessions. They agree that mother's interaction with, and her view of, the baby may be marred by ghosts (Fraiberg), attributions (Lieberman), projections (Cramer), or fantasies (Lebovici). Yet, they criticize these methods for downplaying the *infant's* part in therapy. They ask the mother to get down on the floor, observe the baby, and interact with him at his initiative. She becomes an "observer of her infant's activity, potentially gaining insight into the infant's inner world and relational needs" (Cohen et al., 1999, p. 433). Also, the baby has a "therapeutic experience of negotiating his relationship with his mother, and thus begins to master his environment" (idem). The therapist, finally, engages in "watching, waiting, and wondering about the interactions between mother and infant" (Cohen et al., 1999, p. 437). S/he empowers the mother to describe how she experiences her infant's play and their relationship, and "to examine her internal working models of her relationship with her infant and to modify or revise them to be more in line with her new experiences" (Lojkasek et al., 1994, p. 214). This work occurs during the second half of the session, when therapist and mother discuss what transpired between her and the baby.

To some extent, the WWW is akin to Norman's but differences emerge:

> The therapist does not instruct, give advice, or *interpret* the infant's activity or play but *provides a safe, supportive environment* . . . The mother and the therapist *discuss the mother's observations of her infant's activity* and attempt to understand the themes and relational issues that the infant is trying to master, focusing on the inevitable problems that emerge as the mother begins to struggle with following her infant's lead.
>
> (Cohen et al., 1999, p. 434)

The added italics indicate that the therapist does not address the baby. Rather, s/he and the mother discuss what they think the baby is doing.

The PTIP team at the Anna Freud Centre

These clinicians (Baradon, Biseo, Broughton, James, & Joyce, 2016) are also influenced by attachment theory. They illustrate a wish among PTIP clinicians to integrate Freudian metapsychology with infant research, attachment theory, and developmental psychology. They use a "psychoanalytic framework", implying that "unconscious material is to be understood and, where appropriate, addressed, because it shapes the way a person functions, both in health and pathology" (p. 52) and that "the therapy will address impingements of conflict, f/phantasy, negative affect and maladaptive defences" (idem). This reflects their Freudian anchorage. Another psychoanalytic influence is Winnicott, emphasizing notions such as the good-enough mother, the True Self, etc. A recurrent term is "scaffolding", whereby "the parent recognises, labels, and structures the baby's motor, mental and emotional experiences ahead of his capacity to do this himself" (p. xxiii). The therapist, too, will scaffold "the parent/s and the baby's experiences and responses" (idem). They concede that "putting such diverse theories together inevitably reveals contradictions and gaps" (p. 3), with which I agree. Their solution is of "roaming between traditions and using each as convenient" (idem). The method was

96 Part I: Clinic

submitted to an RCT (Fonagy, Sleed, & Baradon, 2016), which will be referred to in the next chapter.

The London authors often mention the baby's *needs* to engage the parent to help him with *attachment* and *emotional regulation*. They are more hesitant to speak of his *wish* to enroll a parental *object* to become the target of his *drives*. One might link this to a greater emphasis on object-relational thinking à la Winnicott and a lesser Freudian influence. This is also evident in their use of the term sexuality, by which they refer to that of the parent, not of the child. Although they also address the baby, this seems to occur less insistently than in Norman's and Dolto's techniques. This certainly does not preclude them from observing the infant's contact with the therapist and from using countertransference to understand the baby.

The impact of the setting and the clinical sample

This survey needed to pass by many legitimate candidates. Another fact needs emphasis; most authors worked in public health clinics. In 1972, Fraiberg founded an infant mental health programme in Ann Arbor that later moved to San Francisco. Some years later, Cramer founded a centre in Geneva. Dolto's "Maisons Vertes", still in operation, were walk-in facilities where mothers with babies could get instant, brief psychotherapeutic interventions. In contrast, though Norman worked for some time at a CHC his published cases were mainly from private practice. This enabled lengthy high-frequency treatments, a modality he firmly advocated.

Also, various PTIP modes have been devised for patients living in different circumstances. Many of Norman's parents seemed psychologically minded and similar to the Geneva sample. In contrast, Fraiberg often treated adolescent or immigrant mothers with a low educational and economic status (Dowling, 1982), which also applies to the Anna Freud team in London. The Melbourne therapists treat severely sick children. Such factors will influence the parents' trust in the clinician, motivation for analytic work, and means of taking part in therapy. Thus, it is hard to compare the methods, and this overview is but a skeleton to scaffold major questions that every PTIP method must face. When I refer to the various authors' approaches, we should also recall that their technique was probably not always "according to the book". Norman's technique had more supportive elements, and he addressed the mother's suffering more often, than is evidenced in his writings. I guess similar discrepancies could be found among the other authors.

Conclusions

Two major questions were formulated initially: (1) Which role do various PTIP modes attribute to a baby in therapy? (2) If they claim to work by helping parents come to grips with their unconscious attitudes towards the baby, do they speak of similar struggles – let alone of an Unconscious – in him/her? Our survey indicates that all PTIP therapists view the baby's participation as essential. The main dividing line is (a) if they regard him as a *catalyst* fuelling the therapeutic process in the *mother*, or (b) as someone who needs to *communicate with* the *therapist*. Whichever alternative the therapist opts for, it has repercussions on question (1) and thus on technique. Model (a) inspires the therapist to talk to the mother *about* her baby. Model (b) will rather lead him/her to talk more *to* the baby about his suffering which, secondarily, will help change the relationship with the mother.

As for question (2), no author seems comfortable with attributing to a baby an Unconscious in the *systematic* sense. Norman, however, assumed that "the infant has an unconscious in the *dynamic* sense of the word" (2004, p. 1107, italics added). Questions (1) and (2) are in fact related. The more a therapist is prone to speak of unconscious forces at work in a baby, the more he will intervene directly to her. If he thinks she harbours conflicting affects vis-à-vis mother, then addressing both participants seems logical. In the Lisa case, Norman saw the problem as due both to the depressive mother's lack of emotional availability and the girl's avoidance of mother's eyes.

Fraiberg (1982) was ambivalent about applying the term "unconscious" to a baby. She did regard gaze avoidance as the result of a defensive process, though "something within us resists the word [defence] and its connotations" (p. 614). We will discuss this "something" in Chapter 18 in connection with the defence concept. Whether such a discussion would have led Fraiberg to retain or change her position, she definitely felt that a gaze-avoiding baby has unpleasant representations of a depressed mother, and that the evasion aims to minimize the risk of having them sparked off once again. She and Norman would probably also have agreed that the baby avoids the eyes because mother's depression prevents her from regulating the baby's affects, and thus a vicious interactive circle keeps twirling.

All PTIP therapists would thus concur that a mother can be caught up in unconscious conflicts with her baby, but few would claim that *the baby* is capable of this. If we adhere to basic assertions in Freudian theory we are, as I see it, bound to claim that a baby may indeed have such conflicts. I do not submit this as an argument but to clarify some important divergences. One often hears that we should not attribute unconscious forces to a young baby since her ego is too immature for such advanced mental operations. One example is Stern (1985), whose position on this topic will be presented in Chapters 15 and 17. In his view, sleep and feeding problems "are not signs or symptoms of any intrapsychic conflict within the infant . . . They are the accurate reflection of an ongoing interactive reality, manifestations of a problematic interpersonal exchange, *not psychopathology of a psychodynamic nature*" (p. 202, italics added). His words highlight one position in the ongoing discussions among PTIP therapists. I hope this chapter's rendition of various methods has made the arguments clearer. In the next chapter, we will survey some RCTs of the cited methods.

This chapter is derived, in part, from an article published in *Psychodynamic Psychiatry*: 2014, *42*(2), 203–234. Salomonsson, B. (2014b). Psychodynamic therapies with infants and parents: A critical review of treatment methods. (Reprinted by permission from Guilford Press.)

Chapter 11

Parent–infant psychotherapy
RCTs and follow-up studies

Meta-analyses of PTIP

Many methods described in the previous chapter were tested in randomized clinical trials (RCTs). This chapter reviews results and methodological problems with their design, measures, and interpretation of results. Some meta-analyses, one on "nonbiological interventions" for postpartum depression (Dennis, 2004) and one on Parent–Infant Interaction Interventions (Singleton, 2005), clarified that therapeutic methods are heterogenous and some outcome studies have inadequate designs. Another meta-analysis by Barlow and co-workers (2010) focused on how to organize perinatal psychiatric health care, a topic approached in this book's final chapter.

Specific RCTs

Mother–infant psychotherapy vs. Interaction Guidance

An RCT (Robert-Tissot et al., 1996) compared mother–infant psychotherapy, according to the Fraiberg-Geneva model (see Chapter 10), with Interaction Guidance (McDonough, 2004), which is a more pedagogic and supportive method. Both groups received about six therapy sessions. Follow-ups were made post-treatment and at six and 12 months. Outcome measures were a questionnaire on infant symptoms, an interview with the mother on her representations of the baby, herself *qua* mother, and her partner. Video-recorded dyadic interactions were used to assess her sensitivity and the range of the baby's affects. Significant effects – independent of therapy method – were found at six months on maternal sensitivity, infant behaviour, and symptoms.

The age span (2–30 months) included both non-verbal and verbal children. Another drawback was the absence of an intent-to-treat (ITT) analysis. This method calculates outcomes on the basis of the subjects' initial assignments, regardless of whether they choose to commence these treatments or not. Such a procedure avoids bias in estimating outcomes (Chakraborty & Gu, 2009). In fact, the Swiss outcome statistics excluded one quarter of the sample. Another problem was that subgroup effects were reported, which increases the probability of a type I error (Tukey,

1991). Such "family-wise" or "experiment-wise" errors may lead to false conclusions about treatment efficacy (Olds, Sadler, & Kitzman, 2007; Sun, Briel, Walter, & Guyatt, 2010). Furthermore, treatments were perhaps too brief to show their full potential, which calls into question the reported results; Interaction Guidance brought greater improvement on maternal sensitivity, while mother–infant therapy increased maternal self-esteem. The authors rightly conclude that their results are consistent with common expectations in psychotherapy outcome research: "the effects common to both treatments are greater than their specific effects" (Robert-Tissot et al., 1996, p. 111).

Mother–infant psychotherapy vs. Watch, Wait, and Wonder (WWW)

A Canadian study (Cohen et al., 1999) compared WWW (Chapter 10) with mother–infant therapy (Fraiberg, 1980). Seventy-three dyads with a child mean age of 20 months took part, but six dropped out early in treatment and were not analysed. Many cases were assigned according to the therapists' caseload, which disclaims the label "essentially random" assignment. Therapies were about 14 sessions. Outcome instruments were questionnaires on parental stress, sense of competence, and depression. Infant cognitive behaviour and development were assessed via the Bayley scales (1969), and the quality of mother–infant play was rated via video-recordings (Chatoor, 1986).

Immediately post-treatment, WWW was more efficacious in improving attachments, development according to Bayley scores, and mother-reported satisfaction, but not maternal sensitivity or responsiveness. Both methods equally reduced mother-reported child problems and stress and improved mother–child relationships. The authors hypothesize that WWW was advantageous because these therapists advised mothers to follow the infant's lead, thereby utilizing the child's attachment and developmental strivings. This may in turn have improved the mothers' competence.

Follow-ups were made after six months on the remaining 79% of cases (Cohen et al., 2002). Most outcomes continued to improve, and some new improvements emerged for mother–infant therapy. Perhaps improvements appeared earlier in WWW because of the infant focus. In addition, the insight-oriented work in mother–infant therapy might have left these mothers distressed for a longer period and slowed down outcomes. Cf. the "sleeper" effect in various therapies (for discussions, see Knekt et al., 2016; Kivlighan et al., 2015, Leichsenring, Rabung, & Leibing, 2004; Sandell, 2012). This RCT did not include an ITT analysis. The sample comprised non-verbal and verbal children.

Mother–infant psychotherapy in high-risk samples

The referred studies were made on low-risk socio-economic samples. A Californian study (Lieberman et al., 1991) investigated a high-risk Latino immigrant sample,

100 Part I: Clinic

in which three quarters of the mothers were unemployed. Their mean age was only 25 years. Outcome measures were video-recorded interactions plus home-visitor-rated maternal child-rearing attitudes and the impact of life events (Egeland, Deinard, & Brunquell, 1979). All children were 1 year old at the start, so the researchers could use the Strange Situation procedure (SSI; Ainsworth et al., 1978) for assignment and outcome evaluation. All children who appeared securely attached on the SSI formed the "secure control group." The insecure children were randomized to mother–infant psychotherapy or to the "anxious control group." The control group treatments were unspecified. The mother–infant therapies lasted one year, thus much longer than in the previous studies. At a child age of 2, the index group scored higher on most items of maternal and infant behaviour and interaction. Outcomes were better if the mother seemed involved in the therapeutic process, displayed empathy, initiated interaction, and encouraged reciprocity with the baby. ITT analyses were not made on the 82% of subjects remaining at the follow-up assessments after treatment termination.

British researchers (Fonagy, Sleed, & Baradon, 2016) used a well thought-out design. They recruited a sample of 76 mothers with infants below one year. It was demographically diverse, urban, and from "areas of high levels of socioeconomic deprivation" (p. 101). All mothers had mental health difficulties, and a third of them had bonding difficulties with the baby. The dyads were randomized to either routine care only or in combination with the Anna Freud Centre model of PIP (see Chapter 10). Like many other studies, no between-group effects were found on infant development, attachment or dyadic interaction. In contrast, the PIP mothers developed less hostile and helpless representations of their child, and they reported less stress and depression and more warmth towards the child. Once again, effects on mothers were much more conspicuous than on the babies.

Depressed mothers: comparing four therapies

A group in Cambridge, UK (Cooper, Murray, Wilson, & Romaniuk, 2003; Murray, Cooper, Wilson, & Romaniuk, 2003) investigated if early improvement of maternal depression might enhance dyadic relationships and child development. The sample comprised relatively low-risk but depressed first-time mothers who were randomized with their babies to cognitive-behavioural therapy, psychodynamic mother–infant therapy, non-directive counselling (Holden et al., 1989), or routine primary care.

The three active treatment groups received ten once-weekly sessions at home when the baby was 8–18 weeks, with 83% completing therapies. The ITT analyses revealed improvements for all active therapies on mother-reported relationship problems with the babies, but not on infant behavioural problems. Mothers with high social adversity improved their interactive behaviour with the infants only by non-directive counselling. This finding adds to our understanding of therapeutic specificity: perhaps disadvantaged mothers benefit more from a method that provides advice and support.

When the children were 18 months old, only mothers in the counselling group reported fewer baby problems. No between-group effects were found on measures of attachment and cognitive development. At the five-year follow-up point, no effects were found on mother- and teacher-reported child behaviour problems or cognitive development. Thus, most child outcomes vanished in the active treatments, whereas maternal depression improved from all of them. The authors conclude that "more prolonged interventions may be required," but that "such treatment may not require high-level psychological expertise" (Murray et al., 2003, p. 426). The latter conclusion is based on the positive findings on counselling. Singleton (2005) reached a different conclusion in her meta-analysis; therapist training positively moderated outcomes. This opens up an important debate: is it better that perinatal mental health issues are taken care of by nurses trained in counselling and who support and encourage anxious and depressed mothers? Or, should such care be left in the hands of specialized therapists who aim at searching deeper into the roots of the baby worries? Or, if both alternatives are true, which dyads should receive which kind of help – and how should such care be organized? The book's final chapter will approach these central questions.

Depressed mothers: group therapy

In this US study (Clark, Tluczek, & Wenzel, 2003), 39 mothers with 9-month-old babies were recruited via clinical referrals and selected via a depression questionnaire. Though therapies aimed primarily to help mothers with their depression, the study also examined the effects on infant development. The sample was socially low risk and randomized to mother–infant group therapy, interpersonal individual therapy for the mother (Klerman, Weismann, Rounsaville, & Chevron, 1984), or a waiting list. Treatments of 12 weeks focused on the depression and the baby relationship. Drop-outs were not reported. Outcome measurements were questionnaires on depression and parental stress, development assessments (Bayley, 1969), and dyadic interaction (Clark, 1985).

Follow-up at three months after treatment demonstrated that both active groups were superior in "reducing maternal depressive symptoms, improving mothers' perceptions of their infants' adaptability and reinforcement value, and increasing mothers' positive affect and verbalization" (Clark et al., 2003, p. 441). As in the Swiss study, subscale effects were used to demonstrate general therapy effects, which entail a risk of making family-wise errors. Though babies were present in treatments, effects were found on the mother's but not on the infant's interactive contributions.

Many studies were omitted here, because mothers were treated without their infants (O'Hara, Stuart, Gorman, & Wenzel, 2000), studies were not RCTs (Suchman, DeCoste, Castiglioni, Legow, & Mayes, 2008), or focused on toddlers (Cicchetti, Rogosch, & Toth, 2000; Toth, Rogosch, Manly, & Cicchetti, 2006). The findings

Part I: Clinic

here can be summarized: Index therapies yielded effects on mothers' well-being, while infant effects were not always thoroughly investigated and, if found, were weaker.

An RCT of Mother–Infant Psychoanalytic (MIP) treatment

In 2005, I initiated an RCT in Stockholm that compared Mother–Infant Psychoanalytic (MIP) treatment with CHC care, which we know is an ambitious health care mode. After summarizing our first findings (Salomonsson 2014a, Salomonsson & Sandell, 2011a, 2011b), I will report on the follow-up study when the children had reached 4½ years old.

Study design and protocol

Our methodological considerations drew from the referred RCTs; we studied only non-verbal infants, used questionnaires that covered maternal distress broadly, used ITT analyses, interviewed mother and baby, and video-taped their interactions. We also decided not to report significances on single variables with the aim of supporting general treatment effects. MIP treatments were performed by analysts (not me) trained by Norman (Chapter 10). It had been ideal to compare with another ambitious psychotherapeutic modality, but this proved unfeasible. Since Swedish CHC care is well established and promotes the family members' psychological well-being, using it as a comparison method was reasonable. Mothers were recruited from CHCs and advertisements on parental internet sites and delivery wards. They worried about poor infant sleep, difficulties with feeding or weaning, or that the baby seemed depressed or anxious. And/or they suffered from anxiety, depression, or uncertainty and ambivalence about motherhood. Such "baby worries" were the primary inclusion criteria. Mothers with psychosis or substance abuse were excluded if we doubted their study collaboration. Infants older than 18 months were also excluded.

Outcome measures

Apart from video-taped dyadic interactions, I interviewed the mothers to probe into the roots of their baby worries. An interviewer may be insufficiently reliable, but he can get a first-hand view of the relationship and the symptoms and make qualitative assessments. Mothers and babies were interviewed at intake and again six months later. I also interviewed the therapists post-treatment to study the therapeutic process. Practical circumstances did not allow for interviews with the nurses.

Pre-treatment, I clustered mothers and babies into "Ideal types" (Wachholz & Stuhr, 1999). The mother-report questionnaires were the Edinburgh Postnatal Depression Scale (EPDS; Cox, Holden, & Sagovsky, 1987), the Swedish Parental

Stress Questionnaire (SPSQ; Östberg, Hagekull, & Wettergren, 1997), the General Stress Index (GSI) of the Symptom Check List-90 on general psychological distress (SCL-90; Derogatis & Fitzpatrick, 2004), and the Ages and Stages Questionnaire: Social-Emotional (ASQ:SE; Squires, Bricker, Heo, & Twombly, 2002). Mother–infant relationships were assessed via the Parent-Infant Relationship Global Assessment Scale (PIR-GAS; ZERO-TO-THREE, 2005). Two external raters assessed interactions via the Emotional Availability Scales (EAS; Biringen, Robinson, & Emde, 1998). The therapists' adherence to the MIP method was also assessed plus the mothers' experiences of therapy post-treatment via interviews.

Results

Eighty dyads were randomized. After drop-outs, we could analyse 75 cases. Maternal mean age was 33 years. The sample's social risk was low but the psychiatric risk high, with 50% of previous psychiatric treatment; eating disorders, depression, or anxiety disorders. Almost 80% were primiparae delivered at full-term, but Caesarean sections and vacuum exaeresis were common. The mean baby age at intake was 5 months. Pre-treatment scores on maternal distress and infant behavioural and interaction problems reached clinical significance. The mean EPDS score was 12, doubling the scores among nonclinical Swedish mothers with babies (Seimyr, Edhborg, Lundh, & Sjögren, 2004; Wickberg & Hwang, 1997). These and other measures reflected unequivocally the dyads' distress.

Post-treatment interviews were made six months later. Four mothers declined but their intake scores were included in the ITT analyses. One third of the CHC mothers also had brief therapies, often recommended by the CHC staff. The MIP mothers continued with CHC care while receiving a median of 23 MIP sessions two to three times weekly. To sum up, compared with the group that received only CHC care (the "CHCC group"), *MIP was more advantageous on the EPDS, the EAS sensitivity, the PIR-GAS, and nearly significant on the SPSQ, with small to moderate effect sizes.*

As for the ideal types, the mothers had been classified at intake into five types: the first three were "Chaotic", "Depressed/Reserved", or signalled an "Uncertain Maternal Identity". Their concern was that they somehow contributed, though unknowingly, to the baby worries. They were keen on finding out more about this in therapy. I subsumed them under the overarching type of the "Participator" mother. The fourth and fifth types were different: The "Anxious/Unready" mothers' wish to be cared for competed with their resolve of taking care of the baby, and mothers who were "Conflicting with the Partner" brooded on the relationship with the father rather than with the baby. I grouped them under the overarching type of the "Abandoned". Both treatment groups contained two thirds Participators and one third Abandoned. It emerged that Participators in MIP became more sensitive to the child's signals (EAS) than did their peers in CHC care, and we concluded that they capitalized on the analyst's baby focus. No such moderator effects emerged for the Abandoned mothers.

104 Part I: Clinic

I also created two infant Ideal types during the intake interviews: "Affected" babies reacted negatively when mother was distressed, whereas "Unaffected" babies were generally calm. Mothers of Affected babies indicated more baby problems and personal distress, they were less sensitive and structuring, and their babies were less involving and responsive in interactions. These baby Ideal types thus echoed many quantitative measures at intake. Compared with CHC care, MIP proved superior in improving maternal sensitivity and PIR-GAS scores among dyads with Affected infants.

Some findings coincided with the PTIP studies referred to earlier: maternal improvement on depression, stress, and sensitivity. Our non-significant effects on the infants also replicated earlier studies. A novel finding was that the dyadic *relationship* and maternal *sensitivity* improved more by MIP. Also, mothers who sensed that they somehow contributed to the baby worries, as well as babies who seemed affected by the relationship disorder, benefitted more from MIP than from CHC.

The MIP long-term follow-up study

Would the short-term effects of MIP last? To answer, we initiated a long-term follow-up study when the children had reached 4½ years (Winberg Salomonsson, Sorjonen & Salomonsson, 2015a, b). Now, 66 out of the 80 dyads were willing to participate. We sought to get a comprehensive picture of their functioning; an expert child psychotherapist interviewed the children and I the mothers. We retained many instruments from the infant study; all four mother-report questionnaires and the EAS on the interaction videos. We added a Draw-a-person test (Machover, 1949) to assess the child's cognitive and emotional functioning, the Story Stem Assessment Profile (SSAP; Hodges, Steele, Hillman, Henderson & Kaniuk, 2003) for attachment assessments, the Wechsler preschool and primary scale of intelligence for cognitive functioning (WPPSI-III; Wechsler, 2005), and the Children's Global Assessment Scale (CGAS; Shaffer et al., 1983) for rating their daily functioning. Preschool teachers and mothers also rated child functioning on the Strengths and Difficulties Questionnaire (SDQ; Goodman, 1997). Finally, the children's interviewer clustered them into Ideal types, which she boiled down to the "OK" and "Troubled" children. To get a picture of the mothers' attachment representations of the child, I interviewed them according to the Working Model of the Child Interview (WMCI; Zeanah et al., 1986). As seen in Table 11.1, *children who had been in MIP as babies now performed 10 points better than their CHC peers on the CGAS. Also, there were more OK children in the MIP group, and more Troubled children in the CHCC group.*

The initial effects of MIP on maternal depression were maintained throughout the study, as seen in Figure 11.1. Also, MIP mothers' sensitivity levels normalized already six months after therapy started, which was observed only at 4½ years among CHCC mothers. These findings may explain the children's differential effects. The MIP mothers, by remaining less depressed and becoming sensitive faster, may have helped their children to function better than in the CHCC group.

Table 11.1 Between-group comparisons at 4½ years. SDQ-M: Mother's SDQ rating. SDQ-T: Teacher's rating. All other acronyms explained earlier.

Variable	MIP N	MIP Mean	MIP SD	CHCC N	CHCC Mean	CHCC SD	Comparison Statistics	Value	p
ASQ:SE	32	.98	.90	32	.88	.68	t-test	0.480	.633
SDQ-M	32	8.17	5.54	31	7.39	5.19	t-test	0.580	.564
SDQ-T	24	5.71	4.32	27	6.59	5.31	t-test	−0.647	.520
CGAS	31	78.39	12.80	30	68.87	14.74	t-test	2.696	.009
CGAS cases/non-cases	8/23			16/14			χ^2	4.841	.028
Machover formal	31	1.98	.58	29	1.85	.55	M-W	404.5	.431
Machover emotional	31	1.87	.68	29	1.79	.62	M-W	423.5	.671
SSAP Secure	31	2.22	1.05	30	2.32	1.33	t-test	−0.304	.762
SSAP Avoidant	31	1.05	.48	30	1.16	.52	t-test	−0.915	.364
SSAP Ambivalent	31	.96	.73	30	.84	.61	t-test	0.719	.475
SSAP Disorganized	31	.80	.84	30	.63	.58	t-test	0.883	.381
OK/Troubled Children	21/10			8/22			χ^2	10.314	.001

First published as TABLE 3 in Winberg Salomonsson et al. (2015a). Reprinted by permission of the journal and John Wiley & Sons, Inc.

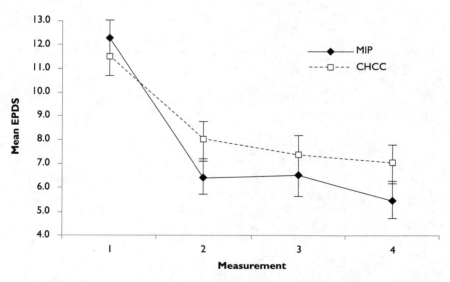

Figure 11.1 EPDS scores at intake, six months later, and at 3½ and 4½ years. The error bars depict 95% confidence interval.

First published as Figure 4 in Winberg Salomonsson et al. (2015b). Reprinted by permission of the journal and John Wiley & Sons, Inc.

How come that we found long-term effects on the children, in contrast to the Cambridge study? One hypothesis is that "the British study recruited mothers who scored high on depression scales, whereas our study recruited those who actively looked for help with their baby worries" (Winberg Salomonsson, 2017, p. 46). Second, the Stockholm therapies were lengthier and of higher frequency and ended only on both parties' agreement. Such freedom reflected clinical judgement but could also be criticized for a lack of standardization. Indeed, we tested if the duration of therapy influenced efficacy, but this was not the case. Another explanation is that the Swedish infants participated in treatment which, according to Norman's theories, would be beneficial. Finally, our comprehensive ratings perhaps detected subtle clinical changes. For example, the Ideal types can be seen as expert clinical ratings based on personal encounters with the child, which may be more sensitive than parental questionnaires.

What works for whom? – On therapeutic specificity

A PTIP therapist may be particularly interested in therapeutic specificity (Blatt & Shahar, 2004; Orlinsky, Rönnestad, & Willutzki, 2004), that is, which mothers and babies profit from which therapeutic techniques. For example, which types of parent–infant interactions are more accessible to psychodynamic interpretations? What roles do academic level, cultural background, and social status play in the parents' acceptance of such techniques? Could one identify babies that are better cases for PTIP or supportive interventions? Our study is one of two (Lieberman et al., 1991; Salomonsson & Sandell, 2011b) addressing such issues. The findings on mothers were similar in both studies; psychotherapy yielded better results if the mother was emotionally involved in the therapeutic process. Our "Participator" mothers appreciated the analyst's probing and sometimes confronting attitude. Frances, in Chapter 3, was such a mother. In contrast, "Abandoned" mothers requested support and advice on child care. With them, the therapist should perhaps be more supportive and self-disclosing. Nora, in Chapter 5, exemplified this category.

Our findings can be compared with studies on "anaclitic" and "introjective" patient categories (Blatt, 2006). Abandoned mothers seemed akin to anaclitic individuals, who are "concerned about trust, closeness, and the dependability of others" (p. 507). The Participator mothers resembled Introjective individuals, who seek to "achieve separation, control, independence, and self-definition, and to be acknowledged, respected, and admired" (p. 508). They are also more "ideational and concerned with establishing, protecting, and maintaining a viable self-concept" (Blatt, 1992, p. 696) . Blatt's group found that psychoanalysis especially helped them, whereas supportive therapy was better for the anaclitic patients. This resembles our results on Participator and Abandoned mothers, respectively. A meta-analysis (Bakermans-Kranenburg, van IJzendoorn, & Juffer, 2003) of sensitivity and attachment interventions showed that brief and less broad interventions that focused on maternal *behaviour* were better in improving parent sensitivity and infant attachment. I wonder if their finding can be explained similarly; was it primarily mothers like our "Abandoned" group who benefitted more from behaviour-oriented interventions, and did their effects cloud the overall effects? The Dutch study does not contain such data on the mothers, so the question remains unanswered.

As for the babies, the negatively affected ones benefitted most from MIP. This seems logical, since the analyst focused on the baby's anxieties. Thus, MIP may especially help distressed babies with gaze avoidance, fretting, mood instability, sadness, insomnia, feeding problems, etc. In contrast, if a mother's depression is not linked with infant symptoms, an excessive focus on her baby might detract from therapeutic work on her sadness, anger, shame, rivalry with the baby, etc. When mother is distressed but the infant relatively healthy, the therapist should be wary of damaging therapeutic alliance by an excessive baby focus.

As in every study, this one had limitations. I merely mention the researchers' allegiance to psychoanalysis and the mothers' demand characteristics. These key topics have been discussed in depth elsewhere (Winberg Salomonsson, 2017).

General conclusions on PTIP efficacy studies

This chapter on RCTs of PTIP highlights that certain conditions must be fulfilled to obtain meaningful results that can influence our development of therapeutic techniques. Studies must be performed under controlled conditions with carefully described measures. Qualitative assessments should be psychodynamically relevant and linked with the quantitative results. If these demands are met, researchers' demands of scientific rigour can harmonize with therapists' demands of studies that reflect and are relevant to clinical practice. Already in the infant study, some MIP therapists said they had now reappraised former notions that focusing on mother's well-being was less important than establishing emotional contact with the baby. The long-term follow-up study also contained qualitative studies, which yielded these conclusions (Winberg Salomonsson, 2017): It seems essential (1) to use a modified MIP technique when the mother needs personal help, (2) to inform her about how MIP therapy works, to enable her to understand and be comfortable with its infant focus, (3) to perhaps invite fathers to a greater extent, and (4) to intervene promptly when problems emerge. "This may help the dyad recover faster, which in turn may give long-term effects on the children" (p. 53).

To end this chapter with a reminder, when comparing the results of all the referred RCTs, we had better recall the words of Cicchetti et al. (2000). Speaking of interventions with toddlers and depressed parents (Lieberman, 1992), they state that it is "too preliminary to make definitive statements about the relative effectiveness of interventions based on social class, type of preventive intervention strategy, or features of maternal depression (i.e., postpartum versus recurrent

108   Part I: Clinic

major depressive disorder)" (p. 137). As always, one size does not fit all, whether in life or in psychotherapy.

This chapter is derived, in part, from an article published in *Psychodynamic Psychiatry*: 2014, *42*(4), 617–640. Salomonsson, B. (2014c). Psychodynamic therapies with infants and parents: A review of RCTs on mother-infant psycho-analytic treatment and other techniques. (Reprinted by permission from Guilford Press.)

Chapter 12

Brief interventions with parental couples – I

Let us return to the CHC. Consultant work there opened my eyes to the challenges and possibilities of couple therapy. Like many analysts, I had been treating individuals in my private practice. At the CHC, I began to see families as well. I never ask the nurse to instruct the parent(s) in which constellation to come to our first appointment. A mother may come alone to vent her troubles, or with her baby since she worries about their contact, or with husband and baby due to a family crisis. The choice indicates what worries her/them the most. Today, one third of my CHC work is couple therapy – often in the presence of the baby, for reasons that I will submit a little later.

I agree with Sager (1976), quoted by Zeitner (2003), that many of my *analytic* patients seek help due to problems in their intimate relationships. My working perspective is then the individual patient; what s/he feels about the partner, why s/he cannot stand up to wishes and conflicts, and which might be his/her contributions *qua* projections in the relationship. This lens is also turned towards my countertransference. I think it is a bit simplistic to intimate, as do Forster and Spivacow (2006), that in couple therapy we focus on problems that reside in an aspect of psychic functioning beyond "the Freudian psychic apparatus", namely, "the link between the members of the couple (the 'intersubjective')" (p. 255). Every psychoanalytically oriented therapy with a group, a family, or an individual takes place in an intersubjective sphere. As an analyst, I am not an omniscient observer who puts my patient/object under the microscope. I am a *participating subject* who interprets the patient(s) by observing, out- and in-wards, the interplay of transference and countertransference.

The clinical challenge for analysts working with couples is not that they lack awareness of the intersubjective dimension but how to deal with it when it is played out by two spouses. It is one thing to listen to an analysand: "You never listen when I am critical of you". My instrument gets going and I reflect on her and my feelings, how this situation arose, how I shall respond, etc. When I hear the same words from a spouse to a partner who then retorts, "Because you always nag at me", to be followed by a new accusation, "You never do what you promise", the situation is different. I feel like a reporter in a war zone unable to stop the combat. If the spouses then, which sometimes happens, join in accusing me, the countertransference gets even more weighty. Such situations "involve matters that arouse more emotional responses in the therapist" (Aznar-Martinez, Perez-Testor, Davins, & Aramburu, 2016, p. 17); one's personal experiences of parenthood, the couple, and family of origin are awakened. True, analytic training leaves us with little experience of sitting with *two* partners and handling their complaints and accusations. In response, I have built on the war metaphor to elaborate a technique for couple consultations. Some characteristics diverge from individual therapy. Or, perhaps I am downplaying the potential of acquiring couple therapy competence through one's training in psychotherapy or analysis? Let us follow up this suspicion.

During my psychiatry residency in the 1970s, couple therapy with two therapists was *en vogue*. We met the family, often in a video-recorded session. Afterwards, we discussed what transpired. I never felt comfortable with this setting. It was time-consuming and, to my taste, a bit pretentious and circumstantial. Then I worked with individual therapies, until one day the CHC experiences forced me to ask: Is there any essential difference between individual and couple therapy? In couple therapy, I analyse interactions of two "external objects" who affect each other in various beneficial and/or destructive directions. They also interplay with me in sundry constellations. In contrast, in individual therapy all this traffic is played out between one patient and me. But what about similarities? In both therapy modes, I focus on containing anxieties that, basically, stem from each person's "internal family of objects". Think of Debbie and Mae from Chapter 9: Mother and I had a crisis, little Mae was upset in parallel to Debbie's embitterment with grandmother's insensitivity. Mae continued crying at home, the family went to the ER, the next session she was upset with what she felt was my coercion of high-frequency treatment. I did not defend myself and claim that her accusations were unjust. Rather, I contained – or acknowledged – her struggle; fighting against an unaccommodating introject forcing her to obey me and and Grandma. Indeed, this was intersubjective work.

In couple therapy, each participant is preoccupied with similar internal struggles, but the therapist mainly focuses on how they are played out in the spousal relationship. Containing anxieties thus occurs in individual *and* couple therapy. In the former, the battle of the introjects is played out in the transference–countertransference relationship. In couple therapy, they emerge between the spouses, with the therapist being a "boxing match commentator". Such roles are also attributed in individual therapy, but here the therapist is one of the boxers, so to speak. Once I grasped that such phenomena were played out *between* the spouses, my experiences of individual work helped me do couple therapy – and without a co-therapist. The challenges were similar; *grasping how internal reality was played out in relationships*. To illustrate, we will now meet with a couple.

Tilde and Salih: a hailstorm of projections

Tilde is a young mother who told the CHC nurse that her partner fears she has a postnatal depression. Their son Kevin is 6 months old. The nurse suggests that Tilde sees me. I expect to meet a sad woman and a worried husband, perhaps also a whining baby. But this happens: A blond Swedish girl enters my office followed by a dark-haired man. No baby in sight. She glares at him: "He's Salih". "Well, yeah, I'm from Lebanon." They sit down, in two corners of the room.

Salih:	*"You're a doctor? You've got to check this up. She's got a postnatal depression, all the signs from the internet are there. What kind of medication will you prescribe?"*
Tilde:	*"Medication? You're the problem, not me! God, this man is choking me! I should never have got this child with him."*
Salih:	*"See what I mean, doctor? Absurd! You wanted this baby, not me! You've got to take responsibility."*
Tilde:	*"Responsibility? I do nothing else the entire day, while you're cuddling with your parents."*
Salih:	*"Cuddling? You're talking shit about me with your dad on the phone!"*
Tilde:	*"I call it talking Swedish. But you and your folks speak Arabic, how do you think I feel? But that's not the worst thing . . ."*
Analyst: (finally managing to cut through the duel)	*"So what's the worst thing for you, Tilde?"*
Tilde:	*"His mum is doing superstitious things with Kevin, poking her finger on his forehead and saying things I don't understand. 'It's to keep him safe and sound', she says. I want my baby to be safe, too, but not with her mumbo jumbo."*
Analyst: (into the war zone again)	*"Tilde told us what's worst for her. What's worst for you, Salih?"*
Salih:	*"That she'll move back to her home town. I never thought I'd have kids. I have many friends who got divorced, and their children commute all over town. Now she's talking about divorce."*
	Salih's lower lip is quivering and his voice is breaking. Tilde tries to calm down.
Tilde:	*"I just said it when I was upset. But sometimes, all this feels like a bloody mistake!"*
Salih:	*"One minute you're upset and say things you don't mean. The next minute, everything you said should be forgotten. If this isn't depression, then what is!?"*
Analyst:	*"I'm not sure if we gain much by calling Tilde's state a depression. I'd say that she has a rough time – and so do you, Salih. By the way, how's Kevin?"*

Depression, marital conflict, or cultural tensions?

Every marriage now and then becomes a cogwheel of mutual projections. Tilde cannot handle her disappointment with Salih and her conflict with the mother-in-law. By threatening with divorce, she seeks to get rid of these issues by "exporting" them to Salih. When I observe his quivering lip, I intuit that her threat has struck a soft spot. In response, he threatens her with a depression diagnosis that he flings in her face without much understanding or warmth. I could investigate this hypothesis further in the next session. They arrived with Kevin, a charming boy eager to get in contact with me. When another round in their battle started, he started whining. Tilde breastfed him, he calmed down while she glared at Salih. Kevin's presence had another effect; they tried to talk in a kinder way. They explained that their relationship was rather new, the baby was not planned but they were quite happy about the pregnancy. When their families were informed her parents, living in another town, waited until the upcoming holidays to come see the newborn, whereas his parents "stormed into our apartment on day one", as Tilde put it. "They wanted to check me out, in front and behind, God it was embarrassing." Salih objects, "They were just happy". Here, Kevin starts whining and I assume this is his reaction to the strained climate.

> Analyst: *"OK, things are rough. You seem to like each other, too. One more thing: When you start fussing, he starts whining. You have a choice. Divorce is easy-peasy. But you say you want to stay together. All right, then you've got to work. Backbiting leads nowhere. To me, the great danger seems that you're so terribly scared, both of you! And you don't know why."*

Fears beneath projective identifications

Staggered, Tilde and Salih stop short at my comment. My aim was to clarify their responsibilities about the future of their relationship and of Kevin. I also pointed at their use of the divorce weapon. And, I ended by digging up their fears in the trenches of mutual projections. I now continued encouraging them to investigate these trepidations.

> Analyst: *"Salih, your greatest fear is that Tilde will move with Kevin to her home town. OK, I get that. But tell me more about your background, perhaps we can understand this a bit better."*

> Salih: "I came to Sweden when I was 15. My parents moved here earlier, so I lived with an uncle on the Lebanese countryside. After four years, my Dad got a job in Sweden so I could join them."
>
> Analyst: "So you didn't see your folks for four years. How was that?"
>
> Salih: "No problems, I'm used to taking care of myself. Problems should be solved. But it wasn't easy here at first, being called an Arab wog and stuff like that. But never mind, it's over now."
>
> Tilde: "Is it over, really? You sound so self-assured, but I wonder . . ."

Tilde sounds warm and eager to know more about the Lebanese boy hiding inside her big, tough partner. We continue talking about Salih. I guess that he is angry with his parents for having abandoned him. Yet, such feelings seem far away from consciousness. But when I suggest he is a "family guy", especially since he was without his folks for four years, he hums cautiously and looks tenderly at Kevin. These two parents started by accusing each other of lacking responsibility, but now they seem accountable and concerned. I turn to Tilde to ask about her background.

> Tilde: "I come from an ordinary family. No battle, no mumbo jumbo, no divorce, nothing."
>
> Analyst: "Swedish harmony against Lebanese chaos. Wow! But, if you were so happy about this perfection, why did you choose this wog?"

I am deliberately using challenging language to get behind Tilde's one-sided image of her family of origin. She continues that her father was the strong person in the family with his wife doing whatever he commanded. Time is up, so there is no time to follow-up on this. They are eager to come again.

The third session there is more warmth between the parents. They are embarrassed about their previous mudslinging and share an earnest intention to get their relationship on foot again. I am surprised at the speedy development; from a war in the trenches to what seems not a mere armistice but peace built on mutual understanding and care. They say they want to continue on their own now. So, we part after I have said they're welcome back one day if they wish. To comment on this phrase, when a patient wants to end treatment, it is also a step towards autonomy that I respect. Accordingly, I do not actively welcome back every patient. But at the CHC, things are different. Parents and children develop rapidly and unexpected things may turn up around the corner. The child's transition to a new developmental phase may wake up a dormant ghost from the parent's nursery. Or, a disease may afflict a family member, renewing the need to work through old or new issues. One might object that my comment is redundant; of course, the couple

Part I: Clinic

feels free to call me again! But this is not always the case. They might think they've had their fair share of treatment and thence, my welcome-back comment.

From couple therapy to individual sessions

Two months later, Salih calls me:

> You've got to help me. Is it normal to suddenly decide to leave home with one's child? And having a dad who pops up at our place ordering Tilde and Kevin to return home? Could you give her an appointment?

I suggest we stick to our setting and that both come to me. Salih accepts reluctantly. One day, when their appointment is due, he is alone in the waiting room because "Tilde has got fever and could not come". I do not know if this is true. Perhaps their communication is derailed and no one knows what the other is doing. During our session, his arguments are the same as on the phone: I should cure Tilde. But I suggest we go on working together and I set up an appointment for the couple.

The next week, Tilde is alone in the waiting room. She says she did not know about Salih's appointment last week.

Tilde:	*"I wanted to come alone. There's one thing I don't grasp – and I won't nag at Salih. I want to understand myself: Why am I so afraid of the Princess? I mean, my mother-in-law! OK, her mumbo jumbo, I don't like it. But she scares the hell out of me!"*
Analyst:	*"You were afraid of her superstitious practices with Kevin. Now she's the Princess . . .?"*
Tilde:	*"I've got a little sister. My parents gave her everything. I learnt to take care of myself. Today, I see my advantage. Regina, that's her name, is so pampered that no guy's good enough for her. Salih and me, at least we're still together!"*
Analyst:	*"Regina means queen. But you talked about a princess."*
Tilde:	*"When I was mad at Regina I used to call her "Princess" to drive her crazy."*
Analyst:	*"She was a spoilt Princess and you were mad at her. Were you also afraid of her? It may seem strange to link your mother-in-law with your sister, but that's what you just did."*
Tilde:	*"I was afraid of my sister, well no, of my parents. They got enraged with me when I teased Regina. Then I turned silent. Cowardice, I guess . . ."*
Analyst:	*"So what do you do with Salih's mother when she does her mumbo jumbo?"*

> *Tilde sighing:*   *"I keep quiet! I think, 'You go on with your stuff, soon we'll be home again and there it's me who decides'. But I feel spineless when I shut up with her."*

Tilde is now far from projecting various shortcomings onto Salih. She is working on herself and wants to see me for some sessions. Salih's command was that I cure Tilde. Now, *she* wants to understand herself. This is a much better position to work from in psychotherapy. Her five-session-therapy focused on her cowardice with two subthemes. One was her rage against the little sister and the ensuing fear that her parents would reject her, which led Tilde to become chicken and yellow. The second subtheme concerned the relationship with her own mother, whom she thought was cowardly vis-à-vis her husband. Tilde began to reassess her previous views.

> *Tilde:*   *"It's true that Dad settled everything at home. One day he said we should move to Croatia. So we went there, the four of us. But Mum got homesick and wanted to return to Sweden. He dismissed her but one day she said, 'I'm moving home now with the girls. Either you follow along, or you'll stay here.' And she did! After some months, he came slouching home to Sweden. Since that day, something happened between them. They started discussing with each other."*

Tilde is sighing. She has often felt powerless towards Salih. Now she realizes that she has been acting like her mother did until that day in Croatia. Tilde has brought up her opinions with Salih in ways that enabled him to ignore them and ride roughshod over her without realizing his impact. The next session, Tilde says she has spoken clearly with Salih.

> *Tilde:*   *"His uncle is an optician, so he's provided my contact lenses. But why have I gone to the other end of town to his shop only because he's related to Salih!? I want someone nearby to get my lenses swiftly. I told Salih I'm going to swap optician to the mall near our house. He got a bit sore but then said, 'OK, it's your decision', and that was it."*
>
> *Analyst:*   *"So your mum decided on Croatia, and you decided on your optician."*
>
> *Tilde:*   *"Maybe I didn't risk as much as my mother did, but I'm proud anyway."*

116 Part I: Clinic

This case started as a husband's request to cure a wife from her postnatal depression. I met a couple at war. Behind their mutual aggressive projections, they were frightened and not only because they had just become parents. Parenthood had activated childhood conflicts and wounds. Salih was devastated lest he should be abandoned by Tilde – as he was in his teens by his parents. Tilde's fear of being deserted was related to anxiety when the parents rejected her because she was an angry big sister. Was this a treatment of postnatal depression, of a marital crisis, of parental ghosts, or of cultural conflicts in a couple? The answer is yes for every alternative but the first; Tilde did not seem specifically depressed. The cultural tensions were interwoven with conflictual themes from their personal backgrounds. Was it a couple therapy or an individual therapy? Yes, to both. As for Kevin, though he initially showed some distress when the parents quarrelled, it did not persist. Had this been the case, I would have brought it up.

Technical points in couple therapy with young parents

The baby's participation

When a therapist treats a family with a baby, s/he aims to "explore its defensive structures, basic assumptions, and underlying anxieties" (J. S. Scharff, 2004, p. 260). This is easier said than done: "we must be able to talk and play at the same time and to work with groups and not just individuals. We must also be willing to tolerate noise, mess and confusion" (idem). Scharff speaks mostly of children beyond infancy. What are the gains of having a baby in family sessions? I have argued that it is essential when there is a disturbance between him/her and a parent. Fair enough, but why have a well-functioning boy like Kevin participate when we address issues within or between his parents?

One answer emerges once we compare the baby to a therapist. To explain, I must make a detour to the concept of *transference*. There are many reasons why psychoanalysts facilitate, ferret out, and draw conclusions from such phenomena. Experience has taught us that a distressed person will inevitably ascribe traits, experiences, opinions, facts, and habits to the one whom s/he asks for help: the analyst. Whether these attributions are fantastic, blind, correct, or contradictory, they are often emotional to an extent that merits the epithet "childish". This is logical, since transference theory suggests that an individual will paste schema from his/her childhood onto the therapist – provided s/he uses a technique that fertilizes the transference and pays attention to its manifestations. The patient may experience the therapist as powerful or helpless, harsh or kind, loving or hateful, indifferent or compassionate, that is, similarly to how a child experiences the parents.

A baby in therapy sessions often kindles emotions in the parents that they wish to avoid, but which need to be brought on the table. I agree that "the youngest children make deeper problems more visible and therefore intervention can happen earlier" (J. S. Scharff, , 2004, p. 261). The baby ignites the parents' infantile world of emotions and experiences and he is thus bound to conjure up the "intruders from the parental past" (Fraiberg, Adelson, & Shapiro, 1975, p. 387). These "ghosts" are not seen by the parents but have become part of their psychological make-up. When Salih urged me to cure his wife's "postnatal depression", he was not aware that he was copying his mother's *Weltanschauung* of dividing people into sane and insane. Neither did he recognize his sense of abandonment in Lebanon. It was I who facilitated it by asking how he felt about not seeing his folks for four years. And, I also think Kevin was my "assistant therapist". The presence of a helpless creature inspired Dad to get in contact with delicate feelings which, otherwise, his hard-boiled attitude did not let through. Thus, Kevin helped change his father's transference to me, from a diagnostician doctor to someone he could talk with about his feelings of weakness and confusion. All in all, Kevin and I worked, though in dissimilar ways, to enhance the parents' transferences to me and each other, and to encourage them to see these patterns and work them through.

The baby's presence also reminds his parents about the gravity of the situation. Here, too, his role is akin to the therapist's, who maintains the setting and contains anxieties emerging as accusations, fears, misgivings, etc. Indeed, his/her very presence will unleash the emotions that make up the transference. Meanwhile, the baby may sleep in the pram or scream at the top of his lungs. Either way, he will make it more difficult for the parents and the therapist to talk about him in abstract. Babies have a talent of attracting our attention and readiness to engage. In therapy, they exert this "magnet" function by forcing the parents to approach a problem which, if unsolved, can jeopardize his future. To phrase it differently, he brings out more adult parts of his parents' personalities.

How are we to reconcile this contradiction? First, I suggested that the baby brings out more infantile emotional layers in the parent. Then I claimed that s/he calls forth their adult aspects! Yet, I think both statements are true. Parent–infant consultations seem to run in consecutive acts. Mutual projections emerge first, as in Salih's words to Tilde: "You wanted this baby, not me!" Second, I intervened to assist them getting in contact with the infantile emotions that their mutual projections served to cover. My question, "What's worst for you?" led to Salih's pain of abandonment and Tilde's fear of her mother-in-law rooted in her childhood. Here, Kevin exerted his "therapist" function simply by being there, little and helpless. In a third phase, his presence served more to evoke adult and responsible facets in the parents. This function I wanted to bring out with my words, "When you start fussing, Kevin starts whining". We must not hasten through and quench the parents' infantile emotions. If I were to begin by admonishing them to behave like adults, it would be upbringing and not therapy. When I told them, "divorce is easy-peasy", I did appeal to their adult facets. But I only did this after having let their projections and helplessness be clearly expressed – and after letting some countertransference vexation sift silently inside of me.

118 Part I: Clinic

A final argument for the baby's presence could be formulated in a provocative sentence; it is because of him/her that the parents are in trouble. Now, don't get me wrong, I do not accuse the baby, but in the Unconscious of many distressed parents, resentments and accusations are roaming: "If it wasn't for the baby we'd still have a wonderful relationship." Such feelings take some time to emerge. As Bell et al. (2007) discovered in interviews with parents, after birth they hastened to establish a unit working according to the motto, "We do everything together". But at 6 weeks of age, there was a new organization of the family system, "characterized by the negotiation of ways of being with the infant as mothers and fathers" (p. 189). Now, each parent felt that his/her relationship with the baby was evolving differently and sometimes in conflict. Indeed, Kevin's parents did not consult with me after delivery, when they were adapting to a new situation and establishing a unitary entity. After some time, it fractured due to Tilde's fear of her mother-in-law, Salih's worries of being stranded, and the mutual projections. Then it was time to appeal to the nurse: "Help us!"

The surgical metaphor

Freud (1910) discusses the "special obstacles to recognizing psycho-analytic trains of thought". One factor, he states, is that "people are afraid of doing harm by psycho-analysis . . . [They] notice that the patient has sore spots in his mind, but shrink from touching them for fear of increasing his sufferings." He objects that "a surgeon does not refrain from examining and handling a focus of disease, if he is intending to take active measures which he believes will lead to a permanent cure". The analyst can make similar claims since the increase in suffering which he causes the patient "is incomparably less than what a surgeon causes, and is quite negligible in proportion to the severity of the underlying ailment" (all quotes p. 52). I disagree with Freud about the negligible suffering caused by a therapist. An insensitive or distanced therapist can cause unnecessary harm and/or the patient may feel they are getting nowhere (Werbart, von Below, Brun, & Gunnarsdottir, 2015; Sandell et al., 2000). But, he is right in pointing to our unwarranted fears of being honest and touching the sore spots – once we have assessed our relationship with the patient reasonably well.

Freud (1912b) returned to this comparison of the psychoanalyst and the surgeon, "who puts aside all his feelings, even his human sympathy, and concentrates his mental forces on the single aim of performing the operation as skilfully as possible" (p. 115). I believe he realized that when a patient seeks help, a contrary voice protests: "Don't dig into this, forget it, things will be all right." Freud (1913a) quotes a French adage: "*Pour faire une omelette il faut casser des œufs*" (p. 135; "to make an omelette you must crack eggs"). Helping another person, whether as therapist or surgeon, demands not only warmth and empathy but also a sort of friendly and robust resolve that is incisive and uncompromising. The analyst needs to be conscious of such currents and use them with good intentions; to help the patient get in contact with emotions that s/he fears and cause trouble.

Brief interventions with couples – I   119

In psychoanalysis, we have plenty of time for preparing "the operation" and seeing to "the postoperative wounds", often already the next day. In brief consultations, sessions are few and sparse. One might conclude that the clinician needs to apply special caution and tardiness in such work. Yet, certain factors contribute to scuppering this inference. Parents at the CHC seek help in a desperate situation, fearing that the relationship between them and/or the baby is cracking. Adult personality facets, which want to build up and secure attachments in the family, conflict with other parts that make egoistical and unrealistic claims. The latter incite the building up of narcissistic defences: "I have no responsibility in this; it's all the fault of my baby or partner". Indeed, Tilde and Salih blamed each other, which made me opt for an incisive or "surgical" intervention: "You say you want to stay together. All right, then you've got to work. Backbiting leads nowhere."

In a classical paper, Greenson and Wexler (1969) claimed psychoanalysis implies four procedures: confrontation, clarification, interpretation, and working through. My comment to Tilde and Salih was a confrontation aimed at disrupting their narcissistic defences. I did not intend to "to add insight into the unconscious per se, but strengthen those ego functions which are required for gaining understanding" (p. 29). I realized that it might also be experienced as offensive. The art of psychotherapy is to gauge how much confrontation is needed – and tolerated – to unsettle the patient's prescribed version of the problem, and how to formulate it frankly and warmly.

There remains one final application of the surgical metaphor that has to do with the time frame. In another paper, Freud (1912b, p. 115) quotes a French surgeon who, when being complimented for his achievements, said, "*Je le pansai, Dieu le guérit*" ("I dressed his wounds, God cured him"). The doctor sutures the dilapidated tissues and nature heals the wound. Transferring this imagery to therapy with a couple, I prefer seeing them three or four times, with an interval of two or three weeks. If my interventions can be seen both as opening the wound and sewing it up, during one and the same session to be sure, the couple need to go back home and "heal the wound". I do not refer to any passive suffering. I often suggest they go home and talk and reflect on themes we addressed. I do not give "homework" as in CBT, but I make it clear that I can only do small bits of work with them and that the bulk of it lies on their shoulders. Most new parents are strongly motivated to work together. To be sure, I could continue with couples for a lengthy stretch of time but I am not convinced this is optimal – apart from the fact that such therapies are not feasible at the CHC.

Unconscious beliefs vs. thinking together

All spouses harbour "unconscious beliefs about what a couple relationship is" (Morgan, 2010, p. 36). These fantasies are brought into the therapy session. Morgan clarifies that such beliefs (Britton, 1998) are felt to be facts "until we become aware that they are in reality only beliefs" (Morgan, 2010, p.37). In a couple, one member's fantasies may dovetail with the other's. Morgan exemplifies with a couple who shares a fantasy that intimacy leads to being taken over by the

120   Part I: Clinic

other. In response, they erect a shared defence and find a third person, often the baby, to function as a barrier against intimacy. I come across this when I ask parents if they have resumed their intimate life. "We're too tired because of the baby", say the two in chorus. After some work they admit, "We spend our evenings on the sofa, each one with a smartphone . . . Not much heat there." This leads to talking about why they fear taking initiatives and expressing yearnings for intimacy.

"Intercourse", this wonderfully ambiguous word is used by Morgan (2012) to refer not only to the sexual act but also to a slow process, in which "the couple increasingly gain a sense that it is possible to discover something new by thinking together" (p. 74). One object of such joint thinking is of course the baby; the parents need to develop a capacity for thinking and dreaming about their baby: "Why is he screaming? Did you check the temperature of the formula? His chin, exactly like your father's, maybe he'll be as stubborn one day!" For such intercourse to come about, each member needs to have a sense that a relationship is:

> something from which one can get help, in which it is alright not to know or understand, in which it is possible to acknowledge getting things wrong, and in which it is possible to share one's uncertainties in reasonable safety.
>
> (p. 75)

The paradox is this; to function in an adult way *qua* parent, one's need of being parented by the partner must also be met. Each partner thus needs to be allowed a space in which fears and weaknesses are listened to by the other. As long as the couple is childless, such needs are not so hard to satisfy. But when a child is born, the new parents are transferred to a relationship with an emotional intensity like the one of the primary mother–baby relationship. Now it is more difficult to be generous. She complains at being alone with a cranky baby the entire day. He is dead tired after a rough working day and wants to go to the gym. She: "What about me, I feel like a sloppy shit and you don't care a damn." He: "I had nine hours at the office while you had café latte with your pals!" Behind such grievances, one discerns two babies who feel distressed and not attended to. To sum up, the challenge for all new parents is to combine the roles of *Partner, Parent and Progeny*. In Tilde's and Salih's case, these roles were hurled between the two in a criss-cross manner. In the next chapter, we will look into therapeutic work with a couple where the roles were more cemented.

Chapter 13

Brief interventions with parental couples – II

In the previous chapter, I applied the concept "unconscious belief" to couple work. Here I will link it to the concept of *transference*, also described in that chapter. Any psychoanalytically oriented therapy, whatever its target group and setting, must account for how it appears and how we handle it. The transference has a therapeutic leverage. As Freud (1912a) wrote in another belligerent formulation: It is on that field that "the victory must be won" (p. 108). In this arena, we aim to help the patient reap laurels in the battle against neurosis. We do this by inviting her to analysis, a "highly specialized form of playing in the service of communication with oneself and others" (Winnicott, 1971b, p. 41). During this play – here we shift to a more prankish metaphor – the patient discovers distortions of herself and others and acquires a truer view of herself and the people around her.

The classical conception of transference was born in treatments with one patient and one therapist. Can we also apply it to marital relationships? A spouse may voice accusations, expectations, and praises that seem exaggerated. We also know they can lead to hassles and quarrels. Have they anything to do with transference? The distortions that form its base emanate from wishes that are modelled on "infantile prototypes" (Laplanche & Pontalis, 1973, p. 455) and rooted "in the deep layers of the unconscious" (Klein, 1952b, p. 55). Freud (1912a) emphasized that transference does not cover impulses which have "passed through the full process of psychical development", or are "directed towards reality", and stand "at the disposal of the conscious personality" (p. 100). If a spouse says the partner is self-centred and heartless, is this built on such mature considerations? If so, we cannot call it transference. Or, have the emotions taken up a "regressive course and [revived] the subject's infantile imagos" (p. 102)? If so, we could indeed speak of inter-spouse transference.

Susanne Abse (2014), a Tavistock therapist, suggests that spouses may exhibit such transferences in that they re-enact "patterns of relationship generated from childhood experiences" (loc. 1108). Yet, she does not develop this use of the term as an inter-partner phenomenon. Another author in that volume on analytic couple therapy (D. E. Scharff & J. S. Scharff, 2014) agrees that "transference is already established between the members of a couple . . . They have a projective identificatory system already" (J. S. Scharff, 2014, loc. 3439). Yet another therapist

(Zeitner, 2003) uses the term "collusion" when a couple's dysfunction is a manifestation of the spouse's "externalization of intrapsychic difficulties onto each other" (p. 349). This closely resembles D. E. Scharff's "projective identificatory system" and my views on inter-partner transference in the case of Eric and Louise, whom we will now learn more about.

Eric and Louise: husband and wife or son and mother?

On a humorous note, Fred Sander (2004) explains the transference aspect of marriage as follows: It

> begins with courtship, if not before. 'I want a girl just like the girl that married dear old Dad.' Each person's unconscious radar screen is looking for an 'other' to complement his or her psychological structure. In the elaborate idealizing, denigrating, jealous fantasies about a loving and/or persecuting other, we are already in the realm of intrapsychic fantasies and their associated conflicts soon to be played out in courtship.
>
> (p. 379)

As the couple therapists Barbara and Stuart Pizer (2006) express it, such fantasies can build up to "interlocking transferences" and "terrorizing demons" that the partners co-construct "as their individual histories have joined to shape (or distort) a shared history" (p. 83). The next case shows that though such transferences are played out between partners of the same generation, the corresponding unconscious characters are rooted in the previous generations.

Eric and *Louise* arrive with their 2-month-old twins, who remain asleep during the first interview. He is approaching 50, is a bit overweight, and has a face marked by hard work and a rough life style. She is younger, in good shape, and with eyes that still seem to look at the world like an astonished child. There is some glow between them, but they immediately start accusing each other.

Louise:	"I don't know what to do with him. He gets up late, never fulfils his promises, he said he was going to find a job but he can't because of his disease . . ."
Analyst:	"Disease?"
Eric:	"Yeah, I'm bipolar, it's hell, I'm on Lithium and antidepressants, in and out of hospitals."
Louise:	"I understand it's hard for you sometimes. But why don't you take your pills!?"
Eric:	"I take them. I only forgot last Tuesday."
Louise:	"You forget quite often. Don't contradict me 'cause I see the pills on your bedside table. Could you please tuck your shirt into your trousers? We're staring at your belly."

Eric:	*"Sorry." (He tucks in the shirt and straightens up a bit.)*
Analyst:	*"Louise, you have a lot of critique against Eric."*
Eric:	*"Yeah, that's just my problem with her. She's running after me like a bitch."*
Louise:	*"I hate being a bitch. This wasn't the life I dreamt of! I was in the UK for 15 years, waiting for a real man. But he never came. I longed for home, met you and now I'm stuck in this swamp."*
Eric:	*"You didn't seem to think of me as a swampy guy when we met . . ."*
Louise:	*"No, I was attracted and fell in love on the spot."*
Analyst:	*"So what happened? How did two lovers end up being a slouch and a bitch? None of you like your role. To me, you seem more like a mischievous boy with his mother yelling at him."*
Eric smiles:	*"I can recognize that. My relationship with my mother is shit. And I know Louise hates it when I don't put my shirts in order . . ."*
Louise:	*"Yeah, you should see his cupboard. Like a bombshell. And he doesn't fix it. By the way, I've told you to take up your gym again. The reason I'm nagging about the shirt is not that I want you to behave properly. It's because you don't look very attractive!"*
Analyst:	*"Eric, you could take that as another complaint – or as an invitation."*
Eric smiles:	*"The second alternative seems nicer. It's not only that I am attracted to you, Louise. You know that! I'm grateful to all the things you've done for my teenage son. (He's from my first marriage.) Wow, he adores you."*
Analyst:	*"And so do you?"*
Eric:	*"Yeah. I don't understand why I do this . . . mischief – or, why you love to harp on at me."*
Louise:	*"I don't love it. I HATE IT!"*

This couple shares a conscious belief in making love, having children, and forming a family with two captains on the bridge deck. Unconsciously, they share a different belief; men are sloppy, irresponsible, and mischievous boys who must be overseen by a distrustful and grouchy wife-mother. Sometimes, being together is fun and pleasurable until a forgotten pill or a shirt outside the trousers sets the mother–son-game in motion. The turning point was when I renamed their roles, her as prosecutor and him as defendant, into her as mother and him as her son. Now there was intercourse and a flash of interest sparkled in their eyes: "Why do we get on this track, over and over again"?

124   Part I: Clinic

Individual or couple therapy?

"When we see one member of a family or couple who chronically monopolizes the flow of conscious and unconscious communication, we recommend individual therapy either instead of or in addition to family therapy" (D. E. Scharff, 2003, p. 260). I agree and add the question: How do we detect when one partner's character structure exerts such oppression on the family members that joint work will be a meaningless roundabout? One might argue that Louise and Eric were not suitable candidates for couple therapy. He had a bipolar disorder, was on medication and occasionally hospitalized. After all, it was *he* who lost his jobs and *he* who did not tuck in his shirts! So why did I not suggest he return to his psychiatrist or seek personal therapy? Indeed, in some cases one spouse has such grave emotional problems that it seems improbable to erect a joint platform for couple therapy. But in my experience, what characterizes such cases is not that one spouse has a psychiatric disorder but that s/he is affronted by the commitment of parenthood and cannot rise to the occasion and get hold of immature and self-centred character traits. Here, one spouse's unconscious belief is not shared by the other partner at all. Like when one mother said, "I thought we were building a family!", and he responded, "I don't want to change my life simply because we've got a child!"

One may retort that such announcements need not be the end of the road. In joint therapy, the couple may discover that their unconscious beliefs beneath the official incompatible statements are rather similar. The initial declarations by Eric and Louise were totally dissimilar, but it was plain to see that there must be more of unison and love underneath – which they confirmed. But then again, was Eric not too ill for couple therapy? Might he not be offended by interpretations about being Louise's "son" and then regress and end up in hospital? Bell and co-workers (2007) described initial family relationships and parenting like "'messy processes' out of which new ways of being together are created. This disorganization plays a fundamental role in the establishment of early family relationships" (p. 179). It can be detrimental to a brittle parent and elicit a psychotic episode, but it may also awaken a need to open up for psychological development. The question is: How do we sift the wheat from the chaff? I will submit some ideas in the following paragraphs.

When I meet with husband and wife at the CHC I take it for granted that – since the two are sitting in my consulting room – they share at least one belief; that it is reasonably possible to make things work better. It is important not to interpret this as the spouses' vow to stay together. Sometimes, they come to about talk their impending separation and how to handle it in the best way for the child. In other cases, a mother comes on her own to complain about her spouse. Often, I suggest she bring him along the next time. At yet other times, a mother might tell me about a partner who deserted her by running away, or by continuing a bachelor's life and turning in at home now and then. Then I am more prone to investigate if she were in similar relationships earlier and, if so, suggest an individual therapy to find out why. Most often, however, couples who come together want to do something about their tedious, angry, boring, saddening, and disappointing relationship. And then we can set up a contract for work, like with Eric and Louise.

How is one to select those parental couples where it seems reasonable to work in a brief consultation? To me, the *balance of evacuation and introjection* is decisive. In all relationships, these two phenomena function as relational modes and practices of maintaining self-esteem and well-being. When we are frustrated, humiliated, or tired we find fault in the other. Like babies we evacuate our distress and plight into the nearest recipient, and the spouse is an easy and accessible target for such drainage. This was plain to see with Tilde and Salih, and Louise and Eric; accusations, ironies, complaints, and wry faces were hurled to and fro. The other side of the coin implies to introject the partner's loving and healthy aspects. When Salih talked dismissively about his lonely years in Lebanon, Tilde voiced her concern: "You sound so self-assured, but I wonder . . ." Beyond her care, she also showed that she was introjecting an aspect of him; she showed empathy, *Einfühlung* (Freud, 1921) or "feeling-in" (Krause, 2010) with the lonely boy. Perhaps, it also resonated with a girl inside Tilde who feared her witch-mother-in-law. Now, the direction changed; projections turned into introjections. The traffic was reversed, which was moving and promising to witness.

One could also describe such a changeover in terms of "hate→love". I am not referring to a swift change of mind: "Let's forget the whole thing and start all over again". I'm rather pointing at the tremendous work in bringing about this shift. It presupposes that one becomes truly *interested* in the other. This happened to Tilde as just mentioned, and it occurred with Eric and Louise when they were taken aback by my comment about mother and son. In both cases, I gauged that the balance of evacuation/introjection was in favour of the latter and therefore, therapy was worth trying.

In contrast, there are some couples at the CHC, luckily quite rare, whom I call "The Strindberg couples". I refer to the author's sombre visions of married life in dramas like *The Dance of Death*, *The Father*, and *Miss Julie*. In such couples, evacuation runs persistently as a sluggish, dark, and monotonous current of hate. Their concern for the child is easily drowned by narcissistic issues. In such cases, individual therapy for each partner might be better (Links & Stockwell, 2002), though I often take leave of such couples with pessimism and misgivings.

Another approach to the question of individual versus couple therapy is to split it up into themes. Some themes need a joint approach. Tilde and Salih needed to investigate ensemble what made them resort to projecting fears onto their partner. But as the ensuing individual therapy with Tilde indicated, it was also essential for her to personally explore why she was so afraid of witches and princesses. With Eric and Louise, there was a similar bi-sectioning of themes. The mother–son theme demanded an investigation in couple work. Then, we intuited another theme related to Eric's background that seemed more fit to pursue in individual therapy. The next session, Eric reported that he had taken up gym training and felt "much better". The two had talked about the mother–son theme and discerned its impact on married life. I asked if they intuited why they took up these roles so steadfastly.

Louise mentioned a poor relationship with her mother, "a harping hag". Eric filled in: "Her mother is a pest. I wonder how you became such a generous person. You saved my life! I was shit when we met. You don't have any idea where I come from!" Eric related a dim and dark story. His father spent his childhood amid the horrors of WW2. "He never talked about it, but I know it destroyed him." Eric and his siblings were sent to foster families. "I'm still bitter about all this."

My guess was that Eric's tendency to adopt the role of the mischievous son to a witch mother was linked with his childhood scars. In addition, here was a man with a long history of manic and depressive episodes, and who knew very little about essential facts from days gone by. Perhaps he feared a mental breakdown if he were to know more. I did not push this point in the couple therapy setting but went on to talk about their present hassles and how to find better ways to deal with them. After another bout of instability, when Eric stopped his medication, got verbally aggressive with Louise, then repentant and exhausted, he said:

> I've never understood why I have these bouts of illness. I'm scared of myself. Why don't I dream at night? Something frightens me about myself, and I suspect it has to do with what happened when I was a boy.

Now, Eric was motivated for individual therapy and asked for it at the psychiatric unit. Still later, Louise learnt more about her tendency to devalue herself. "It's as if I've lost myself. I don't think I'm entitled to having a good life." Now, she became interested in a personal therapy.

Research arguments for a family perspective in perinatal psychotherapy

When I told Tilde and Salih, "When you start fussing, your son starts whining", I relied on clinical experience. This section will submit quantitative research investigating links between marital quality and the development of the infant and child. Clinicians and researchers in perinatal psychology, and I am no exception, have focused on dyadic relationships, especially the mother–infant *dyad*. Of late, many argue that such a focus can obscure "the role that triadic, family-level processes may play in socializing young children's adaptive skills and perspectives on relationships" (McHale & Rasmussen, 1998, p. 40). A widened focus does not imply a mere study of the *three dyads* in a family of mother, father, and baby. We must also focus on the *triadic system* (McHale & Fivaz-Depeursinge, 1999), in which the "higher whole is much more than the sum of the corresponding parts at a lower level" (Emde, 1994, p. 94). We must also distinguish between the spouses' functioning as husband and wife from their coparenting. Until the first child is born, they were two partners in a love relationship. Now they are "coparents", which will overturn their previous roles.

It has been shown that marital satisfaction decreases after childbirth (Rosan & Grimas, 2015). Zemp, Bodenmann, and Cummings (2016) review the literature and cite studies from the UK (Hanington, Heron, Stein, & Ramchandani, 2011) and the US (Gottman & Notarius, 2002). Couple conflict is reported to rise by a factor of 9 after transition to parenthood. Such conflicts cannot be hidden from the children and, in fact, constitute a stronger risk factor than divorce. Gottman and Notarius summarize what may happen with the arrival of the baby: the parents "revert to stereotypic gender roles; they are overwhelmed by the amount of housework and childcare; fathers withdraw into work; and marital conversation and sex sharply decrease. There is also an increase in joy and pleasure with the baby" (p. 172). It has been argued that "it is not whether couples argue but how they do that is most relevant to children" (Zemp et al., 2016, p. 100). Conflicts between parents are, of course, unavoidable (Cummings & Davies, 2002). Katz and Gottman (1997), for example, emphasize the risk when spouses show contempt or withdraw from one another. According to the Emotional Security Theory (Cummings & Davies, 2010), risks to children emerge when they feel that their security is threatened by the conflicts or if they mistrust the parents' abilities to resolve them. The term "conflict" does not only comprise hostility or violence: "Infants' exposure to discordant, but non-violent, parental conflict also exerts negative effects" (Rosan & Grimas, 2015, p. 11).

McHale and Rasmussen (1998) bring out three qualities in a couple's relationship that predict the child's future adjustment: *hostility* and *competition* in coparenting, *discrepancies* in the parents' involvement, and *warmth*. They assessed parents and their infants playing together. They found that hostility between parents at this early stage predicted aggression in the children, even as assessed by their preschool teachers, when they had reached the age of 4. A similar link was found between early inter-parent discrepancies with later child anxiety. Since there was also a continuity of marital quality from infancy to preschool years, the authors found "evidence for the coherence of certain family 'themes' over time" (p. 52) which, also, were linked with child development from infancy to childhood. A more recent study (Gallegos, Murphy, Benner, Jacobvitz, & Hazen, 2016) extends these associations backwards by also assessing *expectant* parents' negative affects. They found a continuity from prenatal marital negativity to mother- and father-withdrawal from the infant at 8 months old. These links continued, especially among fathers, up to the children's emotion regulation at 2 years old.

The studies show that the qualities of marital life and of coparenting are essential for the well-being of the spouses *and* their children. Parents sometimes believe that infants are too young to grasp when they are quarrelling. The referred studies refute this belief. Infants do suffer from negative parental relationships, and their development is also affected. Swiss researchers (Favez et al., 2012; Fivaz-Depeursinge, 2011; Fivaz-Depeursinge & Corboz-Warnery, 1999) devised an instrument, the Lausanne Trilogue Play, in which infant and parents play together. It revealed that babies can interact competently with several people at a time. They are also sensitive to emotional cues when interacting directly with a parent or watching him/her interact with the spouse. They (Favez et al., 2012) followed parents from pregnancy up to a child age of 5. Half of the couples showed a "high-stable" alliance throughout, and their children performed better on affective and cognitive (Theory-of-Mind) tests at 5 years old. Temperament measured at three months also predicted the results. The authors conclude:

> When there are tensions in the couple during pregnancy, it is likely that family interactions will also be difficult once the baby is born and that the development of the child will be affected even several years later. This calls for preventive interventions.
>
> (p. 554)

Similar results were obtained by McHale and Rasmussen (1998) and Gallegos' group (2016).

Since some studies brought out the continuity in marital qualities from pre-pregnancy up to some years afterwards, and that this could affect the child's development, one might conclude that nothing specific happens to a relationship when the partners become parents. If it was fine before it will continue to be so, and vice versa. Yet, this is to simplify matters since *parental development is not linear*. Many factors within and between the parents join with the infant's constitutional setup and his/her helplessness and need of care. Together, they make the infancy period one of the most taxing in relations between the partners. Many couples find themselves far away from the paintings of Virgin Mary and Joseph looking in bliss at little Jesus in the manger. In an American qualitative study (Paris & Dubus, 2005), new mothers reported that they felt isolated and lonely: "Sometimes I'm ready to tear my hair out. At the beginning, I was just sitting here breastfeeding and staring at the walls, and just so terribly uncomfortable in my entire body" (p. 77). They missed their own mothers and felt their husbands did not understand their suffering. Many were "unprepared for the intense feeling of loneliness and the inability to share it with anyone who would understand" (p. 78). To this was added a sense of being disconnected from other adults, including their spouses.

What about fathers? Here, research is less conspicuous and a Practitioner Review (Panter-Brick et al., 2014) suggests that health care professionals and researchers should set out for a "game change" in this area; reports should clarify if fathers participated or not in intervention programmes. When designing them, one should ask "how to make parenting interventions culturally compelling to both fathers and mothers as coparents" (p. 1206). To facilitate fathers' participation, this attitude should be implemented already at the delivery ward. A metasynthesis (Chin et al., 2011) of studies on the transition to fatherhood yielded three main themes: *detachment, surprise, and confusion*. The men viewed their role as "the approachable provider" and wished to become more approachable to their child than their own fathers. They also tended to redefine themselves and the relationship with their partner into becoming a "united tag team". Chapter 2 contains more food for thought on fathers.

According to a literature survey (Genesoni & Tallandini, 2009), fathers' redefinition in terms of "reorganization of the self" (p. 305) was especially demanding during pregnancy. Yet, the periods that were reported to be the most demanding emotionally were labour and birth. These themes could be summarized under the rubric of "change in life", a core category emerging in a Swedish study (Fägerskiöld, 2008). The men felt ill prepared for this change. Fägerskiöld's explanation is that "midwives at antenatal clinics mostly focused on the delivery and the woman who gave birth, and rarely about the man and his feelings" (p. 68). After the baby's arrival, many overwhelming adaptations await the father. He can feel disappointed at not being able to work *and* be with the baby as much as he likes, at the decrease in sex life and freedom, and at feeling clumsy when taking care of the baby. Many men respond to these challenges by taking control over the situation and becoming champions of diaper-changing. We can call it an adaptive defence against helplessness if we wish. But it comes as heaven-sent for the mother and strengthens coparenting!

How do infants contribute to making life difficult for some parents? One oft-mentioned factor is sleep. A Canadian study (Loutzenhiser & Sevigny, 2008) found associations between 3-month-old infants' sleep patterns, parent-rated child negativity, and, particularly, father-reported psychological functioning. The researchers explained the latter finding with the conjecture that "fathers' ratings of parenting stress are more influenced by infant sleep patterns than mothers due to their employment outside of the home" (p. 15). Another stress factor is that if an infant's sleep does not improve over time, the parents may begin to interpret this "as reflective of their parenting skills" (p. 15). It is as if they were thinking "he can't sleep . . . I can't make him sleep . . . I'm a bad parent".

The baby's insomnia disrupts the parents' sleep. A Dutch study (Meijer & van den Wittenboer, 2007) showed that insomnia was more salient among mothers. On the other hand, if the husbands were supportive then the wives felt alright even if they continued to sleep less than their partners. There is also an interplay between infant and parental sleep. A review (Sadeh, Tikotzky, & Scher, 2010) cites studies confirming experiences among CHC nurses; parents' excessive attention to the baby when s/he is about to fall asleep is linked with disrupted infant sleep. This also creates tensions among the spouses. Teti's group (Teti, Kim, Mayer, & Countermine, 2010) brought out that maternal sensitivity, specifically, is linked with infant sleeping problems; it promotes feelings of safety and security when the child is about to fall asleep and thus, sleep will be better regulated. If this aim is not achieved, sleep problems may persist into toddlerhood, sometimes with a prevalence of more than 30% (Lam, Hiscock, & Wake, 2003).

This chapter started by exploring why spouses end up in quarrels when their dreams of a child is fulfilled but meets with realities; not only external restrictions in freedom, finance, etc., but also internal ones arising when unconscious beliefs crash with conscious intentions. In Eric and Louise, we found a man and a woman who became a father and a mother but ended up functioning, on an unconscious level, as a rebellious son and a harping mother. To avert the impression that discord is unusual in families with infants, or that when it does occur it has no impact on an "ignorant infant", I cited research studies. They traced lines beginning prenatally and ending up in childhood, which showed that marital quality is important for the spouses *and* the babies. I end with paraphrasing the biblical story:

> In the beginning the parents conceived a child. Life with the baby was good and it was bad. When it was good, it was all delight and they rejoiced. When life was bad, darkness came into their eyes and the feud started. And the baby sensed it all.

When these parents seek help, there is good potential for helping them in couple therapy. With the baby acting as a kind of cheerleader, they can revise earlier beliefs, conscious and unconscious, about aspects of family life including parenting, sex, upbringing, fun, conflict solution, money, and the division of duties.

Chapter 14

Extending the field to therapy with toddlers and parents

For some while, psychoanalysts have extended their work to groups, families, children, infants, etc. This chapter is about such an extension: therapy with children of 2–4 years and their parents. As with PTIP work, I actively invite both generations to treatment. I address the toddler about what I intuit are the unconscious motivations beneath his behaviour and what I guess he feels about me for the moment. In parallel, the parent's emotions towards me are vehicles promoting the therapeutic process – once we get to talk about them. An apt metaphor is *couple therapy* though, evidently, the child's and the parent's developmental levels and motivations for therapeutic work diverge.

The bases for parent–toddler and PTIP work differ. An infant does not speak or understand words, whereas a toddler allows a reasonably comprehensible dialogue. Babies depend on the parent's continued presence, whereas a toddler might be alone with a stranger. But, being with a *therapist* for more than a few seconds will elicit anxiety. Since toddlers in therapy are often insecurely attached, it would be counterproductive to work without the parent. These factors can be turned into an advantage if we offer parent and child a well-contained setting. There, they may enact individual and shared fantasies underneath that which the parent feels is *the child's* disorder, but which therapy may reveal to have a more complex genesis.

Once I direct my attention to a distressed baby, he may seek to involve me for containment (Salomonsson, 2014a). Agitated interactions like the ones between baby and *mother* sometimes commence between him and *me*. This can form an important leverage for therapeutic work (Salomonsson, 2013). This observation inspired me to extend PTIP technique to toddlers and mothers at the CHC. Problems were unruliness, quarrels, defiance, and sleep problems, and the parents' difficulties with limit-setting and exhaustion. Consultations were a mix of interpretations of the parents' issues and advice on upbringing. Or, the child seemed to have more problems on his/her own. Some such cases lead to lengthy therapies, which enabled me to investigate how a child's disturbed behaviour is linked with his internal world and the interaction with his parent. This chapter describes such a therapy, discusses the technique, and compares it with that of other authors.

132 Part I: Clinic

Background to the case

Bridget is a grey-hued woman who, I conjecture, has once looked happier in life. Emotions pass swiftly across her face: despair, joy, concern, fear, sadness, and exhaustion. She does not sleep well and has a hard time managing her boys. When she only had *Walter*, now 2½ years old, it was OK. But since *Bruno* was born nine months ago she has no energy left. In our first consultation at the CHC, she speaks cautiously since she dislikes "poking about" in her worries, gastritis, stress, exhaustion . . . She is a gym teacher and describes herself as dutiful and a bit stern towards herself. *Ron*, her husband, is a colleague with whom she has many interests in common. "But I have no go nowadays, so marriage isn't much fun. That goes for my Mum-feelings too." She adds that she has never seen a psychiatrist or a therapist before.

Walter cannot fall asleep on his own and often wakes up. A light sleeping drug has been of little help. One parent must sit with him for hours, otherwise he lies awake. "Something seems to worry him," she says. Bridget adds that the troubles started "when Walter returned from the hospital." During pregnancy, a routine ultrasound showed an intestinal malformation, which would require an operation to enable the passage of food. Delivery went well and the operation was performed instantly without complications. "We returned home after two weeks. Since then he has never slept normally." They were not recommended psychological support and did not ask for it. "Everything was OK, I was breastfeeding, and he gained weight and developed normally, except for his sleep." At one year, a CAMHS psychologist suggested the parents should sit close to Walter until he fell asleep and then cautiously move towards the door. "It worked so-so."

Bridget continues, "Then Bruno was born and the second problem arose"; Walter's violence towards his little brother and her feelings about it: "I show Walter love and attention. But he's jealous anyway. So, I feel guilty about Bruno and upset with Walter." When I suggest she come next week and bring both boys along, she willingly accepts. Her depression is apparent – a lack of zest and joy; feelings of guilt, anxiety, and stress; symptoms of gastritis and insomnia; and a temporal connection with Bruno's birth. True, one might recommend antidepressants. In addition, we know of associations between prenatal stress and sleep disturbances in newborns (Field et al., 2007; Glover, Bergman, & O'Connor, 2008; Marcus et al., 2011). Applying a biological explanatory model, one could suggest that Walter's stress tolerance is decreased because Bridget's worries during pregnancy affected the HPA-axis and secondarily his cortisol levels. I might explain this to her and that things will probably be better in the future.

But, the interview also invites psychodynamic musings on Bridget's worries about a foetal malformation, her anxiety about the operation, Walter's insomnia and her exasperation, anger, and guilt that she cannot protect Bruno from attacks. Not only do I ponder on how the parents' fantasies about their future child were affected by the diagnosis of a malformation, I also wonder about the impact of Walter's operation. His insomnia might indicate that anxieties – in him, in the

Therapy with toddlers and parents 133

parents and/or in their relationship – were never properly allayed. If so, this might cast a shadow – though the mechanism is yet unclear – on his fraternal relationship. This model seems important to investigate in psychotherapy, especially since Bridget does not ask for drugs or explanations. She wants to grasp "why things turned out this way" and seems interested in pursuing this path with me.

Meeting with the two brothers

Next week at the CHC, I discover Bridget playing with her sons in the waiting room. Walter runs into my office while Mum is tidying up. During the one minute I am alone with him, he exhibits fierce jealousy and possessiveness. He sees a box of crayons and yells, "MY box!" He sees another one, "MY box too," and tears it open. He is sitting with 30 crayons triumphing, "MY crayons!", while I am reflecting on my feelings of repugnance and provocation. Mum and Bruno now enter the room. Walter exclaims, "MY crayons!" and kicks Bruno. Mum looks aggrieved and I feel ill at ease with Walter's violence. Bruno seems accustomed and smiles. Mother exhorts Walter in vain to share the crayons with Bruno. I start addressing Walter with two aims. One is to convey how I think his behaviour is ruled by affects that he seems to ward off. Another is to create a setting where the affects can be investigated and not be acted out via violent behaviour.

Analyst to Walter:	*"You want all the crayons. Bruno shouldn't have any. I guess you're mad at him."*
Walter:	*"MY crayons!"*
Analyst:	*"Well, they're my crayons. But you may borrow them. You want them all. I'd also like Bruno to borrow some."*
	Walter looks grumpy as I give Bruno crayons. Unexpectedly, a truck is heard. He looks at the window to see what is humming. He wants to have a look and I lift him up. Suddenly, he weeps and panics.
Walter:	*"I go away. Away!"*
Mother:	*"I don't recognize this . . ."*
Analyst:	*"Walter, you got scared and want to run away. I think it's better if you stay and we try to find out what's so scary."*

When Bridget reflects that she is unfamiliar with his behaviour she is already an interested participant in therapy. I might therefore share with her my speculations about Walter's behaviour. But I prefer to enlist him as an active participant by clarifying to *him* the setting and by following up on the emotions that my stance elicits. The rules and the logic of the setting are as follows: we will remain in my office, violence is unaccepted, everyone's rights will be attended to, the crayons are mine but I willingly lend them to Walter as tools of our joint investigation of the emotions behind his unruly behaviour. I thus *preside* over the transference

(Meltzer, 1967). This kindles a negative transference, as evidenced by his sulkiness and perhaps also by his reactions to the truck. The next interchange indicates that a parallel positive transference is nascent as well.

> *Analyst to Walter:* *"You wanted all the crayons. Then you kicked Bruno. Mum and I saw it. Then the truck came. You got scared . . . Now you're scared of my room. It's spooky in here . . . But it's better you stay, then we can talk about it."*
> *Walter is listening attentively. Mum gives him the pacifier and he calms down. She suggests, "If you take out the dummy you can tell us what's scaring you." But no, Walter wants to suck it.*

Bridget's suggestion that Walter take out the dummy to talk with us reflects her nascent identification with my analytic perspective. As for his attentive listening, I interpret it as a dawning positive transference. I now suggest to her that Walter perhaps met with an "ugly" feeling in my office, and the lorry turned into a kind of "policeman" roaring, "I know your ugly thoughts about Bruno". She listens but does not comment. A little later, she says it is difficult to think at home, where she must make peace between the boys. "But I can think here." I muse that the parents do think and talk at home, but here she is offered a different form of thinking. Her son is now more incomprehensible to her, but she has also become interested in a new way of thinking together.

A new quarrel follows about a pencil that Bruno is holding in his hand. When Walter fails to snatch it, he grabs eight soft cuddly toys and refuses to give any to Bruno.

> *Analyst to Walter:* *"You want everything for yourself. Nothing to Bruno! You're mad at him, that's why you kick him. Then you get afraid . . . Now you put your dummy in your mouth, but you don't need it, actually. Why don't you take it out again so we can talk?"*
> *To my surprise, Walter follows my suggestion. Later I add, "You think Bruno is silly. You wish there was no Bruno. But he's here. So, what should you do?"*

My sentences are interspersed with Walter's attentive nodding. I do not think he understood the interventions' literal content but their crucial ingredients: he is angry with Bruno, I have noticed it and take an interest, and I do not condemn him but I want to prevent the violent consequences. Thus, Walter grasps that there is something inside that disturbs him and that I accept him as an angry boy.

Walter lets go of his brother. He empties the toy-box to use it like a hat. He looks happy and Mum is laughing. He grabs a fish and Mum sings a fish song. Right now, Walter has forgotten his jealousy. He sees a pair of slippers and checks if he may play with them. I nod in consent. He exclaims, "Your shoes!" and tries to put them on me. We are laughing that they are too small. He puts them on himself and walks proudly across the room. I tell him, "Earlier, you wanted to be a little boy. Now you're feeling better. It feels good to be bigger, almost as big as me." Bridget smiles warmly.

Walter is "walking in my shoes", identifying with aspects he perceives in me; being big and friendly, and having fun and sharing interesting thoughts. I now suggest that Bridget should bring her husband next week. I also suggest that she and Walter start a joint therapy once weekly. I point out that he has shared fierce feelings with us; he suffers from them and has noticed my interest in understanding them. She consents. "Just one thing: we will soon be moving to X (a faraway town)."

I have several arguments for suggesting mother–toddler therapy. Walter can only handle his jealousy and anger through fighting. His mood and ego-functioning change swiftly. His insomnia persists. I also assume he has a dictatorial superego who "saw" him kicking his brother. I guessed this was why he wanted to run away when he heard the lorry. Cathy Urwin (2008) reminds us about the suggestions by Klein (1934) and Winnicott (1956b) that a ruthless child may suffer from an intolerable guilt that is induced by his violence. He then tries to invite the parents to inflict punishment, "which would at least be time-limited and tolerable" (Urwin, 2008, p. 146). This seems to explain Walter's anxiety except that the truck, not the parents, is cracking down on him.

Walter's relentless superego parallels his unstable perception of psychic reality. Neither I, my room, nor the truck are objects with which he can engage in a pretend mode (Fonagy & Target, 1996). Instead, he has a hard time differentiating external from internal reality. The truck is inside and outside him – and it is all very frightening. His unconscious internal monologue can be sketched:

> I'm mad at my brother. I kick him. He cries and I get scared. I'm a bad boy. My parents don't like me and I can't stand that. No, I'm not bad – the truck's bad and haunts me! The truck is me as well.

Is the superego harshness not only nourished by his fraternal jealousy, but also from the operation in infancy and the anxious climate then? This remains an unproven speculation. Right now, I am convinced that a few consultations will be insufficient. I suggest we work until the family leaves town. This will amount to 14 sessions.

Crocodiles

When I meet with the parents Ron, the father, is angrier with Walter than Bridget. He feels sorry for her and Bruno when Walter behaves badly. He describes him as reckless and wild. When I suggest Walter is scared of his rage they are surprised.

Part I: Clinic

They have never thought about him this way, probably because they are down in the trenches and find it hard to empathize with him.

For the first therapy session next week, I have arranged a toy-box. I want to offer Walter a space where he can express himself as freely as possible. There is a sketch-book, crayons, some little dolls (a sailor boy, king, queen, witch, bumble-bee), a pig family, and a German shepherd with open jaws. This will enable him to express fantasies which I assume centre around oral-aggression, tenderness, family life with its tensions, fears and aspirations, and himself as a cheerful sailor boy.

Walter steps right into my office: "Hi Björn." I respond and show him the toys in the box. He picks out the dolls and throws them at me, one at a time, with a mixture of force and happiness. "Soft things", he says, as if assuring me of his good intentions. Finally, I am holding all the dolls and he tells me to throw them at Mum. Then he orders her to throw them at him. This triangular play goes on until he picks up the sketch-book saying, "Draw crocodile," which he does. He orders me and Mum to do the same and delights when we do it. Bridget seems to enjoy her son's exultant and intrepid attitude.

My contemplations of this interaction bring me to *orality*. Ever since Freud (1905) and Abraham (1927), analytic theory has assumed that experiences during an infant's "oral phase" will leave an imprint on his personality. The term goes beyond stating the obvious; a baby uses the mouth for ingestion and investigation. "Oral" rather signifies that the first mode by which a baby interprets and organizes emotional and cognitive experiences is built up according to a "grammar" or matrix that parallels the mouth's functioning. We do not only refer to its sensorial aspects like sucking and kissing, but also to modes of work such as ingesting, chewing, swallowing, or spitting out. These physiological events are then imbued with psychological meaning. Many embodied metaphors (Lakoff & Johnson, 1999) illustrate this transfer from bodily matters to primal mental experiences. We "devour" our beloved but give our enemy "biting" comments. The ignoramus "swallows" any information, whereas the cynic excels in "bitter" and "sour" comments. Such "conflations" (p. 46) between sensorimotor mouth experiences and emotions are, psychoanalytically speaking, oral metaphors. More about this in Chapter 19!

Another route to exemplifying the oral world and its throng of pleasures and fears proceeds from child therapy. To exemplify with Walter, two stressful events occurred when the oral zone still carried a major significance: his insomnia and his violent aggression after Bruno's birth. I thus imagine that the crocodiles with their perilous teeth symbolize Walter's savage and much-feared anguish and rage. I also think they correspond to the truck in the first interview. His anxiety about the vehicle appeared after he had been pitiless with Bruno and grumpy with me due to our crayon conflict. His anger was transformed into an avenger towards himself; the roaring truck that seemed to represent both his rage and the superego's austere penalty for his "ugly" feeling. I formulate these hypotheses to myself while I address Walter.

Analyst to Walter:	*"Yes, crocodiles are scary. You're afraid of them. You want to draw many crocodiles so they won't be scary. Mum and I should draw them, too."*
Walter:	*"Draw crocodiles!"*
Mother:	*"We were at the Zoo, he saw some crocodiles. I guess that's why he's fascinated by them."*
Analyst:	*"You may be right, but I also think Walter wants to tell us something. We know he's angry. Maybe he wants to bite like a croc but doesn't dare to."*
	Walter goes on drawing, his eyes becoming increasingly warm and enthusiastic. Bridget looks warmly at her son. I suggest, "You like that chap, don't you?" She smiles tenderly.

The technique of gathering Walter's desires and fears into the transference (Meltzer, 1967) already pays off. Before therapy, Walter had no phobias. He was just ruthless and sleepless. Therapy unsettles this balance; I set limits but do not punish, I take an interest in his violence but do not condone it, and I am attentive to his emotions without impugning his right to harbour them. The setting provides a sanctuary (Britton, 1998) where I can put tentative words to the underlying meanings of his experiences and behaviour. His fear of the truck and anguished fascination of the crocs reveal that underneath his violence, anxieties are rampant. When they are met with containment and interpretations, Walter relaxes somewhat and his warmth and enthusiasm emerge. Until now, such traits have been smothered beneath his temper tantrums. In parallel, my countertransference is changing. At first, I felt repulsed by his greed and violence. These issues are far from being solved, but now I also feel that I have a charming fellow in front of me. Thus, the countertransference has become more varied, with positive and negative feelings.

Walter whines again

The next session, Walter enters protesting and whining, "Not go to Björn! Go home!" Mother responds, "But Walter, when I picked you up at preschool you said you wanted to see Björn!" I assume his behaviour reflects a regressive retreat, as if he is declaring, "No, I'm not an angry and violent chap. I am a sad little baby to be taken care of. I wanna go home and sleep!" He avoids looking at his toy-box saying sulkily, "Have dummy." Bridget explains, "Walter wants a pacifier when he is tired." I suggest she wait to allow us time to understand why Walter is afraid: "You're right that the pacifier will soothe him – but it can also function as a 'plug' for his thinking." The two might feel I am cruel in not condoning the dummy, but I dare take this risk after Bridget's positive reactions to Walter's progress during the last session. Meanwhile, he is glaring at me.

138   Part I: Clinic

> *Analyst to Walter:*   *"You got angry with me when I asked Mum to wait with your dummy. I understand it . . . I wonder why you didn't want to enter my room. Did something scare you here?"*
>   *Walter casts a quick glance at his toy-box. I suggest we open it. Another furtive glance, this time on the crocodile drawings. Then he avoids them – and me. He seems baffled.*
>
> *Analyst:*   *"You drew crocodiles. You liked them. Now you're afraid of them."*
>
> *Walter:*   *"Draw croc. You too! They must have eyes!"*
>
> *Analyst:*   *"So they can see if anyone has done any mischief?"*
>   *Walter does not answer but goes on drawing crocs.*
>
> *Analyst:*   *"When you arrived today you were whining and afraid. Now you're happier. Crocs are scary. They bite and their eyes see the silly things people have done. But they can be good, too! Vroom!" (In a playful mood, I push my crocodile drawing towards him. He smiles and does the same to me.)*
>
> *Analyst:*   *"When you're whining, a croc may help you to bite – in a pretend way. Earlier, you were scared. Not anymore . . . It's good not to be scared."*

My "Vroom" game can be labelled an *enactment* ("*mise en acte*"; Lebovici et al., 2002). The term has acquired a certain negative connotation, but this need not be so. The Vroom conveyed to Walter the functioning of a benevolent and just superego; wild games are OK and fun but violent rows are not. Chapter 19 explores how such enactments can help us grasp what is going on underneath the surface and thus promote the therapeutic process. This vignette also shows Walter's fear of entering my office. In my interpretation, he projects his fears and desires on my person and belongings. They become clad with his projections and the counter-projections which he fantasises emanate in me. The illusory advantage to this phobic mechanism is that, as long as he avoids my room, all is OK. But, his interior dilemma remains and the regression entailed in the phobia damages his self-esteem. Soon, the crocodile will come to help; not as an avenger but as a symbol of force, brute but tamed.

A new verve in Walter

Some sessions later, Walter enters my office whining and protesting again. He wants the dummy but Bridget says no, resolutely and friendly. He draws a croc, gets tired of it and switches to the pig family. He groups them together and places the dog aside. I comment, "The dog is guarding the pigs so that nothing bad can happen to them." Walter moves the dog inside the pig family. I comment again, "Now the dog is in the family. Earlier, the pigs were afraid of him. Now he's allowed to play with them. I guess they like the dog though he bites sometimes." Walter looks at me happily. Then he starts whining.

Walter pleading to mother:	*"Throw soft animals!"*
	Mother, gently throwing the animals to him: "It's been a long day today."
Analyst to mother:	*"You often have an excuse at hand when Walter is whining. You don't want to see the German shepherd inside of him."*
Mother with some vexation:	*"But he is tired!"*
	Analyst, while I throw a soft witch doll to her: "And he is angry, too, you know!"
	Mother in surprise, playfulness and irritation, throwing the animal back at me: "Hey, you there!"

My throwing the doll at Bridget is another enactment or spontaneous gesture (Winnicott, 1960a) that denotes many things; my vexation with her resistance to seeing Walter's oral aggression, my display that anger is not dangerous, and my invitation to do psychotherapy like "two people playing together" (Winnicott, 1971b, p. 38). When playing is impossible, the therapist should help bring the patient "into a state of being able to play" (idem). This I do now with Bridget. Walter is watching our play closely. Then he starts whining again. With renewed energy mother addresses him.

Mother to Walter:	*"But Walter, what do you want? Talking is better than whining!"*
Analyst:	*"I think you're whining when you're angry or afraid, Walter. You don't have to be afraid of being angry. A guy who's angry may be liked anyway. The pigs liked the dog though he bites sometimes, didn't they?"*
Mother:	*"That's right!"*
	At this point, Walter walks up to me, looking straight into my eyes. He bangs the witch doll resolutely on my knee, smiling warmly and fearlessly.
Analyst laughing:	*"I got what I deserved, didn't I?"*
Walter:	*"Draw croc, Björn. Croc silly!"*
Analyst:	*"Why?"*
Walter:	*"'Cos it bites."*

Analyst to Walter:	*"But crocs have to eat, don't they?"*
	Walter gets pensive and I address Bridget: "Walter is probably using the crocs to show his anger with Bruno – and how scared he is of it."
Mother:	*"Funny you mentioned Bruno. I was thinking they're getting along better now. When Bruno grabs one of his toys, Walter tells him not to do it – instead of giving him a beating. It works most of the time. And one day Bruno will be bigger and hit back!"*

This section exemplifies some advantages of joint parent–toddler work. Our interchange about the pigs and the dog might have occurred in an individual child therapy but here, the mother's contributions were included in therapeutic work; her defensive avoidance of Walter's anger, a mechanism addressed by Parens (1991), Parker (1995), and Hoffman (2003). When I address her "excuse", she gets annoyed. Indeed, these therapies are replete with transferences from toddler *and* parent. Authors like Miller (2008), Wittenberg (2008), and Lieberman and Van Horn (2008) advise against interpreting parental transferences since it may be "unhelpful to encourage infantile dependency at a point in a couple's lives when they are being called upon to be at their most adult" (Wittenberg, 2008, p. 29). I agree regarding treatments where parents seek advice and the child is not directly addressed. But, I take a different view on a "couple therapy" like Bridget's and Walter's. Both put their conscious and unconscious urges on the table. He fears his aggression and she fears acknowledging and understanding it. Consequently, she develops a negative transference when I remind her of this challenge. This provides therapeutic leverage to help her *and* Walter coming to terms with his internal German shepherd or crocodile.

When I threw the witch at Bridget I was explicit only about her refusal to acknowledge Walter's anger, whereas I was implicit about interpreting her anger with me. I could have said, "I think you're angry with me, Bridget" but in lieu, the witch game emerged spontaneously. She accepted it and showed she had integrated my message when throwing the witch back at me and then telling Walter, "Talking is better than whining!" When he banged the witch on my knee, he confirmed that he was learning that anger is not perilous. He understood this, not only from his interchange with me, but also from the one between his mother and me.

A glimpse of the primordial trauma?

One argument for a lengthy therapy was Walter's early operation, which I surmised constituted an emotional trauma. But until now, our work has focused on his rage, jealousy, violence, and his mother's ways of dealing with this. As the session just reported is about to end, something occurs which perhaps refers to the events after birth. I am sitting pondering if any such traces remain in Walter. Meanwhile, he is sitting silently on my desk chair. He begins to slide down, as if getting under my writing desk. He talks to himself: "Into Mum. Into Mum! . . . They took me away, they took me away."

Walter's comments and funny ballet on my chair make me wonder; is he enacting a fantasy of returning, back "into Mum"? If so, is it a reaction to the fact that they "took him away" for the operation? I say nothing, but I notice that Bridget is fascinated. I share my thoughts: "We've never spoken about Walter's operation . . ." She starts telling me, visibly moved and pained, about the worries during pregnancy and before the operation, and how she missed him during the surgery.

Mother:	*"When we returned home, I wasn't sure I could trust the doctors that everything would be OK. I thought something bad was going to happen anyway."*
Analyst:	*"It must have been a very hard time. I was thinking of this period now that Walter said, 'Into Mum' and 'They took me away'."*
Mother:	*"I also noted it. I've been talking with some mothers at the CHC about attachment. I wondered if the operation affected his attachment to me."*
Analyst:	*"Maybe your attachment to him as well?"*
Mother:	*"I've always thought he's sensitive. Maybe I've been pampering him. Sure, it's related to his start in life. It was terrible! And I felt so sorry for him . . . Maybe I've let him have his way too much when is he fighting with Bruno."*
Analyst:	*"That's why I don't think your excuses are of much use. It's more straightforward if you tell Walter if it's OK or not when he wants to do something. I know this is easier said than done . . ."*
Mother:	*"I'm working on it! Another thing, and this is no excuse: We used to change lodging quite often before, but we've decided to cut that down now. He doesn't like changes. Such things we can respect of course, but not when he hits Bruno!"*

Sometimes a child exhibits an enigmatic utterance or behaviour. The parents had told me about the operation, so it was tempting to link Walter's chair play and comments with it. Yet, it would be easy to refute this link; if any memories should persist, they must be implicit and nebulous. I have addressed (Salomonsson, 2014a) the problems with imputing recollections of early memories that we cannot recall explicitly. Yet, Bridget's comments reveal that they have been, indeed still are, part of the family canon and colour the parents' relationships with him: how they view him, handle him, and what they expect from him. Cf. her comment that Walter was always sensitive. He may have heard of the surgery and fantasized of getting "into Mum" so that "they" would not take him away. Or, he may never have heard about it but observed Mum's eyes when her old fears suddenly re-emerged. "Into Mum" might then be his fantasy of getting into a safer place inside her, where he is unaffected by her anguish. Or, finally, the scene may be a mere insignificant whim. If so, it nevertheless sparked not only my, but also Bridget's, imagination and emotional response.

Clinical epilogue

Our once-weekly therapy of 14 sessions ended when Walter was approaching the age of 3. Half a year after the family had left Stockholm, I received a letter from Bridget. Walter had started preschool and was enjoying it. Recently, his sleep pattern had improved. He told his parents when he was tired, "and that has never happened before! We stopped his sleeping drug and he sleeps through the night. Then he quit the diapers without problems. Walter is a big boy now." Bridget added that the move had upset him. He often had "breakdowns" and was whining a lot. At preschool he was getting more stimulating challenges, which was of help. Mother ended by saying, "I have more patience with Walter because I understand him better." Thus, all problems have not vanished but important advantages are reported and no mention is made of the brothers' fights.

Four years later, the father phoned me. Walter was now 7 years old and diagnosed with ADHD. "He cannot control his impulses very well, he nags at his mother, and gets frustrated if things don't go his way. The school teachers manage these challenges quite well. He is on stimulant medication." He continues, "I was the same when I was a kid, a jittery boy". Walter is also "empathic, a lot of feelings, well-liked by his pals, and gets along OK with his brother". I ask to speak with the mother. She says, "Walter has a super power, he must learn to handle it". She confirms his warmth and enthusiasm. She feels much better today. When I ask what she thinks about our therapy in hindsight she says, "You were the first professional to take our problems seriously. I am very grateful."

My professional super-ego staggered when I heard about the ADHD diagnosis. Had I overlooked such signs? Should he have had another treatment? On reflection, I respond no to both questions. One does not diagnose ADHD in a 3-year-old, and I did not perceive or learn about such symptoms in Walter or his father. To be true, I might have asked about hereditary factors, but the thought never occurred since the parents showed no such signs. I did perceive that Walter was entrenched in an internal turmoil which upset him and the family. This was all played out in therapy. Analyses (Salomonsson, 2004, 2006, 2011b, 2017b) with older boys with ADHD have shown that whatever the backgrounds to their symptoms, they can benefit from psychotherapy to understand the links between emotions and ADHD symptoms, especially deficient impulse control and attention.

Walter's ADHD picture of today, plus his father's similar symptoms from boyhood, suggests a hereditary factor whose influence a brief therapy in toddlerhood could not restrain. Donald Meltzer once said in a supervision that "slices" of psychotherapy can be beneficial when new life challenges confront the child. The arrival of a little brother was one crucible and to help Walter with it, I recommended joint therapy. His school start was another trial and the child psychiatrists, in the town where he now lives, suggested medication and pedagogic measures. From our telephone conversation, I gathered that the previous therapy helped the parents look at Walter, not as an unintelligible and disordered child but as a boy well worth understanding. It would be riveting to meet Walter again, to determine how he looks at himself and to what extent he can connect and talk about his symptoms, emotions, and fantasies. Who knows, maybe he will look me up one day?

One final thought: Earlier, I cautioned against equating present behaviour with very early life events. When Walter said, "into Mum" and "they took me away", I did not interpret it as a memory of the newborn's wish to return to mother's body. But, I do assume that his persistent insomnia was related to early anxiety. We might think of him as a boy with a hereditary sensitivity but we cannot overlook the early separation's effects on him and the parents. Signs of distress already appeared in the form of a very early insomnia. In retrospect, it would have been wise if he and his mother had begun PTIP soon after his return from the operation. I cannot claim it would have forestalled any ADHD symptom, but it might have lessened the risk that his early distress settled into the symptoms in toddlerhood, and which perhaps reflected primal repressions of the trauma (Freud, 1915c; Salomonsson, 2014a).

The literature on toddler–parent psychotherapy

What are the similarities and differences between my mode of parent–toddler work and other traditions? At the end of the day, all therapists "may be indistinguishable from one another when observed clinically even if they use different theoretical terms to describe their work" (Lieberman & Van Horn, 2008, loc. 2104). The summaries to follow are derived from publications and some differences may be greater in writing than in real practice. Let us read them as the authors' personal distillates, not as objective accounts, and yet try to chisel out and compare the essential differences.

Lieberman and Van Horn, San Francisco: Attachment in focus

In an early paper, Lieberman (1992) recommends the therapist to flexibly switch between parent–child sessions, parent-only sessions, and/or hours with the child. She speaks "toddlerese" to explain to the child his feelings. In joint sessions, this will also reach the "child . . . inside the parent" (p. 570). A parent may affect the child via projective identifications of disowned but ego-syntonic aspects of herself, which can make the child feel pushed to comply and identify with them. Perhaps, Bridget's caution with aggression was projected into Walter, which then made it harder for him to deal with his anger. Lieberman emphasizes that "the child's contribution to the affective tone of the interaction is particularly salient in the

144   Part I: Clinic

second year of life" (p. 561). Yet, she seems reluctant to address the child about it. This is, evidently, another take than mine with Walter.

A later volume (Lieberman & Van Horn, 2008) describes therapies mostly with underprivileged families. Improving the child's attachment is the unifying theme. "Attachment problems face parent and child with dilemmas about what is safe and what is dangerous, what is allowed and what is forbidden, that need to be resolved through interpersonal communication, internal accommodation, or a combination of both" (p. 11). The emphasis on danger may reflect the authors' experiences with children exposed to threat and violence. They use a hands-on approach, such as practical advice to families living under imminent threat. Interventions often have a supportive and encouraging quality. The authors also speak with the child to understand what unconsciously drives him/her, which illustrates their heritage of Fraiberg. To exemplify, 2-year-old Maria refuses to clean up as the session ends (p. 75). Mother demands the therapist to stay out of the power struggle with her daughter. In response, the therapist acknowledges to Maria Mum's good intentions and the girl's anxiety at separating from the therapist. She speaks slowly and quietly, claps her hands when the girl picks up the toys and then answers the mother lightly. The possible anger behind Maria's refusal is hardly mentioned. This seems to differ from how I addressed Walter about his rage.

Presumably, my technique would be unsuitable for Lieberman's and Van Horn's population. Walter's family was middle-class with two committed parents. Indeed, how do we adapt technique to a family's educational level, therapy motivation, and socio-economic situation? *No technique can be transferred unmodified to all cases*. To gauge, we must keep an eye on whether parent and child find interventions interesting and conducive to new thoughts – or meaningless and even insulting.

Harel and coworkers, Haifa: reflective functioning in focus

A group in Haifa focuses on *reflective functioning* (Harel, Kaplan, & Patt, 2006). Some parents find it difficult to understand the child's behaviour because their own feelings or thoughts are too much at odds with that of the child. The Israeli model seems developed for families with less reflective functioning than Walter's. Consequently, it aims to facilitate "mental processes that generate representations" (loc. 4844), whereas I provided more of symbolic and transference-oriented interpretations to Walter and Bridget. The different emphases on facilitating reflective processes and interpreting content may thus be due to differences in the population characteristics.

In the same volume, Arietta Slade (2006) describes therapy with a toddler and his mother whose reflective functioning is inhibited. There is little mentioning of therapist–child dialogues. Here, I suspect that it is not only the different levels of ego-functioning and reflective functioning in our populations that lead to different techniques. One also discerns a conceptual difference; I attribute more agency to the child in his relationship with me, and thus I highlight more consistently his/her transference onto me (Salomonsson, 2013).

Tavistock's Under Fives Service: a post-Kleinian approach

Louise Emanuel (2006, 2011), Elizabeth Bradley (Emanuel & Bradley, 2008) and colleagues offer a handful of parent–toddler consultations. Emanuel's conceptualizations cover the experiences of both mother and child. She often interprets a topic brought up by the parents or a behaviour by the child as a symbolic expression of a wish, fear, or conflict. Like me, she uses Kleinian and post-Kleinian conceptual models. In contrast, she seems to seldom address the child about session events (see, however, 2011, p. 683, where she addresses a 13-month-old girl about her angry fantasies). She rather tends to address (Emanuel, 2006) the parents on how to understand the emotions beneath the child's behaviour.

One patient, Douglas, was obsessed with batteries. Emanuel suggests that he "was like a battery, getting charged up and running and running, until he collapsed" (2006, p. 257). She also intuits that as a baby, he might have felt he should "bring Mother to life, to charge her up, so to speak, with his lively activity" (idem). Her guess seems credible, though I would also consider addressing him directly – and it is quite possible that Emanuel would agree – to help him link behaviour and emotions. I might tell him, piecemeal and according to his reactions, "You like batteries. Batteries make cars run quickly . . . It's like you've a battery inside. It makes you run about. . . . I wonder why you run about much." Douglas would only understand a fraction but probably grasp my struggle to understand his obsession with batteries and to draw his attention to this enigma. Emanuel (2011) and I would agree that such understanding is largely based on countertransference. Also, we would be in unison that neglecting negative *parental* transference might risk therapeutic work. I would focus on the *child's* negative transference as well and convey that it can and should be talked about.

One of my arguments for a dialogue with the child is that his responses will help convince the parents about the unconscious intentions beneath his behaviour. One Tavistock clinician, Meira Likierman (2008), comes close to this view. She picks up the child's behaviour as an intention to communicate with her and replies with verbal comments. A 16-month-old boy gets afraid as she is moving closer to him. She retracts her chair telling him, "Look, I am moving *back*" (p. 218). She presumes that he perceives her interest in understanding his fears. I ponder if he might also listen to an interpretation of how he feels about the therapist: "I think you want to get to know me but you're also scared of me. I move back my chair wondering what scares you."

Serge Lebovici, Centre Alfred Binet, Paris: a modified Freudian approach

In the earlier section "Walter whines again", Serge Lebovici was cited as a catalyst for my use of the Vroom game. His technique (Lebovici et al., 2002) implied interpreting explicitly to parents their drive impulses and resistances. Internally,

146   Part I: Clinic

he also considered the child's "imaginary, fantasy, mythic, and narcissistic representations" (de Mijolla, 2009). Often, problems between toddler and parents emanated from the latter's "fantasmatic interactions" (Lebovici & Stoléru, 2003) with the child, which stymied their understanding of the unconscious implications of his symptoms. In his view, the internal worlds of mother and child are intertwined and enmeshed.

Lebovoci used an active technique but disliked giving "advice simply to satisfy the wishes of the parents" (Lebovici et al., 2002, p. 170). Instead he interpreted, with frankness and humour, how their unconscious sexuality coloured the relationship with the baby. He confirmed that the therapist "can also have a direct therapeutic effect on the baby" (Lebovici et al., 2002, p. 180) but DVD recordings (Casanova, 2000) suggest he mostly sought to inspire the *parents'* thinking about the child's feelings.

Summary of the technique and conclusions

The work with Walter and Bridget and other such cases is a natural extension of PTIP experiences. In both areas I initiate a dialogue with parent and child, interpret their unconscious motivations, and contain the child's anxieties (Bion, 1962a, 1970; O'Shaugnessy, 1988). The child address draws from Melanie Klein's ideas (1961, 1975) but with some crucial differences: (a) it opens up for a playful and less threatening atmosphere and enables me to remain more relaxed, probing, and inquisitive; (b) the interplay between external and internal objects becomes more visible by seeing child and parent together; (c) watching this happening in the session helps the three of us to talk about it as an effect of our emotional interchange and thus to learn from it. In Chapter 15, we continue discussing Klein's observations and conceptions.

I finish this chapter with a summary of this mode of parent–toddler therapy:

1/   It is an extension of psychoanalytically informed parent–infant psychotherapy or PTIP.
2/   Parent and toddler are viewed as active therapy subjects. The metaphor is "couple therapy".
3/   A psychoanalytic external and internal frame should be set up from the start. This will clarify the aim – to explore conscious and unconscious urges at the root of the present disorder.
4/   These urges will manifest in derivative forms: play, words, body language, tone of voice, etc.
5/   Parent and child seek containment for such urges and will involve the therapist to achieve it.
6/   They also try to defend against displaying and having them explored.
7/   These urges should be addressed early on in a curious and explorative manner. This will lessen the anxiety of parent and child.

Therapy with toddlers and parents 147

8/ The focus on unconscious communication clarifies to the child that therapy differs from play-time and to the parent that it differs from child guidance.

9/ Interventions often start by a spontaneous pun or a game building on the therapist's grasp of the situation. In a second step, one may shift to explicitly addressing emotions or conflicts that one thinks motivate a certain behaviour.

10/ The work presupposes the parent's motivation and interest in therapy. Should it be lacking from the start, alternative treatment need be considered. Should it decrease during therapy, any possibility of a negative transference burgeoning – in parent or child – should be explored and addressed.

11/ Concerning which parent should participate, this is decided by who is most involved in the relationship struggles. Triadic therapy could also be relevant, though I have less experience of such a setting that includes simultaneous and deep work with the toddler.

12/ This mode is most suitable when a child's disorder entails a concomitant disturbance in the parent–child relationship. Symptoms amenable to therapy include conduct problems, power-struggle with the parents, petulance, depression, fidgetiness, and hyperactivity.

This chapter is derived, in part, from an article published in *Journal of Child Psychotherapy*: 2015, *41*(1), 3–21. Salomonsson, B. (2015a). Extending the field: Parent-toddler psychotherapy inspired by mother-infant work. Available online: www.tandfonline.com. DOI: 10.1080/0075417X.2015.1005383. (Reprinted by permission of Taylor & Francis Group.)

Part II

Theory
The mind of the baby –
continued investigations

Psychoanalysts have been theorizing about adult patients since the end of the 19th century, child patients since the 1920s, but clinical infants and parents received attention only in the 1960s. In Chapter 10, I discussed why delivery was delayed for the latter group. If we now ask about the relative paucity of *theories* emanating from such work, we could answer that psychodynamic therapy with infants and parents, PTIP, is a rather new clinical field. Yet, it is odd that we have not seen more books and papers. I guess there are several reasons. I have mentioned organizational factors which prevent these families from getting in contact with therapists. Accordingly, we often get in contact with baby worries only indirectly, as when a woman in therapy becomes pregnant. Nowadays, therapy is seldom interrupted due to the birth of the child; the mother brings the baby along and continues her treatment. This may give the therapist insights into how the mother's Unconscious is intertwined with that of the baby (Kite, 2012; Stuart, 2012).

I would vote for more reasons why theoretical studies on PTIP are scant. Analysts feel less familiar with this patient combination and how to conceive of such work. Our theory rests on some major tenets: The mind is rooted in the body, it is inaccessible to us in its entirety, it is built up from infancy and onwards, and it is influenced by our genetic heritage and experiences with our dear ones. This mind becomes palpable to us as the patient addresses us about it directly and, also, via our relationship. The main tool for conveying how we think this mind works, how it causes the patient trouble, and how we can help her with it, is *the word*. PTIP is also a talking cure, but to a lesser extent. First, the baby cannot speak. Second, much communication in PTIP conveys meaning through channels other than words. Non-verbal communication is essential in adult therapy, but even more so in parent–infant work. This might baffle an analyst, not only concerning what to say or do with a baby and a parent, as we discussed in the book's first section. Another challenge is how to formulate theoretically the clinical process and the therapeutic mechanisms. Analysts are trained in conceiving their work with adult patients, for example, "based on what emerged in the transference–countertransference relationship, we worked through his resentment at his mother". It is harder to conceptualize what happened when "the baby went on crying, and the mother was on the verge of a breakdown, I spoke of their resentment, until one day the baby calmed down and smiled at Mum". In the adult case, we may link the resentment to childhood events and observe its parallels in the clinical relationship. In PTIP, such insights are opaquer. Did the baby calm down due to my attention, my relationship with him, mother's relationship with me, or . . .?

Another explanation of the theoretical paucity is that PTIP treatments are onerous for the clinician. Few situations can evoke so much bewilderment, frustration, fright, and pity! I may be working with a dyad in despair and sense the parents' expectations of having their catastrophe rectified. Meanwhile I feel, "What on earth is wrong with this baby? Maybe the paediatrician missed a serious problem? Maybe the parents never wanted her?" This weighs on the counter-transference and all strata in my personality are challenged. Adult parts fear making a professional mistake and harming the family. Infantile parts identify with the baby and feel helpless. On video-recorded sessions I see how my face, voice, and body language express such fleeting yet strong identifications.

Yet, analysts take an increasing interest in PTIP treatments. The reasons are the same as the ones for our avoidance; a growing interest in the non-verbal aspects of therapy and a greater openness to submit ourselves to a profound therapeutic relationship. Also, more analysts have discovered, and decided to deal with, a curious paradox: Freud connected adult psychopathology with what the patients had told him about childhood. Many of his theories relied on intuitions about infantile mental life. Still, few analysts have applied his concepts consistently to troubled babies and their parents. It is as if the advent of infant research and attachment theory has dazzled or scared analysts from applying our theory to infants. Not until I began working with PTIP did I ask myself: "Perhaps what I am witnessing now exemplifies Freudian concepts such as 'infantile sexuality' (Freud, 1905), 'defence' (Freud, 1894), 'the baby's hallucinated satisfaction at the breast' (Freud, 1900), 'transference' (Freud, 1912a), and 'primal repression' (Freud, 1915c)?" I even posed the paradoxical question: "Was Freud a Bionian?" (Salomonsson, 2018), as I explored Freud's intuitions about a baby's emotional life. Later, Klein, Winnicott, and Bion set out to conceptualize similar observations in a more comprehensive and elaborate way. Freud was thus ahead of his time but lacked concepts for grasping dyadic relationships. Furthermore, infant research was non-existent and thus could not investigate any overt expressions of his intuitions about the baby's emotional reactivity.

These deliberations fuelled my efforts at integrating Freudian theory with PTIP experiences. My first book sought to conceive of the communicative levels in these treatments. It emphasized that every human communication contains, simul-taneously, messages at various levels. I also elaborated on Norman's (2001) ideas that babies may be sensitive to the non-lexical impact of analytic communication. Since I could sometimes observe this in the baby's relationship with me, I began wondering if babies, similar to adults, could develop a transference onto me. I also focused on primal repression, Freud's concept for explaining that our earl-iest and excruciating experiences can never be recalled but lie buried in our mind and, though irretrievable, can affect our personality and worldview. The final investigation described infantile sexuality as an essential component of what today is called "mother–infant attachment" and investigated its role in certain breastfeeding problems.

The following chapters pursue the track in the first book. Chapter 15 is based on Klein's observations of her grandson, where she studied in vivo the applicability of her theories on how the infant's inner world developed and was played out with his family. My colleague Joseph Aguayo discovered her notes in an archive in London. We wrote a paper (Aguayo & Salomonsson, 2017), of which the chapter is a modified version. Chapters 16 and 17 address a question that has become compelling as I work with distressed babies: What goes on in their minds when they are screaming helplessly, being totally dependent on the parent and discovering that s/he cannot take it away instantly? The answers must, of course, rely on guesswork and various authors provide different answers. In the beginning, the distressed baby requests help from the parents, but soon her/his mind becomes more autonomous in handling the anxiety. This implies, in my reading, that babies create primitive defences early in life. One example is gaze avoidance vis-à-vis the mother, as discussed in Chapter 18.

Chapter 19 is based on the observation that I often come up with metaphors in PTIP therapies. Together with the slips and parapraxes mentioned in Chapter 18, they indicate a regressive tendency when I am confronted with the dyad's despair. The French analyst Lebovici, introduced in Chapter 10, helped me utilize such phenomena to understand the ailment of mother and baby. The book ends with a chapter in which I discuss how to organize and perform perinatal mental health care. It is true that much research remains to investigate the efficacy and the effectiveness of PTIP. Yet, now that we also have studies indicating some long-term effects of similar treatments (Winberg Salomonsson, Sorjonen & Salomonsson, 2015a, b), we have many arguments for providing easily accessible, high-quality therapy at CHCs and similar units around the globe. The book ends with spelling out my vision.

Chapter 15

A baby's mind
Empirical observation versus speculative theorizing

The literature on parent–infant therapy contains many controversies. We have already discussed some: Which roles do mother and father play in the baby's development? Should a distressed baby be treated with both parents or with the mother? Which observational modes should we use when explicating a baby's experiences? Infant research, psychoanalytic speculations, infant observations, and parent–infant therapy provide various entries. Our choice of observational mode affects our choice of theoretical corpus for conceptualizing the observations – and vice versa. Some view lab research and attachment experiments as the "royal road" to understanding the baby. Others rely on intuitions about the transference/countertransference interplay. This chapter brings in Melanie Klein, who belonged to the latter category, albeit with her important reservations about the role of the countertransference. Her observational notes of her grandson will be summarized and discussed. We will then reflect on which method to use to conceive of what goes on in a baby's mind: empirical observation or speculative theorizing – or both, or some other combination.

Klein has been criticized, by analysts and infant researchers, for being speculative and far-fetched in her conclusions. Stern (1985) oppugns her belief that a baby's anxiety-attacks parallel the adult psychotic's view of the world in terms of good and bad. No, he says, such attacks are "simply promiscuously triggered by expectable, everyday stimulation arising from almost anywhere" (p. 189). While Klein's statements about a baby's *affects* seem credible, she writes their *ideational content* in words which raises the question on what she bases such conclusions. Her style bears the stamp of the controversial discussions (King & Steiner, 1991) that rattled and enlivened the London psychoanalysts during WW2. This gave it a categorical character that maybe obfuscated other more tentative and open-minded traits in her thinking. The question thus remains what she thought goes on in a distressed baby's mind. When Dr Aguayo researched Klein's archive at the Wellcome Institute in London, he found her observations of her grandson that were written without any intention of publication. He invited me to a joint investigation: Did the notes add anything new to Klein's conceptions of infant development? How did they concur with today's experimental and clinical findings on infants? Finally, could they help us clarify an eternal epistemological

154   Part II: Theory

problem: Which method(s) should we use to gain entrance into the internal world of the baby?

Klein (1932) established her child analytic work at the Institute of Psycho-Analysis in London. More than a decade later, mother–infant observation became part of the curriculum at the Tavistock Clinic and the British Institute (Bick, 1964). Prior to such observations, conjectures about early infantile states of mind were deployed in the analyses of young children. We know that Freud posited that adult patients' neuroses were rooted in early childhood. Klein now postulated the importance of *infantile conflict* in disturbances in young children and adult patients alike. She (Klein, 1935) had brought out the "depressive position" as central during infancy and attributed theoretical importance to developmental milestones like weaning. She conceptualized mother's breast as the source of the infant's first pleasure and frustrations. The infant was thus challenged with what she later (Klein, 1975) named its "double relation to the breast". Klein's scientific problem was the paucity of data on what infants were like with their mothers. This contributed to making her theories seem far-fetched and speculative.

In the late 1930s, Klein (1938/39) began to remedy this deficiency by observing three grandchildren. The oldest was a male grandson born on October 17, 1937. She observed his developmental milestones, maturation in play, and interaction with family members. Her observations revolved around his unfolding behaviour, rather than retrospective reconstructions as in her child analyses. The notes contain no data on either breastfeeding or weaning. But in a later publication that drew upon material from the notes, Klein (1952a, p. 113) wrote about this boy (now called "Infant D"): "There had been difficulties in breast-feeding almost from the beginning, since the mother's milk gave out, and when a few weeks old he was entirely changed over to bottle-feeding."

From 1935 to1939, Klein supervised Winnicott, who had recently become a psychoanalyst at the British Society. An enthusiast for her child analytic technique from 1935 to 1945, he followed her theories of the depressive position and manic defences. Probably, he shared with her his vast paediatric experiences. As he learned analytic play technique, Klein learned about the need to base observationally what in fact were her theoretical conjectures about infant mental life. This reciprocal influence is evident in Winnicott's paper (1941) *The observation of infants in a set situation.* He drew upon Klein's postulations about the early origins of a maternally driven super-ego. He observed dyads in consultations where he was paediatrician. Here, at last, one could get an empirical basis for Klein's hypotheses. He sat behind his desk, with the baby in mother's lap and a spatula on the desk. He observed how s/he related to this new object. Did he approach and handle it, or was s/he shy and hesitant about it, turning to his/her mother for approval? He linked the babies' "hesitation anxiety" to early super-ego manifestations, which could be self-generated or a reaction to parental disapproval (Aguayo, 2002). He concluded, like Klein, that babies could be ridden by primitive guilt, expecting mother as disapproving. He thus supported her idea that they are "minded".

Klein's observations

Klein's interest grew and was stimulated by Winnicott's empirical research, which could test out her hypotheses about infant mental life. Her youngest patient was Rita, 2¾ years old (Klein, 1932). She would thus have been interested in observing babies and toddlers directly to substantiate her theories. The option of observing her grandson must have ignited her passionate interest. We will see how far she capitalized on this precious situation, and what may have jeopardized her efforts. Her notes mirror a loving grandmother who yet retains an analytic eye on the boy, his father who is Klein's youngest son, and his mother. While metapsychological terms are scarce, it contains warm and evocative details of everyday life and emotions like love, longing, rage, jealousy, dishonesty, etc. Melanie's grandmotherly fondness does not detain her from conceiving of his internal world objectively and soberly. The style differs from her publications, where theoretical concepts are sometimes stacked with little room for the reader to reflect and take a personal stand.

Affects and fantasy content

The material from the boy's first four months is presented less systematically than the ensuing observations. It does not cover the boy's assumed fantasy content but centres round his behaviour and affects. He recognizes faces at 6 weeks old and looks for certain people at 9 weeks old. Affects are noted from the age of 3 months; he has some toys which he gets angry with, takes pleasure in, and uses to comfort himself. Klein (1938/39) lists his facial affective expressions at 3 months old, though only in retrospect: "distress, contentment, laughter, anger" (p. 8). Some notes foreshadow Winnicott's (1953) notion of the transitional object: When the 4-month-old is going to sleep, "he often cries . . . it seems that the toy replaces the company and gives him comfort" (Klein, 1938/39, p. 4). At 5 months old, she sees other behaviours that reduce his frustration: scratching, caressing mother, and tapping people. At 6 months old, he shows "the first signs of love" towards Teddy Bear.

Why is Klein rather silent on affects and fantasies during the boy's first half year? One would consider three reasons that stem from her theoretical development, her personal involvement with the boy, and the setting of these observations. A decade later, she published *Notes on some schizoid mechanisms* (Klein, 1946), which delineated the infant's fantasy life from birth onwards. She focused on that period which she was silent about concerning the boy, that is, when paranoid-schizoid anxieties were dominant. When she observed him, this concept was not born, whereas Winnicott (1941) had begun theorizing on this period earlier. Today, we can utilize Klein's 1946 concepts and speculate that the 3-month-old boy's anger with the toy resulted from projective identifications. He experienced it as replete with his anger and bad self, and harbouring vengeful wishes towards him. His bedtime crying at 4 months old might reflect schizo-paranoid anxieties due to such attacks on the internal objects, with an ensuing sense of desertion.

156 Part II: Theory

Second, Klein's personal involvement might also explain the silence on her grandson's earliest fantasies. The portrait of her son, the boy's father, is rather vague whereas one senses her sometime vexation with mother's low-keyed mood and tendency to pamper the boy. One discerns a grandmother who has views about the boy's upbringing but avoids meddling with the family relations. His mother is influenced by her mother-in-law's thinking, as when she says her son seems to work out aggression on his toys. Despite her impact in the family, she can hardly have felt that she had the parents' unambiguous or unreserved mandate to observe their son. A present-day author (Rustin, 2014) suggests that an infant observer should offer the family a "friendly, non-intrusive, interested presence", while being "aware of the thoughts and feelings around her without being swayed by them into intervening" (p. 99). This is taxing because an observer learns, "sometimes in shocking and surprising ways" (p. 100), about her unconscious preconceptions and memories of her own family life. Such factors must have impacted even more on Klein observing her grandson, for whom she also felt some concern. Thus, the few data on breastfeeding might reflect a wish not to disturb the intimacy of a feeding situation that was difficult.

Third, various intricacies were involved in the relationships among family members and patient–analyst pairs. The boy's father was in analysis with Winnicott, her supervisee and colleague, with whom she was developing theories about infant mental life. His critique (Winnicott, 1962c) of her theories appeared only later. The observations were thus written by, and dealt with, people who were entangled with one another in multifarious ways. This must have constricted Klein's freedom of thought and ability to observe objectively. Finally, she had little experience in parent–infant observation and was unaccustomed to deal with infants clinically. Thus, in the beginning of her grandson's life, Klein was a cautious observer, both regarding her behaviour and her conclusions.

Separation anxiety, loss, and destructiveness

When the boy is somewhat older, Klein begins to submit more clearly her notions about his fantasy world. One theme is *separation*. Eighteen months old, he is left by the parents for an Easter vacation journey. He becomes distressed, falls and cries, and eats voraciously. Klein interprets that he is preoccupied with if it is his fault that the parents are gone, if he may take out his anger on the nurse, if she can put up with it or if he is a bad boy who deserves to feel guilty. In her view, separation anxiety is less caused by the loss per se than by his destructive fantasies. Shortly after the vacation trip, the imminent war forces the family to be evacuated from London. This aggravates the separation pain since the 1½-year-old boy's father is often away and mother is working as well.

In one moving observation the boy has been told, around the time of the parent's vacation, that he must not pick flowers. Standing with his grandmother at a flower-bed, he obeys and just scratches some earth into the water. The landlady witnesses the scene and lauds the good boy. She picks some flowers and hands them to him.

A baby's mind: observation vs speculation   157

Horrified, he avoids touching them and wants to put them back into the earth. Another time, his uncle is playing with him. The boy scratches him and the uncle pretends to cry, whereupon he cries inconsolably. To Klein, the incidents reflect how easily guilt is awakened. Every mishap is his fault; a crying uncle, a flower being picked, and a broken toy.

Klein's interpretations imply that separation reactions are not merely driven by the child's loss and anguish at the parents' coming and going. Today, a discussant might claim that the boy reacted because his attachment relationships were ruptured. Klein would likely contend that to fully understand his ailment we must include his destructive wishes and ensuing guilt. The observations do reveal that he misses his parents, especially the father, but Klein guesses he also wishes to injure them. This follows a theme in *Notes on some schizoid mechanisms* (Klein, 1946). The destructive and hated part of the self is split off and projected to the loved object. The child fears this endangers the object and the sequence gives rise to guilt (p. 12). She concludes this after the boy plays with some flower pots. To Klein the big pot, which he puts on top of the others, represents the father. When some pots get broken, she sees it as a wish to injure him. The example shows Klein's acuity in intuiting the boy's affects, though her claims about their *ideational* content exemplify a habit of attributing to a child the kind of fantasies that her theory suggests he must have. Thus, there is a problem with validating her speculations, which will be tackled in the theoretical discussion.

Klein assumes her grandson has an advanced knowledge about intercourse and reproduction. He puts a little table on top of the other and places them side by side with the top of one overlapping the other. Klein sees a wish to keep the parents together; first, the father on top of the mother as in intercourse, then the two arm in arm. In another case, a lady wants to dissuade him from throwing stones at people on the beach. She shows him "teeny weeny stones". He replies, "teeny weeny babies" and throws them in the sea. To Klein, this is an intercourse scene with the sea as mother, big stones as father, and small stones as the babies. To us, her interpretations of ideational content seem a bit like ready-mades. It is not that we demand "exact data" for validation, which would merely result in a "pseudo-scientific approach, because the workings of the unconscious mind, and the response of the psycho-analyst to them, cannot be submitted to measurement nor classified into rigid categories" (Klein, 1961, p. 12). What we do need is a reference to empirical material gleaned from analytic work and reported so we can follow up how interpretations are received. Such a project was, however, unachievable given the framework of Klein's observations.

The boy's separation anxiety recedes, which Klein attributes to the advent of sphincter control, an increasing mastery of language, and an ability to recruit his parents as good objects. When he is about 1½ years old, he accepts the potty. Klein connects this with her observation that he has begun to show less concern, unhappiness, and guilt about broken things. Defecating in the potty has become a way of releasing anger *and* receiving praise. This lessens his guilt of having damaged toys and things and, at bottom, the parental objects. Also, his increasing

158   Part II: Theory

language mastery helps him tackle the separation anxiety. Only 18 months old, he went into a wordless mix of anxiety, sadness, and anger when the parents parted for Easter. Eight months later, he repeats when father is leaving for London, "Daddy Lunnon". Like a magic formula, these words diminish his anxiety.

Finally, as for the boy's recruitment of his loved ones as good objects, the document abounds with such descriptions. If one may doubt Klein's speculations about his sexual fantasies, one can hardly question her descriptions of his insistent efforts at bringing his parents together in various games. But as always, love is fraught with ambivalence. After Christmas, the father must return to London. His son, 2 years old, misses him badly which, according to Klein, is due both to love and guilt. He wants to be carried around, trips and falls, becomes passive, and cries at bedtime. His mother acknowledges to Klein that she is depressed due to her husband's absence and that this has had a bad effect on him. Mother said he "cried in such a heartbreaking way, that she took him into her bed at night" (Klein, 1938/39, p. 95b). This brings up the question of how, as reported in Klein's notes, external and internal objects impact on each other. Further on, it will lead us to discuss the relation between empirical observation and psychoanalytic models of infant psychology.

Observations of family interactions and speculations on their impact on the baby

At the beginning of 1940 when the boy is past 2 years old, his mother relates to Klein that her depressive mood, which is linked to missing her husband, influences him negatively. Klein mentions mother's problems with "accepting his difficulties" and a "fear which she had when he was a baby and cried more, that she spoils him through giving in . . . her less patient attitude worries him and increases his difficulties" (Klein, 1938/39, p. 99–100). This is a rare report on how family interactions impact on him. It shows her view that "actual conflicts between parents or people who play an important part in the child's life (such as nurse, maid, or teacher) cause much anxiety in children at any age" (Klein, 1961, p. 52). Consequently, we need to analyse "the interaction of internal and external situations" (Op. cit., p. 105). We will soon investigate to what extent her publications contain such analyses.

Klein's grandson in child analysis a decade later

Klein's observations offer a unique opportunity for a follow-up in his latency period. A paper by Milner (1952) refers to an analysis with a boy aged 11. According to her biographer (Letley, 2014, p. 47), this boy was Klein's grandson and she supervised Milner on this case. The paper discusses symbolism, but we wish to connect its vignettes with Klein's observations and draw conclusions about his latency problems. He was referred due to a loss of talent for school work,

A baby's mind: observation vs speculation 159

which he earlier had liked a lot. His play with Milner contains warfare and bombing between two villages. At first, she interprets them à la Klein; school work implies entering mother's body, which on the one hand is demanded by "the schoolmaster-father figure but [on the other hand is] forbidden under threat of castration by the sexual rival father" (Milner, 1952, p. 186). Milner conceives of symbolism as a defence, "because the school had become the symbol of the forbidden mother's body this was then a bar to progress" (idem). This is a classical Kleinian interpretation (Klein, 1930).

But, Milner also intuits that the boy has "difficulties in establishing the relation to external reality as such" (1952, p. 186). School work implies suffering the orders of an external world that impose on him to learn what each symbol should symbolize. She links his sense of "the unmitigated not-me-ness of his school life" (p. 187) to the agonies of his infancy: father's recruitment to war, the birth of a younger brother, and the loss of a beloved rabbit toy. The sense of union, to which a little child is entitled, was thus disrupted. As a result, "subjective unreality and objective reality" could not fuse harmoniously and the boy was unable to "allow illusions about what he is seeing to occur" (p. 190). Milner relates this to his infantile history, inspired by a poem that he brings to a session: *The Parrot* written in 1839 by Thomas Campbell (in: Ingpen, 1903). A beautiful bird must bid adieu to his homeland Spain and arrives in a "heathery land and misty sky". His wings grow grey and his voice turns silent, until one day a Spaniard arrives and addresses him in Spanish. "The bird in Spanish speech replied / Flapped joyously around the cage / Dropped down and died."

Milner links the boy's fascination with the poem with the parents' reports about feeding difficulties in infancy. His mother had too little milk, and the nurse did not give supplementary food in time, so he was in great distress – just as when he, years later, must wait for an analytic session with Milner. This "environmental thwarting in the feeding situation" had confronted him with a "separate identity too soon or too continually" and the illusion of union was experienced as "catastrophic chaos rather than cosmic bliss" (p. 192). Milner's emphasis of the environmental influence is in line with Winnicott (1953) and Bowlby (1969). They emphasized the importance of a total environmental provision and a secure attachment. To Milner, a healthy symbolic capacity can only develop if the child tolerates the difference of one- and two-ness. For this to come about, the environment must allow the child "a recurrent partial return to the feeling of being one . . . by . . . providing a framed space and time and a pliable medium" (Milner, 1952, p. 192). Therefore, it is essential to study whether the environment might have facilitated or interfered with a child's critical experience of fusion.

Milner assures his mother was "very good" (p. 187) and that he had "in general a very good home and been much loved" (p. 191). Like in our cautionary notes on Klein's familial involvement with the boy, we bring out Milner's bias. She was supervised by Klein, whose grandson she was now treating and whose son, the boy's father, had been analysed by Milner's analyst Winnicott, who had been supervised by Klein. Like Klein, she was in a vulnerable position to maintain a

160   Part II: Theory

sober analytic stance. As outsiders two generations later, we are less biased. Milner seems to downplay a probable non-facilitating aspect of her young patient's environment; his mother might have been depressed at times during his infancy. She does mention his early feeding problems but seems to underestimate that the boy might have felt he did *not* have a good enough mother and that he felt unloved at times.

Some passages in both texts point to distress in the mother–child relationship, such as the mother's report to Klein that her depression due to her husband's absence affected her son negatively. Also, Klein reported on the mother's impatience towards her baby's crying and a fear that she would spoil him through giving in. Finally, the parents reported to Milner on their son's initial feeding difficulties. To us, they suggest that the mother–infant and –toddler relationships were not all sunny. Thus, one can read *The Parrot* as a parable of a baby's response to such discord between mother and child. The bird lives in a primeval mother-tongue paradise but becomes caged and must leave. He arrives in a faraway and forbidding land where he wanes into silence. The poem might have caught the boy's imagination because unconsciously, it reminded him of an infantile distressful relationship with the mother. One might naively assume that when the Spaniard addresses the bird in his mother-tongue, he would rejoice and become well again. But it is too late, the shock is unbearable, or he is struck by painful recollections of a vanished Eden. Perhaps this stanza illustrates the breakdown in the boy's symbolization. School has demanded, as it does of every child, that he abandon his "mother-tongue"; to forgo the erudition he has acquired earlier and learn new knowledge. But the boy cannot give up yearning for paradise lost and school becomes infernal. Milner mentions this "environmental thwarting in the feeding situation" but seems to shy away from giving it full weight.

Mother–infant interaction: its status in Klein's theory

One problem with Klein's suggested ideations beneath her grandson's affects and fantasies is, as said, her habit of attributing to a child ideas that her theory suggests he must have. There is a validation problem with how to take up a position on theories about infantile mental life that are based on reconstructions of material from older patients. For similar reasons, one could certainly question our linking the school boy's problems with a hypothesized mother–infant relationship disturbance; that it is based on lofty speculations. These issues impose a detour.

We have quoted Klein (1961) that conflicts between adults can cause the child anxiety. This being said, her main conceptualizations of pathology focused on what went on in the child's "interior", that is, how he transformed his experiences internally. In contrast, descriptions of how family interactions impact on internal objects are brief; food problems may arise due to "adverse feeding conditions, whereas difficulties in sucking can sometimes be mitigated by the mother's love and patience" (Klein, 1952a, p. 96). In a footnote, she adds that "the impact of the

A baby's mind: observation vs speculation 161

environment is of major importance *at every stage* of the child's development" (idem). Similarly, a child's "monstrous and phantastic images of his parents" (Klein, 1933, p. 250) result from projections of aggressive instinct onto the parents and ensuing vengeful attacks, whereas reality perceptions are exiled to a footnote: "The infant has, incidentally, some real grounds for fearing its mother, since it becomes growingly aware that she has the power to grant or withhold the gratification of its needs" (idem). We are not told how a mother exerts such power. To speculate, a mother may unconsciously withhold gratification, to which the infant can react with bewilderment, depression, rage, etc., to which the mother might reciprocate with vengefulness and narcissistic hurt. If such a negative circle is cemented, we are in the domain of mother–infant relationship disorders – but that concept goes beyond classical Kleinian theory.

Klein does not deny that a mother's personality can influence the baby. Her love and understanding is his "greatest stand-by in overcoming states of disintegration and anxieties of a psychotic nature" (Klein, 1946, p. 10). A decade earlier (Klein, 1937) she described the unconscious roots of maternity in terms of reparation and guilt, love, hate, and emphasized a mother's relationship with her own mother. Some mothers exploit "the relationship with the baby for the gratification of their own desires" (p. 318). Others put themselves in the child's place, they look at the situation from his point of view and use their wisdom "in guiding the child in the most helpful way" (p. 319). Yet, we are not told how this is played out in the mother–infant interaction.

An essential question is why Klein played down the mother's impact and provided no model of how it works on the baby. Winnicott (1962c) wrote that she "claimed to have paid full attention to the environmental factor, but it is my opinion that she was temperamentally incapable of this" (p. 177). An alternative explanation of Klein's side-stepping of the environmental factor (Van Buren, 1993) is that she did not have a theory to cover *the interactions between external objects and how they impact on the participants' internal worlds*. It would need to be anchored, not only in reconstructions that evolve in psychoanalytic treatments with verbal children or adults, but *also* in empirically observed mother–baby interactions. True, observations are not identical to hermeneutical interpretations of the internal world (Green, 2000), and we agree that analysis does not deal with "exact data" (Klein, 1961, p. 12). Yet, when she observed the baby she must have thought they added to her analytic understanding, a point we certainly agree with.

Bowlby (1958) requested empirical data to understand infant mental life. He was critical of the "discrepancy between formulations springing direct from empirical observations and those made in the course of abstract discussion", so common among analysts with "first-hand experience of infancy" (p. 354), among which he mentioned Klein. After his supervision with her in the late 1930s, his critique of her theory became adamant due to its "lack of scientific rigour" and "emphasis on the role of unconscious phantasy in the aetiology of neurotic and psychotic symptoms at the expense of environmental factors, especially in relation to clinical issues of separation and loss" (Renn, 2010, p. 146). This gave birth to

162   Part II: Theory

attachment theory and a research tradition based on empirical observations. Analysts have taken different positions on it, from critical (Zepf, 2006) to positive (Fonagy, 2001). Seligman (1999) is one analyst who suggests we rely more on the data of infant observation. He suggests this need not yield simplistic explanations if we recall that "the processes by which 'actual' events become internalized as stable elements of the psyche remain very complex" (p. 133). *Yet, to us the risk of reductionism is equal whether conclusions rely on observations or on reconstructive speculations. Our suggestion of diminishing – but not annihilating – this risk is, as will be argued in the following, to combine various empirical methods.*

Gaps in the jigsaw puzzle

If we want to build an analytic theory of the infant's internal world and how it builds up in interaction with the primary objects, we must grapple with the problem just outlined: the reductionism in *any* method we rely on, be it observations or reconstructive speculations. To this list of "myopic" methods we should add infant observation, PTIP, and analyses with children and adults. The last method has generated reconstructions for intuiting infantile experience and deriving metapsychology. Yet, there is a distance between empirical data (let's say, a patient's overt separation anxiety) and reconstruction (linking this fear with abandonment during infancy). Infant research yields sophisticated data from behavioural observations. But it remains mute on the Unconscious of infant or parent which, as Green (2000) claims, can only be studied by someone – the analyst – who involves his Unconscious to intuit that of the other. Are we then trapped between either leaning on infant research – empirically exact but superficial in its coverage of internal experience – or on psychoanalytic reconstructions that are imaginative but devoid of empirical data of actual infants? Green states that infant researchers study only *observable behaviour*. Stern (2000) refutes this. He proceeds from infant research and ventures beyond observable behaviour and asserts what goes on in the baby's internal life.

Seligman (1999, 2006) seeks to integrate research findings and Kleinian theory. The former teach us that infant and parent are continuously "monitoring, influencing, and determining each other's behavior and meaning" (1999, p. 133). He recommends we start in this tradition by observing details of such interactions and then return to the Kleinian concepts, "rather than starting from the concepts and trying to push the observations into them" (p. 132). He retains the concept of instinct, which he claims can be reached via *direct observation of interactions* "at the most basic psychophysical levels: affects; kinesthetic, proprioceptive, and other bodily experiences" (p. 144). But "instinct", as Freud used the term (1915a) – we are using this mis-translation of *Trieb* (drive) whenever a cited author does so – is a concept "on the frontier between the mental and the somatic, as the psychical representative of the stimuli originating from within the organism and reaching the mind" (p. 122). One *cannot* observe an instinct/drive but only interpret it with an instrument that also covers the analyst's instinctual life and

A baby's mind: observation vs speculation 163

countertransference. To us, Seligman's effort at grounding a psychoanalytic theory on an empiricist platform seems as little – or as much – credible as one relying on a hermeneutics built merely on the interpreter's subjective experiences.

One easily finds other examples of researchers and analysts who unwarily traverse the gap between observation and experience. Beebe and Lachmann (2002, 2014) report on elegant experiments (Meltzoff & Moore, 1997) demonstrating the young infant's imitations of, for example, tongue protrusion. These observations of *behaviour* are incontrovertible but do not *prove* that "the infant's perception of these correspondences provides the infant with a fundamental relatedness between self and other" (Beebe & Lachmann, 2014, p. 26). Similarly, we caution against construing *mind* as "expectancies of procedurally organized action sequences" (idem) that spring from such instances of imitation. We do believe that infants have minds and that parent–infant therapy must proceed from this assumption. But, we know we speculate when we deduce from a baby's behaviour that s/he is sad, distressed, or annoyed, and we are invariably prepared to develop or dismantle our conjectures. Thus, behavioural research cannot prove what the baby's drive or internal world look like. Indeed, experiences cannot be observed except by oneself – but they can be suggested by a mother to her baby, or an analyst to the patient: "Perhaps you feel sad now". Or, they can be noted in a research protocol: "Baby shows signs of sadness". Both comments reflect *assumptions*, not *empirical facts*, about the other's internal world. Thus, a researcher's statements about the infant's internal life are as easy to refute as Klein's proclamations about innate drive conflicts in the baby.

Must we then give up anchoring analytic theories of the infant's internal world in empirical observations? We think not, provided one combines methods. Objective observation belongs to the tasks of infant researchers. They have discovered, with astounding acuity, signs of emotions and cognitions in babies that were unknown until a few decades ago; their emotional reactivity (Tronick, Als, Adamson, Wise, & Brazelton, 1978), participation in proto-conversational communication (Aitken & Trevarthen, 1997), imitation tendency (Meltzoff & Moore, 1997), sensitivity to mother's sensual attributes (Delaunay-El Allam, Soussignan, Patris, Marlier, & Schaal, 2010; DeCasper & Fifer, 1980) and her depression (Field, 2010).

Psychoanalytic therapists can contribute via infant observation and PTIP. The former yields assumptions about "the states of mind and feeling which permeate and shape the relationships of babies and their caregivers, and which also give rise to experiences 'in feeling' in observers and others within the infant's environment" (Rustin, 2006, p. 39). Yet, infant observation is neither a *via regia* to the baby's internal world nor an instrument for systematic research, but "an adjunct to the teaching of psycho-analysis and child therapy" (Bick, 1964, p. 558). PTIP therapists have integrated clinical observations, infant research, and theoretical development. Their reports indicate that a parent's distress can impact negatively on the baby, and that the baby takes part in developing the relationship disorder. Still they rely heavily, as do therapists working with adults, on countertransference, which we know is a subjective and ambiguous method of confirmation.

Freud used his intuitions about the baby's mental life as pieces in a jigsaw puzzle, which he sought to bring together into a coherent theory. Other analysts added their experiences with adults and children to enlarge theory and bring the pieces closer together. Then infant research, infant observation, and PTIP arrived to study real babies. If all these modes today have made the jigsaw pieces come closer and the picture become more complete, the gaps between them are still visible and will always remain, due to the nature of our study object; the subjective experiences of an infant interacting with the primary objects.

This chapter is derived, in part, from an article published in *Psychoanalytic Quarterly*: 2017, *86*(2), 383–408. Aguayo, J., & Salomonsson, B. The study and treatment of mothers and infants, then and now: Melanie Klein's 'Notes on Baby' (1938/39) in a contemporary psychoanalytic context. (Reprinted by permission from Wiley.)

Chapter 16

Naming the nameless

On anxiety in babies – I: Freud

The life of Freddie Mercury, singer and composer in Queen, was a mix of fame, self-destruction, warmth, and friendship. Towards the end of his life, he and Brian May wrote the song "Mother Love". The singer compares the love he is yearning for now to a mother's love for her child. The record ends with two sound clips: a cheering crowd at a rock concert and a babbling baby. He seems to say that the admiration of millions of fans cannot replace what he wants – to retrieve in adult life the love of mother and baby. Such idealizations of the infant–mother relationship are not infrequent and can be disastrous when they function as an unconscious template of adult love. One evident reason is that adults are not babies, and the demands and joys in marriage are not the same as the ones in infancy. Another reason is that such idealizations aim to substitute the excruciating feelings of a panicking baby with the idyllic idea of adult romance. We find another example in Tristan, the lover in Wagner's opera *Tristan und Isolde*, who was orphaned as a baby (Salomonsson, 2014a).

The following two chapters will look at what we guess happens in the baby's mind when s/he fails to encounter "sweet mother love". The topic may seem abstruse and speculative. I agree but cannot stop thinking about what goes on in a baby's mind. Encounters with clinical babies have made me wonder what they experience when grunting, flailing, screaming, and crying. To answer I, indeed all of us, need to observe the baby, ask the mother, and guess. I will try to transgress those "limitations in our ability to identify with the baby" (Meltzer & Harris-Williams, 1988, p. 16) that make us conclude that he has no mental life. Our imaginations about the emotions and representations beneath a baby's behaviour "cannot aspire to any status other than that of being credible". Yet, they are "at least as credible as such unimaginative formulations as 'constitution', 'heredity', or 'just like his father was as a baby'" (Op. cit., p. 18), those everyday expressions we use about babies. The chapters will draw together such intuitions into a psycho-analytic theory of infant distress. One author to be cited, Bion (1962a), labelled it "nameless dread". My aim is to ascribe terms, or names, to this dread. Thence the title of the two chapters: *naming the nameless*. I will first submit vignettes of babies and then review analytic models of infant anxiety and apply them to these babies.

Vignettes

1/ A baby on YouTube

YouTube has a video of a 4-week-old girl with colic, www.youtube.com/watch?v=_AUtYTaYMrE. The mother holds the screaming girl in her lap while trying to comfort her. As she moves the girl closer, she meets mother's eyes briefly and calms down. After a second she starts screaming again. The girl's despair, the mother's helplessness, and the father's presence behind the camera make the scene heart-breaking. The parents write that "the first few months of her life [was a] damaging, life-altering, heart-breaking experience. There was absolutely nothing we could do to soothe her." I recommend the video to induce a feel for infant distress as I now move on to research interviews and therapy cases.

2/ Nancy and her son Brent, 4 weeks old

This example is from our RCT. Nancy, 35 years old, says that Johnny, 2½ years old, never posed any problems, but with 1-month-old Brent she worried from the start. "He didn't want to come out. Delivery was induced at week 41½." It went well,

> but he slept 23 hours per day! Awake, he kept looking at us like 'What's the point, why did you do this to me?' He got a respiratory infection and we were hospitalized from day 10 to 14. Then Johnny, our eldest, got sick while my husband resumed work. We did want Brent, but I had no time to adjust . . . If delivery hadn't been induced he wouldn't have had the infection! . . . Life was easier with one child. I can't feel he's *my* baby. I nearly forgot him in the pram in town.

Brent has difficulties coming to rest and only falls asleep in Nancy's arm, "because he's not feeling welcome".

Their interaction video is like a still-life. Brent is lying in her arms, squirming, grunting, and looking at the ceiling. She looks tender, concerned, bewildered, and tearful. She tries to comprehend why the boy squirms, then closes her eyes, sighs, and offers him the breast. As I look at the video, an image enters my mind: I am standing by my car at a gas station and filling up the tank while absent-mindedly staring in the distance.

The analyst explained to me in an interview: "Brent was really ill, struggling for his life while giving Nancy very little contact". She attributes mother's ambivalence to Brent's brittle state rather than to any unconscious resentment. The analyst was afraid Brent might die: "He couldn't understand why he should go on living. Nancy hadn't seduced him into life. He often had a frown on his forehead."

3/ Mae crying

This case is from Chapter 9 – the therapy session when Debbie was angry with her mother, her sister-in-law, me, and 1-month-old Mae. Mae's distress mounted in parallel to mother's annoyed comments and bumping efforts at consoling her. During the diaper change, Mae stopped crying and looked at me. I told her, "Your mum is angry with everybody today, with you too, and that scares her. It scares you, too, and you cry. Both of you are in distress." As I told Mae this, she listened, calmed down a bit, and then resumed crying. After the session, the family went to the ER to be told that Mae probably had gases.

4/ A whining girl: Beatrice and her 5-month-old daughter Fran

Like case 2, Beatrice and Fran participated in the RCT. When I meet the girl, her face seems old and concerned. Since Fran's second week, Beatrice's "old depression" has come back with anxiety, fears of harming Fran, a sense of unreality, anhedonia, discontent with her husband, and helplessness. She cannot be alone with the girl and asks Grandma to come over. "I wanna lie down and let the girl be on her own." Beatrice gave up breastfeeding after seven weeks. Fran is calm, sometimes fingering a toy or looking at me but on the video, she starts whining and her mother seems offended. Fran picks up a ball and Mum responds, but her rapid movements prevent Fran from joining in. "Nothing's good enough for you, eh? Come on, li'l whiner!" As Mum's sensitivity and tolerance diminish further, the girl whines more. "Starting to rub your eyes, eh? Getting tired of this? What are you talking about? I'll put you in the pram, you slept too little today." I ask the mother to describe her baby. "Fran's a very secure baby, no problems in seeing other people." As we continue, Fran is screaming. "When she doesn't have it her way, she sure can speak out, screaming because her food isn't coming quickly enough." She does not connect Fran's state to the previous play situation on the video.

All these babies are distressed. What goes on in their minds? The answer depends on which conceptual model we apply. Psychoanalytic theory is not one homogenous block but a set of complementary bricks with some common basic assumptions. My plan is to review those "bricks" that have focused most cogently on the infant's internal world.

Freud: the baby as egg and chick

We have already learnt that babies abound in Freud's metapsychology, but it is not clear how he views their anxiety. First, he did not submit systematic baby observations. Second, his formulations of drive theory are hard to translate into

168 Part II: Theory

what the baby is experiencing. Third, he does not portray how the child interacts with the object, that is, the person towards whom s/he directs the drives. This makes it difficult to translate his metapsychological ideas into clinical thinking. Yet, I will research if today's PTIP work can be integrated with classical theory, since it emphasizes one aspect of psychic life often neglected by other theories: *the unconscious experience*.

Freud shifts between two visions of early mental life. I call them *the egg* and *the chick*. In the egg metaphor the baby lives in a world of his own, shut off from the environment. In contrast, the chick simile signifies that he wants nourishment *and* an object to invest with his drives. To illustrate the egg metaphor, Freud suggests that the infant satisfies her "nutritional requirements autistically" (1911, p. 219), as if she were an unhatched bird embryo in an egg. The metaphor relates to narcissism (Freud, 1914), the "original libidinal cathexis of the ego, from which some is later given off to objects", like an amoeba sending out its "pseudophodia" (p. 75). Primary narcissism (Freud, 1914, 1923, 1938) implies that the newborn is uninterested in or ignorant about the external world. In quantitative terms, he has not deployed libidinal cathexis onto it.

Infant researchers (Stern, 1985) and psychoanalysts (Balint, 1952; Lichtenberg, 1983) criticize the notion of primary narcissism. They argue that the newborn has a primary relatedness or intersubjectivity and "is organized as a psychological subject at birth – one who is seeking to enter into regulated engagements with subjective processes in other human beings" (Aitken & Trevarthen, 1997, p. 654). To them, once the baby is born, there is no "egg". Green (1975) notes that Freud defined narcissism inconsistently. In some situations, the baby seeks "to come as close as possible to the zero degree of excitation" (p. 15). This would correspond to primary narcissism. Infant researchers investigate other situations when the baby screams, recalls, smiles at or avoids the mother, and reacts to her coming and going. Green (1995a) notes that "at the beginning of life the encounters between the baby and its object take place in a very limited period of time of the day" (p. 876). Mostly, "the baby is by himself, sleeping, resting, or crying, shouting, in a world which one has every right to call narcissistic" (idem). He alternatively reaches for the mother like a peeping chick – or retreats into primary narcissism like an unhatched bird inside the egg.

Case 2, Brent, illustrates what may happen when an illness interrupts the everyday motions between primary narcissism and object relating. Though Freud's quantitative terminology may clarify how libidinal cathexes are deployed, it does not illuminate Brent's *experiences*. The interview with his mother Nancy shows her fantasies, which spring from an "unconscious oneness that is based on the unconscious of the mother and of the child being in so close relation to each other" (Klein, 1959, p. 248). To intuit Brent's experiences, we must not brush off Nancy's ideas as mere projections. We will return to this topic but merely note that when she says, "Brent didn't want to come out", she assumes he had preferred to remain inside the "egg". The reasons for her notion will become clearer later. Thus, though Freud's terms give a metapsychological and metaphoric vision of Brent's distress, we still need to grasp his *representations* and *feelings*.

Quantitative vs qualitative perspectives

When a baby "egg" aims at zero excitation, his psyche follows the *principle of constancy*. But the baby "chick" also harbours impulses, which originate "in the cells of the body and give rise to the major needs: hunger, respiration, sexuality" (Freud, 1895/1950, p. 297). For them, the *pleasure principle* is the master. The mind harbours an *antagonism* between the two, or rather, "between a state of psychic rest equivalent to a total discharge of external stimuli [the principle of constancy], and forces represented by endogenous stimuli that will disturb this rest and provoke a process of complexification [the pleasure principle]" (Balestriere, 2003, p. 42). Had the baby only to handle *external* stimuli he could just fend them off, reach zero level and satisfaction, and return to the narcissism "in the egg". But strivings for satisfaction also come from *inside*, from the drives. Their aim is to reach out towards objects to get satisfaction.

Freud intimates that the drives are influenced by the child's interactions with the parents. But his description is vague since he wavers between the egg and the chick metaphors. He suggests the distressed baby is screaming for "extraneous help" from an "experienced person" (Freud, 1895/1950, p. 318). Mother hears it, comes to his aid, and he feels better. But which mother is Freud talking about? Is she an agent of the principle of constancy trying to annul the baby's excitation? Or is she working for the pleasure principle, offering herself as an object for fantasies stimulated by the baby's drives? The answer is both – with a temporal precedence of the principle of constancy.

Balestriere seeks to solve the confusion between the principles of pleasure and constancy by observing that "satisfaction" is an oblique translation of Freud's term *Befriedigung*. Together, they cover the two components of an experience of contentment: the quantitative and the qualitative. "Satisfaction" contains the Latin "*satis*" or "enough". A certain amount is needed to achieve contentment: An infant is breastfed, looks drowsy and mother says, "He's had enough, he wants to sleep". She may be right. In this interpretation, she provided milk and worked according to the principle of constancy. The other trajectory is indicated by *Befriedigung*, related to *Friede* or peace. This meaning adds detention and contentment born in an interpersonal relationship. In this reading, the baby found *Friede* at his good-enough mother (Winnicott, 1971b) providing "active adaption" and granting him her "easy and unresented preoccupation" (p. 10). In Wordsworth's (1850) words:

> . . . blest the Babe
> Nursed in his Mother's arms, who sinks to sleep
> Rocked on his Mother's breast; who with his soul
> Drinks in the feelings of his Mother's eye!
> For him, in one dear Presence, there exists
> A virtue which irradiates and exalts
> Objects through widest intercourse of sense
>
> (loc. 67777)

170   Part II: Theory

This baby sinks to sleep, so perhaps zero excitation was achieved. But his *soul* also "drinks in the feelings of his Mother's eye". Through an "intercourse of sense" she exalts various objects and helps him towards contentment and curiosity about the world. The two are also engaged, the poet says later, in an "intercourse of touch" and "mute dialogues with my Mother's heart" (loc. 67797). He relates this to the infant's discovery of the world: "What happiness to live / when every hour brings palpable access / of knowledge, when all knowledge is delight / and sorrow is not there!" (idem).

Yet, our focus is not the baby's happy moments but those that brim with sorrow and panic. Freud's principles of constancy and pleasure yield different conceptions of such distress. Were we to rely on the former, anything above zero excitation would amount to dissatisfaction. However, Freud (1895/1950) adds a qualitative explanation of the baby's *Befriedigungserlebnis*. The mother is "simultaneously the [child's] first satisfying object and further his first hostile object, as well as his sole helping power" (p. 331). His experience could be written: 'Mum, you were once good and helped me, but now I am screaming helplessly. My scream is bad like *you*. In my mind, you're bad to me as long as my discontent lasts!' Here, the child's distress is not only explained by not having *satis* of mother but also by his hostile and ravaging *internal* object. In terms of our avian metaphors, the "chick" is peeping desperately. When mother arrives at the nest and all would seem fine according to the principle of constancy, she is felt to be bad and inimical according to the pleasure principle. The meaning of the term "object" has now become more complex; even if the external "real mother" is good and provides satisfaction, the internal mother may be felt as bad and experienced as hostile.

Brent's (Case 2) extensive sleep is perhaps an effort at charging his infantile self with *satis* narcissistic libido. But the picture is complicated; his squirming in Nancy's arms indicates that his *Friede* is precarious. Why this is so we do not know, but Freud's idea about the hostile object possibly applies. Evidently, such a guess triggers Nancy's guilt, as if it is her fault that he is squirming. The colicky girl (Case 1) may fit in here as well. Colic has been attributed to gastrointestinal dysfunction (Treem, 1994 quoted in DelCarmen-Wiggins & Carter, 2004, p. 81), maternal distress (Levitzky & Cooper, 2000; Maxted et al., 2005; Twomey, High, & Lester, 2012), migraine (Gelfand, Thomas, & Goadsby, 2012), or a poor fit between infant and parental behaviour (Carey, 1990). Whichever the case for this girl, Freud's model indicates that she may experience mother as hostile, merely by dint of *her own* distress. If we add the mother's distress – pre-existing or starting when her baby was screaming – we end up in a model of the baby's distress:

My bad scream characterizes *you*. You're bad as long as my discontent lasts. My tummy aches and you've got that frown and a bad way of holding me. I search your eyes to retrieve my old mum. I find her for a second, but then that horrible image reappears and I can't stop crying.

"Infant Sorrow", by William Blake (1994, p. 125), captures this struggle:

My mother groaned, my father wept!
Into the dangerous world I leapt,
Helpless, naked, piping loud,
Like a fiend hid in a cloud.

Struggling in my father's hands,
Striving against my swaddling bands,
Bound and weary, I thought best,
To sulk upon my mother's breast.

Representations and affects

If we want to grasp a distressed infant's experiences, we must go beyond Freud's notions of libido distribution and ask: What is he thinking about? What does he feel? Which objects, external and fantasized, are involved? The next two sections will approach these questions. Freud (1900) suggested that when a need arises in the baby, for example of food, she will charge the memory of the perception and "re-establish the situation of the original satisfaction" (pp. 565–566). She recalls the bliss of satisfaction, in other words, re-evokes some sort of *representations.* Judging from her screams, they seem charged with strong emotions. Freud speculates about their content but does not emphasize their affective dimension, maybe because his concept of affect is still couched in quantitative terms, "comparable to the electric charge of a nervous impulse" (Green, 1977, p. 130), which is released via the memory of a painful event. At this stage, Freud views such memories as charges, not as representations. Consequently, defences are viewed as *biological* events, as when our bodies defend against a toxic substance. In this model, Brent's mum has got it wrong; he has painful memories of dyspnoea. The frown may signify affective cathexes that he tries to ward off, but the main thing is their "electric charges" and his attempts at getting rid of them. There is nothing reproachful about his frown; it is a bio-physical signal like fever in an inflammatory process.

This line of thought is, however, artificial because we cannot dissociate clearly quantitative and qualitative aspects of an affect (Green, 1999). There is yet another suspicion: *Why* does Brent fret? He is not infected anymore, so why waste energy on what is now a mere memory? Freud thought the infant linked the pain with a hostile mother, and Fraiberg (1982) said he must ward off the person "on whom he is absolutely dependent and who is associated with pain and disappointment" (p. 614). We note how she blends "pain", perhaps a more biological term, with a psychological term, "disappointment". Yet, Green does not criticize Freud's affect theory because of its alleged biological slant but because of the notion that "all presentations originate from perceptions and are repetitions of them" (Freud, 1925, p. 237). Green argues that *the psyche can register traces of affective experiences before it can establish "mnemic traces of perceptions"*. Its task is to "separate out the representations from the contradictory affective infiltrations,

172 Part II: Theory

whose general tendency is towards diffusion, whilst the representations seek articulation" (Green, 1977, p. 152).

Allow me a metaphor: As you enter your office in the morning, you meet some colleagues. An unpleasant sensation arises in you and escalates to anxiety. Slowly, you discern your colleagues' ironic looks. Finally one of them says, "The people at the department you initiated a while ago are approaching a burnout. Do you have some new super project in mind?" These venomous words cast a limpid light on your earlier discomfort. In Green's terms, initially you merely registered some "traces of affective experiences", but as your "aha"-moment arrived you could create articulated representations: "Why are they surly? That department wasn't *my* idea, it was *ours!*" The infant's psychological state may resemble the first seconds in your office; it cannot tell affects from representations. To Green (1977), such representations are cast according to a "primary symbolization" and based on a "primary logic", a "minimal unconscious semantic" with "the figures of psychoanalytic rhetoric" such as "repetition-compulsion, reversal (turning into the opposite and turning against the self), anticipation, mirroring, inclusion, exclusion, formation of the complement . . . the constitution of movable limits, temporary splitting, the creation of substitutes, the setting up of screens and finally projective identification" (p. 152).

In the infant's world, nothing is steady, logical, or unequivocally defined. Experiences are symbolized "in affective perceptual and action modalities" (Rizzuto, 2003, p. 308). He cannot handle them until they have become "accessible to verbal interactions with a responsive adult intent on understanding the child's experiences" (idem). In our simile, this occurred when your colleague voiced what annoyed them. Initially, you did not grasp what went on; also because no "responsive adult" helped you solve the puzzle. The idea of Rizzuto, and many others from Freud onwards, is that the baby's representations do not arise in a mind vacuum. They are also communicated to an object whom she hopes is willing to receive and translate the message: *Representations also have an intersubjective dimension.*

But, there is a problem: The baby does not tell you, "I'm hungry, gimme a good feed!" Many things take place in his mind that he cannot signify through words. How does he do it? French analysts have investigated how phenomena beyond words are signified. Rosolato (1985) spoke of "demarcating" – as opposed to linguistic – signifiers. The former have a "natural" or analogic basis, some resemblance to what they are signifying; when we are angry our voices rise and our muscles get tense. Our organs behave *as if* beating up somebody. Freud's screaming baby in *The Project* thinks mother is hostile, a conclusion s/he bases on analogic parallels; 'my cry's hostile tension is identical to that of Mum'.

If this argument seems enigmatic, it merely reflects the peculiar logic of primitive signification forms, which are so hard to express in words. Yet, the reason why most of us conjecture that a sulking and frowning baby is in a bad mood must be that we act likewise when we feel that way. In Rosolato's terms, such "reciprocal identifications" (p. 69) function so well because they rely on a bodily expressive "language". Thereby, they nourish both the baby's and the mother's fantasies. Nancy's self-accusations rested on her identifying Brent's frown with her own, and not until she vented them with a "responsive adult", her analyst, did they diminish.

Another Frenchman, Jean Laplanche (1999), coined the concept "enigmatic signifier" to explicate how the parent's unconscious communication impacts on the baby. Especially, it explains how infantile sexuality is born in the mother–infant interaction. Roussillon (2011), yet another French analyst, makes an observation which we will return to in the section on the pictogram: There is no clear-cut distinction between perception and representation (p. 136). The latter is merely a more complex and structured form of the former. As for our office metaphor, Roussillon would suggest that there is a fluid border between your initial unease and the following verbal explanations and comprehension. The baby is in more dire straits; verbal explanations are not accessible to him as they were to you at the office. In Brent's case, how can we phrase the representations that accompany his distress? No words will do justice to them. *I wish these pages could sulk, cry, or scream* – but we are all powerless in such efforts! I would sketch his representations in these words: 'Bad. Pain. You bad. Bad everything, everywhere, everytime. Bad go away!' The primitive semantic of such sentences reflects that he has very little sense of continuity, subjectivity or agency.

The role of the object

The *object* is the most volatile component of the drive in Freud's model (1915a), since it links with the drive almost haphazardly, "only in consequence of being peculiarly fitted to make satisfaction possible". But, once again Freud is contradictory. In the passage quoted already (Freud, 1895/1950), the object is an "experienced person" or a "helping power". Gradually, he describes it in more personal terms, such as "maternal care" (*Mutterpflege*; Freud, 1911, p. 219). Still later (Freud, 1925–1926), he links the baby's anxieties even more specifically to separation from the *mother* (p. 138). But, since he wanted to erect a consistent metapsychology – his moniker was *die Hexe,* or the Witch (Freud, 1937, p. 224) – with a drive psychology couched in terms of mechanical forces rather than human relations, he could not account for how the mother–child *interaction* affects the infant psyche.

Some French analysts have developed Freudian drive psychology and opened up for a more diversified rendition of the object's nature. They focus on *intersubjectivity*, a term they use a bit differently from US analysts (Benjamin, 2000; Levenson, 2005/1983; Renik & Spillius, 2004; Stolorow, 1997). The Frenchmen stress that what goes on between and inside two people also has many unconscious "drive-related and sexual dimensions" (Roussillon, 2011, p. 29). Thus, *A's object B is also a subject whose responses bear the stamp of B's drives towards A.* The drive is not a mere force inside an individual pushing him to reach for satisfaction, it does not spin around as in a merry-go-round to land on anyone in the funfair.

174 Part II: Theory

True, from the perspective of the drive's "owner", it is received by an object. But, that object is also a subject with its drive impulses. The drive is thus a messenger (Grotstein, 1980) that impacts on sender and receiver. The *meaning* of a baby's drive impulse emerges only once he *and* the mother-object have interpreted it, as when a mother says, "Come now baby, are you sad today?" and he feels contained. In Roussillon's words, "there is no predetermined meaning attached to the message independently of the object's response" (2011, p. 36).

Brent and Nancy illustrate that once we grasp that an object is also a subject and we apply an intersubjective framework, we understand better how his symptoms affect Nancy and how her unconscious fantasies influence him. When she interprets his frown as a reproach, "Why did you do this to me?", she reveals her gloomy prospects for him. Perhaps this is influenced by her panic at his disease and mourning his upcoming death. It might also be a deferred reconstruction after he fell ill. Maybe she also projects onto Brent, her second child, the complicated relationship with her own younger brother. The idea that Brent didn't want to come out of her might reflect an unconscious fear that once he was born, her resentment against this brother would reawaken and be projected onto Brent. This, of course, frightens her. Then, how do Nancy's unconscious fantasies influence him? This is more difficult to answer and we need other theoreticians to tackle it. Maybe his grunting and squirming are not mere signs of biological distress but also indicate representations of distress and a relationship with a mother who involves him, via projections, in her unconscious universe.

To sum up, Freud's metapsychological account of infant distress has various problems. First, it delineates better the development of the drive than of the object relationships and eclipses the object's interactive contributions. Second, if his rendering of the baby's primary narcissism were his exclusive view – which we now know it was not – of her position in the object world, we would have a hard time explaining the object's contributions. Third, an analytic model of the baby's experiences must account for his representations – but Freud does not do this consistently and thoroughly. Fourth, to comprehend a baby's distress we need a viable affect theory. Freud's version is couched in quantitative terms and divides the affect into motor and ideational components. This seems fair enough; an affect occurs in the body *and* is about something. The challenge is to account for *preverbal* ideations. Freud's "hostile" object is such an effort, but we need more sophisticated concepts to get behind infant distress. To this end, the next chapter will account for post-Freudian theoreticians.

Chapter 17

Naming the nameless

On anxiety in babies – II:
after Freud

Klein and the content of anxiety

Klein departed from Freud's drive concepts to study the *content* of anxiety (Hinshelwood, 1989). We will investigate how far her approach helps in understanding our babies' distress. She agreed with Freud (1925–1926) that anxiety is tied to specific provoking situations, such as the loss of love and of object, and castration. But, she disagreed that it would reflect the ego's efforts at quenching id eruptions. Instead, she radicalized Freud's concept of the death drive. Primitive anxiety, she stated, is a conflict between Thanatos and Eros. Anxiety as an ego signal – this was Freud's version – was a later mechanism in her view: "Anxiety is aroused by the danger which threatens the organism from the death instinct . . . This is the primary cause of anxiety" (Klein, 1948, p. 28). "The new-born infant suffers from persecutory anxiety aroused by the process of birth and by the loss of the intra-uterine situation" (Klein, 1952a, p. 95). Thanatos aims to kill the baby and Klein thus uses the term annihilation anxiety literally.

To survive the mortal threat of Thanatos, the baby diverts it onto the external world. Klein does not depict this as a mere traffic of drive cathexes. Rather, her descriptions of projective and introjective cycles, and of the dynamics between good and bad and external and internal objects, refer to *psychological content* or *representations*. Freud's physical analogies are thus incompatible "with a psychological view of the phantasy content of anxiety" (Hinshelwood, 1989, p. 119). Kleinians refer to *phantasies* "as the primary content of unconscious mental processes" (Isaacs, 1948, p. 82). (Kleinians use the spelling "phantasy" to denote unconscious mental activities. I use it here to be true to that tradition. At other parts in the book, I only spell it fantasy.) They originate as early impulses of and defences against Eros and Thanatos. The mental processes involved are "far removed from words and conscious relational thinking and determined by the logic of emotion" (Op. cit., p. 84). While Freud set fantasy against reality, in Klein's view, unconscious phantasy constantly accompanies reality-oriented behaviour and conscious fantasizing. Since such phantasies are object-directed from the start, Kleinians reject the notion of primary narcissism, the "egg baby"

176 Part II: Theory

in Chapter 16. Klein says that both "auto-erotism and narcissism include the love for and relation with the *internalized* good object which in phantasy forms part of the loved body and self" (1952b, p. 51, italics added). To illustrate, think of the old tune, where Gershwin asserts that somebody loves him and then queries, "I wonder who, I wonder who she can be". To explain narcissism, a Kleinian would answer, "I know who: It's an inside *she* that makes you love yourself".

Klein was criticized by Winnicott (1962c) for paying "lip-service to environmental provision" (p. 177), as if the child's development relied mainly on drive impulses and only insignificantly on the object's contributions. In Chapter 15, we teased out Klein's views on empiricism and theorizing. Though she wanted to ground theory in observations, they were not done in the systematic and unbiased manner that researchers apply today. As we also argued, her descriptions of how a mother's behaviour and attitudes influence the child's experiences were vague and marginal. Paraphrasing Freddie Mercury we can state that in Klein's view, even if a baby received "comfort and care" and "mother love" it might not quench his panic. The anxiety of Thanatos would still threaten his calm.

Let us revert to the four baby cases in Chapter 16; non-Kleinian analysts speculating on their internal worlds would probably set young Brent aside and claim that he had hardly any object to cathect when the respiratory infection hit him. In contrast, they would see the other babies as already involved in object relationships. Klein, however, would claim that the basic threat to *all four* emanated from the death instinct. Anxiety was thus instilled immediately and Brent's dyspnoea confirmed to him that life is unliveable. Not only did he fear that he would die but also that he, or rather his Thanatos, *aimed* at his death. Since the good object had had so little time to be established, it could not pose a counterweight to his death anxiety. To paraphrase the Psalms, he was walking through the valley of the shadow of death but had no shepherd. This interpretation can only apply to the time of his illness. The ongoing distress after his recovery would indicate, in Klein's view, an ongoing war between the grand instincts, which tilted in favour of Thanatos and was aggravated by his negative experiences of the object. As for the origin of such experiences, Klein would have emphasized his projections more than his mother's behaviour. It fell upon Winnicott (1949b, p. 245) to stress the impact of a "bad environment" towards whose "impingement . . . the psyche-soma (i.e. the infant) must react".

As for the girl with colic, as well as Mae and Fran, Klein would claim they were in the throes of complicated object relations to external and internal objects. But, though Klein surely would have sensed the mother's covert hostility towards Fran, I guess she would focus more on the girl's innate death anxiety than on their interaction, that is, how mother's ambivalence aggravated Fran's internal objects. The situation was similar with Mae, but with a notable exception: Debbie's projections had not got a hold on Mae, whose distress thus was temporary. Negative internal objects had not petrified and she was often a happy girl – despite her mother's belief in the contrary.

Winnicott and unthinkable anxiety

Winnicott came to differ from Klein mainly on three issues: how to conceive of the baby's earliest state, his anxiety, and the impact on him by the object's handling. His key terms are *unintegration, unthinkable anxiety*, and *holding*. Unthinkable anxiety appears when the baby is in a state of unintegration and the environment fails in "holding in the stage of absolute dependence" (Winnicott, 1962a, p. 61). Such anxiety is like "(1) Going to pieces, (2) Falling for ever, (3) Having no relationship to the body, (4) Having no orientation" (p. 58). To imagine, hold a heap of pebbles and spread out your fingers. As you watch the tiny stones seep through and fall to the ground, this is like when a mother fails to hold her baby and he tumbles into unintegration. Klein attributed such experiences to the baby's death instinct, whereas Winnicott (1960b) emphasized the mother's *holding*, a term that denotes "not only the actual physical holding of the infant, but also the total environmental provision" (p. 589). He also stressed her "tremendous task" in "preventing clinical breakdown from which recovery occurs only through organization and reorganization of defences" (Winnicott, 1962b, p. 239).

The baby defends against unthinkable anxiety through *disintegration*, "a sophisticated defence . . . an active production of chaos in defence against unintegration in the absence of maternal support . . . it has the advantage of being produced by the baby and therefore of being non-environmental" (Winnicott, 1962a, p. 61). In contrast to unthinkable anxiety, "it is analysable" (idem). To continue the pebble metaphor, such analysis would clarify to the baby when she is opening her hand and letting out all the pebbles. It is possible that Mae's acute distress, up to the ER call, was such an instance. One month old, Mae was still dependent on the hand/mother to hold her pebbles/anxiety. When mother's vexation became palpable yet incomprehensible to Mae, she defended against unthinkable anxiety by "an active production of chaos" (p. 60) or disintegration; she screamed and yelled and was inconsolable. Disintegration thus supplants unintegration but precedes anxiety that results from "instinct tension or object loss" (Winnicott, 1960b, p. 588). Mae's challenge was not to repress drive impulses, nor did she suffer the pangs of being abandoned by an object she clearly recognized.

Winnicott (1960b) uses the term *annihilation* in connection with unthinkable anxiety. It has nothing to do with death, which has "no possible application" (p. 591) to a baby. Rather, it occurs when her sense of "continuity of being is interrupted by reactions to the consequences of [maternal] failure, with resultant ego-weakening" (p. 594). Thus, "the term death instinct [is] unacceptable in describing the root of destructiveness" (p. 591). The threat does not concern the infant's life but "an annihilation of the infant's self" (Winnicott, 1956a, p. 304).

As for unthinkable anxiety, Winnicott's formulations "going to pieces" and "falling forever" are not mere metaphors but cover the baby's actual experiences. However, before an ego has been established, "the infant is not yet an entity having experiences" (Winnicott, 1962a, p. 56). Thus, it must be the ego that creates notions like going to pieces and falling forever. So why does he call the anxiety

178 Part II: Theory

"unthinkable"? It has content and the baby's experiences are described in fairly precise words. If he is not thinking about them, what is he doing when he fears falling and going to pieces? As we will see, we encounter a similar challenge in Bion's writings. But before leaving Winnicott, we recall another phenomenon linked with infant anxiety; the False Self (Winnicott, 1960a). If a mother repeatedly fails to meet the infant's "spontaneous gesture" and instead "substitutes her own gesture" (p. 145), the baby can only give sense to these events via compliance. This can pave the way for developing a False Self, a "false set of relationships . . . a show of being real . . . [and] grow to be just like mother" (p. 146). If Debbie's unconscious ambivalence towards Mae had continued, perhaps the girl might have developed in a similar direction. Thus, when mother exclaimed, "Mae's fussiness is her temperament", I think it mirrored that she was now able to appreciate her daughter's spontaneous gesture.

Bion and nameless dread

Bion (1962) describes an infant's panic as a "nameless dread" (p. 96). Not only does it suffer from what he calls a fear of dying. Even worse, this fear is stripped of any meaning and is thus "nameless". James Grotstein (1990), a US analyst strongly influenced by Bion, describes such experiences as "neither mental nor truly somatic" (p. 272), an "organismic panic" which has not "been transformed into signal, anticipatory, specific anxiety" (1984, p. 305). Britton, a British analyst also inspired by Bion, summarizes such experiences in one formula: they occur when "the uncomprehended has become the incomprehensible" (Britton, 2000, p. 62). Returning to the office metaphor in the previous chapter, if your colleagues had continued their twisted dialogue and you remained ignorant of their concealed critique, you might end up in a Kafkaesque nightmare: "What's wrong with me!?" This would exemplify Britton's idea.

In line with our discussion of Winnicott's "unthinkable anxiety", Bion's term "fear of dying" is problematic since I agree with Winnicott that the notion of death has no application to an infant. As for Bion's term "nameless", the problem is not that a baby does not master language and cannot name objects. Bion is of course aware of this. He refers to an emotional state, which the baby fears both because it is gruesome and he cannot assign a "name" to it. Consequently, he cannot think about it. Let us agree that babies think in terms of non-verbal mental signs. If so, "sign-less dread" would be a more apt term. But can a baby know anything at all about X if he cannot attach some sign to it? I would answer no since, as Charles Peirce has formulated, "we think only in signs" (Kloesel & Houser, 1998, p. 10). Nothing is mental until the mind can link it with a sign, no matter how primitive. If a baby sees his still-faced mother (Tronick et al., 1978), he will panic because he interprets her face as a terrifying icon. His anxiety is thus not sign-less. To conclude, neither "nameless" nor "sign-less" seem apt terms in connection with infantile panic.

Perhaps we can rescue Winnicott's claim about unthinkable anxiety by consulting with Green (1998). He states that "thinking is often confused with

Naming the nameless: II: after Freud 179

psychical activity" (p. 651). He sets aside "psychic events . . . rooted in the body" or "thoughts without a thinker" in Bion's terms. This is different from *thinking* performed by a thinker and communicated to another thinker. Green (2004) clarifies his ideas about *thought* by bringing in Peirce's semiotics, which focuses on how signs are constructed, experienced, and communicated. Peirce introduced a third factor beyond sign–object dyad: the *interpretant* or the "mental sign of the object" (Kloesel & Houser, 1998, p. 13) is the mind's notion of how object and sign are linked. It is "an organizing agent" (Green, 2004, p. 113) outside the sign–object relationship and it recognizes the distance between object and sign.

To shed light, let us bring in a simple example. What goes on in a crying baby's mind? In translation it might be something like, '*She* silly'. He thus recognizes the connection between the object Mother, his sign for it, and his emotional interpretant of the sign–object link. We have here a non-verbal thought with a thinker. Unthinkable anxiety is a different experience, but not because the baby cannot relate it to words. After all, all babies are non-verbal. So how are we to understand that he fears "falling", "going to pieces", or "dying"? Why do Winnicott and Bion not call such fears thoughts? The answer has to do with how we define representation. Green (2004) suggests representation is a unified concept "that is applied to heterogeneous material and is related to meaning, from the earliest and most primitive expressions to the highest and most complex psychic activities" (p. 114). We are now dealing with a problem that Wordsworth (1850) was struggling with, immediately before the "blest Babe" cited in Chapter 16:

> Hard task, vain hope, to analyse the mind,
> If each most obvious and particular thought,
> Not in a mystical and idle sense, But in the words of
> Reason deeply weighed,
> Hath no beginning.
>
> (loc. 67768)

Can we grasp, with our deeply weighed reason, the beginnings of a baby's thought? The crux is that, as Green (2004) puts it, "our deepest inner reality" is "unrepresentable" (p. 121) and comes to us as a category of thought which Peirce called *Firstness*. Here, there is "no comparison, no relation, no recognized multiplicity . . . no change, . . . no reflexion, nothing but a simple positive character" (Kloesel & Houser, 1998, p. 150). To quote Peirce: "Assert [Firstness] and it has already lost its characteristic innocence" (Kloesel & Houser, 1992, p. 248). Green says that in contrast, "the representation of realities through perception" (Op. cit., p. 121) comes to us via *Thirdness*. This category brings in a perspective from the outside world and introduces new relations within the sign–object dyad and thus new interpretants. "The three-party relationship is the matrix of the mind [whereas] . . . a dual relationship . . . does not do justice to the complexity of communication in terms of thought processes" (Green, 2004, p. 132). Other analysts (Grotstein, 1982; Duarte, 2015) have also introduced the figure of the third, some without specifically referring to Peirce (Benjamin, 2005; Britton, 1989).

180   Part II: Theory

To understand *Thirdness* in relation to infant anxiety, let us look at Brent (Case 2). I believe he feels secluded in a dyadic universe where no third can rectify his chaos. Squirming, he turns to mother but feels she has no outlet of *her* anxiety other than towards himself. The two are caught in *a ping-pong of anxieties*. Brent's father could play a crucial role, and he does try to help mother and child, but in vain. Not until the analyst comes in as a third pillar does the construction show some flexibility. Now, they can leave "primary symbolization" (Green, 1977) and start building signifying chains on higher levels to enable ordinary thinking. Fran and her mother Beatrice also demonstrate an absence of *Thirdness*. Beatrice speaks in clichés: her husband "*never* wants to see any problems", her "*old* depression" has come back, and "nothing's good enough for you, *li'l whiner!*" She blocks new perspectives; perhaps her spouse does see her problems, maybe her depression is not one old uniform disease, and possibly, Fran whines because Mum's rapid movements prevent contact.

To sum up, the concepts of nameless dread and unthinkable anxiety seek to capture those primitive experiences that beset a distressed baby. Terms like "going to pieces" and "fear of dying" must be read as metaphors. They do not refer to someone thinking, "I am falling apart" but to psychic events arising in the body. The subject does not recognize himself as creating them – but they are his mental activities that comprise a working through of objects, signs and interpretants. *"Unthinkable anxiety" and "nameless dread" are similes for the interpretants in those psychic states where Thirdness is felt to be absent*; each sign–object dyad has but one meaning, and baby and parent cannot introduce a third perspective on the ongoing panic.

Gaddini

Eugenio Gaddini (1992) begins his investigations of development at an even earlier stage than the authors referred so far. He studies how the mind is born and develops as a "highly differentiated function of the body" (p. 120). He proceeds from an idea of a "complex and concomitant mind-body activity" (idem), an approach resembling the psychosomatic school of Paris (Aisenstein, 2006). The development of the mind starts during intra-uterine life, before "the impressive caesura of the act of birth" (Freud, 1925–1926, p. 138). The foetus lives in a seemingly boundless space. As he discovers its physical limits his bodily memory registers it. Now he has acquired the prerequisites for "mental learning about physiological functions . . . [This is] the fundamental knowledge of body existing at birth" (p. 123). To get an image of this state you may step into a cramped WC, lock the door, and turn off the light. Your hands start pressing the walls, the floor, and the objects. Sounds from the water pipes and smells from the closet reach your ears and nostrils. Sensations arise out of tensions created through perceptions beyond zero; the feel of your hand, a sound, a smell. This illustrates the baby's knowledge of body existing at birth. The Norwegian author Karl Ove Knausgaard (2018) speaks of his baby daughter in his book *Spring*: "What is the world like

Naming the nameless: II: after Freud 181

for a newborn child? Light, dark. Cold, warm. Soft, hard" (p. 7). Contrasts are the first entities that give some "meaning" to a baby's "experiences", though these descriptors go beyond the raw phenomena we are studying here.

As yet, the baby has no mental self-image and his mind is subjugated to his physiological functioning. When the parents hold the newborn, they help create a "boundary environment" (Gaddini, 1992, p. 125). The walls, sounds, and smells of our metaphorical WC are replaced by a parent's hand, breast, and eye. Gaddini also acknowledges the impact of physical imitation, through which the baby first tries to "perceive" (p. 109) and then to "become" or "be". He cites Meltzoff's (2007) "like me" hypothesis based on experiments on babies imitating adult facial movements (Meltzoff & Moore, 1997), such as tongue protrusion. This ability is now substantiated by fMRI studies showing that the brains of babies only a few weeks old have cortical connections between different sensory areas, for example visual, auditory, and sensorimotor (Sours et al., 2017). The studies reveal the brain architecture of "cross-modal" or "multisensory" integration (Stein, Stanford, & Rowland, 2014). They thus help explain neonatal imitation and confirm that the baby's brain is pre-wired to instantly replace the "WC walls", that is, his memory of body and borders, with perceptions of real people.

During this first phase of extra-uterine life, body and mind form one "organism, whose physiological learning process, at a certain point, because of the differentiation of the mental function, becomes aware of itself . . . [and organizes] into a mental 'self' and creates a mental image of the corporal self" (Gaddini, 1992, p. 126). This initial sense of self is a space marked by bodily functioning. Such a "first totality of self" (p. 110), a "space of things", has no psychic structure, boundary, form, or time; it is a Universe. Since the baby experiences 'All is me, I am all' he cannot conceive of a non-self. He is, so to speak, locked in the WC and knows of nothing outside. Every satisfaction is thought to be auto-generated within the Universe, and every dissatisfaction – also felt to be auto-generated – threatens its existence. The experience of time and the use of symbols are beyond reach. Instead, experiences are *things* and memory is the recall of such things. A pang of hunger could be written as 'Here it is again, that thing I fabricated earlier and recognize. If it does not vanish, the Universe will implode and explode'. Gaddini also applies the term "memory" to body functions before they have acquired "a mental quality" (1992, p. 126). Knausgaard (2018, p. 7) renders an evocative imagery:

> You don't know what air is, yet you breathe. You don't know what sleep is, yet you sleep. You don't know what night is, yet you rest in it. You don't know what heart is, yet it beats steadily in your chest, day and night, day and night, day and night.

Of course, this state of things cannot continue. Soon the baby discerns that something escapes his omnipotent control in the space of the total self. Someone is, so to speak, knocking on the toilet door. Now begins the birth of the individual self (Gaddini, 1992, p. 112). All the omnipotence of the total self – with its bliss

182   Part II: Theory

and catastrophe – is now attributed to the object, the first non-self. In response, the baby creates an "instinctuality of the self" (p. 114) which is omnipotent, dismissive of temporality, and conservative. All that matters is the "security and maintenance of the internal space of the self" (idem). To return to our WC metaphor, the baby thinks 'OK, I hear someone knocking, but I don't care. I'm busy getting *my* satisfaction'. Only during this third stage of "instinctual activity of the ego" do we see a drive activity that acknowledges external reality and the object. Our WC occupant now acknowledges: 'I hear you, come in, I need you to get what I want.' To frame it in Peircean terms this object comes in, not only to still his needs, but also to introduce Thirdness to him, that is, mother's internal world and the external world.

A conclusion from Gaddini's model is that we must sort the infant's anxieties according to which level he has reached of differentiating body/mind and subject/object. At first, anxiety is about the Universe going to pieces. Then comes a fear that the individual self or "planet" – as opposed to other selves or "planets" – will perish. This dread also comprises that the baby fears he will lose the affection from someone he has cathected with his drive. The more this "instinctuality of the self" charges an object, the more it becomes an "instinctuality of the ego" (p. 114). This is the birth of the drive in the Freudian sense. The baby is now out of the WC, he recognizes objects and requests satisfaction from them. He soon discovers that this meets with obstacles and, therefore, he develops defences to nip in the bud his yearning for gratification. He has now arrived in the world of *infantile defences*, which we will deal with in Chapter 18.

Brent's (Case 2) squirming and grunting continue after he is well again so, as we stated earlier, they cannot reflect a mere biological reflexive activity. When he was ill, he had to ward off the fundamental threat to his "space of things". Now he has recovered and such warding off is not needed anymore. But, since the primitive mind cannot "distinguish the actual repetition of an experience from its mental reactivation by memory" (Gaddini, 1992, p. 127), it does not matter that there are no more repetitions of somatic distress. His mind creates it anyway via memory; a process we guess is promoted by the anxieties of his mother. Her distress, guilt, and unconscious resentment make it harder for her to help him heal the rift in his universe.

As for Case 1 from YouTube, infant colic begins when body and mind still form a unity. Perhaps the pain is felt as a Universe imploding: 'Pain. Cry. Annihilation forever.' Or, if the baby has begun to create a mental image of the corporal self, this image is distorted: 'I pain. I cry. I am Pain. I am Cry.' The mother comforts, but we do not know how much the colicky girl takes her on board. We can assume that crying evokes anxieties in every mother. Her fear that the baby is dying resonates with anxieties from her own infancy. The abler she can handle them and the less she panics, the more the baby's ego can charge her with libido and make use of her holding: 'I pain. I cry. She here. She counterpoise to my bad.' These are the moments when parents of a colicky baby feel they can comfort and get in contact with the baby amidst the crying fits.

Stern

Daniel Stern was an infant researcher and a psychoanalyst. Over the years, he distanced himself from aspects of Freudian theory. The specific topic of infantile anxiety occurs rarely in his writings. The focus is on the baby's *interpersonal* world (Stern, 1985) and his "sense of self-and-other, [which] has as its starting place the infant's inferred subjective experience" (p. 26). This process is rarely portrayed in the dramatic colours from the authors earlier. As an intersubjectivist, Stern rejected Klein's idea that anxiety derives from the death drive. Rather, it is triggered by expectable and banal stimulation. This parallels his objection that an infant would experience, as Klein said, the world as good or bad, or connect "'pleasurable' and 'good' or 'unpleasurable' and 'bad' at the level of core-relatedness" (p. 252). Such abilities enter later in development, he says. The baby's "reality experience precedes fantasy distortions in development" and is "unapproachable by psychodynamic considerations" (p. 255). Klein would surely protest.

In *Diary of a baby* (1990) Stern depicts Joey, 6 weeks old, who "experiences objects and events mainly in terms of *feelings* they evoke in him, and the opportunities for action they offer him" (p. 13). These feelings are described in terms of sensuousness, rhythm, duration, discontinuity, intensity but not in terms of *content*. He compares them to "weatherscapes" and refrains from speculating about any ideas connected with them: "Full-throated crying is not a state of disorganization . . . [but a] separate and distinct organization of the central nervous system" (p. 33). Green (1995b) concludes that Stern's concept of affects is "in the behavioural sphere" and is "unconnected to drives" (pp. 208–209). Presumably, Winnicott or Bion would also have disagreed and described the crying baby as having an attack of annihilation anxiety or nameless dread. In contrast, Stern's descriptions harmonize with Gaddini's most primeval stages in terms of the first totality of self, the space of things, and the Universe.

Stern's hesitation in describing what babies' feelings are *about*, that is, which representations are embedded in them, has two roots. As a researcher, he avoids speculating on what goes on in someone who cannot confirm the thoughts or ideas that we attribute to him. As an intersubjectivist he emphasizes, like Reddy (2008) and Beebe (Beebe & Lachmann, 2014), that representations have *interactive* meanings and cannot be studied from outside, from a "third-person perspective" (Reddy, 2008, p. 79). This is why his description of baby representations comes off as rather bleak and unspecific (Stern, 1995), in my mind. As stated in Chapter 17, Roussillon also speaks of intersubjectivity but he includes the *unconscious* levels of the participants' minds. The baby's representations arise in touch with corresponding levels in the other person. If s/he is an analyst, s/he will use his/her Unconscious to make conjectures about representational content. This is precisely what Stern criticizes.

Mae (Case 3) screams helplessly. I, the analyst, tell her that Mum is distressed and angry and that it makes Mae distressed as well. My reflections on the meanings

184 Part II: Theory

of her crying stem from an identification with her and my analogic (Rosolato, 1985) understanding; I also get distressed in front of tense and angry people. To add, my interpretations stem from listening to Mother's story and seeing them interacting; Debbie acknowledges her ambivalence towards Mae. I suggest Mae finds Mother incomprehensible; her words, facial expressions, tone of voice do not coalesce into an unequivocal message. Stern might have agreed on my technique but differed on how to conceive of Mae's anxiety. My intervention stems from how I view her representations of a "bad", "hostile" mother. In contrast to Stern, I do make assumptions about their content and hedonic tone.

Aulagnier

To get past the difficulties in wording wordless experiences, we need theories of signification that cover the whole spectrum of human experience. Each referred author contributed with building blocks to such a theory – and each has some missing links. Freud's explanations of anxiety as transformed libido or an ego signal, as well as Klein's attributing it to the death drive, are evocative metaphors but do not make infantile panic easy to grasp. Gaddini's focus is on the birth of the mind rather than on the content of anxiety. Winnicott's and Bion's notions of unthinkable anxiety and nameless dread are poignant, but semiotic theory pointed to logical problems. If we wish to apply such theory to the baby's experiences we find elaborate contributions by French analysts.

Piera Aulagnier (2001) focuses on the infant's *representative* function, which she compares to a metabolic function; it processes not a physical body but an "element of information" (p. 3). These elements undergo a rapid evolution via *the primal, the primary, and the secondary processes*. In each stage, the represented object is linked with the agency that creates the representation. This function starts when the newborn's psyche is plunged into a "heterogenous" (p. 8) space: the mother's psyche. Still, her otherness is not recognized, there is no "she" denoting the mother, only a universal "we". I believe this stage comes a bit later than Gaddini's stage when primal experiences are things and the baby is the Universe.

Following Freud (1900), Aulagnier speaks of the screaming baby who tries to bypass distress by hallucinating satisfaction. When, finally, nipple and mouth meet and the need is satisfied, the primal (*originaire*, not to be confused with primary) process creates an image of a *complementary object zone* or a *pictogram*. It could be translated as 'I am mouth and nipple, I created both representations, they are pleasurable and I want to retain them'. Still, the baby vaguely recognizes that the nipple comes from outside. The positive affect in a pictogram arises (1) because it was created during satisfaction and (2) *the representative activity is pleasurable per se*. There is also a parallel track, ignited by dissatisfaction and energized by Thanatos. The result is a "radical hate" (p. 20) or *the desire not to desire*. Aulagnier's conception of Thanatos is more akin to Freud's "conservative" death drive striving to "return to the quiescence of the inorganic world" (1920, p. 62) than Klein's visions of agonizing dying. In line with both these authors, she thinks there is a balance between Life and Death instincts, as well as a balance between the baby's experiences of satisfaction and frustration.

In the pictogram, an experience of pleasure implies that the sense organ and the perceived phenomenon coalesce: 'This feels good. My seeing feels good, and so does the breast. I am it all.' In contrast, "unpleasure entails the desire for self-mutilation of the organ and the destruction of the corresponding objects of exci-tation" (Aulagnier, 2001, p. 37). The idea that the pictogram "taking-into-oneself" is pleasurable whereas "rejecting-outside-self" is unpleasurable, is reminiscent of Freud's (1915a) views. One could suspect that Aulagnier emphasizes the role of visual perception (Valabrega, 2001), but any sensory perception may yield a pictogram. The sound of breastfeeding, its odour, vibration, taste, touch, or sight all may be represented as pictograms and therefore, I think *sensogram* is a more apt term.

The pictogram also covers the subject that produces the representation and the pertaining activity: 'Representing nipple + mouth + satisfaction + the pleasure in representing = me-hood'. During the reign of the pictogram, the outside world can only be given as "image-of-self" (Aulagnier, 2001, p. 24), a notion resembling Gaddini's "totality of the self". Specifically, the pictogram is a representation constituted of an object and a complementary erogenous zone in an affective link. The concept is enigmatic because it is self-referential and inexpressible, but it helps us grasp the most primitive editions of "the laws that govern the activity of representation" (da Rocha Barros, 2000, p. 1094).

The primal is superseded by the primary process. When the psyche recognizes that a body and a psychic space other than its own do exist, the primary process starts functioning. To be the pawn in the other person's game is shattering to the baby, and a comforting solution opens up of being the object of *her* desire: 'So we're separate. OK, I must accept it. But, *she* wants me! Her nipple wants my mouth.' This enables satisfaction on a grander scale but also makes life riskier; the baby is subjected to the other's presence or absence, love or hate, commitment or indifference. The baby begins to suspect that the other human being desires yet another; a triangle is created and the oedipal drama has begun. This would correspond to a stage that Gaddini covers with the term "instinctual activity of the ego". The baby now recognizes the other as being separate and having intentions towards him/her. Such assumptions were non-existent during the era of the primal process.

Conclusions

I have sought to name the nameless, or to explicate what a panicking baby might feel. This enticing question in perinatal psychology is abstruse and meets with deep resistances, but it also needs our theorizing the most. Various authors devoted deep thinking to this topic. Like all of us, they had to base their conclusions on observations, intuitions, and existing theories. My main point, besides discuss-ing their contributions, was to argue that infant panic is not only a neurological or

186 Part II: Theory

biological event but also involves representations: *A baby's anxiety is about something*. The word "is" is not identical to when I say, "My anxiety is about Carla and our upcoming date. Maybe she'll dismiss me." There, I grasp what my anxiety is about, at least those levels that are reasonably available to my consciousness. The baby's panic "is" also about something, but it is linked with representations that we can only portray in metaphors: death, annihilation, Universe exploding, pictogram, etc. The mothers of Brent, Mae, and Fran figure that their babies' distress "is" about something, but their guesses are coloured by projections. This obstructs the baby from sorting out his representations to make them less threatening by experiencing that someone "on the other side" can imagine, feel into, and translate them into more succinct and explicit messages. After all, that is what containment or holding is all about. The next chapter will look at these distressful situations from another vantage point. I will argue that the baby seeks to counter the parent's projections by erecting psychological defences. The difficulty is similar to when two nations mobilize military forces; tensions escalate and peace is endangered.

Chapter 18

Babies and their defences

Eyes have magical powers as mirrors of the soul and messengers of emotions. More accurately, it is the *interchange of looks* that works. If interrupted, the experience can be catastrophic. This may befall parents looking into the eyes of their baby who turns away the gaze. At the CHC, I meet mothers with the baby in her lap. The child looks at things in the room, at me, and at the father if present. The only object avoided is the eyes of mother, whose face turns sad or dismayed. The father often takes it less seriously: "It'll pass away soon, dear". What motivates such gaze avoidance? Is it a simple reflex beyond the baby's control? Or, is it related to mechanisms that we, with older persons, name *psychological defence*? What does this term imply? If a country builds up a defence against its "hostile" neighbours, we get the logic. If the enemy resides within the nation, similar actions are taken. But when a civil war rages *inside our mind*, our conceptions get vaguer. How can we conceive of such forces when they fume in ourselves? How do we detect and avert them?

Cain envied his brother Abel, Sarah was jealous of young and fertile Hagar, and Oedipus, as Freud intuited, unconsciously avoided discerning that his bride was his mother. These characters suffered an emotional pain so weighty that they must make *interior* changes to avert it. They, and we all, deny personal shortcomings or blame others. We commit acts that our conscience forbids and then close our eyes: "I didn't see it". Or, we vacillate and procrastinate, abjuring the consequences. Freud's theory comprised, from its inception, the notion of such "psychological civil war". He coined the bellicose metaphor of *defence* (1892, 1894, 1895/1950, 1896) hand in hand with another metaphor, that of the drive. We are subjected to constantly combatting forces; our drives seek satisfaction – and we erect defences which allow outlets that are acceptable to ourselves and to society. It fell upon his daughter, Anna Freud (1937), to systematize these "defence mechanisms".

What have psychological defences got to do with babies? If a mother looks at her baby and he turns away his eyes, does this signify a defensive manoeuvre? That would imply that we see him as an intentional agent who can accomplish internal changes to ward off some inner turmoil. We will investigate if this might

188 Part II: Theory

be a valid assumption and if so, whether it can be consistent with the classical psychoanalytic view of defence mechanisms. On a larger scale, we will ask if the defence concept applies to disordered behaviours in infants. If our answer proves positive, new challenges await. If everything that goes on in a baby's mind involves his parents, had we not better conceive of "defence" as an *inter*-subjective and not an *intra*-subjective phenomenon? Wouldn't that concur with Winnicott's (1975) wise argument: "There is no such thing as an infant. Whenever one finds an infant one finds maternal care, and without maternal care there would be no infant" (p. XXXVII). My repartee is that he did not ban the study of babies in their own right. And, the fact that we do PTIP does not prevent us from focusing on the psychological mechanisms beneath *the baby's* behaviour.

The study of defences in babies continues our trajectory of investigating if concepts that psychoanalysts apply to older individuals also cover infants. It starts from the view of the infant as a subject; he feels, remembers, wants, thinks, and has some sense of self-reference or "This is I". True, we cannot determine the mental life of someone who neither understands nor produces speech. But the previous chapters showed that both therapists and parents seem to assume that babies do have representations. To get food for the discussion, let us return to my consulting-room at the CHC.

Kirsten and her parents Myra and Don

Myra, the mother of 3-month-old Kirsten, is worried and unhappy. She accuses herself that their contact is not good. Two years ago, pregnancy was terminated in the 20th week because the foetus had a lethal heart malformation. Half a year later, she miscarried in early pregnancy. After some months she and her husband Don conceived a child, and Kirsten was born in due time. Development and breast-feeding went fine, but at 3 weeks old the girl got colic and Myra could not comfort her. This made her feel distressed and helpless.

As I am listening to Myra's story, Kirsten looks at me with a serious, though not sad, look. Some objects capture her interest, but she never looks at Mum. Little by little, she gets distressed and starts screaming. During the mother's efforts at comforting her, she avoids Mum's face by closing her eyes tightly. Myra's comforting is friendly, though slightly jolting and tense, as in her jaunty comment, "Hey girl, let's be happy, shall we". As Kirsten's gaze avoidance and screaming continue, my countertransference distress and sense of impuissance is mounting. I suggest to Myra to search out the baby's eyes. The girl looks at the ceiling lamp but not at Mum, which makes her devastated.

Their CHC nurse has reported that the father, Don, is also worried so I invite the entire family to the next session. This time the atmosphere is more defensive. When I point out that Kirsten looks at me but does not smile, Mum interjects, "she smiles at home". Kirsten starts screaming and Myra has a hard time consoling her. Don says he noted Kirsten's gaze avoidance towards Myra but not towards himself.

He has been on Google and asks if Kirsten has "an attachment disorder". Today's parents consult the internet on baby-care problems. Often, they get confused and worried after dozens of blogs and expert recommendations, which portray these conditions in a static manner, as if there were one concrete solution to each problem. Questions are not discussed in interactional terms that might raise the parents' curiosity as to how they might be involved in the baby's anxiety. To get past such currents beneath Don's question, I answer: "I tend not to think in such labels. I'm wondering, how could you all enjoy being together more." The parents receive this as a critique that they do not play enough with the girl. They appear ambitious, orderly and sympathetic, anguished and touchy.

In general, I find it difficult to get in contact with a baby when both parents participate. A relationship disorder often centres around the baby and one parent, often the mother. Indeed, Kirsten's gaze aversion is restricted to Mum. Yet, I invite the entire family because both parents worry and fear that Kirsten has an attachment disorder or even autism. I suggest she is a girl with a difficult temperament born into a family with two concerned parents who want the best for her. I focus on their guilt and anxiety and do not feel I have a mandate for a deep-reaching therapy. After some once-weekly consultations, Dad is relaxed: "The girl is OK and Myra is more spontaneous with her." He shows a home video where Mum is dancing and singing with the laughing girl.

One day Myra says: "I have always felt awkward when meeting people's eyes. I feel uncomfortable, like they're staring at me." She adds that this also occurs with me, though I never noticed it. She thinks Kirsten's eyes are sad, which increases her guilt. She continues: "My mum does not understand how worried I am." Here, I decide to switch to mother–daughter therapy because Kirsten's gaze avoidance involves Mum only, concretely and emotionally. I wish to apply a technique that will allow more anxiety to emerge, and I no longer feel satisfied with talking about her "difficult temperament", since this cannot explain why she looks at *me* and *her father* while shunning her mother's eyes. I suggest to Myra, "Something seems to be troubling you and Kirsten – and we need to approach it". Myra confirms her pain and regrets that the girl's avoidance has not been taken seriously by the CHC staff. We thus change the therapeutic setting and I add that Don will be welcome back later. Therapy will last five months. The very first few weeks we meet four, then two, and finally one time per week.

Mother–baby therapy: the first two sessions

Mother and child arrive for their first joint session. Kirsten shuns her mother's eyes but looks at me with a persistent and curious, sometimes a blank and sad, gaze. Myra reports that after delivery she felt happy. Finally, her first child! When the colic started she felt helpless and exhausted. As Kirsten started avoiding her eyes Myra accused herself but could not specify any error on her part. Meanwhile, Kirsten's whining grows into a heart-breaking sobbing and crying with her eyes closed.

190   Part II: Theory

Analyst to the baby:	*"Kirsten, you don't want to look Mum in her eyes. I don't know why. I think you got scared of Mum. Maybe she's like a ghost to you now. It gets even worse, for you and for Mum, when you don't look in her eyes. She feels pushed away and as if she's a bad mum. I think you two love each other, but your 'loves' don't come through."*
	Kirsten is looking at me attentively.
Mother:	*"In the beginning I was so happy, like intoxicated! But when she stopped looking at me I felt she didn't love me anymore."*
Analyst:	*"This is hard on you, Myra. I see now that you, Kirsten, are looking at the ceiling lamp but never at Mum. This is hard on you both."*

The second session, Kirsten starts squirming.

Analyst to the baby:	*"Mum is afraid you don't like her. Yes, there is probably a Mum you don't like, one you got scared of when you were little. That's why you don't look into her eyes. You make yourself lonely when you don't look at her. You turn off Mum's comfort . . . I see a racoon on your sweater, with big, black and scary eyes. Maybe that's how you feel about Mum's eyes. You just want them to get away. But when you turn away from Mum, things get even worse . . . What luck you've got a lonely mother!"*
	The last sentence was a slip. Instead of "persistent" (envis in Swedish) I said "lonely" (ensam).
Analyst to the mother:	*"I said 'lonely' instead of 'persistent'. I wonder why."*
	Mother appealing to the screaming baby: "Kirsten, why are you so sad?!"
Analyst:	*"Did you notice my slip?"*
Mother:	*"Yes, I did."*
Analyst:	*"Why did I say lonely? . . . Do you feel lonely?"*
Mother:	*"Sometimes . . ."*
Analyst to the baby:	*"You get lonely, too, Kirsten, when you turn off Mum. Now you are looking at Mum! And now you stopped."*

Analyst to the mother:	*"What about your loneliness?"*
	Mother, with notable emotion: "It's difficult for me to look at you. Sometimes, I'm looking at her while speaking to you. I hope it's OK with you that I don't look at you then."
	At this point – as Myra gets in contact with her feelings – Kirsten starts looking into Mum's eyes with a steady, calm gaze. Suddenly, it is a serene and calm scene.
Mother:	*"It's hard for me to open up with people. I guess I'm a bit lonely. I don't really talk to people, except to my husband."*
Analyst:	*"Kirsten, you look Mum in the eyes now. Did you see, Mum? Yes, Mum smiled at you. It's like you're drinking Mum's eyes."*
Mother:	*"Soon I can't look at her anymore! It's hard for me being looked at. I must rest my gaze. I get embarrassed . . . Don asked if we had talked about my mother. I answered no. I feel . . . and I guess I told her . . . that I am not satisfied with myself. But I don't judge her . . . she's like me. She did her best out of her conditions in life . . ." (Myra is holding back her tears, groping for words, her voice quivering.)*
Analyst:	*"Kirsten, do you see Mum's face, it's so lively. She's sad when speaking of your Granny. Myra, I was thinking about your mother. I had an image of her being here, holding you in her lap like a baby. I was inspired by how you're holding Kirsten now. Earlier, you were moving her up and down, looking stressed. Now you slowed down, swaying your body from side to side, more relaxed."*
Mother:	*"My mother is the kind of person . . . I'm the same I guess . . . one learns from one's parents . . . I guess she and I are . . . cold. If one stumbles and falls she responds, 'Up you go again'."*
Analyst to mother:	*"Are you cold, really? Isn't it more that you're shy? And you Kirsten, you are shy when you don't dare looking at Mum to get comfort."*
	Myra continues talking about her mother. When voicing some critique she adds, "Mother did her best".

Analyst to mother:	*"Do you defend her because you fear that I might think she's a bitch?"*
Mother:	*"I fear you'll make* me *think she's a bitch! . . . I was so sad when Kirsten was screaming. So much carrying and comforting, it became kind of automatic. I forgot what I was feeling, swinging her up and down, staring into nowhere."*
Analyst:	*"Perhaps you wanted to tell me your mother is auto . . ."*
Mother:	*"An autopilot, that's the word! My mother worked with children all day. When she came home she was tired and had to turn on her autopilot with us kids."*

Comments to the vignette – The analyst's running theory

The vignette illustrates influences from many traditions described in the book. Mother–infant psychoanalytic treatment or MIP (Norman, 2001) appeared when I addressed Kirsten: "You don't want to look Mum in her eyes." Another source was Lebovici (Lebovici et al., 2002; Lebovici & Stoléru, 2003), who inspired me to see the slip as suggesting my unconscious awareness of Myra's loneliness. He also valued the therapist's spontaneous metaphors to grasp unconscious undercurrents in a conversation, as when I used the racoon on Kirsten's sweater to portray her fright. Finally, I was inspired by Fraiberg (1980), as when I investigated how Myra's cumbersome relationship with her mother was a "ghost" in her relationship with Kirsten.

Analysts are taught not to let theoretical preconceptions obscure perceptions in clinical work but listen with "evenly suspended attention" (Freud, 1912b, p. 111) and utilize "negative capability" (Bion, 1970, p. 125) to refrain from asserting beforehand what goes on in the patient. Yet, such ideals are impossible to constantly maintain (Strenger, 1997). I was not able to perceive the session as a Lockean tabula rasa. Indeed, "theory-free" observations are a mirage. Rather, we are "writing" internal scripts with which we order observations. Mine were mainly Freudian, Kleinian, and Winnicottian. I guessed Kirsten's avoidance intended to protect her from unpleasant experiences. I assumed her perceptions of Mum were negative and influenced by the colic and Myra's ways of handling her. In this, I relied on Freud's idea (1895/1950) about the baby's hostile mother object, referred to in Chapter 16. Her primal representation (Salomonsson, 2014a) could be sketched: 'Mum's bad and makes me bad. I avoid looking at her to feel less bad.'

In Kleinian terms, Kirsten's perceptions were subjected to splitting and projective distortions, which resulted in a terrifying internal maternal part object. Any contact with the external Mum, specifically her eyes, might put Kirsten in contact with the feared internal object. Thus, *by circumventing her mother's eyes she sought to avoid a scary emotional experience*. This was also fuelled by how Myra perceived her daughter; her despair about the colic and the gaze avoidance amplified her tension with Kirsten. Further, Myra's dislike of people's eyes presumably linked with her brittle self-esteem. Finally her grief, worry, and lowered self-esteem also sprang from the abortion of a malformed foetus and the miscarriage.

Myra had longstanding problems with her own maternal identifications. Therese Benedek (1959), introduced in Chapter 1, stated that "the mother, through introjecting the gratifying experience of successful mothering, establishes self-confidence in her motherliness" (p. 393). In parallel, the infant will develop confidence in himself. But, such happy circumstances had neither dominated Myra's life nor her relationship with Kirsten. Winnicott (1971b) suggests that a baby looking at Mother's face sees "herself". But Myra rather reflected "her own mood or, worse still, the rigidity of her own defences" (p. 112) when being with Kirsten. To me, Myra seemed more downcast by the colic and her own somewhat closed character than by the loss of the two babies.

One might object that my speculations about Kirsten's internal world were circular arguments scaffolding my theoretical preconceptions. Let us then get back to the consulting room. I heard about foetal catastrophes, Kirsten's birth, the colic, the mother's misery, and the father's worries. The gaze avoidance I observed myself. Was it a mere reflex behaviour? If Myra's eyes had been harrowing, hostile, or avoidant, Kirsten would react to them as to a barking dog or a flash of light. But, Myra did *not* have such eyes. Another option was that the baby harboured an earlier frightening representation of Mum. If so, she was actively defending against Mother's eyes. Then we could enter the legitimate domains of psychoanalytic exploration and explore Kirsten's internal world. Let us call this viewpoint "Kirsten as subject". Yet, Myra reported personal difficulties with looking into people's eyes. Maybe Kirsten was a minor character involved in Myra's difficulties? Consequently, Kirsten would be an "inter-subject". So, what kind of subject is Kirsten actually?

The baby as subject or inter-subject?

In my view, we must either accept that analytic theory is based on clinical observations, dialogues with the patient, ideas stemming from countertransference, and conjectures about the "baby within the patient" and how it was formed in infancy. Especially Chapters 15–17 listed thinkers with such a perspective. Alternately, we discard such speculations – but then our theory is no longer psychoanalytic in any traditional sense. Freud clearly refers to babies as subjects; they feel, wish, react, recall, cognize, and represent to themselves. One could protest that we cannot isolate and study a human subject – infant or adult – *in itself*. Intersubjective theorists argue that an analysand is not an entity that we study from our side of the couch, so to speak. The analyst cannot escape his/her "system participation"

(Levenson, 2005/1983, p. 79) and the patient's emotional reactions are not mere intrapsychic events; they are also "the result of participation in larger social systems" (idem). Viewing the therapeutic relationship as one observing analyst + one observed patient is a fallacy; we cannot "stand outside of what we observe" (Op. cit., p. 8).

The intersubjective perspective provides new meanings to psychoanalytic concepts like neurosis (Levenson, 2005/1983, p. 65) and countertransference (Gerhardt, Sweetnam, & Borton, 2000; Renik & Spillius, 2004, p. 1054). What about Kirsten? If I investigate her gaze avoidance as a defence, I view it as an intra-psychic process and thus, she is a *subject*. Do then intersubjective theorists disclaim human subjectivity? Certainly not. Owen Renik (in Renik & Spillius, 2004) defines it as an individual's "various personal, idiosyncratic assumptions, concerns and motivations – including those that arise from membership in particular cultures and subcultures" (p. 1054). This definition concurs with classical analytic theory. Problems rather emerge from intersubjective theories of *how the analyst gains knowledge* about the subject. Jessica Benjamin (2005) writes that an interaction:

> creates a space for both subjects' separate but recognizable centers of feeling and initiative. In that space there can be some consensual validation, not of the objectively true, but of *what we think we are talking about, what feelings and meanings we believe we are trying to convey about one another in this moment.*
>
> (p. 449, italics added)

Such moments have been termed the "intimate edge" (Ehrenberg, 1992) or "the present moment" in the therapeutic relationship (Stern, 2004).

Benjamin's claim that we cannot achieve objective truth is hopefully shared by every analyst. What is new is her emphasis on what the two analytic participants believe they are conveying *about one another*. The classical perspective is: Analyst → Patient (→ = observes). The intersubjective perspective is: Analyst/subject ↔ Patient/subject (↔ = interacts with). In my view, every analyst oscillates between ↔ *and* →, between interacting as subject with the patient/subject *and* forming hypotheses about the patient/object. I am no neutral observer-analyst and I am coloured by my "power, freedom, and desire" (Benjamin, 2000, p. 46). The reported vignette is suffused with my subjectivity, such as the slip and the racoon metaphor. But, this subjectivity went parallel to forming ideas – it even added to these ideas – about my two patients as subjects.

A German analyst, Werner Bohleber (2010), has elucidated how intersubjective thinkers' views on the subject differ from those of traditional psychoanalysts. In the former, the human mind is "no longer considered independent and isolated" (loc. 340) but as a "continuous, reciprocal mutual influence system in which each partner is contextualized by the other" (Beebe & Lachmann, 2002, p. xiii). These two latter authors avoid the concept of psychic structure and prefer "patterns of experience that are *in process*, that is, organizations that may transform" (Op. cit.,

p. 13). In contrast, traditional psychoanalysis maintains that the self can "be understood and returned to itself by way of a detour through the other" (Bohleber, 2010, loc. 991), that is, via an analyst who listens to his/her subjectivity or countertransference. To Bohleber the subject exists as an entity, whether it is interacting with another subject or not – and we can legitimately say something about it. To me, in the intersubjective view *the subject has a shadow-like quality; not until it falls on an object can we see it.* If, as Benjamin writes, "the analyst and patient are equally participating and observing subjects as well as objects for each other" (2000, p. 47), then with what legitimacy can the analyst say anything about that subject over there, that is, the patient?

This description of the subject's elusive status among intersubjectivists may seem strange to readers familiar with Stern's writings (1985, 1990, 2004). As a clinician, he emphasized the "present moment" in psychotherapy and everyday life. As a theoretician, he presented intersubjectivity as a discrete motivational system. As a researcher, he described "the subjective life of the infant" (1985, p. 5). As an author for a larger audience, he portrayed the inner life of a baby in a more poetic vein (1990). His view of the baby within an inter-subjective matrix appears in terms like "schemas-of-being-together" (1995) or "Representations of Interactions that have been Generalized (RIGs)" (1985, p. 97). In line with Bohleber's and my critique, these terms bypass the baby's subjectivity and reduce it to a *process going on with the parent.* Similarly, when the infant's mind is defined in terms of "expectancies of procedurally organized action sequences" (Beebe & Lachmann, 2014, p. 26), the focus is on what the baby imagines will happen in the interaction with mother, rather than on himself as subject or "This is I".

To illustrate my objection, imagine a baby lying peacefully in the cot looking at a lamp. He is alone and contemplates a flower, a smell, or a memory trace. He may smile to himself, dream, or sigh. At such times, he is creating a subjectivity on his own. At other times, he does it by interacting with others. I argue that we should neither reduce subjectivity to a contingent effect of interactive contexts nor neglect the baby's autochtonous mental activity. Thus, I address Kirsten in words that acknowledge her subjectivity: "I think you got scared of Mum" and "You seem sad".

Do I then deny that the mind originates in dialogue with, principally, the parents? Of course not. The point of disagreement emerges more clearly in our terminologies. Many infant researchers' writings have a certain laboratory-like style, which actually echoes that of Freud, the scientist and nascent psychoanalyst in *The Project.* It risks that they shrink from expressing the baby's passions in simple and subjective language. Furthermore, though I, similarly to infant researchers, regard the baby as an interactor, I also see her as a subject with some stability. A third difference relates to *conflict*, a central psychoanalytic concept (Freud, 1919; Rapaport & Gill, 1959). I apply it to babies as well, whereas Stern's model of self-development contains no such terms. As said in Chapter 17, he focuses on the baby's experiences as "shapes, intensities, and temporal patterns"

196   Part II: Theory

(1985, p. 51). To him, a baby's "intention" (p. 6) is a general direction of the mind but not linked to conflict.

Or, perhaps Stern does speak of conflict in a baby but in other terms? Let us look at his portrait (1990) of a hungry baby:

> The world is disintegrating . . . uneasiness grows. It spreads from the center and turns into pain. It is at the center that the storm breaks out. It . . . turns into pulsing waves . . . [which] swell to dominate the whole weatherscape.
>
> (p. 31)

Then he is picked up by mother and breastfed: "At once the world is enveloped. It becomes smaller and slower and more gentle. The envelope pushes away the empty spaces" (p. 36). Stern's language is more evocative than Klein's blunt terms like "the good breast". Yet, both authors speak of a two-split world in the baby.

My aim is to borrow Stern's poignant descriptions of the hungry baby – but not his theories about what goes on – to illustrate Freud's and Klein's ideas that the child is in a *conflict* due to clashing representations. He loves his "envelope" mother until she shows her inability to immediately delete the pulsing hunger waves. This happens every day, and I agree with Seligman's critique (2006) of Klein, namely that far from every infant suffers from "the terrors of omnipotent destructiveness and deprivation" (loc. 1598). We may only speak of clinical problems and conflicts when a baby like Kirsten has colic and her relationship with mother gets distressed. She must handle the conflict of clashing representations: 'I love my mother, she always comforts me in a wonderful way. No, she can't take my pain away at once. I close my eyes 'cause I want her out of my life.' This is why Kirsten elicits a process that we will now investigate in terms of defence.

Frustration, pain, defence, and hostility in the baby – Freud's views

In Chapter 16, we laid out Freud's scheme (1895/1950) of how the frustrated baby perceives the hostile object. The next time she thinks of or perceives it, unpleasure arises. As if killing two birds with one stone, she tries to discharge that feeling and the object at the same time: 'Blah, I see you again and I feel bad. Get away!' But if frustrations reoccur, the road is paved for the memories of the inimical object to emerge more easily. Since the baby cannot delete them, she must change *internally*. S/he initiates "a repulsion, a disinclination to keeping the hostile mnemic image cathected". On the one hand, she feels a "primary wishful attraction (*primäre Wunschanziehung*)" (p. 322) towards the object that could fulfil her wish. On the other hand, she elicits "a primary defence [fending off, *primäre Abwehr*]". The mental apparatus seeks "to obviate, by means of side-cathexis, the consequent release of unpleasure" (p. 325). If this functions swiftly, unpleasure will be minimal and the need to erect a defence negligible. If not, "there will be immense

Babies and their defences 197

unpleasure and excessive primary defence" (p. 325). To sum up, this is how representations or perceptions of an impotent, then "hostile", object incite the baby to ward them off.

Paradoxically, the hostile object is also the baby's sole helping power: "My enemy is my best friend". The resulting conflict of ambivalence ignites the baby's thinking capacities in relation to a "fellow human-being" (Freud, 1895/1950, p. 331), both in war and peace. She creates tranquil representations, 'Here's my hand, there's Mum's hand. My hand's nice, her hand's nice.' Others are laden with negative affects linked with her scream: 'I scream because I feel bad. I scream to get rid of the bad. You don't help me. You don't take away the bad. *You're just like my scream.*' Since we cannot travel from ourselves, it is harder to withdraw from internal than from external demands. To dampen the former, a "specific action" (Op. cit., p. 297) is implemented, at first via "the attention of an experienced person [who] is drawn to the child's state by discharge along the path of internal change" (p. 318). In the baby's view: 'I feel bad and scream. You/Mum hear it and come to me. You're no longer that bad, you're good'. Screams serve multiple functions; they are communicative, they help bring about the specific action and have an intersubjective and ethical function; "the initial helplessness of human beings is the primal source of all moral motives" (p. 318). The following formula summarizes Freud's idea: *distress + helplessness → effort at discharging distress through scream → internal mother turns bad + external mother perceives distress and rushes to aid → distress alleviated + internal mother turns good → a vision implanted in the child that one is not alone, someone cares, and one day he can do the same to himself and, still later, to others in need.*

If the formula's first steps were valid eternally, the baby would rely on others all his life. So, she must build up defences to deal with the distress. As for Kirsten, does Freud's "primary defence" apply to her gaze avoidance? Should we even call it a defence mechanism – or would that imply capacities non-existent in such a young girl? And, is its purpose to ward off a drive impulse, an unbearable affect or memory? She avoided her mother's eye even when Myra was relaxed and talked friendly, so it must be motivated by something beyond a need to ward off a *present* threat. This "something" probably emerged at the time of the colic. The girl had created a primal representation corresponding to Freud's "hostile object". It lay dormant and then connected with the perception of Mum's eyes. This launched Kirsten's gaze avoidance but since the colic was gone now, it was more like a phobia, where anxiety that is tied "to certain circumstances and conditions is more controllable and therefore less frightening than free-floating anxiety" (Greenson, 1959, p. 663). It was less scary for Kirsten to fear Mum's eyes than her entire person. Her mentation would run something like: 'I'm distressed inside. No, distress is outside. Distress is in Mum, no, in Mum's *eyes*. If I avoid her eyes my distress is gone'. Yet, this solution did not work. Kirsten's subdued character, and her increasing panic in her mother's arms, indicated that her avoidance did not eradicate the internal threat.

Gaze avoidance, infant research, and infant observation

Gaze aversion is no rarity. I will relate findings from infant research and observations and then proceed to Selma Fraiberg who wrote about it. While the prevalence in non-clinical samples is less known, its clinical importance is illustrated by studies connecting it with the mother's emotional state. Infants of mothers instructed to mimic depression (Cohn & Tronick, 1983; Field, 1981) or sadness (Termine & Izard, 1988) tend to react with negativity and gaze aversion. Babies of clinically depressed mothers also tend to avoid their eyes while they look at other familiar people (Pelaez-Nogueras, Field, Cigales, Gonzalez, & Clasky, 1994). Yet, Landesman (2011) did not find this tendency. Even mothers with sub-clinical depressed mood (Feldman, 2007) may have babies with decreased mutual gazing. This may also occur when a non-depressed mother returns after an unexpected separation from the baby (Papousek, 2007).

What does infant gaze behaviour tell us about future development? In a normal sample, a stable gaze towards mother at 4 months old predicted a secure attachment at 1 year old (Koulomzin et al., 2002). These researchers suggested that the future insecure infants' tendency to look away might be an adaptation to maternal intrusion or overstimulation. Temperament might also play a role, they suggest. If we move to maternal depression it may, according to Tronick's (2007b) model, "[disrupt] the mutual regulatory process and [constitute] a break in intersubjectivity" (p. 283). He finds gaze avoidance more often among infants of intrusive mothers than of withdrawn depressed mothers. The former seem to avoid the overstimulation due to mothers' being pushy. Some infant observers also published gaze avoidant cases. Cowsill's (2000) case was a baby boy who, by avoiding mother's eyes, sought to preserve his good internal object. Kernutt's (2007) case was a girl with a mother, a bit like Kirsten's, who was not quite in tune with her emotional self. In Kernutt's interpretation, the girl's gaze avoidance was a reactive response by which she tried to maintain her True self.

Fraiberg's "Pathological defenses in infancy"

In a posthumous article, Fraiberg (1982) discussed gaze avoidance, freezing, and fighting when a baby's "human partners fail in their protective function and he is exposed to repeated and prolonged experiences of helplessness" (p. 614). This leads him to sense that "something is out there", which he vaguely connects with his painful experience. If pain is associated with his mother, he must ward off "the person on whom he is absolutely dependent and who is associated with pain and disappointment" (idem). Fraiberg stops investigating whether the resulting avoidance reflects a defensive process. "The questions seem to lead nowhere: thinking the unthinkable" (idem). The "unthinkable" query is how the baby wards off someone he depends on when his ego is not mature enough to launch any defences. I suggest the baby is facing a conflict; externally vis-à-vis his mother, and internally in that love and dependence crash with anger and frustration. This causes him to react "through a behavior that serves as defense" (p. 613). Note that she avoids the term defence mechanism.

To Fraiberg, gaze avoidance belongs to a "psychobiological system" (p. 621) set in motion because the baby regards his mother as a *real* threat. It seems "summoned from a biological repertoire on the model of 'flight or fight'" (p. 613). Alternately, she says the baby's anticipation of seeing the mother's face functions as a signal anxiety. This perception gets "caught up in conflict in the early months of life, so that registration appears to be closed off selectively" (p. 622). By invoking terms like "signal anxiety" and "conflict", Fraiberg applies a psycho-analytic model. Yet, she avoids using the term repression, which would imply that a painful stimulus is barred from consciousness. Instead, she calls it a "cutoff mechanism *in perception* which selectively edits the mother's face and voice and apparently serves to ward off painful affects" (p. 632, italics added). Fraiberg uses a full-scale psychoanalytic model of signal anxiety, conflict, and the warding off of painful affects – but hesitates between a psychological and a biological theoretical model to explain gaze avoidance.

I concur with Fraiberg's descriptions of gaze avoidance but diverge with her theorizing. In my view, her dependence on ego-psychological models makes her demur at viewing the symptom as a psychologically comprehensible pheno-menon. If "a symptom stands in place of the original conflict" (p. 613) – a traditional psychoanalytic notion – it can only come about if there is an agency to do the substitution. We call that agency "the ego", but Fraiberg thinks gaze avoid-ance can commence in young babies "before there is an ego" (idem). Therefore, it cannot be a symptom in the psychoanalytic sense. Instead, she needs to claim it belongs to the biological repertoire.

Let us see which model shows the best fit on Kirsten. If Myra had maltreated her, her behaviour would be a biological reflex response to danger. But this was not so. Had the girl avoided everybody's eyes we would suspect an incipient autism spectrum disorder. Yet, I met Myra again when Kirsten was 3 years old. She wanted to talk about Kirsten's jealousy towards her newborn brother. Their eye contact was no problem. Mother's story ruled out any grave psychological disorder in the girl. In contrast, during the PTIP there was much pain beneath Kirsten's screaming and Myra's story. According to analytic theory, if a behaviour aims to reduce psychic pain or conflict it is a defence. So, I think it is legitimate to speak of *gaze avoidance as a defence*. To clear the way for this view and check if it fits with traditional analytic theory, I will return to the origins of the defence concept.

The defence concept applied to infants

Freud wanted to link various defence methods to specific mental disorders. When he applied the concept to infants he suggested they use *other* defences than adults:

200   Part II: Theory

> Before its sharp cleavage into an ego and an id, and before the formation of a
> super-ego, the mental apparatus makes use of different methods of defence
> from those which it employs after it has reached these stages of organization.
>
> (Freud, 1925–1926, p. 164, italics added)

Laplanche and Pontalis (1973) hesitate if defence mechanisms presuppose "an organised ego capable of sustaining them" (p. 109). They differ from Fraiberg, who suggested that ego precedes defence. As I see it, though defence modes vary in psychic maturation their basic raison d'être and modus operandi are the same: The mind faces an idea, finds it incompatible, tries to treat it as *non arrivé*, but fails; the memory with its affect cannot be eradicated. Second best for the ego is to aim at "turning this powerful idea into a weak one, in robbing it of the affect – the sum of excitation – with which it is loaded" (Freud, 1894, p. 48).

What about defence *mechanism*? Freud introduced it (1892) and, since Anna Freud (1937), it belongs to common parlance – but its meaning is unclear. Laplanche and Pontalis (1973) suggest it emphasizes that "psychical phenomena are so organised as to permit of scientific observation and analysis" (p. 109). Klein (1975) also spoke of "mechanisms, anxieties, and defences operative in earliest infancy" (p. 53) but without clarifying the first term. One paper (Klein, 1930) reserves it for more advanced defences, but in another (Klein, 1935) she is less clear. Klein (1944/91) did not differ between "defence" and "defence mechanism", maybe because she was less interested in structural topics than in fantasies involved in the defence.

One would expect that Anna Freud had defined "mechanism" but I cannot find she did. Sandler (Sandler & Freud, 1981), in discussing with her, merely states it involves a "sort of mental machinery" that is "independent of the particular object concerned" (p. 238). In another paper (Sandler, 1993b), he suggests it works via "changes in the representational world" (p. 342). Lichtenberg and Slap (1972) give a clearer definition: "The *repetitive* use of a specific cognitive process in a conflict situation establishes it as a *preferred* mechanism by which to regulate conflict; it then may properly be called a *mechanism of defense*" (p. 778, italics added). Now we can ask: (1) is Kirsten's gaze avoidance a "preferred mechanism" by which she regulates a conflict, and (2) is it "independent" of the object? As for question 1, the answer is yes; she repetitively avoids her mother's eyes. As for question 2, it is no; her mother's eyes are avoided selectively. I suggested earlier that the avoidance resembles a phobia in that an internal threat is externalized. Yet, she fears only *one* person's eyes, so the term phobia is not comprehensive. There is a relational component as well; it's all about Mum.

In the end, are we to call Kirsten's avoidance a "psychological defence" or a "defence mechanism"? Laplanche and Pontalis (1973) define *defence* as a group of operations aimed to reduce "any change liable to threaten the integrity and stability of the bio-psychological individual" (p. 103). They are not only directed "towards internal excitation (instinct)" but also towards those "representations (memories, phantasies) [which] this excitation is bound to and to any situation that

Babies and their defences 201

is unpleasurable for the ego" (p. 104). Unpleasurable affects may also become objects of defence. They apply *defence mechanism* to various "types of operations through which defence may be given specific expression". Mechanisms are chosen depending on "the type of illness", "the developmental stage reached", and "the extent to which the defensive conflict has been worked out" (p. 109). The term has so many limitations that I stop at calling Kirsten's avoidance a psychological defence – *not* a mechanism.

Implications for technique

I have applied the defence concept to gaze avoidance. I thus view the baby as a subject with intentions, which contrasts with the intersubjectivist view of a more volatile and interacting subject. Yet, my vignettes contain many elements endorsed by intersubjective therapists; I shared my slip with Myra and I disclosed my affects (Maroda, 2002) when I saw Kirsten meeting Mum's eyes. Am I then not inconsistent using such a technique while questioning the intersubjective concepts?

My response concerns both clinical and theoretical issues. Kirsten's avoidance was part of a relationship disorder, but it was not enough to address how the *mother's* subjectivity coloured their interaction. I also addressed *Kirsten* about her presumed experiences. Had I not spoken to two subjects in the room, we would not have reached the affective breakthrough and the behavioural change in the baby; my slip brought Myra closer to her loneliness, which affected Kirsten's eye contact. In one session, Kirsten had diarrhoea, all diapers were gone, and Myra held her naked in her lap. During this lengthy contact, Kirsten looked at Mum with a steady and calm gaze. The scene was warm and sensual as she was exploring Mum's eyes, fingers, hair, and cardigan. I told Kirsten about her new experience of Mum's warmth, softness, touch, odour, and voice. Kirsten was bathing in Mum's infantile sexuality opening up to that of her daughter. As Myra was relishing her daughter she reflected on her and her mother's stiffness. In one sense, my technique was intersubjective; I attended to the communications between them. In another sense it was "intra-subjective"; I sought to grasp what was going on inside the two, or even, the three of us.

My theoretical response is that to grasp the process of change in PTIP, we need to conceptualize what happens inside mother *and* baby. Today, concepts from baby–mother interaction research are devised to describe the baby's world. I have argued that they do not give full credit to the baby's subjectivity in that it gets concealed behind a focus on the dyadic interaction. I have suggested another language when we theorize about the baby's mind and we address him in sessions; to speak of his passion, lust, anger, despair, sadness, and falling apart, and to tell him what he wants, avoids, hates, yearns, and fears. I utilize and may disclose my subjectivity and this; my technique contains elements of intersubjectivity. But, the ultimate aim is to uncover the subjectivity of mother *and* baby.

I end my investigation of one aspect of the baby's subjectivity; the use of defence. Starting from Kirsten, I postulate she has painful experiences when interacting with

202 Part II: Theory

her primary object. Her symptom aims to relegate these experiences from consciousness to maintain her own calm and her contact with her mother. This follows the classical analytic description of a defence – a concept that I find essential for understanding certain disturbed behaviours in babies. Interventions should also address the baby about why she defends herself and how we can help her deal with scary affects in a healthier way.

From a clinical perspective, I have come across several cases of persistent gaze avoidance in babies. Based on the model in Kirsten's case, I have been able to do substantial therapeutic work with them and, I should add, their mothers; when a baby rejects his mother, *he* becomes a frightening Gestalt to *her* in that she takes his avoidance to prove that he does not love her. This is, of course, gruelling and painful, which makes treatment even more important.

This chapter is derived, in part, from an article published in *International Journal of Psychoanalysis*: 2015, *97*(1), 65–88. Salomonsson, B. (2015b). Infantile defences in parent-infant psychotherapy: The example of gaze avoidance. (Reprinted by permission from Wiley.)

Chapter 19

Metaphors in parent–infant therapy

PTIP work promotes a certain "looseness" in the analyst's mind. In Chapter 18, I utilized the racoon on Kirsten's sweater as a metaphor of her view of Mum's eyes, and then made the slip about the "lonely" mother. Previously, in Chapter 3, I suggested that "co-thinking", metaphors, puns, and parapraxes can enhance our understanding of the emotional tensions in the session. This chapter is inspired by experiences from PTIPs where I came up with a *metaphor* and suggested it to mother and child. It may signify a peculiar emotion, a defence pattern, or sketch the dyad's distress. I will present some metaphors in a PTIP therapy and discuss gains and pitfalls with using them.

Metaphors in psychoanalysis

Metaphor is commonly seen as a poetic device or a linguistic embellishment; "He is a real lion". This "classical view . . . sees metaphor as 'detachable' from language, a device that may be imported into language in order to achieve specific, prejudged effects" (Arlow, 1979, p. 368), such as making it richer and nobler. In another view, language is metaphorical in itself. Today, this perspective dominates linguistic theorizing. Lakoff and Johnson (1999) have uncovered and categorized metaphors that permeate language. An analyst might say: "You felt put off when standing in front of your mother who treated you coldly". Here, many experiences are "embodied" or expressed "in the flesh": "Put off" transfers signification from physical movement to emotional rejection, and "cold" from temperature to hostility. Even "in front of" is a metaphor since in fact, mother and patient were standing *en face* (also a metaphor!) but the patient felt he was standing where her front is located.

In Wallerstein's (2011) words, metaphor "is used effortlessly, and mostly unremarked, in ordinary language . . . It is . . . an inevitable, intrinsic aspect of human thought, reasoning, and speech" (p. 90). One of Lakoff's and Johnson's points is that metaphors are embodied and originate in basic bodily infantile experiences. An infant strives for physical proximity with the primary object. Thence, "put off" becomes a metaphor of what happens when he fails and feels dismissed. A baby prefers warmth and comfort, so "cold" will signify an unfriendly attitude in

204 Part II: Theory

another person. Such *"conflations"* (p. 46) between sensorimotor and emotional experiences yield metaphors.

Simultaneously with development in linguistic theory, psychoanalysis has undergone a shift regarding our aims and the tools to achieve them, moving:

> from the model of an applied science of *discerning and interpreting unconscious meaning* to methods of *promoting new products of mental activity*. . . . Rather than deciphering or translating a disguised text, the analyst participates in a process that creates a text.
>
> (Kirshner, 2015, p. 67, italics added)

In Bion's (1962a) language, we seek to promote the function of knowledge, "K". This shift affects our view of interpretation. Rather than being seen as an authoritative statement about the patient, it refers to our "deconstructive strategy of clearing away the deposit of accumulated meanings to make room for new ones" (Kirshner, 2015, p. 69). This "antiauthoritarian attitude" questions "the privileged nature of the analyst's subjectivity" (Kernberg, 1997, p. 99). We are less inclined to tell the patient what went on in his childhood and to profess what his present-day issues and symptoms actually "mean". We are more engaged in a joint project whose aim is that he becomes more agile and variegated when reflecting on his feelings, attitudes, and actions. Lichtenberg (2016) points out that the power of our interpretations still lies in revealing "the hidden, forgotten, and unformulated", which the patient may perceive as "aha moments" (p. 5), but we are becoming more intent on *facilitating* such moments. And, importantly, we hope to provide the patient with means to achieve it by himself in the future.

This digression relates to metaphors: In Kirshner's "authoritative" position, metaphors are merely valued as arrows pointing to the patient's *real* history. In his "deconstructive" position, they are appreciated as tools for helping the patient express anxieties and reflect on them. In this view, our job is "an enterprise of mutual metaphoric stimulation in which the analyst, in a series of approximate objectications of the patient's unconscious thought processes, supplies the appropriate metaphors" (Arlow, 1979, p. 381). Other US analysts have also ascribed a significant role to metaphor; Modell (2009) suggests using it to "unconsciously interpret our affective world" and that it is "an organizing template that establishes the categories of emotional memory" (p. 8).

It is not evident to what extent Arlow and Modell sanction that the analyst also voice a metaphor to express *his/her* "creationism" (Ahumada, 1994). In contrast, Ogden (1997) is clear on this point: "My interventions very frequently take the form of elaborating a metaphor that the patient or *I have* (usually unselfconsciously) introduced" (p. 723, italics added). Metaphor is "an integral part of the attempt of two people to convey to one another a sense of what each is feeling (like) in the present moment and what one's past experience felt like in the past . . ." (idem). Reider (1972) suggests that a metaphor:

Metaphors in parent–infant therapy 205

enables both patient and therapist to maintain sufficient discontinuity between primary and secondary process, and permits insights that can be tolerated . . . [It] serves the *defensive* function of allowing the patient to keep a necessary distance from conscious awareness, while serving the function of *reducing the distance* between therapist and patient.

(p. 468, italics added)

It is "the most economic condensation of understanding of many levels of experience, several fixations, symbolic connotations, and an aesthetic ambiguity" (p. 469). These traits are covered by Rizzuto's (2009) term "the synthetic function" of a metaphor. Finally, Stern (1985) claims the clinician's task is "to find the narrative point of origin – invariably, the key metaphor(s)" rather than retrieve "the unmasked earliest edition [which] is rarely where theory predicts its origin point should be" (p. 262).

Other "pro-metaphor" analysts adhere to the *field theory* (Baranger & Baranger, 2009; Civitarese & Ferro, 2013; Ferro, 1999). They view therapy as an exchange of metaphor between analysand and analyst. They do not restrict its use to a mere study of "the similarities and differences between two terms/objects thought of as always identical with themselves" (Civitarese & Ferro, 2013, p. 198), as when one analyses a metaphor in linguistic terms. Instead, metaphor itself "generates the relationship". The authors argue that the analyst's metaphor "is a reverie produced on the spot, or rather, one whose discursive formulation arises out of a reverie" (p. 203). They link metaphor with visual imagery or pictogram (Aulagnier, 2001, see Chapter 17). Pictograms capture "proto-emotional states" and thus help the analyst in "naming something which was previously unnamed" (Ferro, 2006, p. 999). The link with early experience is also mentioned by da Rocha Barros (2000), to whom metaphor is a "synthetic representation of experiences coming from the infantile past" (p. 1092).

Is then metaphor a *via regia*, like the dream (Freud, 1900), to understanding the Unconscious? Let us first recall Freud's reservations in his metaphor of *via regia* or "royal road". Allegedly, he claimed that *the dream* is the royal road to the Unconscious, but this is not true. He stated that "the *interpretation* of dreams is the royal road to a *knowledge of the unconscious activities* of the mind" (p. 608, italics added). The dream does not lay bare the Unconscious on a dissection table. It must be interpreted via a procedure; instantaneous and intuitive or continuous and laborious, but always objective in that the analyst follows the patient's rendition of the dream. Also, it is subjective in that s/he contributes to the interpretation; it thus provides pieces of knowledge about unconscious activities but does not reveal the Truth. This uncertainty also applies to the metaphor, and Wallerstein (2011) argues that though it has been "central to the fabric of psychoanalysis from its very beginnings as an emerging science", we must also clarify its "limitations, and its possibility for obfuscation" (p. 93).

The major hazard of the analyst's metaphor is, to me, *narcissism*. We cannot be certain to what extent it captures the patient's and/or the analyst's fantasy world.

Ahumada (1994) warns that if the analyst views treatment as an interchange between his and the patient's "creationism", the two risk colluding about superficial preconscious matters rather than digging up repressed material from the Unconscious. Thus, the focus on therapy as a dialogue sounds inviting but could also blur that actually, it is the analysand who requested help from the analyst to *suggest* truths that s/he dare not, or cannot, perceive. We are thus left with a constant doubt if an analytic metaphor illuminates – or dims – truths about the patient's internal world.

A sensible approach is to utilize the epistemological method suggested by C. S. Peirce (Kloesel & Houser, 1998; Muller & Brent, 2000; Rennie, 2012). I see metaphor as an inductive statement, a summarizing guess about inner reality expressed in a skewed or displaced way. I and the patient then rely on abductions and deductions to establish to what extent it is credible, useful, and maybe even veracious – which helps me further refine my inductions. *Metaphor is thus one of many roads to understanding the Unconscious.* In contrast to dreams that may be condensed, enigmatic, and bizarre but which, nevertheless, are the patient's personal creations, I am also referring to metaphors created *by the analyst* and which may contain elements that do not pertain to the patient. Let us probe the value of such use by bringing in a clinical case.

First vignette with Leonard and his mother Edna

At the CHC, a nurse reports on Edna who is a first-time mother of 3-week-old Leonard. Though everything is fine with him, the mother says breastfeeding is very problematic and that something terrible might happen to him any minute. "There is so little enjoyment in her ways of being with him", the nurse says. I see the mother for a consultation a few days later.

Edna arrives alone. She speaks of motherhood as a work task like her office duties. She felt this way already during pregnancy, a time when she fantasized very little about her future child. In other words her foetal attachment, a concept we discussed in Chapter 2, must have been feeble. Her story and apparition convey much duty and little pleasure.

> Edna: *"In the beginning I could hardly sleep, I must be there for him all the time, be his guardian, please him, stand attention. I didn't have that relaxed relationship with . . . him."*
>
> Analyst: *"I'm thinking of you and Leonard as a dancing couple. If he takes a step, you could respond by another step that suits you. But no, you think this should be settled beforehand. It's as if you're the dance master taking responsibility of all that goes on in the dancing couple."*
>
> Listening to this dance metaphor *she laughs a bit in some relief. It seems to touch her.*

Metaphors in parent–infant therapy 207

> *Edna:* "I thought I was going to feel much safer being a mother. And I think he sometimes senses that I do not feel that way with him. Then I get stressed and tense."

Some years ago, she had CBT when approaching a burn-out. She is married and describes her husband fondly. I ask her to bring her son to the next session and tell her we must move sessions to my private office, due to my tight CHC schedule. She accepts and treatment continues gratis there.

When she arrives with her son to the next session, he peers at her from her lap or moves his head towards her breast in a calm rhythm. He seems OK but mother worries.

> *Edna:* "I worry constantly. I am responsible for his survival. I search on the internet how to secure vacuum . . . Without vacuum, he cannot establish the correct sucking technique."
>
> *Analyst:* "I wonder what would happen if you told your husband that
> *(with a smile)* you have a vacuum and he must use the right technique to fill it up."

I take a risk in linking her adult sexuality with the two infantile sexualities, hers and the boy's, that I assume clash in breastfeeding (Salomonsson, 2012a) and make it so stressful. Still, I dare make this link due to the calm and confidence that she is evincing.

> *Edna:* "I enjoy being with my husband . . . Well, it's a bit hard for me to tell him how I want things."
>
> At this point she wants to leave this track, so I drop it and return to her issues with breastfeeding.
>
> *Analyst:* "I wanted to bring out that breastfeeding could be a mutual delight rather than viewing it as Leonard having a vacuum that you must fill up."

Our dialogue continues. In response to my queries about her background, she says the parents are affectionate but often provide concrete solutions to her worries rather than listening to them. I suggest this parallels her attitude with the boy: "As soon as he whines you must offer a solution."

We now begin therapy twice a week. Once, the father takes part. He seems supportive and reflective and is not worried. Next session, the fifth, Edna feels guilty of not recalling the previous hour. From now on, the entire mother–infant therapy will be video-recorded upon the parents' consent.

> *Edna:* "It's a kind of dumbness inside, I can't put words to what I feel . . . I recognize it from my work. I'm good at control, and I can write reports on concrete matters but not on how I experience things."
>
> Now the boy is distressed, flailing and whining.
>
> *Analyst:* "You're really cramping, Leonard. Mum offers you milk, you suckle intensely and maybe some air gets down as well . . . a real panic. Mum likes to control things at work, but she can't control your flailing so she thinks she's a failure. Oh dear, Leonard, you are cramping and struggling."
>
> I then link his cramps with Mum's dumbness and her inability to recall the previous session.
>
> *Analyst:* "Leonard, when you cry Mum gets this mute thing inside, and matters get worse for both of you. Just as your little body is cramping, Mum's head cramps when she doesn't know what she's feeling or what we've been talking about."

After this *cramp metaphor* is born, Edna speaks of Leonard's arrival as a chock. Overwhelmed by emotions, she responded with a mental "cramp" and a resolve to "secure his survival". I return to the dance metaphor from the first session.

> *Analyst:* "When you and Leonard are together, it is as if you're a dance instructor teaching him according to a manual."
>
> Edna struggles with her tendency to view this intervention as issued by another dance instructor, that is, me. I add that I am not there to instruct her but to help both of them.
>
> *Edna:* "I thought I would feel much safer! I guess Leonard sometimes senses I'm not feeling safe."
>
> Leonard becomes distressed.
>
> *Analyst to Leonard:* "You see, Leonard, Mum's got an issue with dancing. And you, you're not dancing samba today really, it's a bit jittery. Or maybe you want to make poo-poo, I don't know. What's happening inside you, Mum, right now?"
>
> *Edna:* "I was thinking that I don't like dancing or massage. I have no sense of rhythm, actually."

The ensuing sessions she elaborates on her "mental cramp":

Metaphors in parent–infant therapy 209

It's as if I *am* my achievements. If I don't succeed I'm no good, at work or at breastfeeding, and I cramp. When I don't manage, I brood on why I don't succeed! And when Leonard is distressed I feel the same. I wish I could focus more on the . . . soft things.

The cramp also implies, she says, "I can't *desire* anything from Leonard. I was reminded about it when we agreed earlier that breastfeeding is not a one-way thing but something going on between him and me." I add that neither does *she* dare being desired by Leonard: "You often use the pronoun 'one' instead of 'I' when speaking of yourself." She exclaims: "Yeah, other women are mothers to *someone* but I ask myself if it's really me who is his mother."

"Dance" and "cramp": psychodynamics of two metaphors

Edna is low-keyed, cautious, and a bit hard to reach emotionally. She looks at me eagerly when I am speaking but feels awkward when *she* is talking about feelings. This numbness is painful but has also rendered her a reputation of trustworthiness and efficiency at work. Pregnancy was a work project, not an opportunity to fly away in fantasies about the child's future. Leonard's arrival struck like a bolt from the blue. What to do with someone she is responsible for but who cannot express his wishes clearly? She is very tender with him, which suggests that he has awakened her infantile sexuality. Since this clashes with her efficient and massage-detesting persona, he threatens her equilibrium. I feel uncertain if he, too, is distressed on a more continuous basis.

The dance and cramp metaphors both relate to movement that is withheld and stunted. In retrospect, I discern several sources to the dance metaphor: One is texts that depict mother–infant interaction as a dance (Stern, 1985; Trevarthen & Aitken, 2001), another is my interest in music. These sources form a narcissistic component and may thus reveal more about me than about this dyad. A third font is Edna's reports about their distressed interaction. A fourth source might have been the nurse's report but she said mother and son were fine together. She rather worried about *the mother's* emotional state. All in all, *countertransference* seems a more central source. I meet with a suave, sympathetic, and earnest woman. I would like to get closer to help her but I feel hesitant, uncertain, and frustrated by our constrained interchange. When the dance metaphor is born, Edna uses it to speak of her unsafety as a mother and her guess that Leonard perceives her stress and tension. "Dancing with him" is not as enjoyable as she would like.

The birth of the cramp metaphor is different. When I voice it, my conscious aim is to objectively describe Leonard's flailing movements, muscular tension, and desperate crying. Its metaphorical aspect is born only when I link his movements with Edna's difficulties with spontaneity: "Just as your little body is cramping, Mum's head cramps." At this point, she starts speaking of her chock upon Leonard's arrival. Coupling the two metaphors, she responds that she dislikes dancing and massage and has no sense of rhythm. Suddenly we are into deep strata

210   Part II: Theory

of her personality. Perhaps she rejects her body in its infantile sexual aspects, and I wonder if this may affect their interaction. This hunch receives confirmation when she says she would like to focus on the "soft things". She brings in the word "desire" to denote what she yearns for with Leonard. By now she intuits the links between her issues with sexuality (no dance, massage, or rhythm) and her "cramp" at breastfeeding. This also influences her entire sense of being a mother: "I ask myself if it's really me who is his mother."

I suggested that my *conscious* motive for the "cramp" metaphor was just to describe his movements. I now grasp that unconsciously, I was frustrated. Like most people, I enjoy being with a happy and relaxed baby, or with an adult who expresses her feelings and is easy to reach. The unconscious script, already at the birth of the cramp metaphor, was "Come on guys, let's relax and dance together. Loosening up muscles and mind is pleasurable." I assume that the mental leap, from his flailing to her emotional deadlock, and from concrete description to metaphorical signification, was enabled by this script. In other terms, frustration in the countertransference unleashed a creative act; to link his movement pattern with her mindset.

Metaphor in parent–infant psychotherapy

The vignette will now help us investigate specifically metaphors in PTIP. Serge Lebovici (Lebovici, 2000; Lebovici et al., 2002; Lebovici & Stoléru, 2003) advocated spontaneous "metaphorizing interventions" (Lebovici, 2000) that could reveal what he unconsciously assumed was going on in the dyad. Once he voiced such a metaphor, it could help mother improve her symbolic capacities and liberate such dawning capacities in the baby. It also relies on *creativity*: the patient communicates affects to, and tries to affect, the analyst. Only rarely does he explicitly become aware of them. Instead, he intuits a *mise en acte*, an *enaction* (enactment), an urge or an "empathic response", in his body (Lebovici et al., 2002, p. 181). This response finds its way into a metaphor, often with a physical connotation, like "dance" and "cramp". *Mise en acte* and *enaction* risk being misconstrued as a sanction to act out one's impulses vis-à-vis the patient. This is *not* Lebovici's advice. He suggests we utilize such moments "to understand, to realize, to contain, and to interpret" (p. 182) what is being enacted by baby and parent. He recommends the therapist to be "taken over by the situation" (idem) in a *hysterical identification* with the dyad. "Hysterical" denotes an analyst's ability to enter rapid and fleeting identifications with mother and baby, and invent metaphors to be included in an interpretation.

Another explanation for why babies can stimulate metaphoric functioning issues from *intermodal perception*; "the perception of unitary objects or events that make information simultaneously available to more than one sense" (Bahrick & Hollich, 2008, p. 165). Such early skills have been demonstrated across all senses. Young babies' imitation of an adult's tongue protrusion (Meltzoff & Moore, 1997) was mentioned in Chapter 15 on Klein's observations and in Chapter 17 on Gaddini's theories. Meltzoff (2007, p. 36) suggests it relies on "active intermodal matching" (AIM) whereby the baby registers perception and production of human movements within a "supramodal representational system" that helps infants code human acts, perceived and/or performed, in one common framework. "Perception and production 'speak the same language' and are intimately bound at birth" (idem).

We now realize that primary metaphors (Lakoff & Johnson, 1999, p. 49) rely on intermodal perception since they conflate a sensorimotor and an emotional experience. Analysing après-coup the dance metaphor, I realized my frustration with our contact. I wanted to "come closer" to Edna – another conflating metaphor. To dance is to approach somebody and thence my metaphor was born. If intermodal perception is a signature of babies' mentation, one might say that I thought like a baby when I came up with the dance imagery. This would illustrate "hysterical identification" with the infant, which I think we all use with babies. Thence all the metaphors and metonyms we use to address them; "my heart", "sweetie-pie", "honey" . . . Intermodal tokens of love!

Apart from stimulating the analyst's intermodal mentation, the baby's presence brings out infantile material in another way. The sight of diapers, breastfeeding, crying, belching, farting, etc. dissolves the borders between the analyst's "instantaneous, intuitive, nonconscious knowing that affects physiological responses and behaviors" and a "more explicit awareness, usually verbal, of . . . the analysand's current emotions, intentions, values, and goals, past influences, and present context" (Lichtenberg, 2016, p. 6). We criss-cross between imagery and words, between concrete and abstract thinking. Also, it is very stressful to sit with a screaming baby, and our infantile helplessness is awakened. This can push us to ward off affects, look for medical explanations, or wish to escape. Such impulses can be transformed via a metaphor into a better service.

What about the mother? To what extent does her presence incite the metaphoric activity in the analyst? I think this varies. The therapist listens to their expectations for the baby's bright future but also to fantasies of infanticide or suicide. One faces their love for the child but also narcissism, vengeance, and envy. These factors intensify countertransference which, via *mise en acte* or *enaction*, facilitates our metaphoric function. The more the mother tends to repress, the more the onus is on us to create the metaphor. The more the mother is in a state of psychological transparency (Bydlowski, 2001), the easier she may come up with metaphors, to be seen in the next vignette.

Stern (1985) speaks of metaphors in connection with *attunement*. It relates to "sharing affective states", that is, processes that "let other people know that you are feeling something very like what they are feeling" (p. 138). He asks how you can get "'inside of' other people's subjective experience and then let them know that you have arrived there, without using words" (idem). He gives an everyday portrait of a mother exclaiming "YES, thatta girl" to her happy baby waving her arms (p. 141). As Stern says, this illustrates cross-modal matching (mother's raised voice – girl's raised arms) and a match between the feeling states of the two. But, his example is vitally different from Edna and Leonard. Stern's mum is skilled in entering "the intersubjective domain" with her baby, whereas Edna could *not* attune well to her baby. She just cramped.

212 Part II: Theory

Stern's *attunement* seems more related to imitation and playing together – although he emphasizes that the match between the two participants' expressions refers to "expressions of inner state" (p. 142) rather than to observable behaviour. I suggest that attunement – between Edna and Leonard and between her and me – was stiff and cumbersome, and *this stimulated my metaphoric activity*. Stern says it recasts "the experience of emotional resonance" into "another form of expression", without necessarily proceeding towards "empathic knowledge or response. Attunement is a distinct form of affective transaction in its own right" (p. 145). Metaphor would thus, in his view, represent such recasting. My objection is that "attune" connotes a *fit* or *sameness*, as when musicians tune their instruments, while metaphor implies a *leap* from the signified to the signifier. There is a discord between what is explicitly said and Edna's tension. This yields unpleasure, which I seek to discharge by creating metaphors of a stilted dance or a mental cramp. Metaphors therefore condense, in an apt and economic way, many levels of experience (Reider, 1972) and serve a defensive function; they help me to come to grips with a situation that I feel is anguishing and challenging.

Second vignette with Leonard and his mother Edna

Let us apply our theoretical concepts to a third metaphor. It emerged during the 11th session, which I had to transfer back from my private office to the CHC for schedule reasons. Such a change of frame runs counter to ordinary work with older children and adults. Since there is a sense of urgency in parent–infant therapy – to cancel one week may have dire consequences – I take a more flexible attitude to alterations in the setting in PTIP, as discussed in Chapters 7 and 8. In the beginning of this Monday session, Edna spoke about her distress concerning a thrush infection in Leonard's oral cavity. During the weekend, life was boring and stressful and their contact had sagged. She had to give him a bitter-tasting medication and wash her breasts with an anti-mycotic solution before breastfeeding. This uncoupled her intuition and spontaneity with him, and the boy disliked the drug. Today, though, she said their contact was much better again. I suggested this made it easier to trust her intuition when being with Leonard, which she confirmed. Yet, I was struck by her sad eyes.

> *Analyst to Edna:*   *"As we're talking about intuition,* my *intuition tells me you look sad."*
>
> *Edna:*   *"Yeah. I don't know why. I guess when I got here, I saw parents in the CHC waiting-room who don't have to see a psychologist to get a good contact with their baby. Things got different from what I expected . . . I don't understand it! I* know *all parents aren't happy with their babies, and yet . . ."*

Metaphors in parent–infant therapy 213

> *We discuss if her sadness is due to the thrush infection complicating her contact with Leonard.*
>
> Edna: *"When the thrush is getting better I can relax. But yesterday, my only focus was on fixing it. I got so active and busy and I didn't talk to him much."*

I suggest she is now realizing that she is involved in an *interaction* with Leonard, and that her feelings do affect how it develops. While saying this, I am getting concerned about *our* interaction; we are stuck in an intellectual and strained dialogue, so I bring in her affects again.

> Analyst: *"You're sad now, I see it again."*
>
> Edna: *"Yeah . . . it's sad that it's not self-evident for me to seek out a relationship with him. I'm not relaxed, I don't talk with him enough. Well, now I do talk but it's not self-evident for me that . . . when he's not, well he is communicating back to me in his way, but when he doesn't do it via speech, then it doesn't become self-evident for me to stay in contact, though I know it's important to do so. On the other hand, I think it's natural that one isn't as communicative when there is no two-way communication . . . via words, that is."*

Edna speaks in a rapid, conscientious, and monotonous way, like a school-girl presenting her homework to her class.

> Analyst: *"Why are words so important for you? I don't think you communicate just by words. Had I only listened to your words, we wouldn't get in contact. Like now, I think you look sad."*
>
> Edna: *"That's true."*
>
> Analyst: *"Your eyes are sadder than your words . . . For you, words function like a brick wall, they block your feelings."*
>
> Edna: *"How do you mean?"*
>
> Analyst: *"Like a wall with red bricks. Behind it, a girl is sitting crying."*
>
> Edna: *"Yeah, well, I don't know."*
>
> Analyst: *"You look quite sad."*
>
> Edna: *"Precisely."*
>
> Analyst: *"I guess you are afraid of that little girl behind the wall."*
>
> Edna: *"I don't experience myself as a sad person . . . But I do feel*
> (thoughtful   little *sometimes. I've always needed to feel secure, and I*
> at first, then   *worry about things that didn't even happen but that might*
> more eager)   *happen. And I also tend to diminish myself."*

214 Part II: Theory

Analyst: "So that's how you'd describe the little girl; anxious, diminishing herself, searching for safety. Then there is the big girl; appreciated at work for her trustworthy, competent and cheerful achievements in writing her reports. I guess words have become important to maintain that wall. You arrived at a new place today, and Big girl said, 'We're going to do the same thing here as in his office. No worries!' But Little girl said, 'I don't like this new place, I don't feel safe here'."

Edna becomes more and more tearful. I continue.

Analyst: "Enter that little rabbit (pointing at the boy). He leaps over the wall without problems. He whines and cries, and you get staggered and don't know what to do. Little girl has been pushed back by Big girl for many years, so you can't ask her for help. Instead, Big girl prescribes words and solutions and you consult Google on all your worries about Leonard."

Edna: "No no, Google is just positive to me!"

Analyst: "I have another idea: Little girl is very clever and could be of help to you. Big girl taught you to suppress her, but I'm saying, 'Come forward little girl, you can understand this baby boy, you can feel your way into how he's feeling when he's sad . . .' And Leonard, the little rabbit, is perhaps saying: 'Mum, couldn't we bring down that wall a bit? You don't need it anymore'."

Edna: "But the little girl is no good! She makes me worry about everything!"

Analyst: "I'd say the wall is no good. It wants to disconnect Big and Little girl."

Edna: "But I need that wall! Otherwise Little girl triggers my worries and I waste energy on worrying about things that didn't even happen!"

Analyst: "Maybe the wall could be movable. Sometimes, Big girl must have the upper hand and act swiftly. But often, things are not as dangerous or humiliating as you imagine. Then Little girl would be of help. For example, Big girl tries to convince you: 'Many mothers worry about their babies, it's all on the internet. You don't need anybody else to help with your worries.' Yet, her words do not calm you down. Little girl could tell you, 'Never mind if other mothers need a psychotherapist or not. I know that I need help. I think it's good coming to Björn. I want to'!"

Pensive, Edna says she felt ashamed about her worries during the first visits to the health visitor. I suggest she was under the influence of Big girl. Yet, the nurse perceived her problem and reported to me about it, though she couldn't pinpoint its exact nature.

Metaphors in parent–infant therapy 215

> *Analyst:* "*I think 'Little nurse' perceived your worries, perhaps that your eyes were sad. I think she was very professional in using her Little girl. Her 'wall' moved between Big nurse and Little nurse. So the nurse, too, has a Big girl and a Little girl inside her, like we all do.*"

Leonard wakes up and remains sleepy for the rest of the hour. At the end, we couple the imagery of Little and Big girl with the relationship with her mother. Edna describes her as committed and loving, which meets up with Little girl's needs. But she can also be dismissive and suggest concrete solutions to emotional problems, in line with Big girl's ideology. We return to her strong reaction to the new locale of this session. She ends with a pensive remark.

> *Edna:* "*I was quite unprepared for being sad today. I didn't feel sad when I arrived. It had been a good day! Not that it must be a bad day for me to feel sad, but I wasn't prepared to feel this way.*"

The wall: comments to a metaphor

The video-recording of the session shows that the metaphor was accompanied by my hand gestures drawing a wall in the air and a girl behind it. I was thus portraying a situation in sensorimotor terms. Why did this imagery appear just then? Once again, *countertransference* provides the key explanation. The emotional situation could be summarized with other metaphors; we were under *pressure* and I felt *far away* from Edna. Her eyes looked sad but she could not say what tormented her. I sensed her sadness, expressed my empathy about the thrush, tried to alleviate her harsh ego-ideal, and spoke about her contact with Leonard. Yet, our contact was muffled and my countertransference despair waxed. This was probably the prime cause of the wall image. The despair indicated my *narcissistic imbalance*; I was frustrated at not reaching her emotionally. In terms of empathy, it also represented my *hysterical identification* with Edna's isolation, which I transformed into an imagery of a girl crouching behind a wall. This image would not have been born unless I could sense how it is to cower and tremble behind a wall.

The construction of the wall metaphor was similar to the ones about dance and the cramp. To crouch behind an unyielding structure is a sensorimotor experience. Feeling lonely and abandoned is an emotional experience. The two conflate into the wall metaphor. The difference between the two sets lies in the clinical context. When "dance" and "cramp" emerged, Edna was more cautious and muted. True, there was also emotional restraint and stilted interchange in the "wall" session. Yet, her eyes revealed strong emotions, which moved me and inspired a more dynamic metaphor: It started as a wall and evolved to include Little girl, Big girl,

216   Part II: Theory

and the rabbit. It started with signifying loneliness and sadness; the girl behind the wall. Then it waxed to include the conflict between her anxious longing and her harsh ego-ideal; Little girl versus Big girl. Finally, it covered the antagonism with the mother. The significations expanded more easily than previously, when the dance and the cramp similae came up. Edna was now more transparent and curious about her emotions: "I was unprepared for being sad."

Conclusions

The analyst's metaphors may further the clinical process. Their specificity does not lie in their linguistic structure but in their origin; in situations of emotional pressure. This charge, which is part and parcel of every analytic encounter, differentiates the analytic metaphor from others. We need to keep this in mind to understand *why* a clinical metaphor emerges and *what* its utility is. Its value depends on whether (1) the patient feels it is relevant and expresses her personal dilemma, (2) it is private to the analyst and mainly reflects his narcissistic preoccupations, and (3) he is perceptive and courageous in discerning the countertransference. In PTIP, therapist metaphors seem more frequent than in other settings. This is related to (a) the intense countertransference, which awakens infantile strata in the analyst and pushes him towards concrete thinking, (b) the oscillations between verbal and non-verbal communication, which makes him use body language like gestures and facial expressions, and (c) the character of the setting, with its parallels to psychodrama and couple therapy. The concrete and bodily nature of the transactions between mother and child also belongs to this point.

I am ending this chapter by stating the evident; no clinical tool is a panacea. This applies to metaphors as well. I have clarified the risks but wish to end on a positive note: If we use metaphors creatively and with judgement, avoid squeezing out brilliant figures of speech but remain spontaneous, and keep track of the countertransference and the process after the metaphor emerged, we may often find it to be a valuable clinical tool.

Chapter 20

A vision for the future

I hope the biblical imagery of "In the beginning . . ." did not make me appear as an acolyte eager to foist the gospel of perinatal psychotherapy on everybody. Yet, I claim that much suffering exists among young parents and babies and that some could be diminished if certain conditions were fulfilled: Professional competence in perinatal psychology needs to increase and perinatal health care organization should integrate somatic and psychological care and be accessible and of high quality. If all these conditions were fulfilled today, this chapter would be redundant. It is divided in two sections: how to organize a health care that integrates medical and psychological perspectives, and how to amalgamate the two in the mindset of each professional. As we will see, the two topics are interrelated. The chapter is written to inspire the reader beyond the book's clinical vignettes, recommendations, and theorizing; to inform and lobby colleagues, health care officials, and politicians. They need to understand that perinatal psychology is urgent and should be regarded as an ingredient in health care, as self-evident as inoculations and measuring the child's growth.

Organization

To my knowledge, the question of how to organize perinatal psychological care has not received much scientific attention. It tends to be managed according to local traditions, economic factors, political structures, and the power balance between professions. It is of course hard to compare the efficiency of organizational models but that should not subdue our discussion: What are the effects of organizational structures on the well-being of parents and infants, and on the atmosphere and competence of the professionals? Such questions apply to every medical field, but in perinatal psychology some issues are added. The baby cannot voice his demands, and parents do not always discern the psychological undercurrents beneath their baby worries.

Let us sketch two models of health care: the *horizontal* and the *vertical.* They are simplified images of a complex reality. The horizontal, in Figure 20.1, implies that parents with babies visit local centres near their living quarters. This gives them easy access and conveys that regular check-ups are routine yet important.

218 Part II: Theory

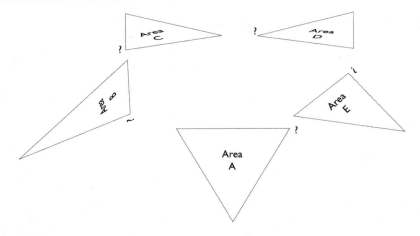

Figure 20.1 The horizontal model. "Area" indicates a housing area. The question marks are explained in the text.

Many symptoms and worries are banal and disappear by themselves. The nurse can do a quick check-up and reassure the parents that things will be all right in a day or two. Local units facilitate personal contacts that make it easier to broach difficult and embarrassing topics. Likewise, follow-up calls can be arranged easily. These advantages are utilized in countries with a well-organized public health system, such as Scandinavia, France, Great Britain, and Israel. Countries with poor resources can also use such a system with units in faraway villages.

The horizontal model in Figure 20.1 has two drawbacks. One applies to all medical services; difficult and complex cases can be overlooked or not treated correctly. Mothers with postpartum psychosis, an ongoing toxicomania, or those living in abject poverty or with a violent partner need more help than a local

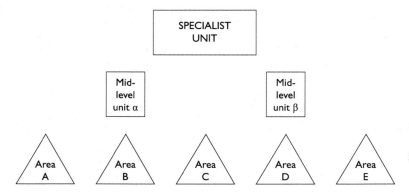

Figure 20.2 The vertical model.

perinatal unit can offer. The second drawback is specific to perinatal psychology, but before discussing it we need to lay out the vertical model.

The vertical model is more hierarchical. Local centres are the base units for "simple" cases. When their resources do not suffice, families are referred to mid-level clinics with more intensive health care, for example, group therapy, play therapy, and social assistance. If a family member is severely disordered, specialist treatment is offered at a unit at the top of the pyramid. This model is common in many medical fields, as when diabetic cases are managed by the local GP and nurse, and only the complicated ones go to mid- or high-level units. One would guess it might function for perinatal psychological disorders, too. "Simple" cases, like a mother worrying about the baby, could be calmed and supported by the nurse. If matters got serious, she could refer them up along the pyramid. Yet, this is only true if several conditions are fulfilled. The nurse needs to be trained in, capable of, and have time for detecting baby worries. Referrals must be smooth and rapid and mothers should not feel intimated or scared by them. Yet, such conditions are seldom fulfilled. In Chapter 7, I listed nurses' problems in detecting emotional issues in families with babies. When they suspect such worries they do not always have the courage, skill, or sensitivity to bring them up with the parents.

Few men and women who just had a child define themselves as psychiatric cases. They have become *parents* and now something happened, which they did not expect and which overwhelmed them. With or without help, some intuit that "it is psychological" but guilt, shame, inability to love, envy, and anxiety threaten self-esteem. The horizontal model seems better for countering the problems – *if a competent psychotherapist is integrated at the base units*. This is the big question raised in Figure 20.1. The need of such therapists is seldom recognized, now that psychiatry seeks to emulate medicine to focus on diagnostics and drugs. Our Zeitgeist risks labelling "baby worries" as a psychiatric disorder rather than a *parental crisis reaction* moulded on the individual's history and present life.

Another quandary is today's interpretation of *evidence-based medicine* or *EBM* (Sackett, Rosenberg, Muir Gray, Brian Haynes, & Richardson, 1996). It was defined as "the conscientious, explicit, and judicious use of current best evidence in making decisions about the care of individual patients . . . [It means] integrating individual clinical expertise with the best available external clinical evidence from systematic research" (p. 71). It should also cover the "thoughtful identification and compassionate use of individual patients' predicaments, rights, and preferences in making clinical decisions about their care" (idem). Sadly, this advice is often twisted into making psychiatric care a buffet of manualized treatments. One forgets *practice-based evidence*, which allows for "variation in patient symptoms and comorbidity, therapist competence, and treatment contexts" (Holmqvist, Philips, & Barkham, 2015, p. 20). Clinics are charged to supply EBM treatment according to the patient's diagnosis – not to her wishes or what the therapist reckons is best. This policy is ill-suited for any psychiatric population, even more so for new parents whose treatment motivation and self-esteem are brittle. Also, symptoms may be volatile and difficult to pinpoint, which make diagnoses uncertain.

220 Part II: Theory

The medical model often triumphs during organizational reforms. The new leadership wants to set up a "state of the art" health care. Such fervour favours a vertical model. Psychologists are now appointed "generalists", but this overlooks the specificity of perinatal therapy; we must be conversant with parents *and* infants and stay in the taxing climate of PTIP. Becoming a "generalist", the perinatal therapist's competence is diluted. If s/he, furthermore, is displaced to a unit higher up in the organization, referrals become more impersonal and cumbersome. The CHC nurse may now have to write up a proper referral instead of speaking informally with the psychologist about a family. In brief, the vertical model widens the gap between nursing and psychological care.

It follows that if the vertical model dominates, it becomes difficult for families to pass smoothly from low-level to specialist-level care. Adult psychiatry at that level does not always observe that when a patient is a parent of small children, his/her disorder involves the entire family. Similarly, child psychiatry may overlook that a distressed child may have parents with mental health problems that must be addressed. Barlow et al. (2010) recommend that perinatal psychiatry be expanded, and that specialists should support "primary care and community professionals and involve consultation, joint assessment, direct clinical work, training, supervision, and the development of protocols and care pathways" (p. 183). Their advice seems to follow more of a vertical model. Based on experiences from the RCT study on MIP and my work with CHC consultations, I take another view. In the RCT, it was not difficult to recruit worried mothers and inspire them to take part. But after the project ended, applications to the analyst group ceased. It emerged that perinatal psychiatry services were not easy to access for families in need. My RCT interviews revealed that these mothers were not always adequately captured by the CHC nurses. Donna, in Chapter 3, said she was never offered the EPDS questionnaire by her CHC nurse. The two did not establish a contact that enabled her distress to show and be talked about. Had Donna not seen the project's internet advertisement, she would not have been recruited to the study.

What are the caveats with the horizontal model? A parallel vertical organization must exist for the problematic cases. A psychotic or addicted mother cannot be treated only at a CHC. Some parents cannot take care of their newborns and need maternity institutions. For sure, some also need medication. All this is self-evident and "only" demands a smooth cooperation between the two models. The second caveat forms the background to my CHC work and is symbolized by the "?" in Figure 20.1. If we want to pick up baby worries and suggest brief and qualified therapy, *we need to place a competent part-time psychotherapist at every local CHC*. With such a mode of work, s/he can:

1/ Provide consultations for parents and infants at their health care unit.
2/ Supervise midwives and nurses to be conversant with addressing parents about emotional problems and with observing signs of infant distress.
3/ Convey to nurses, doctors, and parents that pre- and postnatal emotional problems, whatever their precedence, can be viewed as crisis reactions. True,

they may be severe and need lengthier treatment, medication, and even hospital care. But they indicate that a psychological system is now strained by the special plights of the perinatal period.

The mindset of the health care professional

Doctors' and nurses' curricula and training programmes proceed from a more medical perspective. Symptoms are taught to be signs of an illness that needs to be diagnosed. Even better, its etiology should be established and treatment should proceed accordingly. True, these curricula include courses in psychology, and every physician and perinatal nurse knows of postnatal depression and infant emotional distress. However, many health care professionals do not feel comfortable in addressing such issues with the parents. Some reasons were delineated in Chapter 7, such as their uncertainty, embarrassment, and fear. The medical model risks adding another factor; the demand that a nurse or a doctor should detect an emotional condition and diagnose it and, once this has been accomplished, s/he can supposedly abolish the question mark. This was how nurse Andrea, in Chapter 7, reacted: "Maybe the mother has a postnatal depression!" It was as if this inference terminated the inquiry. Now it was more a question of referring her to a doctor for SSRI treatment, rather than to find out more about the causes and circumstances of this very mother's suffering by talking with her.

The solution to these side effects of the medical focus in the academic education of doctors and nurses is neither to diminish it nor to offer more psychology lectures. A basic psychological knowledge is essential, but their clinical skills need *maintenance* throughout their professional careers. To uphold skills about new drugs, regulations, and therapies, they take regular courses. The need for psychological maintenance is based on another factor: their personalities. *Anyone* who meets with these families gets moved, provoked, anguished, sad, and ambivalent. One takes to psychological defences and becomes distant, unfocused, timorous, bitter, or just fed up. The psychologist at the local CHC should, apart from taking care of families, answer for such psychological upkeep during supervisions. Only regular and repeated sessions can prevent the described defensive phenomena from rusting up. Let me illustrate by recounting an event some years ago. The nurses at my CHC became overbooked and supervisions had to be cancelled for a while. After one month, I had no more referrals! When we resumed supervisions I asked, half-jokingly, if all emotional problems in the neighbourhood had suddenly vanished. We found out that the essential reason was the lack of "maintenance". The psychological perspective sneaked out the backdoor, as it were. Courage and perspicacity slackened, whereas medical duties were duly upheld. After this discussion, referrals started coming in again.

This event can be described in terms of what went on in the minds of the nurses. One can also focus on the relationship between me and the nurses. Regular supervisions had paved the way for their confidence in me. Such trust also needs maintenance. On a deeper level, the nurses may have felt abandoned by me and

222 Part II: Theory

therefore dimmed their psychological spectacles. Here we discern yet another drawback when a psychologist works far away from the CHC: as the geographical and organizational distance increases between nurses and therapist, so do mutual misgivings.

The argument for regular supervisions can be extended one step further. Not only are they essential for inspiring nurses to become interested in a family's emotional climate and how to address its members about it. Also, this outlook is likely to extend indirectly to the family: the nurse receives inspiration during supervisions, and thence she conveys her psychological interest to the parents. They will then find it easier to accept such an outlook on their worries and, when relevant, become interested in a consultation with "our therapist here at the CHC".

This book started with the perspective "in the beginning". Now we have arrived "in the end". I hope to have inspired therapists to work with infants and parents in brief or lengthy treatments. I happen to work in the Swedish model, and therapists in other countries will have to accommodate to their local conditions. But in the end, and in my opinion, the modes of work that I have submitted in this book and the theories supporting them are valid around the globe.

References

Aarts, M. (2000). *Marte Meo: Basic manual*. Harderwijk, Netherlands: Aarts Productions.

Abelin, E. L. (1975). Some further observations and comments on the earliest role of the father. *International Journal of Psychoanalysis, 56*, 293–302.

Aber, J. L., Slade, A., Berger, B., Bresgi, I., & Kaplan, M. (1985). *The Parent Development Interview*: Unpublished manuscript. Barnard College, Columbia University, NY.

Abraham, K. (1927). *Selected papers on psycho-analysis*. London: Maresfield Reprints.

Abse, S. (2014). Intimacy and the couple – the long and winding road. In D. E. Scharff & J. S. Scharff (Eds), *Psychoanalytic couple therapy. Foundations of theory and practice (Kindle edition)* (pp. 35–43, loc. 1054–1262). London: Karnac Books.

Aguayo, J. (2002). Reassessing the clinical affinity between Melanie Klein and D. W. Winnicott (1935–51): Klein's unpublished "Notes on Baby" in historical context. *International Journal of Psychoanalysis, 83*(5), 1133–1152.

Aguayo, J., & Salomonsson, B. (2017). The study and treatment of mothers and infants, then and now: Melanie Klein's "Notes on Baby" (1938/39) in a contemporary psychoanalytic context. *Psychoanalytic Quarterly, 86*(2), 383–408.

Ahumada, J. L. (1994). Interpretation and creationism. *International Journal of Psychoanalysis, 75*(4), 695–707.

Ainsworth, M. S., Blehar, M. C., Waters, E., & Wall, S. (1978). *Patterns of attachment: A psychological study of the strange situation*. Oxford, England: Lawrence Erlbaum.

Aisenstein, M. (2006). The indissociable unity of psyche and soma: A view from the Paris Psychosomatic School. *The International Journal of Psychoanalysis, 87*(3), 667–680.

Aitken, K. J., & Trevarthen, C. (1997). Self/other organization in human psychological development. *Development & Psychopathology, 9*(4), 653–677.

Alhusen, J. L. (2008). A literature update on maternal-fetal attachment. *Journal of Obstetric, Gynecologic, & Neonatal Nursing, 37*(3), 315–328.

Alhusen, J. L., Gross, D., Hayat, M. J., Woods, A. B., & Sharps, P. W. (2012). The influence of maternal-fetal attachment and health practices on neonatal outcomes in low-income, urban women. *Research in Nursing & Health, 35*(2), 112–120.

Alhusen, J. L., Hayat, M. J., & Gross, D. (2013). A longitudinal study of maternal attachment and infant developmental outcomes. *Archives of Women's Mental Health, 16*(6), 521–529.

Aristotle. (1999). Nicomachean ethics (W. D. Ross, Trans.). Kitchener, Ont.: Batoche Books.

Arlow, J. (1979). Metaphor and the psychoanalytic situation. *Psychoanalytic Quarterly, 48*, 363–385.

224 References

Atzil, S., Hendler, T., Zagoory-Sharon, O., Winetraub, Y., & Feldman, R. (2012). Synchrony and specificity in the maternal and the paternal brain: Relations to oxytocin and vasopressin. *Journal of the American Academy of Child & Adolescent Psychiatry, 51*(8), 798–811.

Aulagnier, P. (2001). *The violence of interpretation. From pictogram to statement (La violence de l'interprétation: du pictogramme à l'énoncé, 1975. Paris: PUF).* London: Routledge.

Aznar-Martinez, B., Perez-Testor, C., Davins, M., & Aramburu, I. (2016). Couple psychoanalytic psychotherapy as the treatment of choice: Indications, challenges and benefits. *Psychoanalytic Psychology, 33*(1), 1–20.

Bacon, R. J. (2002). Winnicott revisited: A point of view. *Free Associations, 9B,* 250–270.

Bahrick, L. E., & Hollich, G. (2008). Intermodal perception. In M. M. Haith & J. B. Benson (Eds), *Encyclopedia of infant and early childhood development* (Vol. 2, pp. 164–176). San Diego, CA: Academic Press.

Bakermans-Kranenburg, M. J., van IJzendoorn, M. H., & Juffer, F. (2003). Less is more: Meta-analyses of sensitivity and attachment interventions in early childhood. *Psychological Bulletin, 129*(2), 195–215.

Balestriere, L. (2003). *Freud et la question des origines* (Freud and the question of origins) (2nd ed.). Bruxelles: De Boeck & Larcier.

Balint, M. (1952). *Primary love and psycho-analytic technique.* London: Maresfield Library.

Balint, M. (1979). *The Basic Fault.* London/New York: Tavistock Publications.

Baradon, T., Biseo, M., Broughton, C., James, J., & Joyce, A. (2016). *The practice of psychoanalytic parent-infant psychotherapy – Claiming the baby* (2nd ed.). London: Routledge.

Baranger, M., & Baranger, W. (Eds). (2009). *The work of confluence. Listening and interpreting in the psychoanalytic field.* London: Karnac Books.

Barlow, J., Schrader McMillan, A., Kirkpatrick, S., Ghate, D., Barnes, J., & Smith, M. (2010). Health-led interventions in the early years to enhance infant and maternal mental health: A review of reviews. *Child and Adolescent Mental Health, 15*(4), 178–185.

Bayley, N. (1969). *Manual for the Bayley Scales of Infant Development.* Berkeley, CA: Institute of Human Development.

Beebe, B., & Lachmann, F. M. (2002). *Infant research and adult treatment: Co-constructing interactions.* Hillsdale, NJ: Analytic Press.

Beebe, B., & Lachmann, F. (2014). *The origins of attachment. Infant research and adult treatment.* New York: Routledge.

Bell, L., Goulet, C., St-Cyr Tribble, D., Paul, D., Boisclair, A., & Tronick, E. (2007). Mothers' and fathers' views of the interdependence of their relationships with their infant: A systems perspective on early family relationships. *Journal of Family Nursing, 13*(2), 179–200.

Bellion, E. (2001). Agressivité et grossesse; Pour un cheminement nécessaire vers la naissance de la relation mère/bébé. Le fonctionnement psychique chez la femme enceinte à la lumière du Rorschach et du TAT (Aggression and pregnancy: A necessary progress of the birth of the mother-baby relationship. Psychic functioning in the pregnant woman in the light of Rorschach and TAT). *Devenir, 13,* 67–83.

Belot, R.-A., & de Tychey, C. (2015). Maternal mentalization and the infant's somatic development: A comparative Rorschach study. *Bulletin de psychologie, 5,* 367–389.

References   225

Benedek, T. (1959). Parenthood as a developmental phase – A contribution to the libido theory. *Journal of the American Psychoanalytic Association, 7*, 389–417.

Benjamin, J. (2000). Intersubjective distinctions: Subjects and persons, recognitions and breakdowns: Commentary on paper by Gerhardt, Sweetnam, and Borton. *Psychoanalytic Dialogues, 10*(1), 43–55.

Benjamin, J. (2005). Creating an intersubjective reality: Commentary on paper by Arnold Rothstein. *Psychoanalytic Dialogues, 15*, 447–457.

Benoit, D., Parker, K. C., & Zeanah, C. H. (1997). Mothers' representations of their infants assessed prenatally: Stability and association with infants' attachment classifications. *Journal of Child Psychology and Psychiatry, 38*(3), 307–313.

Berg, A. (2003). Beyond the dyad: Parent-infant psychotherapy in a multicultural society – Reflections from a South African perspective. *Infant Mental Health Journal, 24*(3), 265–277.

Bergman, A. (1985). The mother's experience during the earliest phases of infant development. In E. J. Anthony and G. H. Pollock (Eds), *Parental influences: In health and disease* (pp. 165–180). New York: Little Brown & Co.

Bergman, K., Sarkar, P., Glover, V., & O'Connor, T. G. (2008). Quality of child-parent attachment moderates the impact of antenatal stress on child fearfulness. *Journal of Child Psychology & Psychiatry, 49*(10), 1089–1098.

Bick, E. (1964). Notes on infant observation in psychoanalytic training. *International Journal of Psychoanalysis, 45*, 558–566.

Bion, W. R. (1962). *Learning from experience*. London: Karnac Books.

Bion, W. R. (1965). *Transformations*. London: Karnac Books.

Bion, W. R. (1970). *Attention and interpretation*. London: Karnac Books.

Bion, W. R. (1992). *Cogitations*. London: Karnac Books.

Bion, W. R. (1997). *Taming wild thoughts*. London: Karnac Books.

Biringen, Z., Robinson, J. L., & Emde, R. N. (1998). *Emotional Availability Scales* (3rd ed.). Unpublished manual. Colorado State University.

Blake, W. (1994). *William Blake. Selected Poetry*. Oxford: Oxford University Press.

Blandon, A. Y., Calkins, S. D., Keane, S. P., & O'Brien, M. (2008). Individual differences in trajectories of emotion regulation processes: The effects of maternal depressive symptomatology and children's physiological regulation. *Developmental Psychology, 44*(4), 1110–1123.

Blatt, S. J. (1992). The differential effect of psychotherapy and psychoanalysis with anaclitic and introjective patients: The Menninger Psychotherapy Research Project revisited. *Journal of the American Psychoanalytic Association, 40*(3), 691–724.

Blatt, S. J. (2006). A fundamental polarity in psychoanalysis: Implications for personality development, psychopathology, and the therapeutic process. *Psychoanalytic Inquiry, 26*, 492–518.

Blatt, S. J., & Shahar, G. (2004). Psychoanalysis – with whom, for what, and how? Comparisons with psychotherapy. *Journal of the American Psychoanalytic Association, 52*(2), 393–447.

Bleger, J. (1967). Psychoanalysis of the psychoanalytic frame. *International Journal of Psychoanalysis, 48*, 511–519.

Bleger, J. (2012). Theory and practice in psychoanalysis: Psychoanalytic praxis. *International Journal of Psychoanalysis, 93*(4), 993–1003.

Blos, P. (1985). *Son and father: Before and beyond the Oedipus complex*. New York: Free Press.

226 References

Bohleber, W. (2010). *Destructiveness, intersubjectivity, and trauma: The identity crisis of modern psychoanalysis.* London: Karnac Books.

Bowlby, J. (1958). The nature of the child's tie to his mother. *International Journal of Psychoanalysis, 39,* 350–373.

Bowlby, J. (1969). *Attachment and loss.* London: Pimlico.

Britton, R. (1989). The missing link: Parental sexuality in the Oedipus complex. In R. Britton, M. Feldman, & E. O'Shaughnessy (Eds), *The Oedipus complex today: Clinical implications* (pp. 83–101). London: Karnac Books.

Britton, R. (1992). Keeping things in mind. *New Library of Psychoanalysis, 14,* 102–113.

Britton, R. (1998). *Belief and imagination.* London: Routledge.

Britton, R. (2000). Hyper-subjectivity and hyper-objectivity in narcissistic disorders. *Fort Da, 6B*(53–64).

Britton, R. (2013). Commentary on three papers by Wilfred R. Bion. *The Psychoanalytic Quarterly, 82*(2), 311–321.

Burström, B., Marttila, A., Kulane, A., Lindberg, L., & Burström, K. (2017). Practising proportionate universalism – A study protocol of an extended postnatal home visiting programme in a disadvantaged area in Stockholm, Sweden. *BMC Health Services Research, 17*(1), 91.

Bydlowski, M. (2001). Le regard intérieur de la femme enceinte, transparence psychique et représentation de l'objet interne (The interior look of the pregnant woman, psychological transparency and representation of the internal object). *Devenir, 13*(2), 41–52.

Cannella, B. L. (2005). Maternal-fetal attachment: An integrative review. *Journal of Advanced Nursing, 50*(1), 60–68.

Carey, W. B. (1990). Infantile colic: A pediatric practitioner-researcher's point of view. *Infant Mental Health Journal, 11*(4), 334–339.

Casanova, A. (2000). Serge Lebovici. Eléments de la psychopathologie du bébé (Elements of infant psychopathology). DVD. France.

Chakraborty, H., & Gu, H. (2009). A mixed model approach for intent-to-treat analysis in longitudinal clinical trials with missing values. *RTI Press publication MR-0009-0903.* Retrieved from www.rti.org/rtipress

Chatoor, I. (1986). *Mother/infant/toddler play scale.* Washington, DC: Children's Hospital National Medical Center.

Chin, R., Hall, P., & Daiches, A. (2011). Fathers' experiences of their transition to fatherhood: A metasynthesis. *Journal of Reproductive and Infant Psychology, 29*(1), 4–18.

Chronis, A. M., Lahey, B. B., Pelham, W. E., Jr., Williams, S. H., Baumann, B. L., Kipp, H., . . . Rathouz, P. J. (2007). Maternal depression and early positive parenting predict future conduct problems in young children with attention-deficit/hyperactivity disorder. *Developmental Psychology, 43*(1), 70–82.

Cicchetti, D., Rogosch, F. A., & Toth, S. L. (2000). The efficacy of toddler-parent psychotherapy for fostering cognitive development in offspring of depressed mothers. *Journal of Abnormal Child Psychology, 28,* 135–148.

Civitarese, G., & Ferro, A. (2013). The meaning and use of metaphor in analytic field theory. *Psychoanalytic Inquiry, 33*(3), 190–209.

Clark, R. (1985). *The parent-child early relational assessment. Instrument and manual:* Madison, WI: Department of Psychiatry, University of Wisconsin Medical School.

Clark, R., Tluczek, A., & Wenzel, A. (2003). Psychotherapy for postpartum depression: A preliminary report. *American Journal of Orthopsychiatry, 73*(4), 441–454.

References 227

Cohen, N. J., Lojkasek, M., Muir, E., Muir, R., & Parker, C. J. (2002). Six-month follow-up of two mother-infant psychotherapies: Convergence of therapeutic outcomes. *Infant Mental Health Journal, 23*(4), 361–380.

Cohen, N. J., Muir, E., Parker, C. J., Brown, M., Lojkasek, M., Muir, R., & Barwick, M. (1999). Watch, wait and wonder: Testing the effectiveness of a new approach to mother-infant psychotherapy. *Infant Mental Health Journal, 20*(4), 429–451.

Cohn, J. F., & Tronick, E. (1983). Three-month-old infants' reactions to simulated maternal depression. *Child Development, 54,* 185–193.

Conde, A., Figueiredo, B., Tendais, I., Teixeira, C., Costa, R., Pacheco, A., . . . Nogueira, R. (2010). Mother's anxiety and depression and associated risk factors during early pregnancy: Effects on fetal growth and activity at 20–22 weeks of gestation. *Journal of Psychosomatic Obstetrics & Gynecology, 31*(2), 70–82.

Condon, J. T., & Corkindale, C. (1997). The correlates of antenatal attachment in pregnant women. *British Journal of Medical Psychology, 70*(4), 359–372.

Condon, W. S., & Sander, L. W. (1974). Neonate movement is synchronized with adult speech: Interactional participation and language acquisition. *Science, 183*(4120), 99–101.

Cooper, P. J., Landman, M., Tomlinson, M., Molteno, C., Swartz, L., & Murray, L. (2002). Impact of a mother-infant intervention in an indigent peri-urban South African context: Pilot study. *British Journal of Psychiatry, 180,* 76–81.

Cooper, P. J., Murray, L., Wilson, A., & Romaniuk, H. (2003). Controlled trial of the short- and long-term effect of psychological treatment of post-partum depression. 1. Impact on maternal mood. *British Journal of Psychiatry, 182*(5), 412–419.

Cowsill, K. (2000). 'I thought you knew': Some factors affecting a baby's capacity to maintain eye contact. *Infant Observation, 3*(3), 64–83.

Cox, J., Holden, J., & Sagovsky, R. (1987). Detection of postnatal depression: Development of the 10-item Edinburgh Postnatal Depression Scale. *British Journal of Psychiatry, 150,* 782–786.

Cramer, B. (1997). *The scripts parents write and the roles babies play.* Northvale, NJ: Jason Aronson Inc.

Cramer, B. (1998). Mother-infant psychotherapies: A widening scope in technique. *Infant Mental Health Journal, 19*(2), 151–167.

Cramer, B., & Palacio Espasa, F. (1993). *La pratique des psychothérapies mères-bébés. Études cliniques et techniques (The practice of mother-infant psychotherapies. Clinical and technical studies).* Paris: PUF.

Cranley, M. S. (1981). Development of a tool for the measurement of maternal attachment during pregnancy. *Nursing Research, 30*(5), 281–284.

Crawford, A., & Benoit, D. (2009). Caregivers' disrupted representations of the unborn child predict later infant-caregiver disorganized attachment and disrupted interactions. *Infant Mental Health Journal, 30*(2), 124–144.

Cummings, E. M., & Davies, P. T. (2002). Effects of marital conflict on children: Recent advances and emerging themes in process-oriented research. *Journal of Child Psychology & Psychiatry & Allied Disciplines, 43*(1), 31–63.

Cummings, E. M., & Davies, P. T. (2010). *Marital conflict and children. An emotional security perspective.* New York: The Guilford Press.

da Rocha Barros, E. M. (2000). Affect and pictographic image. *International Journal of Psychoanalysis, 81,* 1087–1099.

Dayton, C. J., Levendosky, A. A., Davidson, W. S., & Bogat, G. A. (2010). The child as held in the mind of the mother: The influence of prenatal maternal representations on parenting behaviors. *Infant Mental Health Journal, 31*(2), 220–241.

228 References

de Mijolla, A. (2009). Serge Lebovici. Retrieved from www.encyclopedia.com/doc/1G2-3435300807.html

DeCasper, A. J., & Fifer, W. P. (1980). Of human bonding: Newborns prefer their mothers' voices. *Science, 208*(4448), 1174–1176.

Delaunay-El Allam, M., Soussignan, R., Patris, B., Marlier, & Schaal, B. (2010). Long-lasting memory for an odor acquired at the mother's breast. *Developmental Science, 13*(6), 849–863.

DelCarmen-Wiggins, R., & Carter, A. (2004). *Handbook of infant, toddler, and preschool mental health assessment.* New York: Oxford University Press.

Dennis, C.-L. E. (2004). Treatment of postpartum depression, part 2: A critical review of nonbiological interventions. *Journal of Clinical Psychiatry, 65*(9), 1252–1265.

Derogatis, L. R., & Fitzpatrick, M. (2004). *The SCL-90-R, the Brief Symptom Inventory (BSI), and the BSI-18.* Mahwah, NJ: Lawrence Erlbaum Associates Publishers.

Diamond, M. J. (2017). Recovering the father in mind and flesh: History, triadic functioning, and developmental implications. *Psychoanalytic Quarterly, 86*(2), 297–334.

Diatkine, G. (2007). Lacan. *International Journal of Psychoanalysis, 88,* 643–660.

Dolto, F. (1971). *Dominique: The analysis of an adolescent.* New York: Outerbridge & Lazard, Inc.

Dolto, F. (1982). *Séminaires de psychanalyse d'enfant, vol. 1 (Seminars on child psycho-analysis, vol. 1).* Paris: Editions du Seuil.

Dolto, F. (1985). *Séminaires de psychanalyse d'enfant, vol. 2 (Seminars on child psycho-analysis, vol. 2).* Paris: Editions du Seuil.

Dolto, F. (1994). *Solitude.* Paris: Gallimard.

Dolto, F. (2013/1971). *Psychoanalysis and paediatrics: Key psychoanalytic concepts with sixteen clinical observations of children* (F. Hivernel & F. Sinclair, Trans.). London: Karnac.

Dowling, S. (1982). Review of "Clinical studies in infant mental health. The first year of life": Edited by Selma Fraiberg. *Psychoanalytic Quarterly, 51,* 430–434.

Draper, J. (2003). Men's passage to fatherhood: An analysis of the contemporary relevance of transition theory. *Nursing Inquiry, 10*(1), 66–78.

Duarte, P. G. F. (2015). *Considerations on the use of Peirce's conceptions in psychoanalysis.* Unpublished paper. São Paulo.

Edhborg, M., Lundh, W., Seimyr, L., & Widström, A. M. (2003). The parent-child relationship in the context of maternal depressive mood. *Archives of Women's Mental Health, 6*(3), 211–216.

Egeland, B., Deinard, A., & Brunquell, D. (1979). *A prospective study of the antecedents of child abuse. Final Report to the National Center on Child Abuse and Neglect* (unpublished).

Ehrenberg, D. B. (1992). *The intimate edge: Extending the reach of psychoanalytic interaction.* New York: W.W. Norton.

Eizirik, C. L. (2015). The father, the father function, the father principle: Some contemporary psychoanalytic developments. *The Psychoanalytic Quarterly, 84*(2), 335–350.

Emanuel, L. (2006). Disruptive and distressed toddlers: The impact of undetected maternal depression on infants and young children. *Infant Observation, 9*(3), 249–259.

Emanuel, L. (2011). Brief interventions with parents, infants, and young children: A framework for thinking. *Infant Mental Health Journal, 32*(6), 673–686.

Emanuel, L., & Bradley, E. (Eds). (2008). *"What can the matter be?" – Therapeutic interventions with parents, infants, and young children.* London: Karnac Books.

Emde, R. N. (1990). Mobilizing fundamental modes of development: Empathic availability and therapeutic action. *Journal of the American Psychoanalytic Association, 38*(4), 881–913.

References 229

Emde, R. N. (1994). Commentary: Triadification experiences and a bold new direction for infant mental health. *Infant Mental Health Journal, 15*, 90–95.

Espasa, F. P., & Alcorn, D. (2004). Parent-infant psychotherapy, the transition to parenthood and parental narcissism: Implications for treatment. *Journal of Child Psychotherapy, 30*(2), 155–171.

Fägerskiöld, A. (2008). A change in life as experienced by first-time fathers. *Scandinavian Journal of Caring Sciences, 22*(1), 64–71.

Faimberg, H. (2014). The paternal function in Winnicott: The psychoanalytical frame. *International Journal of Psychoanalysis, 95*(4), 629–640.

Favez, N., Lopes, F., Bernard, M., Frascarolo, F., Lavanchy Scaiola, C., Corboz-Warnery, A., & Fivaz-Depeursinge, E. (2012). The development of family alliance from pregnancy to toddlerhood and child outcomes at 5 years. *Family Process, 51*(4), 542–556.

Feldman, R. (2007). Parent-infant synchrony and the construction of shared timing; physiological precursors, developmental outcomes, and risk conditions. *Journal of Child Psychology & Psychiatry & Allied Disciplines, 48*(3–4), 329–354.

Feldman, R., Gordon, I., & Zagoory-Sharon, O. (2011). Maternal and paternal plasma, salivary, and urinary oxytocin and parent–infant synchrony: Considering stress and affiliation components of human bonding. *Developmental Science, 14*(4), 752–761.

Feldman, R., Granat, A., Pariente, C., Kanety, H., Kuint, J., & Gilboa-Schechtman, E. (2009). Maternal depression and anxiety across the postpartum year and infant social engagement, fear regulation, and stress reactivity. *Journal of the American Academy of Child & Adolescent Psychiatry, 48*(9), 919–927.

Feldman, R., Weller, A., Leckman, J. F., Kuint, J., & Eidelman, A. I. (1999). The nature of the mother's tie to her infant: Maternal bonding under conditions of proximity, separation, and potential loss. *Journal of Child Psychology and Psychiatry, 40*(6), 929–939.

Ferenczi, S. (1949). Confusion of tongues between the adults and the child (the language of tenderness and of passion). *International Journal of Psychoanalysis, 30*, 225–230.

Ferro, A. (1999). *The bi-personal field – experiences in child analysis*. London: Routledge.

Ferro, A. (2006). Clinical implications of Bion's thought. *International Journal of Psychoanalysis, 87*(4), 989–1003.

Field, T. M. (1981). Infant gaze aversion and heart rate during face-to-face interactions. *Infant Behavior & Development, 4*(3), 307–315.

Field, T. (2000). Infant massage therapy. In C. H. J. Zeanah (Ed.), *Handbook of infant mental health* (pp. 494–500). New York: The Guilford Press.

Field, T. (2010). Postpartum depression effects on early interactions, parenting, and safety practices: A review. *Infant Behavior & Development, 33*(1), 1–6.

Field, T. (2011). Prenatal depression effects on early development: A review. *Infant Behavior and Development, 34*(1), 1–14.

Field, T., Diego, M., & Hernandez-Reif, M. (2009). Infants of depressed mothers are less responsive to faces and voices: A review. *Infant Behavior & Development, 32*(3), 239–244.

Field, T., Diego, M., Hernandez-Reif, M., Figueiredo, B., Schanberg, S., & Kuhn, C. (2007). Sleep disturbances in depressed pregnant women and their newborns. *Infant Behavior & Development, 30*(1), 127–133.

Field, T., Healy, B., Goldstein, S., & Guthertz, M. (1990). Behavior-state matching and synchrony in mother–infant interactions of nondepressed versus depressed dyads. *Developmental Psychology, 26*, 7–14.

230 References

Fivaz-Depeursinge, E. (2011). A systems perspective on the integrative child psychiatry approach. Discussion of paper: "Working here and now with the individual and family system: A case of a traumatized child". *Infant Mental Health Journal, 32*(6), 666–672.

Fivaz-Depeursinge, E., & Corboz-Warnery, A. (1999). *The primary triangle. A developmental systems view of mothers. fathers, and infant.* London: Basic Books.

Fivaz-Depeursinge, E., & Favez, N. (2006). Exploring triangulation in infancy: Two contrasted cases. *Family Process, 45*(1), 3–18.

Fonagy, P. (1996). Discussion of Peter Wolff's paper "Infant observation and psychoanalysis". *Journal of the American Psychoanalytic Association, 44*(2), 404–422.

Fonagy, P. (2001). *Attachment theory and psychoanalysis.* New York: Other Press.

Fonagy, P., Sleed, M., & Baradon, T. (2016). Randomized controlled trial of parent–infant psychotherapy for parents with mental health problems and young infants. *Infant Mental Health Journal, 37*(2), 97–114.

Fonagy, P., Steele, H., & Steele, M. (1991). Maternal representations of attachment during pregnancy predict the organization of infant-mother attachment at one year of age. *Child Development, 62*(5), 891–905.

Fonagy, P., & Target, M. (1996). Playing with reality: I. Theory of mind and the normal development of psychic reality. *International Journal of Psychoanalysis, 77*, 217–233.

Forster, Z. R. D., & Spivacow, M. A. (2006). Psychoanalytical psychotherapy for/with couples: Theoretical basis and clinical utility. *International Journal of Psychoanalysis, 87*(1), 255–257.

Fraiberg, S. (1980). *Clinical studies in infant mental health.* New York: Basic Books.

Fraiberg, S. (1982). Pathological defenses in infancy. *Psychoanalytic Quarterly, 51*(4), 612–635.

Fraiberg, S. (1987). *Selected writings of Selma Fraiberg.* Columbus, OH: Ohio State University Press.

Fraiberg, S. (1989). *Assessment and therapy of disturbances in infancy.* Northvale, NJ: Jason Aronson.

Fraiberg, S., Adelson, E., & Shapiro, V. (1975). Ghosts in the nursery. A psychoanalytic approach to the problems of impaired infant-mother relationships. *Journal of the American Academy of Child Psychiatry, 14*(3), 387–421.

Frank, M. A., Tuber, S. B., Slade, A., & Garrod, E. (1994). Mothers' fantasy representations and infant security of attachment: A Rorschach study of first pregnancy. *Psychoanalytic Psychology, 11*(4), 475–490.

Freeman, T. (2008). Psychoanalytic concepts of fatherhood: Patriarchal paradoxes and the presence of an absent authority. *Studies in Gender and Sexuality, 9*(2), 113–139.

Freud, A. (1937). *The Ego and the mechanisms of defence.* London: Hogarth Press.

Freud, H. C. (2011). *Electra vs. Oedipus: The drama of the mother-daughter relationship.* London: Routledge.

Freud, S. (1892). *Draft K. The neuroses of defence. From "Extracts from the Fliess Papers". SE I* (pp. 220–229). London: Karnac Books.

Freud, S. (1894). The neuro-psychoses of defence. *SE 3* (pp. 41–61).

Freud, S. (1895/1950). Project for a scientific psychology. *SE I* (pp. 281–391).

Freud, S. (1896). Further remarks on the neuro-psychoses of defence. *SE 3* (pp. 157–185).

Freud, S. (1900). The interpretation of dreams. *SE 4–5*.

Freud, S. (1905). Three essays on sexuality. *SE 7* (pp. 123–246).

Freud, S. (1910). Five lectures on psycho-analysis. *SE 11* (pp. 1–56).

References 231

Freud, S. (1911). Formulations on the two principles of mental functioning. *SE 12* (pp. 213–226).

Freud, S. (1912a). The dynamics of transference. *SE 12* (pp. 97–108).

Freud, S. (1912b). Recommendations to physicians practising psycho-analysis. *SE 12* (pp. 109–120).

Freud, S. (1913a). On beginning the treatment (further recommendations on the technique of psychoanalysis I). *SE 12* (pp. 121–144).

Freud, S. (1913b). Totem and taboo: Some points of agreement between the mental lives of savages and neurotics. *SE 13* (pp. 1–162).

Freud, S. (1914). On narcissism: An introduction. *SE 14* (pp. 67–102).

Freud, S. (1915a). Instincts and their vicissitudes. *SE 14* (pp. 109–140).

Freud, S. (1915b). Observations on transference-love (further recommendations on the technique of psycho-analysis III). *SE 12* (pp. 157–171).

Freud, S. (1915c). Repression. *SE 14* (pp. 141–158).

Freud, S. (1919). Introduction to psycho-analysis and the war neuroses. *SE 17* (pp. 205–216).

Freud, S. (1920). Beyond the pleasure principle. *SE 18* (pp. 1–64).

Freud, S. (1921). Group psychology and the analysis of the ego. *SE 18* (pp. 65–144).

Freud, S. (1923). The ego and the id. *SE 19* (pp. 3–66).

Freud, S. (1925). Negation. *SE 19* (pp. 233–240).

Freud, S. (1925–1926). Inhibitions, symptoms and anxiety. *SE 20* (pp. 87–178).

Freud, S. (1930). Civilization and its discontents. *SE 21* (pp. 57–146).

Freud, S. (1937). Analysis terminable and interminable. *SE 23* (pp. 209–254).

Freud, S. (1938). An outline of psychoanalysis. *SE 23* (pp. 139–208).

Gaddini, E. (1981). Bion's "catastrophic change" and Winnicott's "Breakdown". *Rivista di Psicoanalisi, 27*, 610–621.

Gaddini, E. (1992). *A psychoanalytic theory of infantile experience*. London: Routledge.

Gallegos, M. I., Murphy, S. E., Benner, A. D., Jacobvitz, D. B., & Hazen, N. L. (2016). Marital, parental, and whole-family predictors of toddlers' emotion regulation: The role of parental emotional withdrawal. *Journal of Family Psychology, 31*(3), 294–303.

Gelfand, A. A., Thomas, K. C., & Goadsby, P. J. (2012). Before the headache: Infant colic as an early life expression of migraine. *Neurology, 79*(13), 1392–1396.

Genesoni, L., & Tallandini, M. A. (2009). Men's psychological transition to fatherhood: An analysis of the literature, 1989–2008. *Birth: Issues in Perinatal Care, 36*(4), 305–318.

Gentile, J. (2007). Wrestling with matter: Origins of intersubjectivity. *Psychoanalytic Quarterly, 76*, 547–582.

George, C., Kaplan, N., & Main, M. (1985). *The Adult Attachment Interview.* Unpublished manuscript. University of California, Berkeley, CA.

Gerhardt, J., Sweetnam, A., & Borton, L. (2000). The intersubjective turn in psychoanalysis: A comparison of contemporary theorists: Part 1: Jessica Benjamin. *Psychoanalytic Dialogues, 10*(1), 5–42.

Glover, V., Bergman, K., & O'Connor, T. (2008). The effects of maternal stress, anxiety, and depression during pregnancy on the neurodevelopment of the child. In S. Dowd Stone & A. Menken (Eds), *Perinatal and postpartum mood disorders. Perspectives and treatment guide for the health practitioner* (pp. 3–16). New York: Springer Publishing Company.

Gonzalez, A., Jenkins, J. M., Steiner, M., & Fleming, A. S. (2012). Maternal early life experiences and parenting: The mediating role of cortisol and executive function. *Journal of the American Academy of Child & Adolescent Psychiatry, 51*(7), 673–682.

232 References

Goodman, R. (1997). The Strengths and Difficulties Questionnaire: A research note. *Journal of Child Psychology & Psychiatry & Allied Disciplines, 38*(5), 581–586.

Gottman, J. M., & Notarius, C. I. (2002). Marital research in the 20th century and a research agenda for the 21st century. *Family Process, 41*(2), 159–197.

Green, A. (1975). The analyst, symbolization and absence in the analytic setting (On changes in analytic practice and analytic experience) – In memory of D. W. Winnicott. *International Journal of Psychoanalysis, 56*, 1–22.

Green, A. (1977). Conceptions of affect. *International Journal of Psychoanalysis, 58*, 129–156.

Green, A. (1995a). Has sexuality anything to do with psychoanalysis? *International Journal of Psychoanalysis, 76*, 871–883.

Green, A. (1995b). Summary: Affects versus representations or affects as representations? *British Journal of Psychotherapy, 12*, 208–211.

Green, A. (1998). The primordial mind and the work of the negative. *International Journal of Psychoanalysis, 79*, 649–665.

Green, A. (1999). *The fabric of affect in the psychoanalytic discourse.* London: Routledge.

Green, A. (2000). Science and science fiction in infant research. In J. Sandler, A.-M. Sandler, & R. Davies (Eds), *Clinical and observational psychoanalytical research: Roots of a controversy* (pp. 41–72). London: Karnac Books.

Green, A. (2004). Thirdness and psychoanalytic concepts. *Psychoanalytic Quarterly, 73*, 99–13.

Greenson, R. R. (1959). Phobia, anxiety, and depression. *Journal of the American Psychoanalytic Association, 7*, 663–674.

Greenson, R. R. (1967). *The technique and practice of psychoanalysis.* Madison, CT: International Universities Press.

Greenson, R. R., & Wexler, M. (1969). The non-transference relationship in the psychoanalytic situation. *International Journal of Psychoanalysis, 50*, 27–39.

Grotstein, J. (1980). A proposed revision of the psychoanalytic concept of primitive mental states – part I. Introduction to a newer psychoanalytic metapsychology. *Contemporary Psychoanalysis, 16*, 479–546.

Grotstein, J. (1982). Newer perspectives in object relations theory. *Contemporary Psychoanalysis, 18*, 43–91.

Grotstein, J. (1984). A proposed revision of the psychoanalytic concept of primitive mental states, part ii – the borderline syndrome – section 3 disorders of autistic safety and symbiotic relatedness. *Contemporary Psychoanalysis, 20*, 266–343.

Grotstein, J. S. (1990). Nothingness, meaninglessness, chaos, and the "black hole" I. *Contemporary Psychoanalysis, 26*, 257–290.

Grotstein, J. (1999). Projective identification reassessed: Commentary on papers by Stephen Seligman and by Robin C. Silverman and Alicia F. Lieberman. *Psychoanalytic Dialogues, 9*(2), 187–203.

Hall, G., Hivernel, F., & Morgan, S. (Eds). (2009). *Theory and practise in child psychoanalysis: An introduction to Françoise Dolto's work.* London: Karnac.

Hanington, L., Heron, J., Stein, A., & Ramchandani, P. (2011). Parental depression and child outcomes – is marital conflict the missing link? *Child: Care, Health & Development, 38*(4), 520–529.

Harel, J., Kaplan, H., & Patt, R. (2006). Reflective funtioning as a change-promoting factor in mother-child and father-child psychotherapy. In C. Wachs & L. Jacobs (Eds), *Parent-focused child therapy (Kindle edition)* (Ch. 12). Northvale: Jason Aronson.

References 233

Harris, A. (1997). Aggression, envy, and ambition: Circulating tensions in women's psychic life. *Gender and Psychoanalysis*, *2*, 291–325.

Hart, B., & Hilton, I. (1988). Dimensions of personality organization as predictors of teenage pregnancy risk. *Journal of Personality Assessment*, *52*(1), 116–132.

Hinshelwood, R. D. (1989). *A dictionary of Kleinian thought*. London: Free Association Books.

Hodges, J., Steele, M., Hillman, S., Henderson, K., & Kaniuk, J. (2003). Changes in attachment representations over the first year of adoptive placement: Narratives of maltreated children. *Clinical Child Psychology and Psychiatry*, *8*(3), 351–367.

Hoffman, L. (2003). Mothers' ambivalence with their babies and toddlers: Manifestations of conflicts with aggression. *Journal of the American Psychoanalytic Association*, *51*(4), 1219–1240.

Holden, J. M., Sagovsky, R., & Cox, J. L. (1989). Counselling in a general practice setting: Controlled study of health visitor intervention in treatment of postnatal depression. *British Medical Journal*, *298*(6668), 223–226.

Holmqvist, R., Philips, B., & Barkham, M. (2015). Developing practice-based evidence: Benefits, challenges, and tensions. *Psychotherapy Research*, *25*(1), 20–31.

Holt, R. R. (1968). *Manual for the scoring of primary process manifestations in Rorschach responses* (10th ed.). New York: New York University, Research Center for Mental Health.

Horney, K. (1926). The flight from womanhood: The masculinity-complex in women, as viewed by men and by women. *International Journal of Psychoanalysis*, *7*, 324–339.

Huizink, A. C., Robles de Medina, P. G., Mulder, E. J., Visser, G. H., & Buitelaar, J. K. (2003). Stress during pregnancy is associated with developmental outcome in infancy. *Journal of Child Psychology and Psychiatry*, *44*(6), 810–818.

Huth-Bocks, A. C., Theran, S. A., Levendosky, A. A., & Bogat, G. A. (2011). A social-contextual understanding of concordance and discordance between maternal prenatal representations of the infant and infant–mother attachment. *Infant Mental Health Journal*, *32*(4), 405–426.

Ingpen, R. (Ed.). (1903). *One thousand poems for children*. Philadelphia, PA: George W. Jacobs & Co.

Isaacs, S. (1948). The nature and function of phantasy. *International Journal of Psychoanalysis*, *29*, 73–97.

Jones, C. J., Creedy, D. K., & Gamble, J. A. (2012). Australian midwives' attitudes towards care for women with emotional distress. *Midwifery*, *28*(2), 216–221.

Jones, E. (1955). *Sigmund Freud, life and work, volume two: Years of maturity 1901–1919*. London: Hogarth Press.

Joseph, B. (1985). Transference: The total situation. *International Journal of Psychoanalysis*, *66*, 447–454.

Karmiloff, K., & Karmiloff-Smith, A. (2001). *Pathways to language*. Cambridge, MA: Harvard University Press.

Katz, L., & Gottman, J. (1997). Spillover effects of marital conflict: In search of parenting and coparenting mechanisms. In J. P. McHale & P. A. Cowan (Eds), *Understanding how family-level dynamics affect children's development: Studies of two-parent families* (Vol. 74, pp. 57–76). San Francisco, CA: Jossey-Bass.

Kernberg, O. F. (1997). The nature of interpretation: Intersubjectivity and the third position. *American Journal of Psychoanalysis*, 97–110.

Kernutt, J. (2007). The I, or the eye, and the other: A mother-infant observation vignette analysed using Winnicott's concept of false self. *Infant Observation*, *10*(2), 203–211.

234 References

King, P., & Steiner, R. (1991). *The Freud-Klein controversies 1941–45*. London and New York: Tavistock/Routledge.

Kinsella, E. A., & Pitman, A. (2012). Engaging phronesis in professional practice and education. In *Phronesis as Professional Knowledge* (pp. 1–12). Rotterdam: Sense Publishers.

Kirshner, L. (2015). The translational metaphor in psychoanalysis. *International Journal of Psychoanalysis, 96*(1), 65–81.

Kite, J. V. (2012). A case for analysis with the baby in the consulting room. *Journal of the American Psychoanalytic Association, 60*(3), 501–508.

Kivlighan III, D. M., Goldberg, S. B., Abbas, M., Pace, B. T., Yulish, N. E., Thomas, J. G., . . . Wampold, B. E. (2015). The enduring effects of psychodynamic treatments vis-à-vis alternative treatments: A multilevel longitudinal meta-analysis. *Clinical Psychology Review, 40*, 1–14.

Klatskin, E. H., & Eron, L. D. (1970). Projective test content during pregnancy and postpartum adjustment. *Psychosomatic Medicine, 32*(5), 387–493.

Klaus, M. R., & Kennell, J. H. (1982). Parent-infant bonding (2nd ed.). Saint Louis, MO: C.V. Mosby.

Klein, M. (1928). Early stages of the Oedipus conflict. *International Journal of Psychoanalysis, 9*, 167–180.

Klein, M. (1930). The importance of symbol-formation in the development of the ego. *International Journal of Psychoanalysis, 11*, 24–39.

Klein, M. (1932). *The psycho-analysis of children*. London: Hogarth Press.

Klein, M. (1933). The early development of conscience in the child. In *Love, guilt and reparation and other works by Melanie Klein* (pp. 248–257). London: Hogarth Press.

Klein, M. (1934). On criminality. In *Love, guilt and reparation and other works by Melanie Klein* (pp. 258–261). London: Hogarth Press.

Klein, M. (1935). A contribution to the psychogenesis of manic-depressive states. In *Love, guilt and reparation and other works by Melanie Klein* (pp. 262–289). London: Hogarth Press.

Klein, M. (1937). Love, guilt and reparation. In *Love, guilt and reparation and other works by Melanie Klein* (pp. 306–343). London: Hogarth Press.

Klein, M. (1938/39). *Notes on Baby. An unpublished manuscript in the Melanie Klein Archives, (PP/KLE/A.49-51)*. Wellcome Institute. London.

Klein, M. (1944/91). The emotional life and ego-development of the infant with special reference to the depressive position. In P. King & R. Steiner (Eds), *The Freud-Klein controversies* (pp. 752–843). London: Tavistock/Routledge.

Klein, M. (1946). Notes on some schizoid mechanisms. In *Envy and gratitude and other works 1946–1963* (Vol. 3, pp. 1–24). London: Hogarth Press.

Klein, M. (1948). On the theory of anxiety and guilt. In *Envy and gratitude and other works 1946–1963* (Vol. 3, pp. 25–42). London: Hogarth Press.

Klein, M. (1952a). On observing the behaviour of young infants. In *Envy and gratitude and other works 1946–1963* (Vol. 3, pp. 94–121). London: Hogarth Press.

Klein, M. (1952b). The origins of transference. In *Envy and gratitude and other works 1946–1963* (Vol. 3, pp. 48–56). London: Hogarth Press.

Klein, M. (1959). Our adult world and its roots in infancy. In *Envy and gratitude and other works 1946–1963* (Vol. 3, pp. 247–263). London: Hogarth Press.

Klein, M. (1961). *Narrative of a child analysis: The conduct of the psycho-analysis of children as seen in the treatment of a ten year old boy*. London: Hogarth Press.

References 235

Klein, M. (1975). *Envy and gratitude and other works 1946–1963.* London: Hogarth Press and the Institute of Psycho-Analysis.

Klerman, G. L., Weismann, M. M., Rounsaville, B. J., & Chevron, E. S. (1984). *Interpersonal psychotherapy of depression.* New York: Basic Books.

Kloesel, C., & Houser, N. (Eds). (1992). *The essential Peirce, vol. 1: 1867–1893.* Bloomington, IN: Indiana University Press.

Kloesel, C., & Houser, N. (Eds). (1998). *The essential Peirce, vol. 2: 1893–1913.* Bloomington, IN: Indiana University Press.

Knausgaard, K. O. (2018). *Spring.* New York: Penguin Random House.

Knekt, P., Virtala, E., Harkanen, T., Vaarama, M., Lehtonen, J., & Lindfors, O. (2016). The outcome of short- and long-term psychotherapy 10 years after start of treatment. *Psychological Medicine, 46*(6), 1175–1188.

Koulomzin, M., Beebe, B., Anderson, S., Jaffe, J., Feldstein, S., & Cynthia, C. (2002). Infant gaze, head, face and self-touch at four months differentiate secure vs avoidant attachment at one year: A microanalytic approach. *Attachment and Human Development, 4*(1), 3–24.

Krause, R. (2010). An update on primary identification, introjection, and empathy. *International Forum of Psychoanalysis, 19*, 138–143.

Kris, E. (1956). On some vicissitudes of insight in psychoanalysis. *International Journal of Psychoanalysis, 37*, 445–455.

Künstlicher, R. (1996). The function of the frame: To protect the psychoanalytic room. *Scandinavian Psychoanalytic Review, 19*, 150–164.

Lacan, J. (1966/2006). *Ecrits – The first complete edition in English* (B. Fink, Trans.). New York: W. W. Norton & Company.

Lacan, J. (1998). La forclusion du Nom-du-Père (The foreclosure of the Name of the Father). In J.-A. Miller (Ed.), *Le séminaire vol. 5. Les formations de l'inconscient (The seminar, vol. 5. Formations of the unconscious)* (pp. 143–159). Paris: Editions du Seuil.

Lakoff, G., & Johnson, M. (1999). *Philosophy in the flesh.* New York: Basic Books.

Lam, P., Hiscock, H., & Wake, M. (2003). Outcomes of infant sleep problems: A longitudinal study of sleep, behavior, and maternal well-being. *Pediatrics, 111*(3), e203–e207.

Lampl-De Groot, J. (1928). The evolution of the Oedipus complex in women. *International Journal of Psychoanalysis, 9*, 332–345.

Landesman, P. (2011). *Maternal depression and the management of infant gaze aversion.* (Ph. D.), New York University School of Social Work, ProQuest LLC, Ann Arbor, MI.

Laplanche, J. (1999). *Essays on Otherness.* London: Routledge.

Laplanche, J., & Pontalis, J. B. (1973). *The language of psychoanalysis.* London: Hogarth Press.

Lara-Carrasco, J., Simard, V., Saint-Onge, K., Lamoureux-Tremblay, V., & Nielsen, T. (2013). Maternal representations in the dreams of pregnant women: A prospective comparative study. *Frontiers in Psychology Vol 4 2013, ArtID 551, 4.*

Lebovici, S. (2000). La consultation thérapeutique et les interventions métaphorisantes (The therapeutic consultation and the metaphorizing interventions). In M. Maury & M. Lamour (Eds), *Alliances autour du bébé. De la recherche à la clinique (Alliances around the baby. From research to clinic)* (pp. 223–243). Paris: Presses Universitaires de France.

Lebovici, S., Barriguete, J. A., & Salinas, J. L. (2002). The therapeutic consultation. In J. M. Maldonado-Durán (Ed.), *Infant and toddler mental health* (pp. 161–186). Washington, DC: American Psychiatric Publishing Inc.

236   References

Lebovici, S., & Stoléru, S. (2003). *Le nourisson, sa mère et le psychanalyste. Les interactions précoces (The baby, his mother and the psychoanalyst. Early interactions)*. Paris: Bayard.

Leckman, J. F., Feldman, R., Swain, J. E., & Mayes, L. C. (2007). Primary parental preoccupation: revisited. In L. C. Mayes, P. Fonagy, & M. Target (Eds), *Developmental science and psychoanalysis. Integration and innovation* (pp. 89–116). London: Karnac Books.

Leichsenring, F., Rabung, S., & Leibing, E. (2004). The efficacy of short-term psychodynamic psychotherapy in specific psychiatric disorders. *Archives of General Psychiatry, 61*, 1208–1216.

Letley, E. (2014). *Marion Milner: The life*. London: Routledge.

Levenson, E. (2005/1983). The ambiguity of change. An inquiry into the nature of psychoanalytic reality. In E. Levenson (Ed.), *The fallacy of understanding – The ambiguity of change* (pp. 3–180). Hillsdale, NJ: The Analytic Press.

Levitzky, S., & Cooper, R. (2000). Infant colic syndrome – maternal fantasies of aggression and infanticide. *Clinical Pediatrics, 39*(7), 395–400.

Lichtenberg, J. D. (1983). *Psychoanalysis and infant research*. Hillsdale, NJ: Analytic Press.

Lichtenberg, J. D. (1987). Infant studies and clinical work with adults. *Psychoanalytic Inquiry, 7*(3), 311–330.

Lichtenberg, J. D. (2016). Interpretation revisited. *Psychoanalytic Inquiry, 36*(1), 4–13.

Lichtenberg, J. D., & Slap, J. W. (1972). On the defense mechanism: A survey and synthesis. *Journal of the American Psychoanalytic Association, 20*, 776–792.

Lieberman, A. F. (1992). Infant-parent psychotherapy with toddlers. *Development and Psychopathology, 4*(4), 559–574.

Lieberman, A. F., & Van Horn, P. (2008). *Psychotherapy with infants and young children – Repairing the effects of stress and trauma on early attachment*. New York: The Guilford Press.

Lieberman, A. F., Weston, D. R., & Pawl, J. H. (1991). Preventive intervention and outcome with anxiously attached dyads. *Child Development, 62*(1), 199–209.

Likierman, M. (2008). Spanning presence and absence: Separation anxiety in the early years. In L. Emanuel & E. Bradley (Eds), *"What can the matter be?" – Therapeutic interventions with parents, infants, and young children* (pp. 207–227). London: Karnac.

Lindgren, K. (2001). Relationships among maternal-fetal attachment, prenatal depression, and health practices in pregnancy. *Research in Nursing & Health, 24*, 203–217.

Links, P. S., & Stockwell, M. (2002). The role of couple therapy in the treatment of narcissistic personality disorder. *American Journal of Psychotherapy, 56*(4), 522–538.

Loewald, H. W. (1951). Ego and reality. *International Journal of Psychoanalysis, 32*, 10–18.

Lojkasek, M., Cohen, N. J., & Muir, E. (1994). Where is the infant in infant intervention? A review of the literature on changing troubled mother-infant relationships. *Psychotherapy: Theory, Research, Practice, Training, 31*(1), 208–220.

Loutzenhiser, L., & Sevigny, P. R. (2008). Infant sleep and the quality of family life for first-time parents of three-month-old infants. *Fathering, 6*(1), 2–19.

Machover, K. (1949). *Personality projection in the drawing of the human figure (a method of personality investigation)*. Springfield, IL: Thomas.

Mack Brunswick, R. (1940). The preoedipal phase of the libido development. *Psychoanalytic Quarterly, 9*, 293–319.

References 237

Maddahi, M. S., Dolatian, M., Khoramabadi, M., & Talebi, A. (2016). Correlation of maternal-fetal attachment and health practices during pregnancy with neonatal outcomes. *Electronic Physician*, *8*(7), 2639–2644.

Malone, J. C., & Dayton, C. J. (2015). What is the container/contained when there are ghosts in the nursery?: Joining Bion and Fraiberg in dyadic interventions with mother and infant. *Infant Mental Health Journal*, *36*(3), 262–274.

Manzano, J., Palacio Espasa, F., & Zilkha, N. (1999). The narcissistic scenarios of parenthood. *International Journal of Psychoanalysis*, *80*(3), 465–476.

Marcus, S., Lopez, J. F., McDonough, S., MacKenzie, M. J., Flynn, H., Neal Jr., C. R., . . . Vazquez, D. M. (2011). Depressive symptoms during pregnancy: Impact on neuroendocrine and neonatal outcomes. *Infant Behavior & Development*, *34*(1), 26–34.

Marks, Z., Murphy, S., & Glowinski, H. (2001). *A compendium of Lacanian terms*. London: Free Association Books.

Maroda, K. (2002). No place to hide: Affectivity, the unconscious, and the development of relational techniques. *Contemporary Psychoanalysis*, *38*, 101–120.

Martini, J., Knappe, S., Beesdo-Baum, K., Lieb, R., & Wittchen, H.-U. (2010). Anxiety disorders before birth and self-perceived distress during pregnancy: Associations with maternal depression and obstetric, neonatal and early childhood outcomes. *Early Human Development*, *86*(5), 305–310.

Maxted, A. E., Dickstein, S., Miller-Loncar, C., High, P., Spritz, B., Liu, J., & Lester, B. M. (2005). Infant colic and maternal depression. *Infant Mental Health Journal*, *26*(1), 56–68.

McCauley, K., Elsom, S., Muir-Cochrane, E., & Lyneham, J. (2011). Midwives and assessment of perinatal mental health. *Journal of Psychiatric and Mental Health Nursing*, *18*(9), 786–795.

McDonough, S. (2004). Interaction guidance. Promoting and nurturing the caregiving relationship. In A. J. Sameroff, McDonough, S. C., & Rosenblum, K. L. (Eds), *Treating parent-infant relationship problems* (pp. 79–96). New York: The Guilford Press.

McHale, J. P., & Fivaz-Depeursinge, E. (1999). Understanding triadic and family group interactions during infancy and toddlerhood. *Clinical Child and Family Psychology Review*, *2*(2), 107–127.

McHale, J. P., & Rasmussen, J. L. (1998). Coparental and family group-level dynamics during infancy: Early family precursors of child and family functioning during preschool. *Development and Psychopathology*, *10*(1), 39–59.

Meijer, A. M., & van den Wittenboer, G. L. H. (2007). Contribution of infants' sleep and crying to marital relationship of first-time parent couples in the 1st year after childbirth. *Journal of Family Psychology*, *21*(1), 49–57.

Meltzer, D. (1967). *The psychoanalytic process*. Perthshire, Scotland: Clunie Press.

Meltzer, D., & Harris-Williams, M. (1988). *The apprehension of beauty: The role of aesthetic conflict in development, violence and art*. Perthshire, Scotland: Clunie Press.

Meltzer, D. (1992). *The claustrum*. Perthshire, Scotland: Clunie Press.

Meltzoff, A. N. (2007). The 'like me' framework for recognizing and becoming an intentional agent. *Acta Psychologica*, *124*(1), 26–43.

Meltzoff, A. N., & Moore, M. K. (1997). Explaining facial imitation: A theoretical model. *Early Development & Parenting*, *6*, 179–192.

Miller, L. (2008). The relation of infant observation to clinical practice in an under-fives counselling service. In L. Emanuel & E. Bradley (Eds), *"What can the matter be?" – Therapeutic interventions with parents, infants, and young children* (pp. 30–45). London: Karnac.

238 References

Milner, M. (1952). Aspects of symbolism in comprehension of the Not-Self. *International Journal of Psychoanalysis, 33*, 181–194.

Modell, A. H. (2009). Metaphor – The bridge between feelings and knowledge. *Psychoanalytic Inquiry, 29*(1), 6–11.

Moehler, E., Kagan, J., Parzer, P., Brunner, R., Reck, C., Wiebel, A., . . . Resch, F. (2007). Childhood behavioral inhibition and maternal symptoms of depression. *Psychopathology, 40*(6), 446–452.

Morgan, M. (2010). Unconcious beliefs about being a couple. *Fort Da, 16*, 36–55.

Morgan, M. (2012). How couple relationships shape our world: Clinical practice, research, and policy perspectives. In A. Balfour, C. Vincent, & M. Morgan (Eds), *How couple relationships shape our world: Clinical practice, research, and policy perspectives* (pp. 71–83). London: Karnac Books.

Moskowitz, S. (2011). Primary maternal preoccupation disrupted by trauma and loss: Early years of the project. *Journal of Infant, Child, and Adolescent Psychotherapy, 10*(2–3), 229–237.

Muller, J., & Brent, J. (2000). *Peirce, semiotics, and psychoanalysis*. Baltimore & London: The John Hopkins University Press.

Muller, M. E. (1992). A critical review of prenatal attachment research. *Scholarly Inquiry for Nursing Practice, 6*(1), 5–22.

Muller, M. E. (1993). Development of the prenatal attachment inventory. *Western Journal of Nursing Research, 15*(2), 199–215.

Muller, M. E. (1996). Prenatal and postnatal attachment: A modest correlation. *Journal of Obstetric, Gynecologic & Neonatal Nursing, 25*(2), 161–166.

Murray, L., Arteche, A., Fearon, P., Halligan, S., Croudace, T., & Cooper, P. J. (2010). The effects of maternal postnatal depression and child sex on academic performance at age 16 years: A developmental approach. *Journal of Child Psychology & Psychiatry, 51*(10), 1150–1159.

Murray, L., & Cooper, P. J. (1997). *Postpartum depression and child development*. New York: The Guilford Press.

Murray, L., Cooper, P. J., Wilson, A., & Romaniuk, H. (2003). Controlled trial of the short- and long-term effect of psychological treatment of post-partum depression. 2. Impact on the mother–child relationship and child outcome. *British Journal of Psychiatry, 182*(5), 420–427.

Norhayati, M., Hazlina, N., Asrenee, A., & Emilin, W. (2015). Magnitude and risk factors for postpartum symptoms: A literature review. *Journal of Affective Disorders, 175*, 34–52.

Norman, J. (2001). The psychoanalyst and the baby: A new look at work with infants. *International Journal of Psychoanalysis, 82*(1), 83–100.

Norman, J. (2004). Transformations of early infantile experiences: A 6-month-old in psychoanalysis. *International Journal of Psychoanalysis, 85*(5), 1103–1122.

Norman, J., & Salomonsson, B. (2005). 'Weaving thoughts': A method for presenting and commenting psychoanalytic case material in a peer group. *International Journal of Psychoanalysis, 86*(5), 1281–1298.

O'Connor, T. G., Monk, C., & Fitelson, E. M. (2013). Practitioner review: Maternal mood in pregnancy and child development – implications for child psychology and psychiatry. *Journal of Child Psychology and Psychiatry, 55*(2), 99–111.

O'Donnell, K. J., Glover, V., Barker, E. D., & O'Connor, T. G. (2014). The persisting effect of maternal mood in pregnancy on childhood psychopathology. *Development and Psychopathology, 26*(2), 393–403.

References   239

O'Hara, M. W., Stuart, S., Gorman, L. L., & Wenzel, A. (2000). Efficacy of interpersonal psychotherapy for postpartum depression. *Archives of General Psychiatry, 57*(11), 1039–1045.

Ogden, T. H. (1982). *Projective identification and psychotherapeutic technique.* New York: Academic Press.

Ogden, T. H. (1997). Reverie and metaphor: Some thoughts on how I work as a psychoanalyst. *International Journal of Psychoanalysis, 78,* 719–732.

Ogden, T. H. (2004). On holding and containing, being and dreaming. *International Journal of Psychoanalysis, 85,* 1349–1364.

Olds, D. L., Sadler, L., & Kitzman, H. (2007). Programs for parents of infants and toddlers: Recent evidence from randomized trials. *Journal of Child Psychology & Psychiatry & Allied Disciplines, 48*(3–4), 355–391.

Olinick, S. L. (1985). The primary data of psychoanalysis. *Contemporary Psychoanalysis, 21,* 492–500.

Olson, S. L., Bates, J. E., Sandy, J. M., & Schilling, E. M. (2002). Early developmental precursors of impulsive and inattentive behavior: From infancy to middle childhood. *Journal of Child Psychology & Psychiatry & Allied Disciplines, 43*(4), 435–447.

Orlinsky, D. E., Rönnestad, M. H., & Willutzki, U. (2004). Fifty years of psychotherapy process-outcome research: Continuity and change. In M. J. Lambert (Ed.), *Bergin and Garfield's handbook of psychotherapy and behavior change* (5th ed., pp. 307–390). New York: John Wiley & Sons, Inc.

O'Shaughnessy, E. (1988). W.R. Bion's theory of thinking and new techniques in child analysis. In E. Bott Spillius (Ed.), *Melanie Klein today. Developments in theory and practice. Volume 2: Mainly practice* (pp. 177–190). London: Tavistock/Routledge.

Östberg, M., Hagekull, B., & Wettergren, S. (1997). A measure of parental stress in mothers with small children: Dimensionality, stability and validity. *Scandinavian Journal of Psychology, 38*(3), 199–208.

Paglia, M. (2016). The Maison Verte, a transitional space: introducing the work of Françoise Dolto in the UK. *Infant Observation, 19*(3), 224–237.

Panter-Brick, C., Burgess, A., Eggerman, M., McAllister, F., Pruett, K., & Leckman, J. F. (2014). Practitioner review: Engaging fathers – recommendations for a game change in parenting interventions based on a systematic review of the global evidence. *Journal of Child Psychology and Psychiatry, 55*(11), 1187–1212.

Papousek, M. (2007). Communication in early infancy: An arena of intersubjective learning. *Infant Behavior & Development, 30*(2), 258–266.

Paquette, D., Coyl-Shepherd, D. D., & Newland, L. A. (2013). Fathers and development: New areas for exploration. *Early Child Development and Care, 183*(6), 735–745.

Parens, H. (1991). A view of the development of hostility in early life. *Journal of the American Psychoanalytic Association, 39S,* 75–108.

Paris, R., & Dubus, N. (2005). Staying connected while nurturing an infant: A challenge of new motherhood. *Family Relations, 54*(1), 72–83.

Parker, R. (1995). *Mother love, mother hate: The power of maternal ambivalence.* New York: Basic Books.

Paul, C., & Thomson Salo, F. (2007). Babies in groups: The creative roles of the babies, the mothers and the therapists. In M. E. Pozzi-Monzo & B. Tydeman (Eds), *Innovations in parent-infant psychotherapy* (pp. 134–153). London: Karnac.

Pelaez-Nogueras, M., Field, T., Cigales, M., Gonzalez, A., & Clasky, S. (1994). Infants of depressed mothers show less "depressed" behavior with their nursery teachers. *Infant Mental Health Journal, 15*(4), 358–367.

240 References

Pereira, M., & Ferreira, A. (2015). Affective, cognitive, and motivational processes of maternal care. In M. C. Antonelli (Ed.), *Perinatal programming of neurodevelopment* (pp. 199–217). New York: Springer.

Pines, D. (2010). *A woman's unconscious use of her body. A psychoanalytical perspective (Kindle edition)*. New York: Routledge/Taylor & Francis Group; US.

Pizer, B., & Pizer, S. A. (2006). "The gift of an apple or the twist of an arm": Negotiation in couples and couple therapy. *Psychoanalytic Dialogues, 16*(1), 71–92.

Poh, H., Koh, S., & He, H. (2014). An integrative review of fathers' experiences during pregnancy and childbirth. *International Nursing Review, 61*(4), 543–554.

Porcerelli, J. H., Huth-Bocks, A., Huprich, S. K., & Richardson, L. (2015). Defense mechanisms of pregnant mothers predict attachment security, social-emotional competence, and behavior problems in their toddlers. *American Journal of Psychiatry, 173*(2), 138–146.

Quinodoz, D. (1992). The psychoanalytic setting as the instrument of the container function. *International Journal of Psychoanalysis, 73*(4), 627–636.

Rapaport, D., & Gill, M. M. (1959). The points of view and assumptions of metapsychology. *International Journal of Psychoanalysis, 40*, 153–162.

Raphael-Leff, J. (2005). *Psychological processes of child bearing* (4th ed.). London: Anna Freud Centre.

Raval, V., Goldberg, S., Atkinson, L., Benoit, D., Myhal, N., Poulton, L., & Zwiers, M. (2001). Maternal attachment, maternal responsiveness and infant attachment. *Infant Behavior & Development, 24*(3), 281–304.

Reck, C., Hunt, A., Fuchs, T., Weiss, R., Noon, A., Moehler, E., . . . Mundt, C. (2004). Interactive regulation of affect in postpartum depressed mothers and their infants: An overview. *Psychopathology, 37*(6), 272–280.

Reddy, V. (2008). *How infants know minds*. Cambridge, MA: Harvard University Press.

Reider, N. (1972). Metaphor as interpretation. *International Journal of Psychoanalysis, 53*, 463–469.

Renik, O., & Spillius, E. B. (2004). Intersubjectivity in psychoanalysis. *International Journal of Psychoanalysis, 85*(5), 1053–1064; discussion 1057–1061.

Renn, P. (2010). Psychoanalysis, attachment theory and the inner world: How different theories understand the concept of mind and the implications for clinical work. *Attachment: New Directions in Psychotherapy and Relational Psychoanalysis, 4*, 146–168.

Rennie, D. L. (2012). Qualitative research as methodical hermeneutics. *Psychological Methods, 17*(3), 385.

Rizzuto, A. (2003). Psychoanalysis: The transformation of the subject by the spoken word. *Psychoanalytic Quarterly, 72*, 287–323.

Rizzuto, A. (2009). Metaphoric process and metaphor: The dialectics of shared analytic experience. *Psychoanalytic Inquiry, 29*, 18–29.

Robert-Tissot, C., Cramer, B., Stern, D. N., Serpa, S. R., Bachmann, J.-P., Palacio-Espasa, F., . . . Mendiguren, G. (1996). Outcome evaluation in brief mother-infant psychotherapies: Report on 75 cases. *Infant Mental Health Journal, 17*(2), 97–114.

Roggman, L. A., Boyce, L. K., Cook, G. A., Christiansen, K., & Jones, D. (2004). Playing with Daddy: social toy play, Early Head Start, and developmental outcomes. *Fathering: A Journal of Theory, Research, and Practice about Men as Fathers, 2*(1), 83–108.

Rosan, C., & Grimas, E. (2015). The power of couple-focused approaches in the perinatal period. *Journal of Family Health, 26*(1), 10–13.

Rosolato, G. (1985). *Éléments de l'interprétation (Elements of interpretation)*. Paris: Gallimard.

References 241

Roussillon, R. (2011). *Primitive agony and symbolization*. London: IPA and Karnac.

Rustin, Michael (2006). Infant observation research: What have we learned so far? *Infant Observation, 9*(1), 35–52.

Rustin, Margaret (2014). The relevance of infant observation for early intervention: Containment in theory and practice. *Infant Observation, 17*(2), 97–114.

Rutherford, H. J. V., & Mayes, L. C. (2014). Minds shaped through relationships: The emerging neurobiology of parenting. In R. N. Emde & M. Leuzinger-Bohleber (Eds), *Early parenting and prevention of disorder* (pp. 50–73). London: Karnac Books.

Sackett, D. L., Rosenberg, W. M. C., Muir Gray, J. A., Brian Haynes, R., & Richardson, W. S. (1996). Editorial: Evidence based medicine: what it is and what it isn't. *British Medical Journal, 312*(7023), 71–72.

Sadeh, A., Tikotzky, L., & Scher, A. (2010). Parenting and infant sleep. *Sleep Medicine Reviews, 14*(2), 89–96.

Sager, C. J. (1976). *Marriage contracts and couple therapy*. New York: Brunner/Mazel.

Salomonsson, B. (2004). Some psychoanalytic viewpoints on neuropsychiatric disorders in children. *International Journal of Psychoanalysis, 85*(1), 117–135.

Salomonsson, B. (2006). The impact of words on children with ADHD and DAMP. Consequences for psychoanalytic technique. *International Journal of Psychoanalysis, 87*(4), 1029–1047.

Salomonsson, B. (2007a). Semiotic transformations in psychoanalysis with infants and adults. *International Journal of Psychoanalysis, 88*(5), 1201–1221.

Salomonsson, B. (2007b). "Talk to me baby, tell me what's the matter now". Semiotic and developmental perspectives on communication in psychoanalytic infant treatment. *International Journal of Psychoanalysis, 88*(1), 127–146.

Salomonsson, B. (2011a). The music of containment. Addressing the participants in mother-infant psychoanalytic treatment. *Infant Mental Health Journal, 32*(6), 599–612.

Salomonsson, B. (2011b). Psychoanalytic conceptualizations of the internal object in an ADHD child. *Journal of Infant, Child, and Adolescent Psychotherapy, 10*(1), 87–102.

Salomonsson, B. (2012a). Has infantile sexuality anything to do with infants? *International Journal of Psychoanalysis, 93*(3), 631–647.

Salomonsson, B. (2012b). Psychoanalytic case presentations in a Weaving Thoughts group. On countertransference and group dynamics. *International Journal of Psychoanalysis, 93*(4), 917–937.

Salomonsson, B. (2013). Transferences in parent-infant psychoanalytic treatments. *International Journal of Psychoanalysis, 94*(4), 767–792.

Salomonsson, B. (2014a). *Psychoanalytic therapy with infants and parents: Practice, theory and results*. London: Routledge.

Salomonsson, B. (2014b). Psychodynamic therapies with infants and parents: A critical review of treatment methods. *Psychodynamic Psychiatry, 42*(2), 203–234.

Salomonsson, B. (2014c). Psychodynamic therapies with infants and parents: A review of RCTs on mother–infant psychoanalytic treatment and other techniques. *Psychodynamic Psychiatry, 42*(4), 617–640.

Salomonsson, B. (2015a). Extending the field: Parent-toddler psychotherapy inspired by mother-infant work. *Journal of Child Psychotherapy, 41*(1), 3–21.

Salomonsson, B. (2015b). Infantile defence in parent–infant psychotherapy: The example of gaze avoidance. *International Journal of Psychoanalysis, 97*(1), 65–88.

Salomonsson, B. (2017a). The function of language in parent-infant psychotherapy. *International Journal of Psychoanalysis, 98*(6), 1597–1618.

242 References

Salomonsson, B. (2017b). Interpreting the inner world of ADHD children: Psychoanalytic perspectives. *International Journal of Qualitative Studies on Health and Well-being, 12*(sup1), 1298269. doi:10.1080/17482631.2017.1298269

Salomonsson, B. (2018). Was Freud a Bionian? Perspectives from parent-infant psychoanalytic treatments. To be published in A. Alisobhani & G. Corstorphine (Eds), *Everything we know nothing about: Explorations in Bion's "O"*. London: Karnac.

Salomonsson, B., & Sandell, R. (2011a). A randomized controlled trial of mother-infant psychoanalytic treatment. 1. Outcomes on self-report questionnaires and external ratings. *Infant Mental Health Journal, 32*(2), 207–231.

Salomonsson, B., & Sandell, R. (2011b). A randomized controlled trial of mother-infant psychoanalytic treatment. 2. Predictive and moderating influences of quantitative treatment and patient factors. *Infant Mental Health Journal, 32*(3), 377–404.

Salomonsson, B., & Sandell, R. (2012). Maternal experiences and the mother–infant dyad's development: Introducing the Interview of Mother's Experiences (I-ME). *Journal of Reproductive and Infant Psychology, 30*(1), 21–50.

Salomonsson, B., & Sleed, M. (2010). The ASQ:SE. A validation study of a mother-report questionnaire on a clinical mother-infant sample. *Infant Mental Health Journal, 31*(4), 412–431.

Salomonsson, B., & Winberg Salomonsson, M. (2017). Intimacy thwarted and established: Following a girl from infancy to child psychotherapy. *International Journal of Psychoanalysis, 98*(3), 861–875.

Sandbrook, S. P., & Adamson-Macedo, E. N. (2004). Maternal-fetal attachment: Searching for a new definition. *Neuroendocrinol Lett, 25(Suppl.1)*, 169–182.

Sandell, R. (2012). Research on outcomes of psychoanalysis and psychoanalysis-derived psychotherapies. In G. O. Gabbard, B. E. Litowitz, & P. Williams (Eds), *Textbook of psychoanalysis* (2nd ed., pp. 385–403). Arlington, VA: American Psychiatric Publishing.

Sandell, R., Blomberg, J., Lazar, A., Carlsson, J., Broberg, J., & Schubert, J. (2000). Varieties of long-term outcome among patients in psychoanalysis and long-term psychotherapy: A review of findings in the Stockholm Outcome of Psychoanalysis and Psychotherapy Project (STOPP). *The International Journal of Psychoanalysis, 81*(5), 921–942.

Sander, F. M. (2004). Psychoanalytic couple therapy: Classical style. *Psychoanal Inquiry, 24*, 373–386.

Sandler, J. (1993a). On communication from patient to analyst: Not everything is projective identification. *International Journal of Psychoanalysis, 74*, 1097–1107.

Sandler, J. (1993b). Fantasy, defence and the representational world. *Bulletin of the Anna Freud Centre, 16*(337–347).

Sandler, J., & Freud, A. (1981). Discussions in the Hampstead Index on 'The Ego and the Mechanisms of Defence': V. The Mechanisms of Defence, Part 2. *Bulletin of the Anna Freud Centre, 4*, 231–277.

Sandman, C. A., & Davis, E. P. (2010). Gestational stress influences cognition and behavior. *Future Neurology, 5*(5), 675–690.

Scharff, D. E. (2003). Psychoanalytic models of the mind for couple and family therapy. *Journal of Applied Psychoanalytic Studies, 5*(3), 257–267.

Scharff, D. E., & Scharff, J. S. (Eds). (2014). *Psychoanalytic couple therapy. Foundations of theory and practice (Kindle edition)*. London: Karnac Books.

Scharff, J. S. (2004). Play and very young children in object relations family therapy. *International Journal of Applied Psychoanalytic Studies, 1*, 259–268.

Scharff, J. S. (2014). Establishing a therapeutic relationship in analytic couple therapy. In D. E. Scharff & J. S. Scharff (Eds), *Psychoanalytic couple therapy. Foundations of theory and practice (Kindle edition)* (pp. 131–147, loc. 3372–3785). London: Karnac Books.

Seimyr, L., Edhborg, M., Lundh, W., & Sjögren, B. (2004). In the shadow of maternal depressed mood: experiences of parenthood during the first year after childbirth. *Journal of Psychosomatic Obstetrics & Gynecology*, 25(1), 23–34.

Seligman, S. (1999). Integrating Kleinian theory and intersubjective infant research: Observing projective identification. *Psychoanalytic Dialogues*, 9(2), 129–159.

Seligman, S. (2006). *Projective identification and the transgenerational transmission of trauma (Ch. 4)* C. Wachs & L. Jacobs (Eds.), *Parent-focused child therapy (Kindle edition)*. Lanham: Rowman & Littlefield Publishers.

Seth, S., Lewis, A. J., & Galbally, M. (2016). Perinatal maternal depression and cortisol function in pregnancy and the postpartum period: A systematic literature review. *BMC Pregnancy and Childbirth*, 16(1), 124.

Shaffer, D., Gould, M. S., Brasic, J., Ambrosini, P., Prudence, F., Bird, H., & Aluwahlia, S. (1983). A Children's Global Assessment Scale (CGAS). *Archives of General Psychiatry*, 40(11), 1228–1231.

Shah, P. E., Fonagy, P., & Strathearn, L. (2010). Is attachment transmitted across generations? The plot thickens. *Clinical Child Psychology and Psychiatry*, 15(3), 329–345.

Shapiro, T. (2013). *Discussion of Salomonsson's paper*. Paper presented at the Association for Psychoanalytic Medicine. Columbia University Center for Psychoanalytic Training and Research, New York.

Sherick, I. (2009). A proposal to revive "Parent Guidance": An illustration of a brief intervention with the mother of a toddler. *Psychoanalytic Study of the Child*, 64, 229–246.

Siddiqui, A., & Hägglöf, B. (2000). Does maternal prenatal attachment predict postnatal mother-infant interaction? *Early Human Development*, 59(1), 13–25.

Silverman, R., & Lieberman, A. (1999). Negative maternal attributions, projective identification, and the intergenerational transmission of violent relational patterns. *Psychoanalytic Dialogues*, 9(2), 161–186.

Singleton, J. L. (2005). *Parent-infant interaction interventions: A meta-analysis*. Dissertation Abstracts International: Section B: The Sciences and Engineering.

Slade, A. (2006). Representation, symbolization, and affect regulation in the concomitant treatment of a mother and child. In C. Wachs & L. Jacobs (Eds), *Parent-focused child therapy (Kindle edition)* (Ch. 13). Northvale, NJ: Jason Aronson.

Slade, A., Cohen, L. J., Sadler, L. S., & Miller, M. (2009). The psychology and psychopathology of pregnancy. In C. H. Zeanah (Ed.), *Handbook of infant mental health* (3rd ed., pp. 22–39). New York: The Guilford Press.

Slade, A., Grienenberger, J., Bernbach, E., Levy, D., & Locker, A. (2005). Maternal reflective functioning, attachment, and the transmission gap: A preliminary study. *Attachment & Human Development*, 7(3), 283–298.

Slochower, J. (1996). Holding and the evolving maternal metaphor. *Psychoanalytic Review*, 83, 195–218.

Sorenson, D. S., & Schuelke, P. (1999). Fantasies of the unborn among pregnant women. *MCN: The American Journal of Maternal/Child Nursing*, 24(2), 92–97.

244 References

Sours, C., Raghavan, P., Foxworthy, W., Meredith, M., El Metwally, D., Zhuo, J., ... Gullapalli, R. P. (2017). Cortical multisensory connectivity is present near birth in humans. *Brain Imaging and Behavior*, *11*(4), 1207–1213.

Squires, J., Bricker, D., Heo, K., & Twombly, E. (2002). *Ages & Stages Questionnaires: Social-Emotional. A parent-completed, child-monitoring system for social-emotional behaviors*. Baltimore, MD: Paul H Brookes Publishing.

Stavrén-Eriksson, E. (2016). *Transition to fatherhood in Sweden today (paper presented at a research student's course)*. Karolinska Institutet, Stockholm.

Stein, A., Pearson, R. M., Goodman, S. H., Rapa, E., Rahman, A., McCallum, M., ... Pariante, C. M. (2014). Effects of perinatal mental disorders on the fetus and child. *The Lancet*, *384*(9956), 1800–1819.

Stein, B. E., Stanford, T. R., & Rowland, B. A. (2014). Development of multisensory integration from the perspective of the individual neuron. *Nature Reviews. Neuroscience*, *15*(8), 520.

Stern, D. N. (1985). *The interpersonal world of the infant*. New York: Basic Books.

Stern, D. N. (1990). *Diary of a baby (Kindle edition)*. New York: Basic Books.

Stern, D. N. (1995). *The motherhood constellation: A unified view of parent-infant psychotherapy*. London: Karnac Books.

Stern, D. N. (2000). The relevance of empirical infant research to psychoanalytic theory and practice. In J. Sandler, A.-M. Sandler, & R. Davies (Eds), *Clinical and observational psychoanalytical research: Roots of a controversy* (pp. 73–90). London: Karnac Books.

Stern, D. N. (2004). *The present moment in psychotherapy and in everyday life*. New York: W.W. Norton and Company Ltd.

Stolorow, R. D. (1997). Dynamic, dyadic, intersubjective systems: An evolving paradigm for psychoanalysis. *Psychoanalytic Psychology*, *14*(3), 337–346.

Stolorow, R. D., & Atwood, G. F. (1997). Deconstructing the myth of the neutral analyst: An alternative from intersubjective systems theory. *Psychoanalytic Quarterly*, *66*(3), 431–449.

Strenger, C. (1997). Hedgehogs, foxes, and critical pluralism: The clinician's yearning for unified conceptions. *Psychoanalysis and Contemporary Thought*, *20*, 111–145.

Stuart, J. (2012). Introduction: Babies in the consulting room: What happens when analyst, mother and infant meet. *Journal of the American Psychoanalytic Association*, *60*(3), 493–500.

Stuhr, U., & Wachholz, S. (2001). In search for a psychoanalytic research strategy: The concept of Ideal Types. *Psychologische Beitrage*, *43*(3), 153–168.

Suchman, N., DeCoste, C., Castiglioni, N., Legow, N., & Mayes, L. (2008). The Mothers and Toddlers Program: Preliminary findings from an attachment-based parenting intervention for substance-abusing mothers. *Psychoanalytic Psychology*, *25*(3), 499–517.

Sun, X., Briel, M., Walter, S. D., & Guyatt, G. H. (2010). Is a subgroup effect believable? Updating criteria to evaluate the credibility of subgroup analyses. *British Medical Journal*, *340*, 850–854.

Suri, R., Lin, A. S., Cohen, L. S., & Altshuler, L. L. (2014). Acute and long-term behavioral outcome of infants and children exposed in utero to either maternal depression or antidepressants: A review of the literature. *Journal of Clinical Psychiatry*, *75*(10), e1142–e1152.

Swain, J., Dayton, C., Kim, P., Tolman, R., & Volling, B. (2014). Progress on the paternal brain: Theory, animal models, human brain research, and mental health implications. *Infant Mental Health Journal*, *35*(5), 394–408.

References 245

Termine, N. T., & Izard, C. E. (1988). Infants' responses to their mothers' expressions of joy and sadness. *Developmental Psychology*, *24*(2), 223–229.

Teti, D. M., Kim, B.-R., Mayer, G., & Countermine, M. (2010). Maternal emotional availability at bedtime predicts infant sleep quality. *Journal of Family Psychology*, *24*(3), 307–315.

Thomson Salo, F. (2007). Recognizing the infant as subject in infant-parent psychotherapy. *International Journal of Psychoanalysis*, *88*(4), 961–979.

Thomson Salo, F., & Paul, C. (2001). Some principles of infant-parent psychotherapy. Ann Morgan's contribution. *The Signal. The World Association for Infant Mental Health*, *9*(1–2), 14–19.

Thomson Salo, F., Paul, C., Morgan, A., Jones, S., Jordan, B., Meehan, M., & Morse, S. (1999). "Free to be playful": Therapeutic work with infants. *Infant Observation*, *31*(1), 47–62.

Toth, S. L., Rogosch, F. A., Manly, J. T., & Cicchetti, D. (2006). The efficacy of toddler-parent psychotherapy to reorganize attachment in the young offspring of mothers with major depressive disorder: A randomized preventive trial. *Journal of Consulting and Clinical Psychology*, *74*(6), 1006–1016.

Toth, S. L., Rogosch, F. A., Sturge-Apple, M., & Cicchetti, D. (2009). Maternal depression, children's attachment security, and representational development: An organizational perspective. *Child Development*, *80*(1), 192–208.

Trad, P. V. (1991). From mothers' milk to mothers' dreams: Maternal destructive separation fantasies. *Contemporary Psychoanalysis*, *27*, 34–50.

Treem, W. R. (1994). Infant colic: A pediatric gastroenterologist's perspective. *Pediatric Clinics of North America*, *41*, 1121–1138.

Trevarthen, C., & Aitken, K. J. (2001). Infant intersubjectivity: Research, theory, and clinical applications. *Journal of Child Psychology & Psychiatry & Allied Disciplines*, *42*(1), 3–48.

Tronick, E. (2007a). Infant moods and the chronicity of depressive symptoms: The cocreation of unique ways of being together for good or ill, Paper 2: The formation of negative moods in infants and children of depressed mothers. In E. Tronick (Ed.), *The neurobehavioral and social-emotional development of infants and children* (pp. 362–377). New York: W. W. Norton.

Tronick, E. (2007b). *The neurobehavioral and social-emotional development of infants and children*. New York: W. W. Norton.

Tronick, E., Als, H., Adamson, L., Wise, S., & Brazelton, T. B. (1978). The infant's response to entrapment between contradictory messages in face-to-face interaction. *Journal of the American Academy of Child and Adolescent Psychiatry*, *17*, 1–13.

Tronick, E., & Weinberg, K. (1997). Depressed mothers and infants: Failure to form dyadic states of consciousness. In L. C. Murray, P. (Ed.), *Postpartum depression and child development* (pp. 54–84). New York: The Guilford Press.

Tukey, J. W. (1991). The philosophy of multiple comparisons. *Statistical Science*, *6*(1), 100–116.

Twomey, J. E., High, P., & Lester, B. M. (2012). Colic: What's maternal mental health got to do with it? *Infant Mental Health Journal*, *33*(5), 543–552.

United Nations (2015). *World Population Prospects: The 2015 Revision, DVD Edition*.

Urwin, C. (2008). Where the wild things are: Tantrums and behaviour problems in two under-fives boys. In L. Emanuel & E. Bradley (Eds), *"What can the matter be?": Therapeutic interventions with parents, infants, and young children* (pp. 143–158). London: Tavistock Clinic Series, Karnac Books.

246 References

Valabrega, J.-P. (2001). Les notions de pictogramme et de potentialité – psychotique – dans l'œuvre de Piera Aulagnier (The notions of pictogram and potentiality – psychotic – in the work of Piera Aulagnier). *Topique, 1*(74), (pp. 2119–2122) doi:10.3917/top.074.0119

Van Buren, J. (1993). Mother-infant semiotics: Intuition and the development of human subjectivity –Klein/Lacan: Fantasy and meaning. *Journal of the American Academy of Psychoanalysis & Dynamic Psychiatry, 21*(4), 567–580.

van IJzendoorn, M. (1995). Adult attachment representations, parental responsiveness, and infant attachment: A meta-analysis on the predictive validity of the Adult Attachment Interview. *Psychological Bulletin, 117*(3), 387–403.

Vartiainen, H., Suonio, S., Halonen, P., & Rimón, R. (1994). Psychosocial factors, female fertility and pregnancy: a prospective study — Part II: Pregnancy. *Journal of Psychosomatic Obstetrics & Gynecology, 15*(2), 77–84.

Vik, K., & Braten, S. (2009). Video interaction guidance inviting transcendence of post-partum depressed mothers' self-centered state and holding behavior. *Infant Mental Health Journal, 30*(3), 287–300.

Vreeswijk, C. M. J. M., Maas, A. J., Rijk, C. H., & van Bakel, H. J. (2014). Fathers' experiences during pregnancy: Paternal prenatal attachment and representations of the fetus. *Psychology of Men & Masculinity, 15*(2), 129.

Vreeswijk, C. M. J. M., Maas, A. J. B. M., & van Bakel, H. J. A. (2012). Parental represent-ations: A systematic review of the working model of the child interview. *Infant Mental Health Journal, 33*(1), 1–15.

Wachholz, S., & Stuhr, U. (1999). The concept of ideal types in psychoanalytic follow-up research. *Psychotherapy Research, 9*(3), 327–341.

Wallerstein, R. S. (2011). Metaphor in psychoanalysis: Bane or blessing? *Psychoanalytic Inquiry, 31*(2), 90–106.

Watillon, A. (1993). The dynamics of psychoanalytic therapies of the early parent–child relationship. *International Journal of Psychoanalysis, 74*, 1037–1048.

Wechsler, D. (2005). *WPPSI-III. Manual, del 1. Svensk version. (Original title: Wechsler preschool and primary scale of intelligence*, 3rd ed.) (E. Tideman, Trans.). Stockholm: Psykologiförlaget.

Weinberg, M. K., Olson, K. L., Beeghly, M., & Tronick, E. (2006). Making up is hard to do, especially for mothers with high levels of depressive symptoms and their infant sons. *Journal of Child Psychology and Psychiatry, 47*(7), 670–683.

Werbart, A., von Below, C., Brun, J., & Gunnarsdottir, H. (2015). "Spinning one's wheels": Nonimproved patients view their psychotherapy. *Psychotherapy Research, 25*(5), 546–564.

Wickberg, B., & Hwang, C. P. (1997). Screening for postnatal depression in a population-based Swedish sample. *Acta Psychiatrica Scandinavica, 95*(1), 62–66.

Widlöcher, D. (2001). The treatment of affects: An interdisciplinary issue. *The Psychoanalytic Quarterly, 70*(1), 243–264.

Winberg Salomonsson, M. (2017). *Long-term effects of mother-infant psychoanalytic treatment.* (Ph.D.), Karolinska Institutet, Stockholm.

Winberg Salomonsson, M., & Barimani, M. (2017). Mothers' experiences of mother-infant psychoanalytic treatment – a qualitative study. *Infant Mental Health Journal, 38*(4), 486–498.

Winberg Salomonsson, M., Sorjonen, K., & Salomonsson, B. (2015a). A long-term follow-up of a randomized controlled trial of mother-infant psychoanalytic treatment: Outcomes on the children. *Infant Mental Health Journal, 36*(1), 12–29.

References 247

Winberg Salomonsson, M., Sorjonen, K., & Salomonsson, B. (2015b). A long-term follow-up study of a randomized controlled trial of mother-infant psychoanalytic treatment: Outcomes on mothers and interactions. *Infant Mental Health Journal, 36*(6), 542–555.

Winnicott, D. W. (1941). The observation of infants in a set situation. In *Through paediatrics to psycho-analysis* (pp. 52–69). London: Hogarth Press.

Winnicott, D. W. (1949a). Hate in the countertransference. *International Journal of Psychoanalysis, 30*, 69–74.

Winnicott, D. W. (1949b). Mind and its relation to the psyche-soma. In *Through paediatrics to psychoanalysis* (pp. 243–254). London: Hogarth Press.

Winnicott, D. W. (1950). Aggression in relation to emotional development. In *Through paediatrics to psycho-analysis* (pp. 204–218). London: Hogarth Press.

Winnicott, D. W. (1953). Transitional objects and transitional phenomena – A study of the first not-me possession. *International Journal of Psychoanalysis, 34*, 89–97.

Winnicott, D. W. (1955). Metapsychological and clinical aspects of regression within the psycho-analytical set-up. *International Journal of Psychoanalysis, 36*, 16–26.

Winnicott, D. W. (1956a). Primary maternal preoccupation. In *Through paediatrics to psycho-analysis* (pp. 300–305). London: Hogarth Press.

Winnicott, D. W. (1956b). The antisocial tendency. In *Through paediatrics to psycho-analysis* (pp. 306–315). London: Hogarth Press.

Winnicott, D. W. (1960a). Ego distortion in terms of true and false self. In *The maturational processes and the facilitating environment: Studies in the theory of emotional development* (pp. 140–152). London: Hogarth Press.

Winnicott, D. W. (1960b). The theory of the parent-infant relationship. *International Journal of Psychoanalysis, 41*, 585–595.

Winnicott, D. W. (1962a). Ego integration in child development. In *The maturational processes and the facilitating environment* (pp. 56–63). London: Hogarth Press.

Winnicott, D. W. (1962b). The theory of the parent-infant relationship – Further remarks. *International Journal of Psychoanalysis, 43*, 238–239.

Winnicott, D. W. (1962c). A personal view of the Kleinian contribution. In *The maturational processes and the facilitating environment* (pp. 171–178). London: Hogarth Press.

Winnicott, D. W. (1965). *The maturational processes and the facilitating environment: Studies in the theory of emotional development* (Vol. 64). London: Hogarth Press.

Winnicott, D. W. (1971a). *Therapeutic consultations in child psychiatry*. London: Hogarth Press.

Winnicott, D. W. (1971b). *Playing and reality*. London: Tavistock Publications.

Winnicott, D. W. (1975). *Through paediatrics to psycho-analysis*. London: Hogarth Press.

Wittenberg, I. (2008). Brief work with parents of infants. In L. Emanuel & E. Bradley (Eds), *"What can the matter be?" – Therapeutic interventions with parents, infants, and young children* (pp. 7–29). London: Karnac.

Wordsworth, W. (1850). *The Complete Works* (A. Balloch Grosart Ed.). Amazon: Kindle Editions.

Yarcheski, A., Mahon, N. E., Yarcheski, T. J., Hanks, M. M., & Cannella, B. L. (2009). A meta-analytic study of predictors of maternal-fetal attachment. *International Journal of Nursing Studies, 46*(5), 708–715.

Zeanah, C., Benoit, D., & Barton, M. (1986). *Working model of the child interview.* Unpublished interview. New Orleans: Tulane University.

Zeanah, C., Benoit, D., & Hirshberg, L. (1996). *Working model of the child interview coding manual.* Unpublished manual. New Orleans.

248 References

Zeitner, R. M. P. A. (2003). Obstacles for the psychoanalyst in the practice of couple therapy. *Psychoanalytic Psychology, 20*(2), 348–362.

Zemp, M., Bodenmann, G., & Cummings, E. M. (2016). The significance of interparental conflict for children. *European Psychologist, 21*(2), 99–108.

Zepf, S. (2006). Attachment theory and psychoanalysis: Some remarks from an epistemological and from a Freudian viewpoint. *International Journal of Psychoanalysis, 87*(6), 1529–1548.

ZERO-TO-THREE. (2005). *Diagnostic classification of mental health and developmental disorders of infancy and early childhood (DC 0–3:R).* Washington: DC: ZERO TO THREE Press.

Zlot, S. (2007). The parenthood conflict in the light of mother-infant psychotherapy. *Mellanrummet, 16*, 11–22.

Index

abandonment 73, 103, 106–7, 116–17
abduction 206
Abraham, K. 136
Abse, S. 121
abstinence, rule of 75–6, 78
abstraction 22
accoucher 36
activation relationship theory 20
active intermodal matching (AIM) 210–11
Adam and Eve 6
ADHD 142–3
adolescents 5, 16, 69–70
adrenocorticotropic hormone (ACTH) 14
Adult Attachment Interview (AAI) 25
affect 24, 127–8, 133, 197; baby's mind
    153, 155, 157; metaphors 211–13;
    naming the nameless 171–2, 174, 183–4
Ages and Stages Questionnaire: Social-
    Emotional (ASQ:SE) 103
aggression 127, 133–6, 140, 143, *see also*
    violence
Aguayo, J. 151, 153
Ahumada, J.L. 206
air travel 59
Alhusen, J.L. 24
alpha-elements 17
ambivalence 15, 29, 33–4, 76–7, 158, 178
amygdala 20
anaclitic patients 106
anaesthesia 51
'Andrea' 67, 221
anger 17, 35, 81–3; baby's mind 155–8;
    toddlers 136, 139–40, 143; trauma 41–4
Ann Arbor 96
Anna Freud Centre 95–6, 100
annihilation 175, 177–8
anxiety 47, 127; baby's mind 154–8, 160–1;
    Child Health Centre 61, 64–6, 74;

defences 197, 199; naming the nameless
    167, 175–80, 182–4, 186; primary
    preoccupation 15–18, 33, 35; toddlers
    132, 136, 143; trauma 41–2, 44–5
anxious attachment 25, 100
Anxious/Unready type 103
Aristotle 66
Arlow, J. 204
assessment 54–5
attachment 4, 94–6; baby's mind 150–1,
    157, 162, 189; foetal 14, 18, 24–6, 30,
    206; primary preoccupation 15, 22–3,
    25–7, 33; studies 100–1; toddlers 131,
    141, 143–4
attributions 94
attunement 211–12
Aulagnier, P. 184–5
Australia 94, 96
Autumn Sonata (Bergman) 44
avoidance 25, 93, 97, *see also* gaze
    avoidance

Balestriere, L. 169
Barlow, J. 220
batteries 145
Beebe, B. 163, 183
Befriedigung (satisfaction) 169–71, 184–5
belief, unconscious 119–24
Bell, L. 118
Benedek, T. 5, 193
Benjamin, J. 194
Bergman, I. 44
beta-elements 17
Bible 3–4, 6, 15, 36, 129, 217
biological factors 58, 132, 171, 199
Bion, W.R. 64, 78, 83; baby's mind 150,
    165, 178–9, 183–4, 204; primary
    preoccupation 17–18, 29, 32, 35

250 Index

Blake, W. 170
Blatt, S.J. 106
bliss 13
body 5, 28, 36, 180–1
Bohleber, W. 194–5
Boundless Maternity, Principle of 66
Bowlby, J. 159, 161
Bradley, E. 145
brain 14–15, 20, 181
breast, double relation to 154
breastfeeding 28, 39, 81, 91; anxiety in
    babies 166–7, 169, 184–5; baby's mind
    154, 156, 196; Child Health Centre
    68–9, 74; metaphors 206–10, 212;
    therapeutic technique 49, 52–3
Britain *see* UK
British Institute 154
Britton, R. 64, 178
Bydlowski, M. 16

Caesarean; C-section 9, 37, 49–52, 80,
    103
California 99
Cambridge study 100, 106
Campbell, T. 159
Canada 25, 94, 99, 129
cardiotocography (CTG) 37
caring 33, 43, 70, 81
cathexis 168, 171
causation 6
CBT 72, 207
Centre Alfred Binet 90, 145–6
chick and egg metaphor 168–70, 175
Child Health Centres (CHCs) 9, 11, 37, 80;
    baby's defences 187–9; clinical methods
    88, 96; consultations 50, 53; couple
    therapy 109–10, 113, 119, 124–5, 129;
    external frame 56, 59–60, 62–3; future
    220–2; internal frame 71–9; metaphors
    206–7, 212; studies 102–4; supervision
    64–70; toddlers 131, 133, 141
Children's Global Assessment Scale
    (CGAS) 104
chocolate 84
Cicchetti, D. 107
clarification 119
class *see* socio-economic status
Cognitive Behavioural Therapy (CBT) 72,
    207
colic 166, 170, 176, 182, 188–9, 192–3,
    196–7
collusion 122

communication 35, 71, 124; baby's mind
    149–50, 163, 172–3; clinical methods
    91–3, 97; metaphors 213, 216; toddlers
    145, 147
Condon, J.T. 24
conflict 154, 195–6; marital 103, 127–9,
    158, 160
confluence 4
confrontation 119
confusion 128–9
consciousness 16, 87, *see also* mind
constancy, principle of 169–70
containment 59, 186; methods 93–4;
    primary preoccupation 17–18, 29–30,
    35; toddlers 131, 146
controversy 153
coparenting 126–9
Corkindale, C. 24
cortisol 14, 132
couch 75–6, 78–9
counselling 68, 100–1
countertransference 38–9, 70; baby's mind
    153, 163, 188; clinical methods 88, 96;
    couple therapy 109–10, 117; internal
    frame 73, 76, 78; metaphors 209–11,
    215–16; toddlers 137, 145
couple therapy 74, 77, 109–30; case
    vignettes 110–16, 122–6; metaphor for
    toddler therapy 131, 140, 146;
    projections 110–14; research arguments
    for 126–30; technical points 116–20; to
    individual sessions 114–16
Cowsill, K. 198
Cramer, B. 89–90, 93–4, 96
cramp metaphor 208–10, 212, 215
Cranley, M.S. 24
craving 83–4
crisis 61, 64, 83, 219; brief interventions
    88–9
crocodiles 135–40

da Rocha Barros, E.M. 205
da Vinci, L. 46
Dance of Death (Strindberg) 125
dance metaphor 206–12, 215
data 161–3
death 9, 32, 36–8, 40–1
death drive 175–7, 183–5
deduction 206
defecation 157
defence 41, 74, 97, 119, 150–1, 159,
    187–202, 221; analyst's running theory

Index   251

192–3; anxiety in babies 171, 177, 182; case vignette 188–92; Freud on 196–7; gaze avoidance research 198–9; (inter-) subjectivity? 193–6; mechanism 200–1; primary preoccupation 23, 25–6
deliverance 36
delivery 3–4, 8–9, 23, 32, 43, 45, 49, 51, 129; trauma 36–41
'delossery' 8, 14, 36
demarcating 172
depression 7, 97, 132, 198, 221; anxiety in babies 167, 180; baby's mind 158, 160, 163; Child Health Centre 57–8, 60–1, 67, 73–4; couple therapy 110–12, 116, 126; psychology of pregnancy 14–15, 17; studies 100–2, 104, 107
depressive position 154
desire 66, 184–5, 209–10
detachment 128
detectives 72
Diamond, M.J. 19
Diary of a baby (Stern) 183
differentiation 32
discipline 20–1
discrepancies 127
disintegration 177
distress 54, 116, 160, 197; anxiety in babies 167, 170, 174, 183–4, 186; psychology of pregnancy 15, 24
divorce 111–12, 127
dogs 138–40
Dolto, F. 91–3, 96
Draper, J. 21
dread 165, 178–80, 182, 184
dream 23, 205–6; analyst's reverie 78–9
drive 167–9, 173–6, 182, 187; clinical methods 90, 96; death drive 175–7, 183–5
drugs *see* medication
dummy 134, 137–8
dyadic relationships 126, 150
dyspnoea 171, 176

Ecclesiastes, book of 36
economic factors *see* socio-economic status
Edinburgh Postnatal Depression Scale (EPDS) 72, 102, 220
education 66, 68, 84–5, 221
egg and chick metaphor 168–70, 175
ego 32, 43, 175, 177, 182, 184, 199–201; immaturity 92–3, 97

ego-psychology 88, 90
Einfühlung 125
Electra complex 42–3
Emanuel, L. 145
emotion 4, 9, 163; Child Health Centre 57–9, 64–7, 78; couple therapy 110, 116–18; metaphors 215–16; pregnancy 14–15, 24
Emotional Availability Scales (EAS) 103
emotional regulation 96, 127
Emotional Security Theory 127
empathy 125
empiricism 161–3, 176
enactment 90, 138–9, 210–11
English language 13
enigmatic signifier 173
environment 159–61, 176–7
envy 42, 49–53, 187, *see also* jealousy
Eros 175
errors, type I 98–9
ET 33–5
etymology 13, 36
evacuation 125
evidence 7, 14, 107, 126–8
evidence-based medicine (EMB) 219
evolution 41
excuses 139–41
Exodus, book of 6
expectant 13
external frame 71, 82, 85, 146
external object 43, 110, 158, 161, 175
eyes 187, 212–13, 215, *see also* gaze avoidance

facultative 20
Fägerskiöld, A. 129
falling forever 177, 179
False Self 178
fantasies 16–17, 24, 42, 45, 59; baby's mind 155–7, 161, 174–5; clinical methods 90, 94; couple therapy 119, 122; toddlers 136, 141–2, 146
father 4–5, 18–22, 103, 142, 187; Child Health Centre 62, 76–8; couple therapy 109, 113–15, 117, 127–8; and maternal introject 42–3; Name of 21–2, 30, 66, 70; therapeutic technique 49, 51
The Father (Strindberg) 125
father's father 126
father's mother 122–3, 155–6, 159
fear of dying 178–80
Feldman, R. 20

252 Index

Ferenczi, S. 76
field theory 205
Firstness 179
Flaubert, G. 44
foetal attachment 14, 18, 24–6, 30, 206
foetus 3–4, 11–12, 17, 32–4, 180
förlossning 36
Forster, Z.R.D. 109
Fraiberg, S. 5, 43, 144, 171; clinical
   methods 88–90, 93–4, 96–8; defences
   192, 198–200
frame 71–3, 76, 78, 80, 82–3, 85, 146
France 218
Frank, M.A. 26
Freeman, T. 21
French analysts 19, 87, 90–1, 172–4
French language 13, 28, 36, 118–19
frequency, of therapy 50, 65–6, 82–3, 85,
   106, 110
Freud, A. 187, 200
Freud, H. 42–4
Freud, S. 18–19, 42, 136, 205; anxiety in
   babies 167–75, 182–5; baby's mind 150,
   162, 164; Child Health Centre 62, 75–6,
   78; clinical methods 88, 95–7; couple
   therapy 118–19, 121; defences 187,
   192–3, 195–7, 199–200
Friede 169–70
frustration 75, 196, 210
fusion 32

Gaddini, E. 180–5, 210
Galbally, M. 14
Gallegos, M.L. 128
gaze avoidance 73–4, 77, 97, 107, 151,
   187–94, 197–202
gender 20, 127
general parent-infant health care 56–7
General Stress Index (GSI) 103
generalists 220
Genesis, book of 3–4, 6
Genesoni, L. 19, 21
Geneva 89, 96, 98
Gentile, J. 17
geography 62
German 13, 36–7
Gershwin, G. 176
ghosts in the nursery 5, 8, 43, 88–90, 93–4,
   113, 116–17
gleichschwebende Aufmerksamkeit see
   reverie
going to pieces 177, 179–80, 182

good-enough mother 92, 95, 160, 169
Gottman, J.M. 127
grandmother *see* father's mother; mother's
   mother
Green, A. 22, 162, 168, 171–2, 178–9, 183
Greenson, R.R. 119
grossesse 13, 28
Grotstein, J. 178
group therapy 101
guilt 135, 154, 156–8, 189

Hägglöf, B. 24
Haifa 144
heredity 142–3
Herod 6
hesitation anxiety 154
Hincks-Dellcrest Center 94
Hoffman, L. 29, 140
holding 77, 79, 177, 182, 186
hope 59
horizontal model 217–19
hormones 14, 58
hostility 127, 170, 172, 174, 184; defences
   187, 192, 196–7
hysterical identification 210–11, 215

"I think"-method 68
Ideal types 102–6
ideational content 153, 157
identification: hysterical 210–11, 215;
   maternal 63, 193; projective 64, 122,
   155
identity 16–17
illness 5, 168, 174, 176, 182, 221
imitation 163, 210, 212
immaturity, ego 92–3, 97
incertus 19–21
infancy, definitions 87
Infant D 154
Infant Mental Health Centres 60
infant mortality 57
"Infant Sorrow" (Blake) 170–1
infanticide 6
infantile conflict 154
infantile defences 182
infantile emotions 116–17, 121
infantile sexuality 90, 150–1, 173, 201,
   207, 209–10
infant–parent psychotherapy 89
insecurity 15, 17, 131
"instinct" 162, 182
Institute of Psycho-Analysis 154

Index 253

intent-to-treat (ITT) 98–100, 102
interaction guidance 89, 98–9
intercourse 120, 157, 170
intergenerational transmission 30
intermodal perception 210–11
internal frame 71–3, 76, 78, 80, 146
internal object 43, 146, 155, 158, 170,
  175–6, 193, 198
internal relation 14
internet 74, 102, 189, 214, 220
interpretant 179–80
interpretation 119, 204–5
intersubjectivity 76; anxiety in babies 168,
  173–4, 183; defences 188, 193–5, 198;
  metaphors 201, 211; parental couples
  109–10
intimacy 29, 119–20
introjection 5, 43–6, 58, 106, 110, 125
Iran 25
Israel 144, 218

jealousy 83–4, 133–5, 187, *see also* envy
Jesus 6, 15, 36, 46, 128
Johnson, M. 203

Karolinska Institute 63
Katz, L. 127
Kernutt, J. 198
Kirshner, L. 204
Klein, M. 43, 88; anxiety in babies 175–7,
  183–4; baby's mind 150–1, 153–6,
  158–63; defences 192, 196, 200;
  toddlers 135, 145–6
Knausgaard, K.O. 180–1
knowledge 204–5

Lacan, J. 21, 30, 66
Lachmann, F.M. 163
Lakoff, G. 203
language 92–3, 157–8, 172–3, 203–5
Laplanche, J. 173, 200
latency 158–9
Latin 13, 19, 87, 169
Lausanne Trilogue Play 127
Law 66
Lebanon 113, 117, 125
Lebovici, S. 47, 90–1, 94, 145–6, 151,
  192, 210
LEGO-lady 31
Lewis, A.J. 14
LHPA 14
libido 168, 170–1, 182, 184

Lichtenberg, J.D. 200, 204
Lieberman, A.F. 94, 140, 143–4
Likierman, M. 145
Lindgren, K. 24
London 95–6, 151, 153–4, 156, 158
loneliness 30–1, 125, 128, 190–2, 215–16
loss 8, 36
love 5–6, 47–8, 72; baby's mind 158, 161,
  165, 190; maternal introject 38–40,
  42–3

McHale, J.P. 127–8
Mack Brunswick, R. 42
Madame Bovary (Flaubert) 44
Magic Flute (Mozart) 44
maintenance 221
Maisons Vertes 96
Mama Mia CHC 60
marriage 112, 121–9, 165
masochism 76–7, 90
Maternal Antenatal Attachment Scale
  (MAAS) 24
maternal aspect 78
maternal holding 77, 79
maternal identification 63, 193
maternal introject 43–6, 58
maternal preoccupation *see* primary
  maternal preoccupation
maternal principle 66–7
Maternal-Foetal Attachment (MFA) scale
  24–5
Matthew, book of 6
May, B. 165
mechanism 200–1
medication 15, 80, 84–5, 142, 212; Child
  Health Centre 60–1, 73; future 220–1;
  parental couples 111, 122, 124, 126
Melbourne 94, 96
Meltzer, D. 54, 142
Meltzoff, A.N. 181, 210
memory 141, 143, 171, 181–2
Mercury, F. 165, 176
meta-analyses 98, 101
metaphors 35, 47, 69–70, 85, 90–1, 110,
  121, 136, 151, 186, 203–16; dance/
  cramp 206–12, 215; defence as 187;
  egg/chick 168–70, 175; office 172–3,
  178; royal 42, 74–5; royal road 153,
  205; surgical 118–19; wall 213–15;
  WC 180–2
methods 6–7, 87–97, 161–3
midwives 43–4, 57, 129

254 Index

Miller, L. 140
Milner, M. 158–60
mind 149–51, 165; anxiety in babies 167, 172, 178–81, 184; defences 195, 201; empirics/theories 154–5, 161, 163–4
mise en acte 90, 138–9, 210–11
Miss Julie (Strindberg) 125
Modell, A.H. 204
Morgan, M. 119–20
Moses 6, 15
Moskowitz, S. 18
"Mother Love" (Queen) 165, 176
mother-in-law 112, 114–15, 118, 125, 156
Mother-Infant Psychoanalysis (MIP) 92–3, 192, 220; randomized clinical trial (RCT) 102–7
mother's mother 63, 81–3, 167; couple therapy 110, 126; defences 189, 191; introjection 40–1, 43–7; metaphors 215–16; primary preoccupation 25, 29–31, 34
mourning 89, 91
mouth 136, 139–40
Mozart, W.A. 44
Muhammed 6, 15
Muller, J. 24, 26

Name of the Father 21–2, 30, 66, 70
nameless dread 165, 178–80, 184
naming the nameless 165, 185
narcissism 5, 28, 33, 119; anxiety in babies 168, 174–6; clinical methods 90, 93; maternal introject 42, 44; metaphors 205, 209, 215–16
Netherlands 106–7
neuroscience 14–15, 20, 181
Niederkunft 36
Nom-du-Père 21–2, 30, 66, 70
Non-du-Père 22
Norman, J. 87, 92–7, 102, 106, 150
Notarius, C.I. 127
Notes on some schizoid mechanisms (Klein) 155, 157
nurses 53, 56–7, 59–60, 62–72, 219–22

object 13, 43, 110, 146; anxiety in babies 170, 172–7, 179, 182; baby's mind 155, 158, 161; defences 193, 196–8
object-relations 29, 96, 168
The observation of infants in a set situation (Winnicott) 154
O'Connor, T.G. 15

Oedipus complex 19, 21, 42, 185, 187
Ogden, T.H. 204
orality 136, 139–40
organization 217–21
oxytocin 20

P-group 65
pacifier 134, 137–8
pain 182, 196, 198–9
palimpsest 71–2, 75
panic 10–11, 37–8, 40, 178, 185
Parens, H. 140
Parent Development Interview (PDI) 25
Parent-Infant Relationship Global Assessment Scale (PIR-GAS) 103–4
Paris 85, 90–1, 145–6
Parker, R. 140
The Parrot (Campbell) 159–60
Participator type 103, 106
passivity 13
paternal aspect 30, 78
paternal preoccupation 18, 21
paternal principle 66–7, *see also* father
Paul, C. 94
peace 169–70
Peirce, C.S. 178–9, 182, 206
perception 171–3, 185, 199; intermodal 210–11
personality 5–7, 48, 119, 221
phantasies 175, *see also* fantasies
phronesis 66
pictogram 184–5, 205
pigs 138–40
Pines, D. 16
Pizer, B. & S. 122
play 127, 136, 139, 146–7, 154
pleasure principle 169–70
Pontalis, J.B. 200
pop-up comments 73–5
Porcerelli, J.H. 26
potty 157
poverty *see* socio-economic status
practice-based evidence 219
pregnant, etymology 13
Prenatal Attachment Inventory (PAI) 24
preschool 127, 142
primal process 184–5
primal repression 54, 150
primary maternal preoccupation 5, 15–18, 20, 23–7, 41; circumventing 28–35; external frame 56, 62; therapeutic technique 47, 49, 53

primary narcissism 168, 174–5
primary process 5, 185
Primary Process Integration (PPI) 23
progression 5, 31
The Project (Freud) 172, 195
projection 12, 41, 43, 84, 186; clinical
  methods 90, 94; parental couples 112,
  116–18
projective identification 64, 122, 155
projective tests 27
prudence 66
Psalms 176
psychoanalytic theory *see* theory
psychodynamic therapy with infants and
  parents (PTIP) 87–92, 94–7, 220; baby's
  mind 149–51, 162–4, 168; defences 188,
  199, 201; metaphors 203, 210, 212, 216;
  randomized clinical trials (RCTs)
  98–102, 107–8; toddlers 131, 143, 146

quantitative and qualitative 14, 107,
  126–8, 168–9
Queen (band) 165
Queen of the Night 44

randomized clinical trials (RCTs) 49, 60,
  220; anxiety in babies 166–7; Mother-
  Infant Psychoanalysis (MIP) 102–7;
  primary preoccupation 28, 30; PTIP
  98–102, 107–8; review of clinical
  methods 89, 94, 96
Raphael-Leff, J. 31–2
Rasmussen, J.L. 127–8
reaction formation 41–2, 44
reality 16, 21–4, 135, 159, 161, 175
Reddy, V. 183
reductionism 162
referral 53, 62–3, 219–21
reflective functioning 25, 144
regression 4–5, 46, 64, 121, 151; external
  frame 61–2; internal frame 75, 79;
  primary preoccupation 17, 31, 33;
  toddlers 137–8
regulation, emotional 96, 127
Reider, N. 204
rejection 93
religion 3–4, 6, 36
Renik, O. 194
representation 171–5, 179, 183–6, 197,
  200
repression 54, 90, 150, 199
resentment 29, 33, 86, 149–50

resistances 62, 78, 139
responsibility 69, 82, 113
restlessness 8, 11
reverie 17, 78–9, 205
rigidity 24
Rizzuto, A. 172, 205
Rorschach tests 23–6
Rosolato, G. 172
Roussillon, R. 173–4, 183
royal metaphor 42, 74–5
"royal road" metaphor 153, 205

sadomasochism 76–7
Sager, C.J. 109
salvation 36
San Francisco 96
Sander, F. 122
Sandler, J. 200
satisfaction 169–71, 184–5
scaffolding 95
Scandinavia 57, 218
Scharff, D.E. 116–17
Scharff, J.E. 122
school 7–8, 159–60
screaming 165–73, 183–4, 188, 197
secrecy 63, 65
secure attachment 23, 94, 100, 119, 159,
  198, *see also* attachment
Selective Serotonin Reuptake Inhibitors
  see SSRI
self 181–3, 185; False 178; True 92, 95,
  198
self-esteem 44, 58, 61, 99, 193, 219
Seligman, S. 162–3, 196
semiotics 178–9, 184
Semmelweiss, I. 57
semper incertus 19–21
sensitivity 104
sensogram 185
separation 3–4, 6, 29, 32, 49–50, 143,
  156–8
Seth, S. 14
sexuality 5, 85, 146, 150–1, 173, 201;
  clinical methods 90, 96; metaphor 207,
  209–10
shame 8–9, 57–9, 62
Siddiqui, A. 24
signal anxiety 199
signification 172–3, 178–9, 184
Singleton, J.L. 101
sisters 114–15
Slade, A. 13, 17, 25, 144

256 Index

sleep 90, 129, 132, 135–6, 142–3, 169;
   excessive 166, 170
sleeper effect 99
Slep, J.W. 200
social norms 29, 33
socio-economic status 61, 99–100, 106–7,
   144, 218
specificity, therapeutic 106
Spivacow , M.A. 109
spontaneous gesture 178
Spring (Knausgaard) 180–1
SSRI 15, 60–1, 80, 84–5, 221
Stein, A. 58
Stern, D.N. 56, 97; anxiety 183–4;
   defences 195–6; metaphors 205,
   211–12; mind 153, 162
stimulation 20–1
Stockholm 60, 63, 102–6
Story Stem Assessment Profile (SSAP)
   104
Strange Situation Inventory (SSI) 23, 25,
   100
Strengths and Difficulties Questionnaire
   (SDQ) 104
stress 14–15, 99–101, 129, 132, 207
Strindberg couples 125
subjectivity 13, 188, 193–5, 201, 204
suffering 118
superego 92, 135–6, 138, 142, 154
supervision 63–70, 221–2
surgical metaphor 118–19
surprise 128
Swain, J. 20–1
Sweden 38, 60, 87, 102–6, 113, 115, 129
Swedish language 13, 36
Swedish Parental Stress Questionnaire
   (SPSQ) 102–3
Switzerland 89–90, 96, 98, 127
symbolic order 21, 92
symbolism 158–60, 172
symptom 199
Symptom Check List-90 103

talking cure 88, 93, 149
Tallandini, M.A. 19, 21
Tavistock Clinic 121, 145, 154
teamwork 63
teenagers 5, 16, 69–70
temperament 128
Teti, D.M. 129
Texas 25
Thanatos 175–6, 184–5

themes 125, 127
theory 7, 121, 136; of anxiety in babies
   167–8; clinical methods 87–9, 95; of
   defences 192–5, 199–202; internal
   frame 76, 79; of metaphor 203–5;
   of mind 149–50, 160, 162–3; of
   signification 184–5
therapeutic specificity 106
thinking 178–9; together 120, 134; the
   unthinkable 198
Thirdness 179–80, 182
Thomson Salo, F. 94
timekeeping 65–6, 71
toddlers 92, 107, 131–47; literature on
   143–6; summary of technique 146–7
Toronto 94
Totem and Taboo (Freud) 19
toys 136, 144, 155
Trad, P.V. 29
transference 33, 44, 88, 150; internal
   frame 71, 75; parental couples 109–10,
   116–17, 121–2; therapeutic technique
   48, 54–5; toddlers 133–4, 137, 140,
   144–5, 147
transitional object 155
translation 35, 78
transmission gap 25
trauma 18, 30–1, 37, 41, 50; clinical
   methods 90, 93; toddlers 140–1
triadic system 126, 147, 179–80
Trieb 162, *see also* drive
Tristan und Isolde (Wagner) 165
Tronick, E. 198
Troubled type 104
True Self 92, 95, 198
trust 62–3

UK 25, 100, 106, 127, 218
unconscious: baby's mind 162, 168, 183;
   clinical methods 87, 90–1, 96–7;
   metaphors 205–6; parental couples
   118–24
unintegration 177
unmasking 78
unthinkable anxiety 177–80, 184
Urwin, C. 135
US 99–101, 127–8, 173, 204

Van Horn, P. 140, 143–4
vasopressin 20
vertical model 217–20
via regia (royal road) 153, 163, 205

violence 132–8, 144, *see also* aggression
Virgin and Child with Saint Anne
  (da Vinci) 46
Virgin Mary 13, 46, 128
Vreeswijk, C.M. 19
"Vroom" game 138, 145

Wagner, R. 165
wall metaphor 213–15
Wallerstein, R.S. 203, 205
war 159; metaphor 109–13, 116, 121
Watch, Wait, and Wonder (WWW) 94–5, 99
WC metaphor 180–2
weaning 29, 74
weaving thoughts 65
Wechsler scale (WPPSI) 104
Wellcome Institute 153
Wexler, M. 119
Winnicott, D.W. 47, 76, 80, 135; anxiety in
  babies 176–8, 183–4; baby's mind 150,

154–6, 159, 161; clinical methods 92,
  95–6; defences 188, 192–3;
  primary preoccupation 15–16, 18,
  20, 22–3, 32
witch 125–6, 140, 173
Wittenberg, I. 140
womb 3–4, 12
words 13, 35–6; baby's mind 149, 172,
  178–9; clinical methods 87–8, 91–3;
  metaphors 213–14
Wordsworth, W. 169, 179
work 28, 33, 39, 48–9, 208–9
Working Model of the Child Interview
  (WMCI) 26, 104
working through 119

Yarcheski, A. & T.J. 24
YouTube 166, 182

Zeitner, R.P.M.A. 109